W9-CLW-033

HMH

into Literature™

Front Cover Photo Credits: (outer ring): © Magdalena Kowalik/Shutterstock, (bottom inset): ©Joseph Sohm-Visions of America/Digital Vision/Getty Images, (inner ring): ©Creative Travel Projects/Shutterstock, (c) ©Carrie Garcia/Houghton Mifflin Harcourt, (c overlay): ©Eyewire/Getty Images, (bc overlay): ©elenamiv/Shutterstock

Back Cover Photo Credits: (Units 1-6): ©Diana Ong/Getty Images; ©Roy Scott/Getty Images; ©CliquePhoto/Moment/Getty Images; © Sherry Lachelle Photography; ©Library of Congress/Corbis/VCG via Getty Images; ©Veronika By/Shutterstock

Printed in the U.S.A.

ISBN 978-1-328-47482-7

3 4 5 6 7 8 9 10 0877 27 26 25 24 23 22 21 20 19

4500752607 B C D E F G

GRADE 11
Volume 1

Program Consultants:
Kylene Beers
Martha Hougen
Elena Izquierdo
Carol Jago
Erik Palmer
Robert E. Probst

PROGRAM CONSULTANTS

Kylene Beers

Nationally known lecturer and author on reading and literacy; coauthor with Robert Probst of *Disrupting Thinking, Notice & Note: Strategies for Close Reading,* and *Reading Nonfiction;* former president of the National Council of Teachers of English. Dr. Beers is the author of *When Kids Can't Read: What Teachers Can Do* and coeditor of *Adolescent Literacy: Turning Promise into Practice,* as well as articles in the *Journal of Adolescent and Adult Literacy.* Former editor of *Voices from the Middle,* she is the 2001 recipient of NCTE's Richard W. Halle Award, given for outstanding contributions to middle school literacy. She recently served as Senior Reading Researcher at the Comer School Development Program at Yale University as well as Senior Reading Advisor to Secondary Schools for the Reading and Writing Project at Teachers College.

Martha Hougen

National consultant, presenter, researcher, and author. Areas of expertise include differentiating instruction for students with learning difficulties, including those with learning disabilities and dyslexia; and teacher and leader preparation improvement. Dr. Hougen has taught at the middle school through graduate levels. In addition to peer-reviewed articles, curricular documents, and presentations, Dr. Hougen has published two college textbooks: *The Fundamentals of Literacy Assessment and Instruction Pre-K–6* (2012) and *The Fundamentals of Literacy Assessment and Instruction 6–12* (2014). Dr. Hougen has supported Educator Preparation Program reforms while working at the Meadows Center for Preventing Educational Risk at The University of Texas at Austin and at the CEEDAR Center, University of Florida.

Elena Izquierdo

Nationally recognized teacher educator and advocate for English language learners. Dr. Izquierdo is a linguist by training, with a Ph.D. in Applied Linguistics and Bilingual Education from Georgetown University. She has served on various state and national boards working to close the achievement gaps for bilingual students and English language learners. Dr. Izquierdo is a member of the Hispanic Leadership Council, which supports Hispanic students and educators at both the state and federal levels. She served as Vice President on the Executive Board of the National Association of Bilingual Education and as Publications and Professional Development Chair.

Carol Jago

Teacher of English with 32 years of experience at Santa Monica High School in California; author and nationally known lecturer; former president of the National Council of Teachers of English. Ms. Jago currently serves as Associate Director of the California Reading and Literature Project at UCLA. With expertise in standards assessment and secondary education, Ms. Jago is the author of numerous books on education, including *With Rigor for All* and *Papers, Papers, Papers,* and is active with the California Association of Teachers of English, editing its scholarly journal *California English* since 1996. Ms. Jago also served on the planning committee for the 2009 NAEP Reading Framework and the 2011 NAEP Writing Framework.

Erik Palmer

Veteran teacher and education consultant based in Denver, Colorado. Author of *Well Spoken: Teaching Speaking to All Students* and *Digitally Speaking: How to Improve Student Presentations.* His areas of focus include improving oral communication, promoting technology in classroom presentations, and updating instruction through the use of digital tools. He holds a bachelor's degree from Oberlin College and a master's degree in curriculum and instruction from the University of Colorado.

Robert E. Probst

Nationally respected authority on the teaching of literature; Professor Emeritus of English Education at Georgia State University. Dr. Probst's publications include numerous articles in *English Journal* and *Voices from the Middle,* as well as professional texts including (as coeditor) *Adolescent Literacy: Turning Promise into Practice* and (as coauthor with Kylene Beers) *Disrupting Thinking, Notice & Note: Strategies for Close Reading,* and *Reading Nonfiction.* He regularly speaks at national and international conventions including those of the International Literacy Association, the National Council of Teachers of English, the Association of Supervisors and Curriculum Developers, and the National Association of Secondary School Principals. He has served NCTE in various leadership roles, including the Conference on English Leadership Board of Directors, the Commission on Reading, and column editor of the NCTE journal *Voices from the Middle.* He is also the 2004 recipient of the CEL Exemplary Leader Award.

UNIT 1

FOUNDATIONS AND ENCOUNTERS

PAGE 1

? ESSENTIAL QUESTIONS

- Why are we bound to certain places?
- What motivates people to explore the unknown?
- What does it mean to be a stranger in a strange land?
- What happens when cultures collide?

Key Learning Objectives
- Analyze folk literature
- Make inferences
- Analyze thematic development
- Analyze plot structure
- Analyze and evaluate evidence
- Analyze informational texts
- Analyze voice
- Paraphrase
- Analyze allusions
- Analyze language
- Evaluate author's purpose
- Compare author's purpose

Visit the Interactive Student Edition for:
- Unit and Selection Videos
- Media Selections
- Selection Audio Recordings
- Enhanced Digital Instruction

UNIT 2

BUILDING A DEMOCRACY

PAGE 94

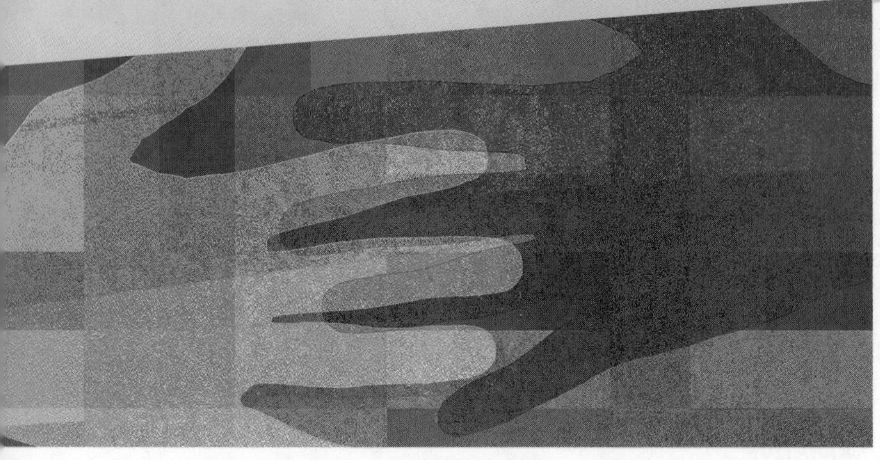

ESSENTIAL QUESTIONS

- What does oppression look like?
- How do we gain our freedom?
- How can we share power and build alliances?
- How do we transform our lives?

Key Learning Objectives

- Analyze argumentative texts
- Analyze text structure
- Analyze informational texts
- Determine author's purpose
- Analyze effectiveness of digital texts
- Analyze literary elements
- Analyze and evaluate plot
- Monitor comprehension
- Evaluate print and graphic features
- Analyze speaker
- Analyze and compare themes
- Compare voice and tone

Online Ed **Visit the Interactive Student Edition for:**

- Unit and Selection Videos
- Media Selections
- Selection Audio Recordings
- Enhanced Digital Instruction

UNIT 3

THE INDIVIDUAL AND SOCIETY

PAGE 204

? **ESSENTIAL QUESTIONS**

- In what ways do we seek to remain true to ourselves?
- How do we relate to the world around us?
- What do we secretly fear?
- When should we stop and reflect on our lives?

ANALYZE & APPLY

COLLABORATE & COMPARE

COMPARE MAIN IDEAS

Key Learning Objectives

- Analyze poetry
- Analyze theme and structure
- Analyze essays
- Analyze development of key ideas
- Analyze figurative language
- Analyze sound devices
- Summarize
- Analyze author's craft
- Compare main ideas
- Analyze literary elements
- Analyze structure
- Analyze mood
- Compare themes

Visit the Interactive Student Edition for:

- Unit and Selection Videos
- Media Selections
- Selection Audio Recordings
- Enhanced Digital Instruction

UNIT 4

THE QUEST FOR FREEDOM

PAGE 324

ESSENTIAL QUESTIONS

- When is self-determination possible?
- What divides us as human beings?
- How do we face defeat?
- What is the price of progress?

ANALYZE & APPLY

COLLABORATE & COMPARE

COMPARE ARGUMENTS

Key Learning Objectives

- Analyze author's purpose
- Analyze letters
- Analyze tone
- Make connections
- Analyze media effectiveness
- Analyze literary elements
- Analyze structure
- Analyze informational texts
- Analyze and evaluate arguments
- Analyze speaker and voice
- Analyze sound devices
- Analyze language
- Compare writer's voice

Visit the Interactive Student Edition for:

- Unit and Selection Videos
- Media Selections
- Selection Audio Recordings
- Enhanced Digital Instruction

UNIT 5

AMERICA TRANSFORMED

PAGE 452

ESSENTIAL QUESTIONS

- To what degree do we control our lives?
- Why do humans cause harm?
- What are the consequences of change?
- What makes a place unique?

COLLABORATE & COMPARE

Key Learning Objectives

- Analyze character
- Analyze setting
- Analyze author's purpose
- Analyze tone
- Evaluate graphic features
- Evaluate counterarguments
- Analyze point of view
- Make and confirm predictions
- Synthesize information
- Compare author's purpose

Visit the Interactive Student Edition for:

- Unit and Selection Videos
- Media Selections
- Selection Audio Recordings
- Enhanced Digital Instruction

UNIT 6

CONTEMPORARY VOICES AND VISIONS

PAGE 568

? ESSENTIAL QUESTIONS

- How do we deal with rejection or isolation?
- For whom is the American Dream relevant?
- When should personal integrity come before civic duty?
- What would we do if there were no limits?

ANALYZE & APPLY

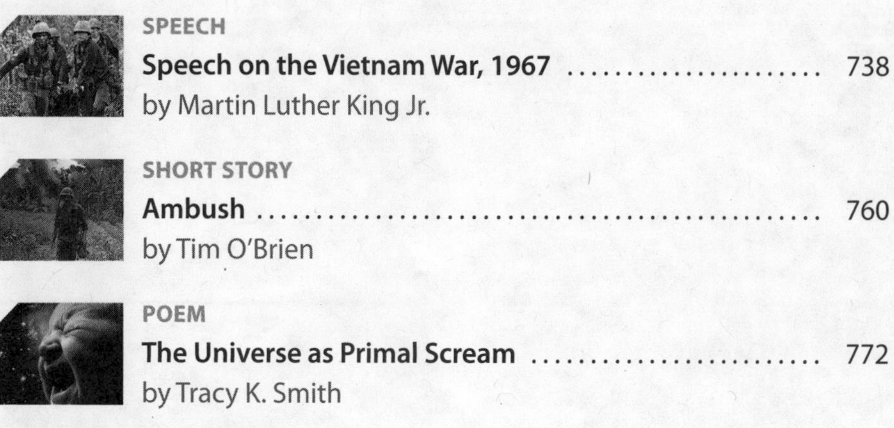

COLLABORATE & COMPARE

COMPARE IDEAS ACROSS GENRES

COMPARE THEMES

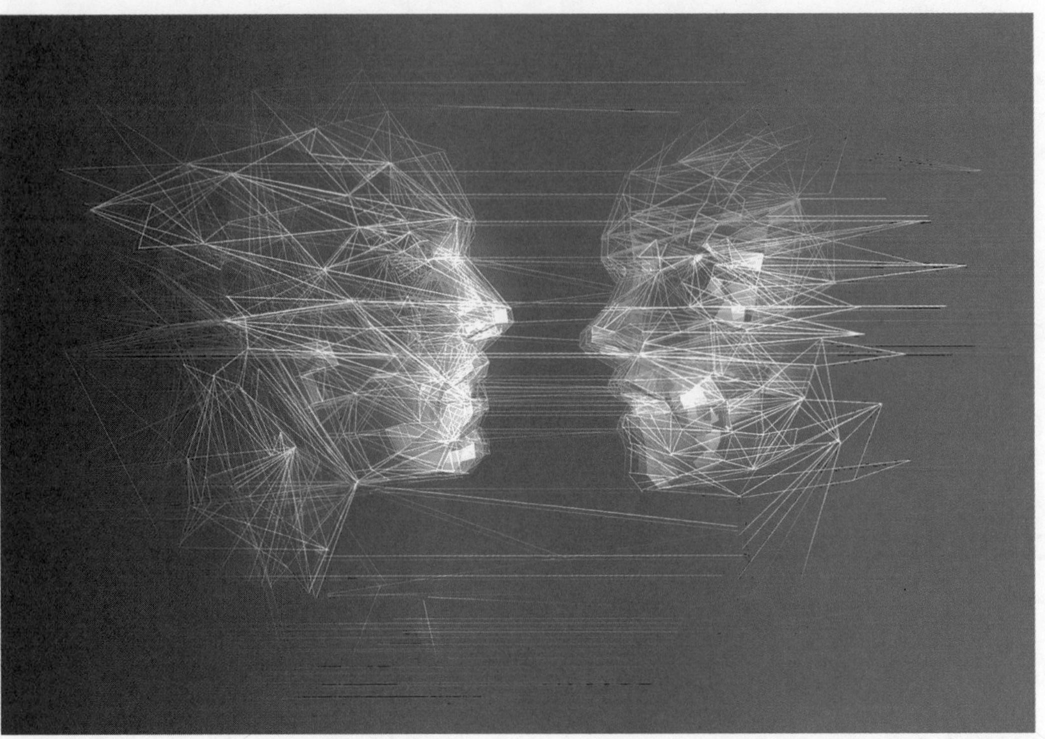

Suggested Novel Connection

Key Learning Objectives

- Make and confirm predictions
- Analyze author's message
- Analyze dramatic elements
- Analyze and evaluate arguments
- Analyze and evaluate rhetorical devices
- Analyze poetry
- Determine theme
- Analyze development of ideas
- Analyze poetry
- Analyze point of view

Visit the Interactive Student Edition for:

- Unit and Selection Videos
- Media Selections
- Selection Audio Recordings
- Enhanced Digital Instruction

SELECTIONS BY GENRE

LETTER/APHORISM

NARRATIVE NONFICTION

SELECTIONS BY GENRE

DRAMA

MEDIA STUDY

HMH

Into Literature Dashboard

Easy to use and personalized for your learning.

Monitor your progress in the course.

Ed your friend in learning | Class 1 | Welcome, Oliver

Discover | Assignments | Data & Reports

Into Literature | View by CONTENT STANDARDS

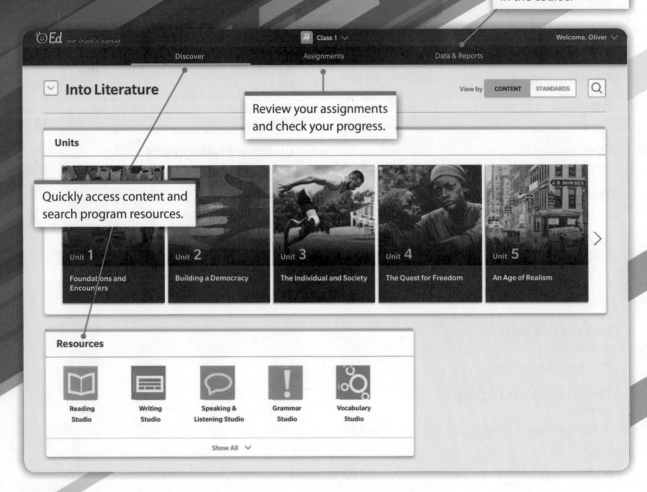

Review your assignments and check your progress.

Units

Quickly access content and search program resources.

Unit 1 Foundations and Encounters

Unit 2 Building a Democracy

Unit 3 The Individual and Society

Unit 4 The Quest for Freedom

Unit 5 An Age of Realism

Resources

Reading Studio | Writing Studio | Speaking & Listening Studio | Grammar Studio | Vocabulary Studio

Show All

Explore Online to Experience the Power of HMH *Into Literature*

All in One Place

Readings and assignments are supported by a variety of resources to bring literature to life and give you the tools you need to succeed.

Supporting 21st-Century Skills

Whether you're working alone or collaborating with others, it takes effort to analyze the complex texts and competing ideas that bombard us in this fast-paced world. What will help you succeed? Staying engaged and organized. The digital tools in this program will help you take charge of your learning.

Ignite Your Investigation

You learn best when you're engaged. The **Stream to Start** videos at the beginning of every unit are designed to spark your interest before you read. Get curious and start reading!

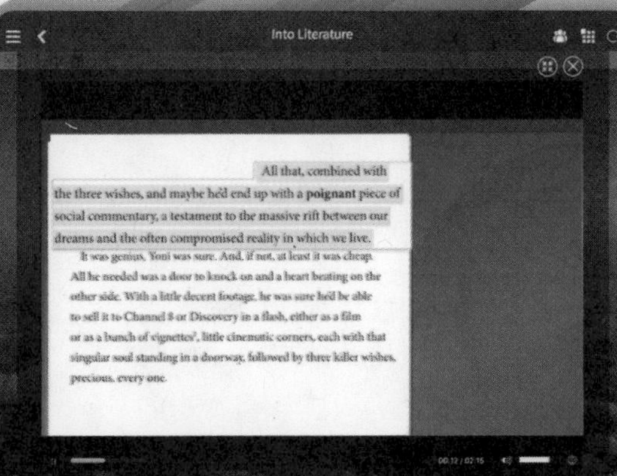

Learn How to Close Read

Close reading effectively is all about examining the details. See how it's done by watching the **Close Read Screencasts** in your eBook. Hear modeled conversations on targeted passages.

Personalized Annotations

My Notes encourages you to take notes as you read and allows you to mark the text in your own customized way. You can easily access annotations to review later as you prepare for exams.

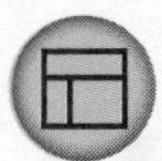

Interactive Graphic Organizers

Graphic organizers help you process, summarize, and keep track of your learning and prepare for end-of-unit writing tasks. **Word Networks** help you learn academic vocabulary, and **Response Logs** help you explore and deepen your understanding of the **Essential Questions** in each unit.

No Wi-Fi? No problem!

With HMH *Into Literature,* you always have access: download when you're online and access what you need when you're offline. Work offline and then upload when you're back online.

Communicate "Raise a Hand" to ask or answer questions without having to be in the same room as your teacher.

Collaborate Collaborate with your teacher via chat and work with a classmate to improve your writing.

HMH

Into Literature STUDIOS

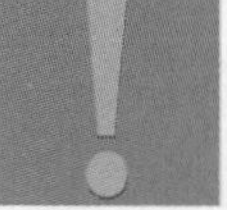

All the help you need to be successful in your literature class is one click away with the Studios. These digital-only lessons are here to tap into the skills that you already use and help you sharpen those skills for the future.

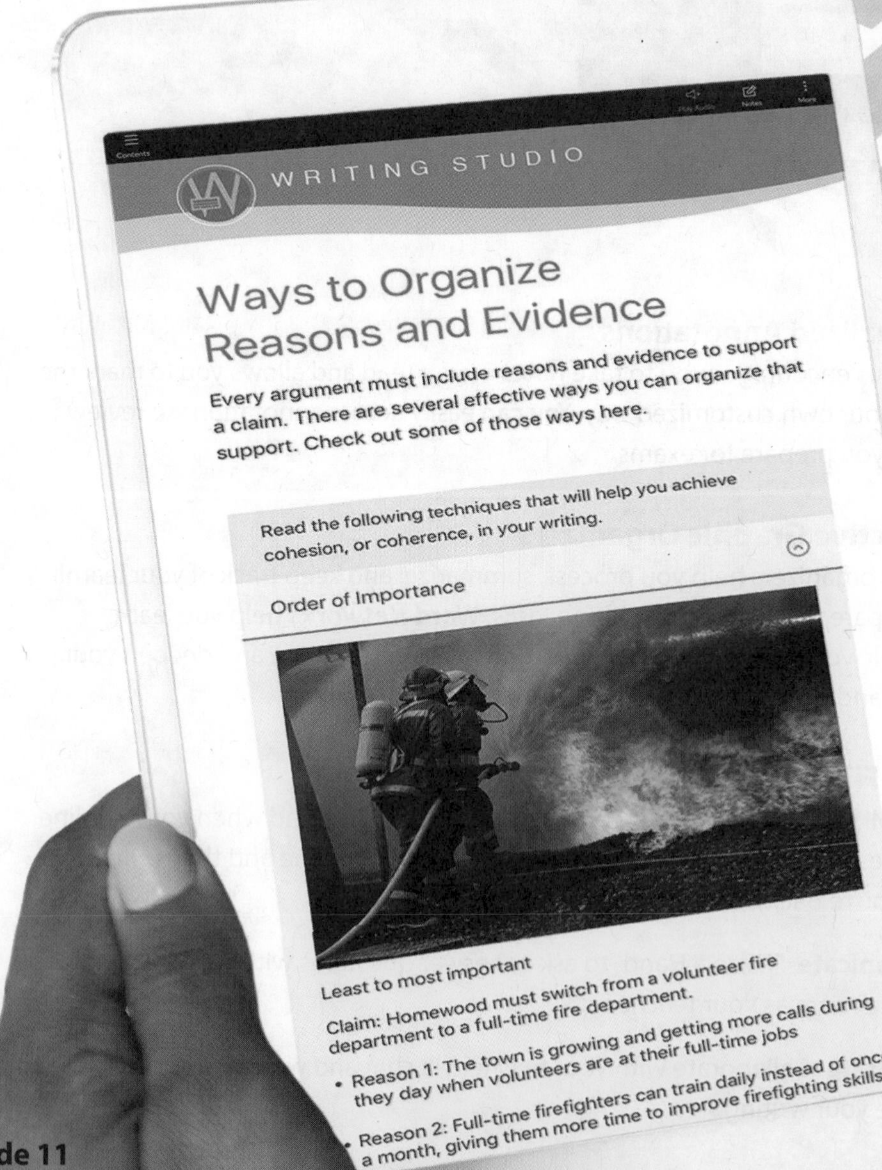

Easy-to-find resources, organized in five separate STUDIOS. On demand and on ED!

Look for links in each lesson to take you to the appropriate Studio.

READING STUDIO

Go beyond the book with the Reading Studio. With over 100 full-length downloadable titles to choose from, find the right story to continue your journey.

WRITING STUDIO

Being able to write clearly and effectively is a skill that will help you throughout life. The Writing Studio will help you become an expert communicator—in print or online.

SPEAKING & LISTENING STUDIO

Communication is more than just writing. The Speaking & Listening Studio will help you become an effective speaker and a focused listener.

GRAMMAR STUDIO

Go beyond traditional worksheets with the Grammar Studio. These engaging, interactive lessons will sharpen your grammar skills.

VOCABULARY STUDIO

Learn the skills you need to expand your vocabulary. The interactive lessons in the Vocabulary Studio will grow your vocabulary to improve your reading.

Dr. Kylene Beers and Dr. Robert E. Probst

In reading, as in almost everything else, paying attention is most important.

You wouldn't stand in the batter's box, facing a hard-throwing pitcher, with your mind wandering to what you may have for dinner that evening. The prospect of a fastball coming toward you at 80 miles an hour tends to focus the mind.

And you wouldn't attempt to sing a difficult song in front of a large crowd with your thoughts on what dress you're going to wear to the dance this coming weekend. The need to hit the high note, without cracking, in front of 500 people evokes concentration.

Paying attention is essential.

It's the same with reading. Of course, if you don't concentrate while reading, you won't suffer the pain of being knocked down by the fastball or the embarrassment of failing to hit the notes in front of the crowd, but you'll miss what the text offers. If you don't pay attention, there is barely any purpose in picking up the text at all.

But there is a purpose in reading. And that purpose, that point, is to enable us to change. The change may be slight, or it might be dramatic. We might, at one extreme, simply get a little more information that we need:

- Where is tonight's game?
- What time is band practice?
- What pages do we need to read for homework?

Reading for that sort of information doesn't dramatically change who we are, but it does change us slightly. Or, at least, it ***might*** change us slightly. Obviously, it is ***we***, the readers, who must do the changing. The text doesn't do it for us. When we read that tonight's game is away, instead of at home, we have to change our plans to let us get to the other school. We have to take in the information and do something with it. If we don't, if we show up at the home field despite what we have read, the reading will have been pointless, a waste of time. And the evening will be wasted, as well. We have to pay attention to the book — what's on the page, and to our heads — what we thought before we read and what we now think. And we have to take it to heart — that is to say, we have to act on what we now know and think.

Other reading, however, might enable us to change more significantly. We might change our thinking about an important problem, or we might change our attitude about an important issue. We can't tell you which text will do that for you or how you might grow and change as a result of reading it. That's much too individual. It's hard to predict unless you know the reader well and know some of the texts that might matter to him or her:

- Some of us might read about child labor in foreign countries and change our minds about what we will buy and what we will boycott.
- You might read *To Kill a Mockingbird*, and change your thinking about race relations.
- You might read about climate change and wonder what you can do to help preserve the earth.

We can't know exactly what book will be powerful for which reader. But we can safely predict that if you don't notice what the text offers, think about it, and take what matters to you into your head and heart, then the reading probably won't mean much to you.

We're going to urge you to pay attention to three elements as you read:

- **The Book.** Or whatever text you have in your hand, whether it is a book, an article, a poem, or something else. We are going to urge you to listen carefully to what it tells you, and we're going to give you some strategies that we hope will make that easy for you to do.
- **Your Head.** We're going to ask you also to pay attention to your own thoughts. If it's an article you're reading, then keep in mind what you thought about the topic before you began, and then think seriously about how you might have changed your thinking as a result of what you've read. If it's a story or a poem or a movie, then think about what thoughts or feelings it brought to mind and how they might have shaped your reaction to the text.
- **Your Heart.** Finally, we encourage you to ask yourself what you want to carry away from the reading. What matters to you? How might you change your thinking? How might you have shifted your attitudes about something, even if only slightly? What do you take to heart?

It all begins with noticing.

But there's a lot in a book to notice, so it might help to keep in mind just a few things that you will probably see in almost any text (unless it is very short). We call these elements "signposts" because they serve readers just as signposts or street signs serve drivers — they alert them to something significant. The careless driver, who doesn't pay attention and misses a stop sign or a hairpin-curve sign, is likely to end up in trouble. The lazy reader, who doesn't notice the signposts, won't end up in trouble — he just isn't likely to know what's going on in the text.

THE FICTION SIGNPOSTS

We want to share 6 signposts that help you when reading fiction.

CONTRASTS AND CONTRADICTIONS

Without a contrast or a contradiction, everything is just the same, just the usual, just what you would have expected. Boring.

But when some event occurs that contrasts vividly with what you would have expected, then you are likely — if you're paying attention — to notice it.

When a friend's behavior suddenly changes and contrasts with what you would expect, you will notice it and ask yourself why. Similarly, when a character in a story does something drastically different from what he has usually done, you should pause and wonder why. Or, when a writer gives you an idea that contradicts the thoughts you have always held, again you might slow down and ask yourself, "Is she right or am I? Should I accept those thoughts or reject them? Is the answer somewhere in between what I have read and what I used to think?" Keep in mind the general question "Why is the character doing or saying that?" and it will lead you to other questions you might ask about the moment of contrast and contradiction, that moment when you bump into something unexpected.

In Nathaniel Hawthorne's "The Minister's Black Veil," a student has noted CONTRASTS AND CONTRADICTIONS and asked this question: Why would the characters act this way?

Text	Student notes
After a brief interval, forth came good Mr. Hooper also, in the rear of his flock. Turning his veiled face from one group to another, he paid due reverence to the hoary heads, saluted the middle-aged with kind dignity, as their friend and spiritual guide, greeted the young with mingled authority and love, and laid his hands on the little children's heads to bless them. Such was always his custom on the Sabbath day. Strange and bewildered looks repaid him for his courtesy. None, as on former occasions, aspired to the honor of walking by their pastor's side. Old Squire Saunders, doubtless by an accidental lapse of memory, neglected to invite Mr. Hooper to his table, where the good clergyman had been wont to bless the food almost every Sunday since his settlement. He returned, therefore, to the parsonage, and at the moment of closing the door, was observed to look back upon the people, all of whom had their eyes fixed upon the minister. A sad smile gleamed faintly from beneath the black veil, and flickered about his mouth, glimmering as he disappeared.	Members of the congregation seem confused, and none of them walk with Mr. Hooper after the church service ends. Even Squire Saunders breaks with his long tradition of inviting Mr. Hooper to dinner. They're staying away from him. Perhaps they're embarrassed or even frightened by Mr. Hooper's behavior, leading him to feel sad and lonely.

AHA MOMENT

Sometimes too many days go by without one of those moments when you suddenly understand something. But when you have such a moment you recognize that it's important and you stop and think about it. One day you might suddenly say to yourself "I'm echoing everything my friends say, but I don't really believe any of it." That's an important moment that may lead to a change in what you do, or at least to some hard thinking about the choices you have made. You've had an insight — an Aha — and you have to ask yourself what it means.

In the same way, the character in the story will almost always come to some insight into his situation, some "Aha" moment in which he realizes, perhaps suddenly, something about himself, his situation, or his life. When you come to such a moment, ask yourself "How will this change things?" Because it almost always will. Aha Moments are usually indicated with phrases such as "I knew," "I understood," "He figured it out," "She slowly realized," or "She nodded, knowing what she had to do . . ."

In Jack London's "**To Build a Fire**," a student has noted an **AHA MOMENT** and asked this question: How might this change things?	
Fifty degrees below zero stood for a bite of frost that hurt and that must be guarded against by the use of mittens, earflaps, warm moccasins, and thick socks. Fifty degrees below zero was to him just precisely fifty degrees below zero. That there should be anything more to it than that was a thought that never entered his head.	The man understands how to survive when it's fifty degrees below zero, but he has never imagined what might happen if it were colder.
As he turned to go on, he spat speculatively. There was a sharp, explosive crackle that startled him. He spat again. And again, in the air, before it could fall to the snow, the spittle crackled. He knew that at fifty below, spittle crackled on the snow, but this spittle had crackled in the air. Undoubtedly it was colder than fifty below—how much colder he did not know.	He has an Aha Moment when he spits and realizes that it's much, much colder than he'd expected. He might be realizing that he's in trouble—that he needs to act quickly in order to survive.

TOUGH QUESTIONS

"Do you want pizza or spaghetti for dinner?" really isn't a tough question, even if you can't make up your mind. Your answer isn't going to change much of anything, and tomorrow you probably won't even remember that you made a choice. You aren't going to think about it for very long or very hard, and no one will ever write a book about the choice between pizza and spaghetti. If they do, we won't read it.

A tough question is one we struggle with, one that might change the course of our lives — one, at least, that will have some serious consequences for us. "Should I play football, as the coach wants me to, or should I join the band, as I want to?" "Should I follow the crowd, as everyone is pressing me to do, or should I respect my own thoughts and let the crowd condemn me for it?" These are tough questions, and how we might answer them will shape the days to come.

Often a story, even an entire book, is built around the tough question. If we ask ourselves "What does this make me wonder about?," we will probably be led into exploring the same issue the character or the writer is exploring. The writer probably wanted to see what would happen if his character answered the question in a certain way. If you notice the tough question, and ask yourself about it, you will probably be looking at the main issue of the book.

In Kate Chopin's **"The Story of an Hour,"** a student has noted a **TOUGH QUESTION** and asked: What does this question make me wonder about?	
She was young, with a fair, calm face, whose lines bespoke repression and even a certain strength. But now there was a dull stare in her eyes, whose gaze was fixed away off yonder on one of those patches of blue sky. It was not a glance of reflection, but rather indicated a suspension of intelligent thought.	In response to news of her husband's death, Mrs. Mallard feels something "coming to her," but she has no idea what it is. She asks a Tough Question, "What was it?"
There was something coming to her and she was waiting for it, fearfully. What was it? She did not know; it was too subtle and elusive to name. But she felt it, creeping out of the sky, reaching toward her through the sounds, the scents, the color that filled the air.	I wonder if she's going to realize something about herself or about what life will be like now that she's alone.

WORDS OF THE WISER

You may think that you have heard too many of these in your own life.

You probably think there is always someone around who wants to offer you advice, teach you how things are, and tell you what to do and how to think. Sometimes these wise words are right, truly wise, and sometimes they are wrong. But they are almost always an effort to guide you, or the character, to teach something about living in the world.

In a story, we usually hear Words of the Wiser in a quiet moment, when two characters are in a serious conversation about a problem or a decision. Usually the one who is — or thinks she is — wiser, will offer a serious lesson about life. The story will be about the character struggling along, unwilling to learn that lesson until the end; or about the character accepting the lesson and following it to whatever adventures it leads; or perhaps, in rare cases, about the words of the wiser not being wise after all.

In any case, when you notice Words of the Wiser in the story you should ask the same question you are likely to ask in your own life — "What is the lesson, and how will it affect the character (or me)?"

In Tim O'Brien's "Ambush," a student has noted WORDS OF THE WISER and asked this question: What is the life lesson, and how might it affect the character?

He fell on his back. His rubber sandals had been blown off. He lay at the center of the trail, his right leg beneath him, his one eye shut, his other eye a huge star-shaped hole. For me, it was not a matter of live or die. I was in no real peril. Almost certainly the young man would have passed me by. And it will always be that way. Later, I remember Kiowa tried to tell me that the man would've died anyway. He told me that it was a good kill, that I was a soldier and this was a war, that I should shape up and stop staring and ask myself what the dead man would've done if things were reversed.	The narrator feels guilty for killing an enemy soldier who posed no threat. Kiowa counsels him with Words of the Wiser, trying to help him understand the reality of warfare. The narrator might accept his own role in the conflict, and he may begin acting without any sense of guilt or regret.

AGAIN AND AGAIN

One teacher I had always called on the second or third person to raise a hand, or perhaps on some student who was looking out the window — never on the first hand in the sky.

It happened again and again. Until, of course, I got clever and decided to shoot my hand up quickly even though I didn't have the foggiest notion what the answer was. That must have been the day that the teacher recognized the lesson of Again and Again, and realized that he had established a pattern. Or perhaps he had been planning the switch all along. In any case, it was the day I shot my hand up first that he decided to change his routine. At my expense. . . .

Something that happens over and over, again and again, establishes a pattern. If we pay attention, we'll notice that pattern and ask ourselves, "Why does this happen over and over, again and again?" In our lives, the again and again moment probably teaches us something about our friends, or our teachers, or, perhaps, about the way the world works. And sometimes it alerts us to something that is likely to change.

In any case, whenever we notice something happening again and again, we should take note of it, and ask ourselves "Why does this keep happening repeatedly?" Our answer may be that it teaches us some consistent pattern that we can rely on. Or it may be that it is setting up expectations that we can predict will suddenly not be met. It may be leading us into a surprising Contrast and Contradiction. That, after all is what my teacher did to me. If I had thought more carefully about the Again and Again, and asked myself why he was always avoiding the first hand that waved, I might have guessed that he was preparing a trick and that one day he would call on that first hand.

In Robert Frost's "Mending Wall," a student has noted an instance of AGAIN AND AGAIN and asked this question: Why might the author bring this up again and again?

My apple trees will never get across And eat the cones under his pines, I tell him. He only says, "Good fences make good neighbors." Spring is the mischief in me, and I wonder If I could put a notion in his head: "*Why* do they make good neighbors? Isn't it Where there are cows? But here there are no cows. Before I built a wall I'd ask to know What I was walling in or walling out, And to whom I was like to give offence. Something there is that doesn't love a wall, That wants it down." I could say "Elves" to him, But it's not elves exactly, and I'd rather He said it for himself. I see him there Bringing a stone grasped firmly by the top In each hand, like an old-stone savage armed. He moves in darkness as it seems to me, Not of woods only and the shade of trees. He will not go behind his father's saying, And he likes having thought of it so well He says again, "Good fences make good neighbors."	The speaker's neighbor says that "good fences make good neighbors" again and again, and the speaker wonders if that's true. I think Frost may be repeating the words to emphasize the idea that people, like the speaker's neighbor, sometimes rely on old sayings and beliefs to guide their actions, even when those sayings and beliefs don't make sense anymore.

MEMORY MOMENT

Sometimes, in a reflective moment, a memory will surprise you. You won't have been trying to remember that day, or that person, or that event. It will just pop up like an almost forgotten old friend who knocks at your door and surprises you.

But something called that memory up at that moment. Something that was happening right now reached into your distant past and pulled that memory into your thoughts. Figuring out why that happened will probably tell you something important. It may explain why you are feeling the way you are feeling. It may even explain why you are acting as you are at the moment.

In a story, the Memory Moment is an author's creation. She has decided to reach back into the past for something that she thinks you, as a reader, need to know. It's easy to skip over these moments. After all, you want to go forwards, not backwards, and the Memory Moment steps back into the past. But it's probably important to ask yourself "Why is this moment important?" Because you can assume that if the writer is any good at all, she thinks you should notice it and take note of it.

In Ambrose Bierce's "**An Occurrence at Owl Creek Bridge**" a student has noted a **MEMORY MOMENT** and asked this question: Why might this memory be important?

One evening while Farquhar and his wife were sitting on a rustic bench near the entrance to his grounds, a gray-clad soldier rode up to the gate and asked for a drink of water. Mrs. Farquhar was only too happy to serve him with her own white hands. While she was fetching the water her husband approached the dusty horseman and inquired eagerly for news from the front.	This section of the story describes events in the past, events that might form a Memory Moment for Peyton Farquhar.
"The Yanks are repairing the railroads," said the man, "and are getting ready for another advance. They have reached the Owl Creek bridge, put it in order and built a stockade on the north bank. The commandant has issued an order, which is posted everywhere, declaring that any civilian caught interfering with the railroad, its bridges, tunnels or trains will be summarily hanged. I saw the order."	I think the exchange with the soldier reveals a lot about Farquhar's motivations. It also explains events described previously in the story: Farquhar had been caught trying to stop Northern soldiers from using the railroads during their advance.

NONFICTION SIGNPOSTS

Nonfiction has text clues as well. Just as in fiction, they invite you to stop and think about what's happening. These clues will help you focus on author's purpose — a critical issue to keep in mind when reading nonfiction. More importantly, these signposts will help you as you keep in mind what we call the Three Big Questions. These questions ought to guide all the reading we do, but especially the nonfiction reading. As you read, just keep asking yourself:

- What surprised me?
- What did the author think I already knew?
- What changed, challenged, or confirmed my thinking?

That first one will keep you thinking about the text. Just look for those parts that make you think, "Really!?!" and put an exclamation point there. The second one will be helpful when the language is tough, or the author is writing about something you don't know much about. Mark those points with a question mark and decide if you need more information. That final question, well, that question is why we read. Reading ought to change us. It ought to challenge our thinking. And sometimes it will confirm it. When you find those parts, just put a "C" in the margin. When you review your notes, you will decide if your thinking was changed, challenged, or confirmed.

As you're looking at what surprised you, or thinking about what is challenging you, or perhaps even as you find a part where it seems the author thinks you know something that you don't, you might discover that one of the following signposts appears right at that moment. So, these signposts help you think about the Three Big Questions. We have found five useful signposts for nonfiction.

CONTRASTS AND CONTRADICTIONS

The world is full of contrasts and contradictions — if it weren't, it would be a pretty dull place to live.

This is the same Contrast and Contradiction that you are familiar with from fiction. It's that moment when you encounter something you didn't expect, something that surprises you. It may be a fact that you find startling, a perspective that you had never heard before, or perhaps an argument that is new to you. We should welcome those moments, even though they may be disconcerting. They give us the opportunity to change our minds about things, to sharpen our thinking. The last person we want to become is that reader who reads only to confirm what he has already decided. That reader is committed to not learning, not growing, and standing absolutely still intellectually.

In Iris Chang's "Building the Transcontinental Railroad," a student has noted a CONTRAST AND CONTRADICTION and asked this question: What is the difference, and why does it matter?

As the railroad neared completion, the Chinese encountered the Irish workers of the Union Pacific for the first time. When the two companies came within a hundred feet of each other, the Union Pacific Irish taunted the Chinese with catcalls and threw clods of dirt. When the Chinese ignored them, the Irish swung their picks at them, and to the astonishment of the whites, the Chinese fought back. The level of antagonism continued to rise. Several Chinese were wounded by blasting powder the whites had secretly planted near their side. Several days later, a mysterious explosion killed several Irish workers. The presumption was that the Chinese had retaliated in kind. At that point, the behavior of white workers toward the Chinese immediately improved.	Initially, the author contrasts the behavior of each group toward the other: Chinese workers ignored the taunts of their Irish competitors. That contrast, when those same workers respond to violence with violence, helps draw attention to how much abuse Chinese workers were willing to take before taking action to defend themselves.

EXTREME AND ABSOLUTE LANGUAGE

We are all guilty of overstatement all the time.

Well, that's an overstatement. We aren't all guilty, and those of us who are probably aren't guilty all of the time. When we hear "all," or "none," or "always," or "never," we can be absolutely certain — let's make that "almost certain" — that we are hearing absolute language. All it takes is one exception to make the claim false.

But we do tend to exaggerate and occasionally overstate our claims. Absolute language is easy to spot, and it's often harmless over-statement. Extreme language approaches absolute language but usually stops short. Much of the time, it's harmless, too. When you tell your buddy you're starving, you probably aren't. Or when you say you just heard the funniest joke in the world, even though that's probably not true, your comment causes no real harm.

Sometimes, however, an extreme statement is potentially dangerous. If, for example, someone in authority were to say something like, "I am 100% certain that the airline crash was caused by terrorists," and we had not yet even found the black box that would explain the cause of the accident, then gullible listeners might believe and form opinions based on that statement, even though the phrase "100% certain" shows us clearly that it is an extreme statement. After all, no one ever claims to be 100% certain unless he isn't. So the question becomes, "How certain is he?" 80%? 40%? 20%?

When we spot absolute or extreme language, we should ask ourselves "Why did the author say it this way?" Sometimes the answer will be revealing.

In Thomas Jefferson's "The Declaration of Independence," a student has noted instances of EXTREME AND ABSOLUTE LANGUAGE and asked this question: Why did the author use this language?

Prudence, indeed, will dictate that governments long established should not be changed for light and transient causes; and, accordingly, all experience hath shown that mankind are more disposed to suffer, while evils are sufferable, than to right themselves by abolishing the forms to which they are accustomed. But, when a long train of abuses and usurpations, pursuing invariably the same object, evinces a design to reduce them under absolute despotism, it is their right, it is their duty, to throw off such government, and to provide new guards for their future security. Such has been the patient sufferance of these colonies; and such is now the necessity that constrains them to alter their former systems of government. The history of the present King of Great Britain is a history of repeated injuries and usurpations, all having, in direct object, the establishment of an absolute tyranny over these States.	Wow! Jefferson uses both absolute and extreme language throughout the text. Not only does his language draw attention to the colonists' suffering, but it also stresses the idea that the government has had only one goal, to establish tyrannical power over the states. His use of language creates a clear sense that the colonists' decision is just.

NUMBERS AND STATS

"If I've told you once, I've told you a million times. . . ."

Those are numbers — 1 (once) and 1,000,000 — though we prefer to see that as Extreme and Absolute Language. Still, it allows us to make the point, which is that numbers are used to make a point. In this case, they reveal that the speaker is annoyed at how often he has to repeat himself for you to get the message. You barely have to ask the anchor question "Why did the writer or speaker use those numbers or amounts?"

But that's the question you should ask when numbers or stats or amounts appear in something you are reading. Writers include them because they think those numbers, which look like hard, objective, indisputable data, will be persuasive. The questions are, "What are they trying to persuade you to think or believe?" And, "Are the numbers reliable?"

When a writer tells you, for instance, that 97–98% of scientists who have studied the issue think that humans are affecting the environment in damaging ways, we probably want to ask what those figures tell us, both about the situation and the writer's purpose. Our answer will probably be that the writer believes the scientists have reached a consensus that we are endangering the planet. The writer might have said "most of the scientists agree," but "most" is vague. It could mean anything from slightly more than half to almost all. But "97–98%" is much more precise. And it's very close to 100%, so it should be persuasive. Numbers and stats help us visualize what the author is trying to show; it's up to you to decide if there's more you need to know.

In Ron Chernow's "Thomas Jefferson: The Best of Enemies," a student has noted NUMBERS AND STATS and asked this question: Why did the author use these numbers or amounts?

Hamilton—brilliant, brash and charming—had the self-reliant reflexes of someone who had always had to live by his wits. His overwhelming intelligence petrified Jefferson and his followers. As an orator, Hamilton could speak extemporaneously for hours on end. As a writer, he could crank out 5,000- or 10,000-word memos overnight. Jefferson never underrated his foe's copious talents. At one point, a worried Jefferson confided to his comrade James Madison that Hamilton was a one-man army, "a host within himself."	Not only could Hamilton speak off-the-cuff for hours, but he could also write incredibly long memos in a single night. The author includes these Numbers and Stats to help illustrate and explain why Jefferson and his allies were "petrified" by the single-handed power and abilities of Hamilton.

QUOTED WORDS

American writer Ambrose Bierce said that quotation is "The act of repeating erroneously the words of another." When writers use quotations they are probably doing one of two things. They may be giving you an individual example so that you can see what some person thought or felt about a certain situation, event, or idea. In that case, the writer is probably trying to help you see the human impact of what otherwise might be an abstract idea, difficult to imagine. A writer might, for instance, tell you about the massive damage Hurricane Harvey brought to the coast of Texas. A description of the widespread destruction will give you a picture of what happened; but the quoted words of someone who heard the hundred-mile-an-hour winds for hours when the storm came ashore or whose house was flooded by the rising waters will give you a feel for the impact of the storm on a real person.

Writers also use quoted words to lend authority to a claim they are making. Quoting the authority adds some credibility to the situation. The

Houston meteorologist who has studied the data and reports, "Harvey dumped more water in a shorter period of time on Houston than any other storm in Houston's history" ought to be believed more than the guy on the street corner who announces, "This is the worst storm ever."

In Abraham Lincoln's Second Inaugural Address, a student has noted QUOTED WORDS and asked this question: Why was this person or text quoted or cited, and what did this add?

The Almighty has his own purposes. "Woe unto the world because of offences! for it must needs be that offences come; but woe to that man by whom the offence cometh." If we shall suppose that American slavery is one of those offences which, in the providence of God, must needs come, but which, having continued through his appointed time, he now wills to remove, and that he gives to both North and South this terrible war, as the woe due to those by whom the offence came, shall we discern therein any departure from those divine attributes which the believers in a living God always ascribe to him?	Lincoln uses Quoted Words from the Bible to suggest that the nation's suffering during the Civil War is the result of divine punishment—a punishment that resulted from the nation's failure to end slavery when it was time for it to end.

WORD GAPS

Unless we read such simple texts that we know everything there is to know about the subject, we will almost inevitably stumble into the gap between the writer's vocabulary and ours. Although that's occasionally frustrating, we might see it as an opportunity to sharpen our understanding. We might either learn a new word or learn how a word we already know might be used in a new way.

If we are in a hurry (and reading in a hurry is probably a bad idea because it doesn't give us time to think), then when we encounter a new word our first question might be, "Can I get by without knowing this word?" If you can, maybe you should make what sense you can of the sentence and move on. When we do that we lose the opportunity to learn something, but occasionally we just don't have the time. At the very least, you might jot down the word on the blank pages at the back of the book as a reminder to look it up later, so that the opportunity won't be completely lost.

A better way to approach the problem of the unknown word, however, might be to strategically ask several questions. Obviously the first step is to see if the word is at least partially explained by the context. For instance, if you read "hard, objective, indisputable data," and you don't know what "indisputable" means, you can easily figure out that it is something close to "hard" or "objective." Perhaps it means "definite," "not arguable," or something similar. Close enough. If you can get that far you can probably go on without losing much. You may want to ask someone later what the word "indisputable" means, or look it up in the dictionary, but at the moment you will be able to read on.

If that easy fix doesn't work, however, you might start with "Do I know this word from somewhere else?" If you do, then you have a place to begin. What the word meant in the context with which you are familiar might be a clue to what it means in this new context. For instance, you know what it means when someone says, "I'm depositing my paycheck in the bank." But then you hear your friend say, "You can bank on me." You know your friend isn't becoming a financial lending institution. But, if you'll give yourself a moment to think about what you know about banks, then you might be able to figure out that this means you can count on your friend.

Sometimes, the word is a technical word, a term used primarily by experts in the field, and if you don't know the language of that field, you'll simply need to look it up.

In Charles C. Mann's "Coming of Age in the Dawnland," a student has noted a WORD GAP and asked this question: Can I find clues in the sentence to help me understand the word?

Armed conflict was frequent but brief and mild by European standards. The *casus belli* was usually the desire to avenge an insult or gain status, not the wish for conquest. Most battles consisted of lightning guerrilla raids by ad hoc companies in the forest: flash of black-and-yellow-striped bows behind trees, hiss and whip of stone-tipped arrows through the air, eruption of angry cries. Attackers slipped away as soon as retribution had been exacted. Losers quickly conceded their loss of status.	I don't know the phrase "casus belli," but the author lists two common reasons for "armed conflict" and war among Native American groups, so I can guess that "casus belli" probably means "reasons or causes for war."

READING AND WRITING ACROSS GENRES

by Carol Jago

Reading is a first-class ticket around the world. Not only can you explore other lands and cultures, but you can also travel to the past and future. That journey is sometimes a wild ride. Other books can feel like comfort food, enveloping you in an imaginative landscape full of friends and good times. Making time for reading is making time for life.

Genre

One of the first things readers do when we pick up something to read is notice its genre. You might not think of it exactly in those terms, but consider how you approach a word problem in math class compared to how you read a science fiction story. Readers go to different kinds of text for different purposes. When you need to know how to do or make something, you want a reliable, trusted source of information. When you're in the mood to spend some time in a world of fantasy, you happily suspend your normal disbelief in dragons.

In every unit of *Into Literature,* you'll find a diverse mix of genres all connected by a common theme, allowing you to explore a topic from many different angles.

GENRE: INFORMATIONAL TEXT

THOMAS JEFFERSON: THE BEST OF ENEMIES

How can we share power and build alliances?

Writer's Craft

Learning how writers use genre to inform, to explain, to entertain, or to surprise readers will help you better understand—as well as enjoy—your reading. Imitating how professional writers employ the tools of their craft—descriptive language, repetition, sensory images, sentence structure, and a variety of other features—will give you many ideas for making your own writing more lively.

GENRE ELEMENTS: SHORT STORY
- is a work of short fiction that centers on a single idea and can be read in one sitting
- usually includes one main conflict that involves the characters and keeps moving
- includes the basic ele of fiction—plot, chara setting, and theme
- may be based on real and historical events

GENRE ELEMENTS: INFORMATIONAL TEXT
- provides factual information
- includes evidence to support ideas
- contains text features
- includes many forms, such as news articles and essays

GENRE ELEMENTS: LITERARY NONFICTION
- shares factual information, ideas, or experiences
- develops a key insight about the topic that goes beyond the facts
- uses literary techn as figurative lang narration
- reflects a persona involvement in th

GENRE ELEMENTS: POETRY
- may use figurative language, including personification
- often includes imagery that appeals to the five senses
- expresses a theme, or a "big idea" message about life

Into Literature provides you with the tools you need to understand the elements of all the critical genres and advice on how to learn from professional texts to improve your own writing in those genres.

Reading with Independence

Finding a good book can sometimes be a challenge. Like every other reader, you have probably experienced "book desert" when nothing you pick up seems to have what you are looking for (not that it's easy to explain exactly what you are looking for, but whatever it is, "this" isn't it). If you find yourself in this kind of reading funk, bored by everything you pick up, give yourself permission to range more widely, exploring graphic novels, contemporary biographies, books of poetry, historical fiction. And remember that long doesn't necessarily mean boring. My favorite kind of book is one that I never want to end.

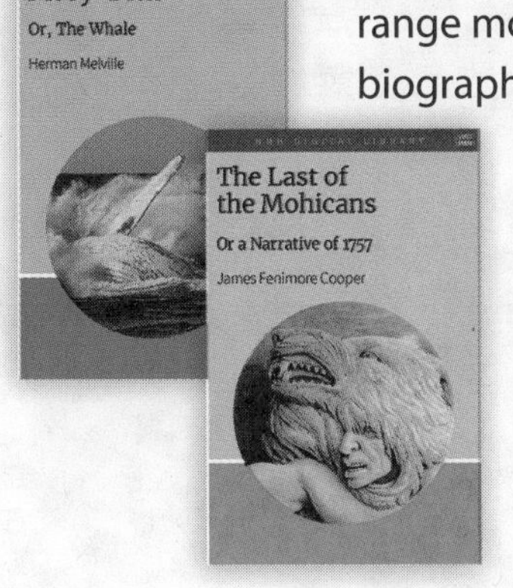

Take control over your own reading with *Into Literature's* Reader's Choice selections and the HMH Digital Library. And don't forget: your teacher, librarian, and friends can offer you many more suggestions.

SHORT STORY
Reality Check
David Brin
Explore the ways humans may continue to evolve when all concrete possibilities have been exhausted.
POEM
Democracy
Langston Hughes
How does a poet express his passionate plea for freedom?
ESSAY
Martin Luther King Jr.: He Showed Us the Way
César Chávez
Find out why César Chávez believes that King's form of protest is the only way to achieve meaningful change.

UNIT 1

FOUNDATIONS AND ENCOUNTERS

EARLY AMERICAN LITERATURE

> "[In America] individuals of all nations are melted into a new race . . . whose labors . . . will one day cause great changes in the world."
>
> —Michel-Guillaume Jean de Crèvecoeur

Discuss the **Essential Questions** with your whole class or in small groups. As you read Foundations and Encounters, consider how the selections explore these questions.

? *ESSENTIAL QUESTION:*

Why are we bound to certain places?

For thousands of years, Native Americans regarded themselves as caretakers, not owners, of the land. The Europeans who began arriving in North America, however, saw things differently. They laid claim to the land and aggressively defended it from Native Americans—and from one another. In the end, the British claim overpowered all others. Yet the question remains: What connects people to the places they live, work, and fight to preserve?

? *ESSENTIAL QUESTION:*

What motivates people to explore the unknown?

America's early explorers traveled for many reasons: to gain glory for themselves or for their countries, to find gold or other riches, to discover new routes for travel and trade. Yet none of these motivators alone seems like enough to make the uncertainties of exploration—unknown destinations, unknown rewards, unknown dangers—worth the risk. What is it that causes people to seek out the unknown?

? *ESSENTIAL QUESTION:*

What does it mean to be a stranger in a strange land?

The first European settlers in America found a land completely foreign to anything they had known in their home countries. For many of them, America was an experiment in hope. However, they first had to make sense of the challenging environment and unfamiliar people with whom they shared it as they forged a new life for themselves. How do our surroundings affect the way we live and view the world?

? *ESSENTIAL QUESTION:*

What happens when cultures collide?

About five hundred years ago, European explorers and Native Americans encountered each other for the first time. In 1620 the first English Puritans landed at Plymouth, Massachusetts. At first, the two cultures were mutually dependent, interacting peacefully and engaging in trade; but as many more Europeans arrived, tensions and conflicts arose. What opportunities present themselves when people from very different cultures meet and engage with each other for the first time? What is lost when those cultures come into conflict?

EARLY AMERICAN LITERATURE

People have been living in the Americas for at least tens of thousands of years, adapting to its diverse environments. Millions of Native Americans lived on the land, in small villages and in large cities, such as the Aztec capital of Tenochtitlán, the site of present-day Mexico City. When Europeans arrived in 1492, there were many Native American cultures in North America with strongly differing customs and about 300 different languages.

Christopher Columbus's voyage to the Caribbean in 1492 marked the beginning of contact between Europeans and Native Americans. Spain, Portugal, England, France, and the Netherlands all staked claims in the Americas. At first, Native Americans were helpful to the Europeans, but it soon became clear that the newcomers intended to take control of the land. However, firearms were not the most dangerous weapons the Europeans brought with them; they also brought new diseases that killed millions.

In the early 1500s Spain conquered the great Aztec and Inca Empires and claimed Mexico, most of South America, and large portions of what is now the United States. The first French settlements in New France were founded in the early 1600s by fur traders along the St. Lawrence River. Eventually, French holdings included the Great Lakes region and most of the land along the Mississippi River, which was named Louisiana.

English Settlers The English were eager to have a colony in the New World and to prevent the northward expansion of the Spanish colony in Florida. A private trading company, the Virginia Company of London, established the first permanent English settlement at Jamestown, Virginia, in 1607. In 1619 the first Africans were brought to Virginia as enslaved persons to work for white slaveholders.

The original settlers of New England were Pilgrims, Protestant reformers who wanted to separate from the Church of England. Among them was William Bradford, who helped organize the voyage of the *Mayflower*, bringing nearly a hundred people to Massachusetts in 1620. Another group who settled in New England were the Puritans, who wanted to "purify" the Church of England. The Puritans' religious beliefs influenced all aspects of their lives, and the values of hard work, thrift, and responsibility led to thriving settlements and financial success.

COLLABORATIVE DISCUSSION

In a small group, review the timeline and discuss which literary or historical events had the most impact and why.

1400

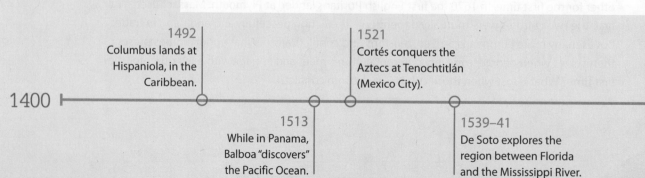

1492
Columbus lands at Hispaniola, in the Caribbean.

1513
While in Panama, Balboa "discovers" the Pacific Ocean.

1521
Cortés conquers the Aztecs at Tenochtitlán (Mexico City).

1539–41
De Soto explores the region between Florida and the Mississippi River.

Native American Oral Traditions Few of the Native American cultures had a written language, but all possessed strong oral cultures and a rich tradition of storytelling. Creation stories—ways to explain how the universe and humans came into being—can be found in every Native American culture. Other forms include legendary histories tracing the migration of peoples or the deeds of cultural heroes, trickster tales, lyrics, chants, songs, healing ceremonies, and dream visions.

Tragically, much of this literature did not survive after so many Native Americans died from European diseases. The surviving works, however, show that diverse Native American groups explored common themes in their spoken literature, including a reverence for nature and the worship of many gods. Contemporary Native American writers, such as Joy Harjo, often incorporate elements of these traditional tales in their writing.

Pre-Colonial Literature While Native American literature offers us a glimpse into the ways and values of America's indigenous peoples, much of our understanding of pre-colonial America comes from the first-person accounts of its early explorers, settlers, and colonists. One of the founders of Jamestown, John Smith, wrote about conflicts with Native Americans, but he also described the "New World" as a paradise with great economic

RESEARCH
What about this historical period interests you? Choose a topic, event, or person to learn more about. Then, add your own entry to the timeline.

1607
First permanent English settlement is founded in Jamestown, Virginia.

1620
Mayflower Pilgrims found Plymouth colony in Massachusetts.

1676
English settlers defeat Native Americans in King Philip's War.

1682
France claims the Mississippi River valley and names it *Louisiana.*

1700

potential. William Bradford, governor of Plymouth Plantation, described North America as "a hideous and desolate wilderness, full of wild beasts and wild men." Bradford and other colonial writers were motivated by their beliefs about their role in God's plan. Their writings included historical narratives, sermons, and poems written in a generally plain style.

Anne Bradstreet was one of the first poets in the American colonies. A volume of her poetry was published in England in 1650 as The Tenth Muse. Some of her best work is on personal themes, such as childbirth and the death of a grandchild.

CHECK YOUR UNDERSTANDING

Choose the best answer to each question.

1 What was North America like before the arrival of Europeans?

A It was an empty continent with abundant resources.

B It was a diverse land with more than 300 well-developed cultures with strongly differing customs.

C North America was a land recently settled by Native American groups that shared a single culture.

D North America was a continent ravaged by disease and warfare.

2 Which statement is an accurate description of Native American literature?

F It was a rich oral tradition focusing on creation stories and a reverence for nature.

G It was written in pictographs similar to Egyptian hieroglyphics.

H It contained many of the same myths and folktales that appear in European cultures.

J It had no literature because Native Americans did not have a written language.

3 We get most of our information about pre-colonial America from —

A modern-day scholars of the historical period

B elaborate written records from ancient civilizations

C first-person accounts of early explorers, settlers, and colonists

D Native American creation myths

ACADEMIC VOCABULARY

Academic Vocabulary words are words you use when you discuss and write about texts. In this unit, you will learn the following five words:

☑ **adapt** ❑ **coherent** ❑ **device** ❑ **displace** ❑ **dynamic**

Study the Word Network to learn more about the word **adapt.**

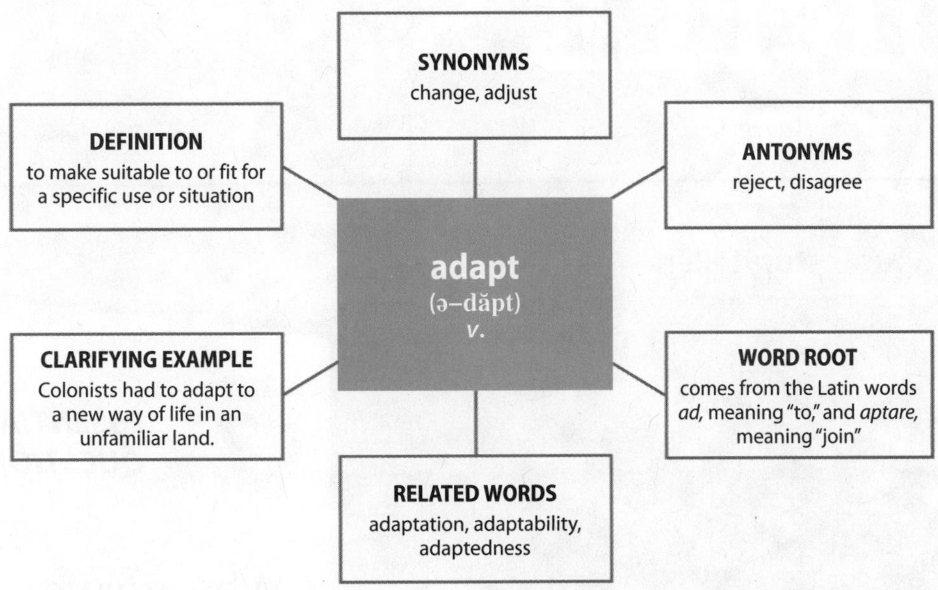

SYNONYMS
change, adjust
DEFINITION
to make suitable to or fit for a specific use or situation
ANTONYMS
reject, disagree
adapt
(ə–dăpt)
v.
CLARIFYING EXAMPLE
Colonists had to adapt to a new way of life in an unfamiliar land.
WORD ROOT
comes from the Latin words ad, meaning "to," and aptare, meaning "join"
RELATED WORDS
adaptation, adaptability, adaptedness

Write and Discuss Discuss your completed Word Network with a partner, making sure to talk through all of the boxes until you both understand the word, its synonyms, antonyms, and related forms. Then, fill out a Word Network for the remaining four words. Use a dictionary or online resource to help you complete the activity.

Go online to access the Word Networks.

RESPOND TO THE ESSENTIAL QUESTIONS

In this unit, you will explore four different **Essential Questions** about early American literature and related texts. As you read each selection, you will gather your ideas about one of these questions and write about it in the **Response Log that appears on page R1**. At the end of the unit, you will have the opportunity to write a **literary analysis** related to one of the Essential Questions. Filling out the Response Log after you read each text will help you prepare for this writing task.

You can also go online to access the Response Log.

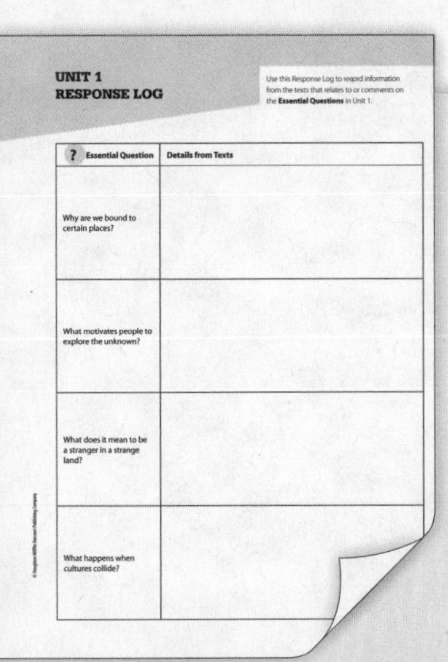

UNIT 1
RESPONSE LOG

Use this Response Log to record information from the texts that relates to or comments on the **Essential Questions** in Unit 1.

? Essential Question	Details from Texts
Why are we bound to certain places?	
What motivates people to explore the unknown?	
What does it mean to be a stranger in a strange land?	
What happens when cultures collide?	

THE WORLD ON THE TURTLE'S BACK

Myth by **Iroquois storytellers**

? ESSENTIAL QUESTION:

Why are we bound to certain places?

QUICK START

Think about creation myths you have heard or read. Do they tell how something began or how something in nature works? Did you believe in the myth? Discuss with a partner.

ANALYZE FOLK LITERATURE

You may already be familiar with **folk literature,** which includes folk tales, myths, fables, and legends passed orally from one generation to the next. A **creation myth** is a traditional folk story with supernatural elements that describes how the universe, Earth, and life began, or explains the workings of the natural world.

Folk literature often include **archetypes,** or characters, situations, or actions that represent universal examples of human nature. For example, the twins in this myth represent two archetypal characters: the hero and the villain. Note other elements that may represent universal examples as you read.

Using the following strategies as you read will help you understand and appreciate the myth's message:

- Read the myth aloud, or imagine a storyteller's voice as you read silently.
- Note mysteries of nature and details about creation that the myth explains.
- Keep track of the ways in which the elements of a creation myth are used. What does this tell you about the genre?

MAKE INFERENCES

This myth articulates the religious beliefs, social customs, and values of the Iroquois culture. However, these beliefs and customs are not directly stated. It is up to you to **infer** them based on the details in the text. The characters' behavior and the way conflicts are resolved suggest the social values and customs that the storytellers wish to convey. As you read, use a chart to note your observations and inferences about what the Iroquois value.

DETAILS ABOUT STORY EVENTS	SOCIAL VALUES AND CUSTOMS	OTHER CULTURAL DETAILS

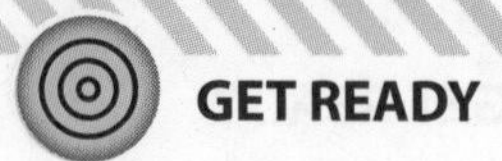

GET READY

CRITICAL VOCABULARY

delicacies **frantically** **vanquish** **pliable**

To see how many Critical Vocabulary words you already know, use them to complete the sentences.

1. Some plastics are hard, while others are as __________ as rubber.
2. The coach __________ ran onto the field to help his injured player.
3. The menu included many __________, such as truffles and caviar.
4. Ultimately, our forces will __________ the enemy.

LANGUAGE CONVENTIONS

Reflexive Pronouns In this lesson you will learn about reflexive pronouns. They are formed by adding *-self* or *-selves* to certain personal pronouns. A reflexive pronoun follows a verb or preposition and reflects back on an earlier noun or pronoun.

> **He wouldn't get any of the roots for her, so she set out to do it herself.**

The reflexive pronoun *herself* refers back to the pronoun *she.* As you read "The World on the Turtle's Back," note the use of reflexive pronouns.

ANNOTATION MODEL

NOTICE & NOTE

As you read, record your notes and observations about the kinds of information you find in this creation myth. You may also mark the details in the text that suggests the social values of the Iroquois. In the model, you can see one reader's notes about "The World on the Turtle's Back."

In the beginning there was no world, no land, no creatures of the kind that are around us now, and there were no men. But there was a great ocean which occupied space as far as anyone could see. Above the ocean was a great void of air. And in the air there lived the birds of the sea; in the ocean lived the fish and the creatures of the deep. Far above this unpeopled world, there was a Sky-World. Here lived gods who were like people—like Iroquois.

The opening words suggest that this is a story of creation.

Gods are supernatural beings, so this is a myth.

Gods appear in human form.

BACKGROUND

"The World on the Turtle's Back" is an Iroquois (ĭr´ə-kwoi´) creation myth filled with conflict and compelling characters. In 1828, Iroquois author David Cusick was the first to write the story down. Today, more than 25 written versions exist.

The term **Iroquois** *refers to six Native American groups that share a culture. Most of them reside in what is now New York state. They call themselves Haudenosaunee, meaning "People of the Longhouse," after the longhouses in which they lived. Between 1570 and 1600, they formed the Iroquois League and managed to remain free from European rule.*

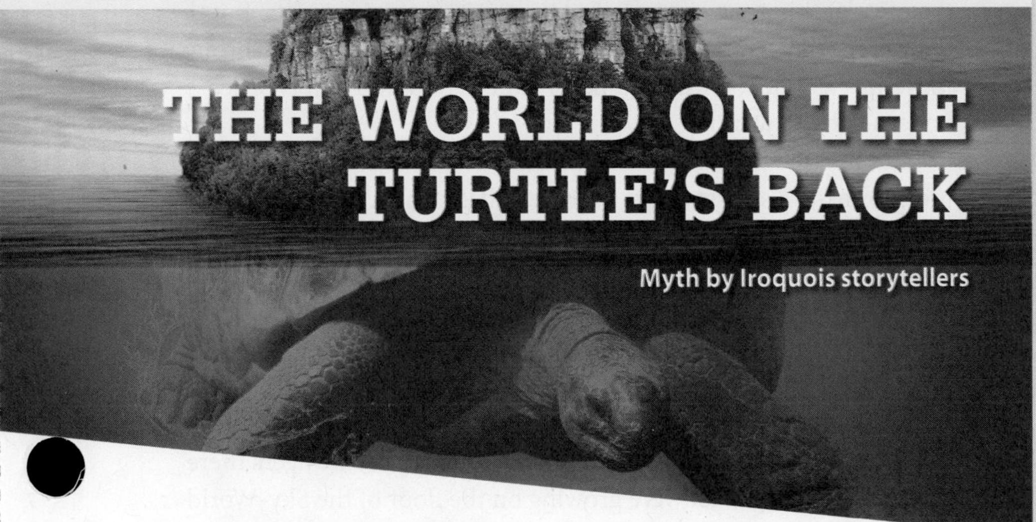

THE WORLD ON THE TURTLE'S BACK

Myth by Iroquois storytellers

SETTING A PURPOSE

As you read, pay attention to the details of this Iroquois creation myth. Note similarities and differences between this account and other tales of creation you are familiar with.

Notice & Note

Use the side margins to notice and note signposts in the text.

1 In the beginning there was no world, no land, no creatures of the kind that are around us now, and there were no men. But there was a great ocean which occupied space as far as anyone could see. Above the ocean was a great void of air. And in the air there lived the birds of the sea; in the ocean lived the fish and the creatures of the deep. Far above this unpeopled world, there was a Sky-World. Here lived gods who were like people—like Iroquois.

2 In the Sky-World there was a man who had a wife, and the wife was expecting a child. The woman became hungry for all kinds of strange **delicacies**, as women do when they are with child. She kept her husband busy almost to distraction finding delicious things for her to eat.

3 In the middle of the Sky-World there grew a Great Tree which was not like any of the trees that we know. It was tremendous; it had grown there forever. It had enormous roots

delicacy
(dĕl´ĭ-kə-sē) *n.* something pleasing and appealing, especially a choice food.

NOTICE & NOTE

that spread out from the floor of the Sky-World. And on its branches there were many different kinds of leaves and different kinds of fruits and flowers. The tree was not supposed to be marked or mutilated by any of the beings who dwelt in the Sky-World. It was a sacred tree that stood at the center of the universe.

ANALYZE FOLK LITERATURE

Annotate: In the first four paragraphs, mark words and phrases that indicate that this is a creation myth.

Evaluate: Explain whether the man and his wife are archetypal characters. In your response, consider details in the text, as well as other accounts of creation you've heard or read.

4 The woman decided that she wanted some bark from one of the roots of the Great Tree—perhaps as a food or as a medicine, we don't know. She told her husband this. He didn't like the idea. He knew it was wrong. But she insisted, and he gave in. So he dug a hole among the roots of this great sky tree, and he bared some of its roots. But the floor of the Sky-World wasn't very thick, and he broke a hole through it. He was terrified, for he had never expected to find empty space underneath the world.

5 But his wife was filled with curiosity. He wouldn't get any of the roots for her, so she set out to do it herself. She bent over and she looked down, and she saw the ocean far below. She leaned down and stuck her head through the hole and looked all around. No one knows just what happened next. Some say she slipped. Some say that her husband, fed up with all the demands she had made on him, pushed her.

frantically
(frăn´tĭ-kəl-lē) *adv.* excitedly, with strong emotion or frustration.

6 So she fell through the hole. As she fell, she **frantically** grabbed at its edges, but her hands slipped. However, between her fingers there clung bits of things that were growing on the floor of the Sky-World and bits of the root tips of the Great Tree. And so she began to fall toward the great ocean far below.

7 The birds of the sea saw the woman falling, and they immediately consulted with each other as to what they could do to help her. Flying wingtip to wingtip they made a great feathery raft in the sky to support her, and thus they broke her fall. But of course it was not possible for them to carry the woman very long. Some of the other birds of the sky flew down to the surface of the ocean and called up the ocean creatures to see what they could do to help. The great sea turtle came and agreed to receive her on his back. The birds placed her gently on the shell of the turtle, and now the turtle floated about on the huge ocean with the woman safely on his back.

8 The beings up in the Sky-World paid no attention to this. They knew what was happening, but they chose to ignore it.

9 When the woman recovered from her shock and terror, she looked around her. All that she could see were the birds and the sea creatures and the sky and the ocean.

10 And the woman said to herself that she would die. But the creatures of the sea came to her and said that they would try to help her and asked her what they could do. She told them that if they could find some soil, she could plant the roots stuck between her fingers, and from them plants would grow. The sea animals said

perhaps there was dirt at the bottom of the ocean, but no one had ever been down there so they could not be sure.

11 If there was dirt at the bottom of the ocean, it was far, far below the surface in the cold deeps. But the animals said they would try to get some. One by one the diving birds and animals tried and failed. They went to the limits of their endurance, but they could not get to the bottom of the ocean. Finally, the muskrat said he would try. He dived and disappeared. All the creatures waited, holding their breath, but he did not return. After a long time, his little body floated up to the surface of the ocean, a tiny crumb of earth clutched in his paw. He seemed to be dead. They pulled him up on the turtle's back and they sang and prayed over him and breathed air into his mouth, and finally, he stirred. Thus it was the muskrat, the Earth-Diver, who brought from the bottom of the ocean the soil from which the earth was to grow.

12 The woman took the tiny clod of dirt and placed it on the middle of the great sea turtle's back. Then the woman began to walk in a circle around it, moving in the direction that the sun goes. The earth began to grow. When the earth was big enough, she planted the roots she had clutched between her fingers when she fell from the Sky-World. Thus the plants grew on the earth.

13 To keep the earth growing, the woman walked as the sun goes, moving in the direction that the people still move in the dance rituals. She gathered roots and plants to eat and built herself a little hut. After a while, the woman's time came, and she was delivered of a daughter. The woman and her daughter kept walking in a circle around the earth, so that the earth and plants would continue to grow. They lived on the plants and roots they gathered. The girl grew up with her mother, cut off forever from the Sky-World above, knowing only the birds and the creatures of the sea, seeing no other beings like herself.

14 One day, when the girl had grown to womanhood, a man appeared. No one knows for sure who this man was. He had something to do with the gods above. Perhaps he was the West Wind. As the girl looked at him, she was filled with terror, and amazement, and warmth, and she fainted dead away. As she lay on the ground, the man reached into his quiver, and he took out two arrows, one sharp and one blunt, and he laid them across the body of the girl, and quietly went away.

15 When the girl awoke from her faint, she and her mother continued to walk around the earth. After a while, they knew that the girl was to bear a child. They did not know it, but the girl was to bear twins.

16 Within the girl's body, the twins began to argue and quarrel with one another. There could be no peace between them. As the time approached for them to be born, the twins fought about their birth.

NOTICE & NOTE

MAKE INFERENCES

Annotate: Reread paragraphs 7–11 and mark the phrases that describe the roles "all the creatures" play in this myth.

Infer: What do these passages suggest about the Iroquois' attitude toward animals?

LANGUAGE CONVENTIONS

Annotate: A reflexive pronoun reflects back on a noun or pronoun. Mark the reflexive pronouns in paragraph 13.

Identify: Identify the word each pronoun reflects back on.

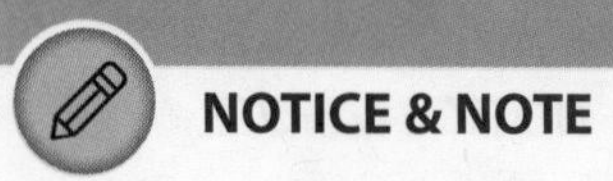

ANALYZE FOLK LITERATURE

Annotate: Mark the phrases in paragraphs 16–18 that describe the twins' relationship.

Predict: Based on the details in these paragraphs, how do you think the twins' conflict will be resolved? Why?

The right-handed twin wanted to be born in the normal way, as all children are born. But the left-handed twin said no. He said he saw light in another direction, and said he would be born that way. The right-handed twin beseeched him not to, saying that he would kill their mother. But the left-handed twin was stubborn. He went in the direction where he saw light. But he could not be born through his mother's mouth or her nose. He was born through her left armpit, and killed her. And meanwhile, the right-handed twin was born in the normal way, as all children are born.

17 The twins met in the world outside, and the right-handed twin accused his brother of murdering their mother. But the grandmother told them to stop their quarreling. They buried their mother. And from her grave grew the plants which the people still use. From her head grew the corn, the beans, and the squash—"our supporters, the three sisters."[1] And from her heart grew the sacred tobacco, which the people still use in the ceremonies and by whose upward-floating smoke they send thanks. The women call her "our mother," and they dance and sing in the rituals so that the corn, the beans, and the squash may grow to feed the people.

18 But the conflict of the twins did not end at the grave of their mother. And, strangely enough, the grandmother favored the left-handed twin.

19 The right-handed twin was angry, and he grew more angry as he thought how his brother had killed their mother. The right-handed twin was the one who did everything just as he should. He said what he meant, and he meant what he said. He always told the truth, and he always tried to accomplish what seemed to be right and reasonable. The left-handed twin never said what he meant or meant what he said. He always lied, and he always did things backward. You could never tell what he was trying to do because he always made it look as if he were doing the opposite. He was the devious one.

20 These two brothers, as they grew up, represented two ways of the world which are in all people. The Indians did not call these the right and the wrong. They called them the straight mind and the crooked mind, the upright man and the devious man, the right and the left.

21 The twins had creative powers. They took clay and modeled it into animals, and they gave these animals life. And in this they contended with one another. The right-handed twin made the deer, and the left-handed twin made the mountain lion which kills the deer. But the right-handed twin knew there would always be more deer than mountain lions. And he made another animal. He made the ground squirrel. The left-handed twin saw that the mountain lion

[1] **the three sisters:** Corn, beans, and squash—the Iroquois' staple food crops—were grown together. The bean vines climbed and were supported by the corn stalks, while squash, which spread across the ground and kept weeds from growing, was planted around the bean plants.

could not get to the ground squirrel, who digs a hole, so he made the weasel. And although the weasel can go into the ground squirrel's hole and kill him, there are lots of ground squirrels and not so many weasels. Next the right-handed twin decided he would make an animal that the weasel could not kill, so he made the porcupine. But the left-handed twin made the bear, who flips the porcupine over on his back and tears out his belly.

22 And the right-handed twin made berries and fruits of other kinds for his creatures to live on. The left-handed twin made briars and poison ivy, and the poisonous plants like the baneberry and the dogberry, and the suicide root with which people kill themselves when they go out of their minds. And the left-handed twin made medicines, for good and for evil, for doctoring and for witchcraft.

23 And finally, the right-handed twin made man. The people do not know just how much the left-handed twin had to do with making man. Man was made of clay, like pottery, and baked in the fire. . . .

24 The world the twins made was a balanced and orderly world, and this was good. The plant-eating animals created by the right-handed twin would eat up all the vegetation if their number was not kept down by the meat-eating animals, which the left-handed twin created. But if these carnivorous animals ate too many other animals, then they would starve, for they would run out of meat. So the right- and the left-handed twins built balance into the world.

25 As the twins became men full grown, they still contested with one another. No one had won, and no one had lost. And they knew that the conflict was becoming sharper and sharper, and one of them would have to **vanquish** the other.

26 And so they came to the duel. They started with gambling. They took a wooden bowl, and in it they put wild plum pits. One side of the pits was burned black, and by tossing the pits in the bowl and betting on how these would fall, they gambled against one another, as the people still do in the New Year's rites.[2] All through the morning they gambled at this game, and all through the afternoon, and the sun went down. And when the sun went down, the game was done, and neither one had won.

27 So they went on to battle one another at the lacrosse[3] game. And they contested all day, and the sun went down, and the game was done. And neither had won.

28 And now they battled with clubs, and they fought all day, and the sun went down, and the fight was done. But neither had won.

[2] **New Year's rites:** Various ceremonies to get ready for the New Year. They often included community confession of sins, the replenishing of hearths in the homes, sacred dances, as well as the gambling ritual.

[3] **lacrosse:** a game of Native American origin wherein participants on two teams use long-handled sticks with webbed pouches to maneuver a ball into the opposing team's goal.

MAKE INFERENCES

Annotate: Mark phrases in paragraphs 19–23 that describe each twin's character and behavior.

Infer: Which twin is characterized as being more admirable? What does this characterization tell you about Iroquois values?

vanquish (văng´kwĭsh) *v.* to defeat in a contest or conflict.

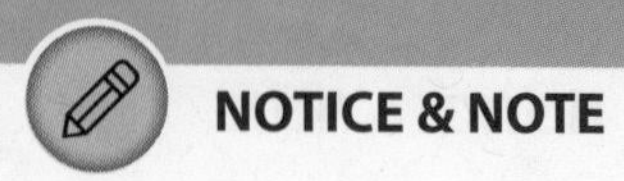

NOTICE & NOTE

29 And they went from one duel to another to see which one would succumb. Each one knew in his deepest mind that there was something, somewhere, that would vanquish the other. But what was it? Where to find it?

30 Each knew somewhere in his mind what it was that was his own weak point. They talked about this as they contested in these duels, day after day, and somehow the deep mind of each entered into the other. And the deep mind of the right-handed twin lied to his brother, and the deep mind of the left-handed twin told the truth.

31 On the last day of the duel, as they stood, they at last knew how the right-handed twin was to kill his brother. Each selected his weapon. The left-handed twin chose a mere stick that would do him no good. But the right-handed twin picked out the deer antler, and with one touch he destroyed his brother. And the left-handed twin died, but he died and he didn't die. The right-handed twin picked up the body and cast it off the edge of the earth. And some place below the world, the left-handed twin still lives and reigns.

ANALYZE FOLK LITERATURE

Annotate: Mark the phrases in paragraphs 32–33 that tell what happened to the left-handed twin and the grandmother.

Analyze: How does this myth explain the fact that the moon is visible mainly at night?

32 When the sun rises from the east and travels in a huge arc along the sky dome, which rests like a great upside-down cup on the saucer of the earth, the people are in the daylight realm of the right-handed twin. But when the sun slips down in the west at nightfall and the dome lifts to let it escape at the western rim, the people are again in the domain of the left-handed twin—the fearful realm of night.

33 Having killed his brother, the right-handed twin returned home to his grandmother. And she met him in anger. She threw the food out of the cabin onto the ground and said that he was a murderer, for he had killed his brother. He grew angry and told her she had always helped his brother, who had killed their mother. In his anger, he grabbed her by the throat and cut her head off. Her body he threw into the ocean, and her head, into the sky. There, "Our Grandmother, the Moon" still keeps watch at night over the realm of her favorite grandson.

pliable
(plī´ə-bəl) *adj.* easily bent or shaped; easily influenced, persuaded, or controlled.

34 The right-handed twin has many names. One of them is Sapling. It means smooth, young, green and fresh and innocent, straightforward, straight-growing, soft and **pliable**, teachable and trainable. These are the old ways of describing him. But since he has gone away, he has other names. He is called "He Holds Up the Skies," "Master of Life," and "Great Creator."

35 The left-handed twin also has many names. One of them is Flint. He is called the devious one, the one covered with boils. Old Warty. He is stubborn. He is thought of as being dark in color.

36 These two beings rule the world and keep an eye on the affairs of men. The right-handed twin, the Master of Life, lives in the Sky-World. He is content with the world he helped to create and with his favorite creatures, the humans. The scent of sacred tobacco rising from the earth comes gloriously to his nostrils.

37 In the world below lives the left-handed twin. He knows the world of men, and he finds contentment in it. He hears the sounds of warfare and torture, and he finds them good.

38 In the daytime, the people have rituals which honor the right-handed twin. Through the daytime rituals, they thank the Master of Life. In the nighttime, the people dance and sing for the left-handed twin.

MAKE INFERENCES

Annotate: Reread paragraphs 36–38. Circle information that tells you about the right-handed twin. Underline information that tells you about the left-handed twin.

Infer: Based on the information contained in these paragraphs, what can you infer about Iroquois customs and values?

CHECK YOUR UNDERSTANDING

Answer these questions before moving on to the **Analyze the Text** section on the following page.

1 How does the turtle help the woman who fell from the sky?

A He brings soil from the ocean floor.

B He carries the woman on his back.

C He breaks the woman's fall.

D He makes the earth grow.

2 What happened when the twins' mother is buried?

F A sacred tree grew from her head.

G Man was created from her ribs.

H The plants that people still use grew.

J She became the light in the sky.

3 What happens to the left-handed twin?

A He kills his brother and mother.

B He kills his grandmother.

C He becomes the Master of Life.

D He becomes ruler of the underworld.

RESPOND

ANALYZE THE TEXT

Support your responses with evidence from the text. NOTEBOOK

1. **Infer** What Iroquois values are revealed by the creatures' actions toward the woman who fell?
2. **Analyze** What characteristics and behaviors suggest that the right-handed twin is an archetypal hero? What characteristics and behaviors suggest the left-handed twin is an archetypal villain? Cite text evidence in your response.
3. **Analyze** How is the conflict between the twins resolved? What does the resolution suggest about the Iroquois' view of both twins?
4. **Draw Conclusions** What elements of the world and human nature does this creation myth explain? Cite text evidence in your response.
5. **Connect** Folk literature often conveys information about a people's culture. From this myth, what do you learn about the Iroquois' attitude toward nature and their view of their gods?

RESEARCH

RESEARCH TIP

You might want to begin your research by learning more about creation myths in general. There are websites or books that include creation myths. Find at least two reliable sources about another culture's creation myth for the information you use.

Almost every culture has an explanation of how the world was created. Research creation myths from a variety of cultures around the world, including other Native American groups. Choose one creation myth to compare with "The World on the Turtle's Back." Write the name of the myth and the culture it comes from in the first column of the chart. Then record two similarities and two differences between the myth you chose and "The World on the Turtle's Back."

CREATION MYTH	SIMILARITIES	DIFFERENCES

Extend Think about what you have learned about creation myths from this activity. Did they have many of the characteristics you learned about in this lesson? What do the two myths you compared tell you about the values of their respective cultures? How do those values compare with the values of modern American culture?

CREATE AND PRESENT

Write a Myth A myth is a traditional story that explains how some aspect of human nature or the natural world came to be. Work with a partner to write a myth.

- ❑ Decide on an aspect of nature or a human characteristic that you want to write about. Start by asking yourself a question, such as "Why do giraffes have long necks?"
- ❑ Create a cast of characters and give them appropriate names. Keep in mind that your characters may be gods, humans, or animals, and may be able to act in exceptional ways.
- ❑ Develop a conflict and resolution that will allow you to provide the answer to your question.
- ❑ As you describe the events in your myth, use vivid imagery that will help paint a mental picture for readers or listeners.

Present a Myth Prepare to present your myth orally with your partner, either before a small group or the whole class.

- ❑ Decide how you will divide your myth for presentation. Will each of you read alternate paragraphs, or will one person read the narration and the other read the dialogue?
- ❑ Practice reading the myth together before you make your presentation.
- ❑ Be prepared to answer other students' questions about your myth and its meaning.

Go to **Writing Narratives** in the **Writing Studio** for help.

Go to **Giving a Presentation: Delivering Your Presentation** in the **Speaking and Listening Studio** for help.

RESPOND TO THE ESSENTIAL QUESTION

Why are we bound to certain places?

Gather Information Review your annotations and notes on "The World on the Turtle's Back." Then add relevant information to your Response Log. As you determine which information to include, think about:

- the role of folk literature in a culture
- the view of humanity expressed by the myth
- Iroquois beliefs and rituals that are revealed through the story

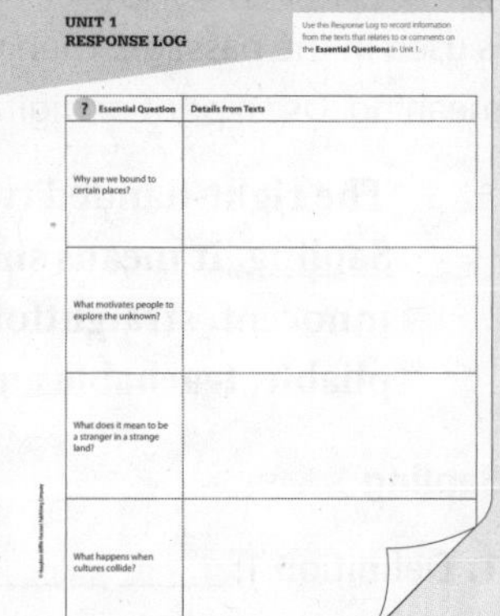

UNIT 1
RESPONSE LOG

Use this Response Log to record information from the texts that relates to or comments on the **Essential Questions** in Unit 1.

? Essential Question	Details from Texts
Why are we bound to certain places?	
What motivates people to explore the unknown?	
What does it mean to be a stranger in a strange land?	
What happens when cultures collide?	

ACADEMIC VOCABULARY

As you write and discuss what you learned from "The World on the Turtle's Back," be sure to use the Academic Vocabulary words. Check off each of the words that you use.

- ❑ **adapt**
- ❑ **coherent**
- ❑ **device**
- ❑ **displace**
- ❑ **dynamic**

RESPOND

CRITICAL VOCABULARY

WORD BANK
delicacies
frantically
vanquish
pliable

Practice and Apply Answer each question with a complete sentence to show that you understand the meaning of each Critical Vocabulary word.

1. How would you respond if you were offered a variety of **delicacies?**
2. How would you feel if you were searching **frantically** for something?
3. What might someone do to **vanquish** an enemy?
4. Would someone who is **pliable** stand firm or be willing to compromise?

VOCABULARY STRATEGY: Multiple-Meaning Words

Go to **Words with Multiple-Meanings** in the **Vocabulary Studio** for more on.

Many words have more than one meaning. For example, when the word *delicacies* is used in "The World on the Turtle's Back," it means "a pleasing or appealing food choice," as in this sentence from the myth:

> **The woman became hungry for all kinds of strange delicacies, as women do when they are with child.**

The word *delicacy* can also mean "fineness in appearance or construction," "frailty of bodily heath," "sensitivity to the feelings of others," or "sensitivity to small changes." When you come across a familiar word used in an unfamiliar way, follow these steps to determine its meaning:

- Look at the word's context to determine its part of speech and infer the correct meaning.
- Consult a print or digital dictionary to look up all the meanings of the word.
- Compare your preliminary determination of the word's meaning to the dictionary definitions to verify the meaning of the word in context.

Practice and Apply Each of the underlined words in the following passage has multiple meanings. For each word, write the definition of the word as it is used in the passage. Then write a definition of the word using a different meaning. Use a print or digital resource to validate your responses.

> **The right-handed twin has many names. One of them is <u>Sapling</u>. It means smooth, young, <u>green</u> and fresh and innocent, straightforward, straight-growing, soft and pliable, teachable and trainable.**

Sapling

1. Definition 1: ______________________________

2. Definition 2: ______________________________

green

1. Definition 1: ______________________________

2. Definition 2: ______________________________

LANGUAGE CONVENTIONS:
Reflexive Pronouns

Go to **Pronouns** in the **Grammar Studio** for help.

Reflexive pronouns are used as direct objects or indirect objects. Reflexive pronouns are used when the subject and object are the same, so they reflect on the subject of the sentence. The following words are reflexive pronouns: *myself, yourself, herself, himself, itself, ourselves, yourselves,* and *themselves.*

Reflexive pronouns can be used to provide emphasis—that the subject did something alone and not with the help of someone else. For example, *Leslie did the experiment by herself.* This sentence stresses that no one helped Leslie.

Reflexive pronouns are also used to avoid awkwardness. For example, it would be awkward to repeat the subject: *Brian made Brian a salad.* Using a reflexive pronoun eliminates the repetition: *Brian made himself a salad.*

Reflexive pronouns are used in the following ways in "The World on the Turtle's Back":

- As an indirect object to tell whom the woman said something to.

  And the woman said to herself that she would die.

- As a direct object to tell whom the woman built the hut for.

  She gathered roots and plants to eat and built herself a little hut.

Practice and Apply Write your own sentences using reflexive pronouns. Use the examples from "The World on the Turtle's Back" as models. When you have finished, share your sentences with a partner.

BALBOA

Short Story by **Sabina Murray**

? ESSENTIAL QUESTION:

What motivates people to explore the unknown?

QUICK START

Is your image of yourself different from the image you want others to see? How so? Does this ever cause conflict with others—or within yourself? Take a few minutes to write your thoughts on these questions.

ANALYZE THEMATIC DEVELOPMENT

Writers of fiction often use their works to communicate insights about life or human nature called **themes.** Most of these themes are not stated; readers must infer them by looking closely at other elements of the work, such as characters, plot, and setting. To identify and trace the development of the themes in "Balboa," ask yourself these questions:

- **Character** How does the main character change or fail to change? What qualities does the main character possess? How do these qualities determine his or her reaction to the conflict? What message does the author convey through how the character's traits influence his or her reactions?
- **Plot** What is the major conflict in the story? How does this conflict lead to other problems? How is the conflict resolved? Is there a lesson to be learned from the way the conflict is resolved?
- **Setting** How does the setting contribute to the problem or challenge a character faces? What qualities does the character reveal as he or she interacts with the setting? What theme might emerge from the way the character solves the problem?

ANALYZE PLOT STRUCTURE

The structure of a story is its organization. Many stories are organized chronologically, following a tale from its beginning to its end. Sometimes, however, authors decide to present the sequence of events out of order to add interest or suspense. They may also seek to achieve a more subtle effect, such as providing information on characters or setting that may be important to the plot. To analyze the structure of "Balboa," look at how the author uses the narrative techniques described in the chart.

FLASHBACK	FLASH FORWARD
A flashback is a scene that interrupts the action to describe events that took place earlier in time. Flashbacks add important background information to help readers gain a new perspective on characters and their motives, understand the causes of events, or see the author's message more clearly. You will see the protagonist in "Balboa" recall significant past events several times.	Flash forward interrupts the narrative to give readers a look at what will happen after the events in the main plot take place. A flash forward may change readers' outlook on events and characters in the story, affect the mood that is created, or illuminate the meaning of the work. In "Balboa," the author chooses to conclude her story with a flash forward focusing on the end of the protagonist's life.

GENRE ELEMENTS: SHORT STORY

- expresses a theme, or insight about life or human nature
- contains literary elements such as character, plot, and setting that develop the theme
- may use narrative techniques such as flashbacks or flash forwards to build interest and suspense

GET READY

CRITICAL VOCABULARY

pristine supplant protrude provision discord distinction cede

To see how many Critical Vocabulary words you already know, work with a partner to complete the following sentence stems.

1. If a landscape is **pristine,** it looks . . .
2. When a seedling **protrudes** from the soil, it . . .
3. If someone **supplants** a leader, he or she . . .
4. When there is **discord** between siblings, the mood in a family is . . .
5. The **distinction** between a blog and an online news source is . . .
6. For a camping trip, I need the following **provisions**: . . .
7. If a knight in a story **cedes** victory to his opponent, he . . .

LANGUAGE CONVENTIONS

Verb Tenses The tense of a verb indicates the time of the action or state of being. An action or state of being can occur in the present, the past, or the future. Short stories are usually told in **past tense** (Sam walked to the store) or **present tense** (Sam walks to the store). However, if the author wants to use plot structures other than chronological order, such as flashback or flash forward, other verb tenses may be used. As you read "Balboa," look for ways the author moves the story around in time by changing the verb tense.

ANNOTATION MODEL

NOTICE & NOTE 

As you read, note details about plot, character, and setting that develop the theme. You may also note any information that seems important to you. In the model, you can see one reader's notes about "Balboa."

Vasco Núñez de Balboa ascends the mountain alone. His one thousand Indians and two hundred Spaniards wait at the foot of the mountain, as if they are the Israelites and Balboa alone is off to speak with God. Balboa knows that from this peak he will be able to see the western water, what he has already decided to name the South Sea. He takes a musket with him. The Spaniards have been warned that if they follow, he will use it, because discovery is a tricky matter and he wants no competition. The day is September 25, 1513.

The word "alone" is repeated; Balboa thinks he is exceptional.

Details paint Balboa as ambitious and arrogant.

Ambition and power are key ideas; probably related to the theme.

BACKGROUND

Vasco Núñez de Balboa (1475–1519) was a Spanish explorer and conquistador who first came to the Americas in 1500 as part of a voyage exploring the coast of present-day Colombia. He is most remembered for being the first European to view the Pacific Ocean in 1513. This event and other facts of Balboa's life form the basis of **Sabina Murray's** *story, published in her book Tales of the New World (2011). Murray lives in western Massachusetts, where she is on the Creative Writing faculty at the University of Massachusetts Amherst.*

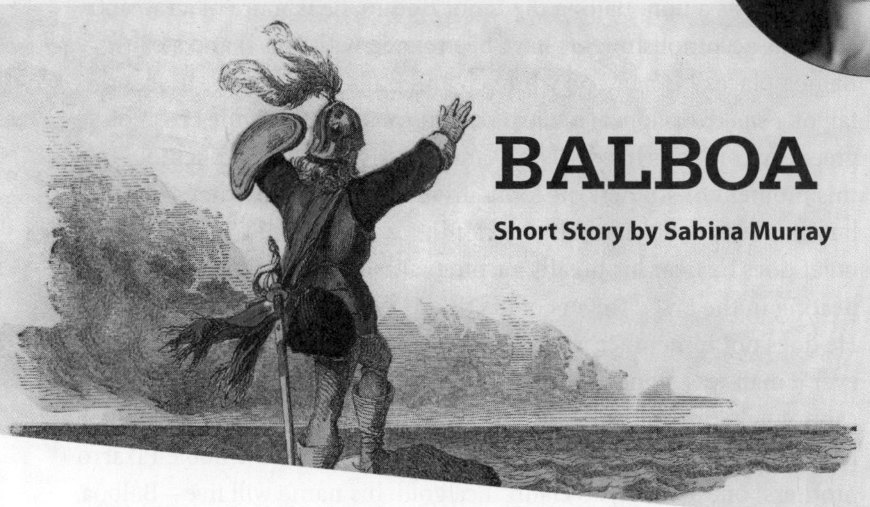

BALBOA

Short Story by Sabina Murray

SETTING A PURPOSE

As you read, pay special attention to Balboa's character traits and any problems he faces. Consider how the author's characterization of Balboa develops the author's message, or theme. Write down any questions you generate during reading.

1 Vasco Núñez de Balboa ascends the mountain alone. His one thousand Indians and two hundred Spaniards wait at the foot of the mountain, as if they are the Israelites and Balboa alone is off to speak with God. Balboa knows that from this peak he will be able to see the western water, what he has already decided to name the South Sea. He takes a musket with him. The Spaniards have been warned that if they follow, he will use it, because discovery is a tricky matter and he wants no competition. The day is September 25, 1513.

2 Balboa ascends slowly. His musket is heavy and he would have gladly left it down below, but he doesn't trust his countrymen any more than he trusts the sullen Indians. So he bears the weight. But the musket is nothing. He is dragging the mantle[1] of civilization up the **pristine** slopes, over the mud, over

[1] **mantle:** a cloak or robe worn by royalty.

Notice & Note

Use the side margins to notice and note signposts in the text.

ANALYZE THEMATIC DEVELOPMENT

Annotate: Mark phrases in paragraphs 1 and 2 that describe Balboa.

Infer: Based on the phrases you marked, what is a character trait that describes Balboa? What might this trait suggest about the story's theme?

pristine
(prĭs′tēn′) *adj.* pure or unspoiled.

the leaves that cast as much shade as a parasol[2] but with none of the charm.

3 Balboa is that divining line[3] between the modern and the primitive. As he moves, the shadow of Spain moves with him.

CONTRASTS AND CONTRADICTIONS

Notice & Note: Mark details in paragraph 4 that suggest a discrepancy between who Balboa is and how he would like to be perceived.

Analyze: How would Balboa like to be viewed by others? Cite text evidence in your response.

4 Balboa steps cautiously into a muddy stream and watches with fascination as his boot sinks and sinks. He will have to find another way. Upstream he sees an outcropping of rock. Maybe he can cross there. He tells himself that there is no hurry, but years of staying just ahead of trouble have left him anxiety-ridden. He would like to think of himself as a lion. Balboa the Lion! But no, he is more of a rat, and all of his accomplishments have been made with speed and stealth. Balboa places his hand on a branch and pulls himself up. He sees the tail of a snake disappearing just past his reach. The subtle crush of greenery confirms his discovery and he shrinks back, crouching. In this moment of stillness, he looks around. He sees no other serpents, but that does not mean they are not there. Only in this momentary quiet does he hear his breath, rasping with effort. He hears his heart beating in the arced fingers of his ribs as if it is an Indian's drum. He does not remember what it is to be civilized, or if he ever was. If ever a man was alone, it is he. But even in this painful solitude, he cannot help but laugh. Along with Cristóbal Colón, backed by Isabel I herself, along with Vespucci the scholar, along with the noble Pizarro brothers[4] on their way to claim Inca gold, his name will live—Balboa. Balboa! Balboa the Valiant. Balboa the Fearsome. Balboa the Brave.

5 Balboa the gambling pig farmer, who, in an effort to escape his debt, has found himself at the very edge of the world.

6 Balboa stops to drink from the stream. The water is cold, fresh, and tastes like dirt, which is a relief after what he has been drinking—water so green that the very act of ingesting it seems unnatural, as though it is as alive as he, and sure enough, given a few hours, it will get you back, eager to find its way out. He has been climbing since early morning and it is now noon. The sun shines in the sky unblinking, white-hot. Balboa wonders if it's the same sun that shines in Spain. The sun seemed so much smaller there. Even in Hispaniola,[5] the sun was Spanish. Even as he prodded his pigs in the heat, there was Spain all around, men with dice, men training roosters, pitting their dogs against each other. But here…then he hears a twig snap and the sound of something brushing up against the bushes. Balboa stands.

[2] **parasol:** light umbrella.

[3] **divining line:** point of separation between ideas.

[4] **Cristóbal Colón . . . Pizarro brothers:** Cristóbal Colón is the Spanish name for Christopher Columbus. Isabel I was queen of Castile (Spain) from 1474 until 1504. Amerigo Vespucci (1451–1512) was an Italian explorer and cartographer. Francisco, Gonzalo, Juan, and Hernándo Pizarro were Spanish conquistadors in Peru.

[5] **Hispaniola:** site of Columbus's first colony; the island containing modern Haiti and the Dominican Republic.

7 "I give you this one chance to turn back," he says, raising his musket as he turns. And then he freezes. It is not one of the Spaniards hoping to share the glory. Instead, he finds himself face-to-face with a great spotted cat. On this mountain, he's thought he might find his god, the god of Moses, sitting in the cloud cover near the peaks, running his fingers through his beard. But no. Instead he finds himself face-to-face with a jaguar, the god of the Indians. He knows why these primitives have chosen it for their deity. It is hard to fear one's maker when he looks like one's grandfather, but this great cat can make a people fear god. He hears the growling of the cat and the grating, high-pitched thunder sounds like nothing he has ever heard. The cat twitches its nose and two great incisors show at the corners of its mouth. Balboa raises his musket, ignites the flint,[6] and nothing happens. He tries again and the weapon explodes, shattering the silence, sending up a big puff of stinking smoke. The cat is gone for now, but Balboa knows he hasn't even injured it.

8 And now it will be tailing him silently.

9 There is nothing he can do about it. He should have brought an Indian with him. The Indians have all seen the South Sea before, so why did he leave them at the foot of the mountain? They have no more interest in claiming the South Sea than they do rowing off to Europe in their dug-out canoes[7] and claiming Spain. But Balboa's hindsight is always good, and no amount of swearing—which he does freely, spilling Spanish profanity into the virgin mountain air—is going to set things straight.

10 He is already in trouble. His kingdom in Darién on the east coast of the New World is under threat, and not from the Indians, whom he manages well, but from Spain. Balboa had organized the rebellion, **supplanted** the governor—all of this done with great efficiency and intelligence. What stupidity made him send the governor, Martín Fernández de Enciso, back to Spain? Enciso swore that he would have Balboa's head on a platter. He was yelling from the deck of the ship as it set sail. Why didn't he kill Enciso? Better yet, why didn't he turn Enciso over to some Indian tribe that would be glad to have the Spaniard, glad to have his blood on their hands? How could Balboa be so stupid? Soon the caravels[8] would arrive and his days as governor (king, he tells the Indians) of Darién will be over. Unless, Balboa thinks, unless he brings glory by being the first to claim this great ocean for Spain. Then the king will see him as the greatest of his subjects, not a troublemaking peasant, a keeper of pigs.

11 Unless that jaguar gets him first.

12 Balboa looks nervously around. The only sound is the trickle and splash of the stream that he is following, which the Indians tell

supplant
(sə-plănt´) *v.* to take the place of.

LANGUAGE CONVENTIONS

Annotate: In paragraph 10, mark verbs that are in the past tense.

Analyze: How do these verbs signal a transition in the plot structure?

[6] **flint:** stone used to create a spark.
[7] **dug-out canoes:** narrow boats made by hollowing out tree trunks.
[8] **caravels:** small sailing ships with two or three masts.

him leads to a large outcropping of rock from which he will see the new ocean. Insects swoop malevolently[9] around his head. A yellow and red parrot watches him cautiously from a branch, first looking from one side of its jeweled head, then the other. Where is the jaguar? Balboa imagines his body being dragged into a tree, his boots swinging from the limbs as the great cat tears his heart from his ribs. He hears a crushing of vegetation and ducks low. He readies his musket again. "Please God, let the damned thing fire." He breathes harshly, genuflecting,[10] musket steady.

13 The leaves quiver, then part. There is no jaguar.

14 "Leoncico!" he cries out. Leoncico is his dog, who has tracked him up the slope. Leoncico patters over, wagging his tail, his great wrinkled head bearded with drool. Leoncico is a monster of a dog. His head is the size of a man's, and his body has the look of a lion—shoulders and hipbones **protruding** and muscle pulling and shifting beneath the glossy skin—which is where he gets his name. "Leoncico" means little lion.

protrude
(prō-trōōd´) *v.* to stick out or bulge.

15 "Good dog," says Balboa. "Good dog. Good dog."

16 He has never been so grateful for the company, not even when he was hidden on board Enciso's ship bound for San Sebastian, escaping his creditors, wrapped in a sail. No one wondered why the dog had come on board. Maybe the dog had been attracted by the smell of **provisions**, the great barrels of salted meat. The soldiers fed him, gave him water. Balboa worried that Leoncico would give him away, but the dog had somehow known to be quiet. He had slept beside Balboa, and even in Balboa's thirst and hunger, the great beast's panting and panting, warm through the sailcloth, had given him comfort. When Enciso's crew finally discovered Balboa—one of the sails was torn and needed to be replaced—they did not punish him. They laughed.

provision
(prə-vĭzh´ən) *n.* food supply.

17 "The Indians massacre everyone. You are better off in a debtors' prison," they said.

18 Balboa became a member of the crew. When the boat shipwrecked off the coast of San Sebastian (they were rescued by Francisco Pizarro), Enciso had been at a loss as to where to go, and Balboa convinced him to try Darién to the north. Once established there, Enciso had shown himself to be a weak man. How could Balboa not act? Enciso did not understand the Indians as Balboa did. He could see that the Indians were battle-hardened warriors. The Spaniards had not been there long enough to call these armies into existence. Balboa's strength had been to recognize this **discord**. He divided the great tribes, supported one against the other. His reputation spread. His muskets blasted away the faces of the greatest warriors. Balboa's soldiers spread smallpox and syphilis. His Spanish

discord
(dĭs´kôrd) *n.* disagreement or conflict.

[9] **malevolently:** with evil intent.
[10] **genuflecting:** bending one knee to the ground.

war dogs, great mastiffs and wolfhounds, tore children limb from limb. The blood from his great war machine made the rivers flow red and his name, Balboa, moved quickly, apace[11] with these rivers of blood.

19 Balboa is loved by no one and feared by all. He has invented an unequaled terror. The Indians think of him as a god. They make no **distinction** between good and evil. They have seen his soldiers tear babies from their mothers, toss them still screaming to feed the dogs. They have seen the great dogs pursue the escaping Indians, who must hear nothing but a great panting, the jangle of the dogs' armor, and then, who knows? Do they feel the hot breath on their cheek? Are they still awake when the beasts unravel their stomachs and spill them onto the hot earth? Balboa's dogs have been his most effective weapon because for them, one does not need to carry ammunition, as for the muskets; one does not need to carry food, as for the soldiers. For the dogs, there is fresh meat everywhere. He knows his cruelty will be recorded along with whatever he discovers. This does not bother him, even though one monk, Dominican—strange fish—cursed him back in Darién. He was a young monk, tormented by epileptic[12] fits. He approached Balboa in the town square in his bare feet, unarmed, waving his shrunken fist.

distinction
(dĭ-stĭngk´shən) *n.* difference in quality.

ANALYZE PLOT STRUCTURE

Annotate: Mark the transition to the flashback in paragraph 19.

Analyze: Analyze the conflict between Balboa and the monk in the flashback. What does this reveal about Balboa's character?

20 "Your dogs," screamed the monk, "are demons."

21 As if understanding, Leoncico had lunged at the monk. Leoncico is not a demon. He is the half of Balboa with teeth, the half that eats. Balboa has the mind and appetite. Together, they make one. It is as if the great beast can hear his thoughts, as if their hearts and lungs circulate the same blood and air. What did the monk understand of that? What did he understand of anything? He said that he was in the New World to bring the Indians to God. So the monk converts the Indians, and Balboa sends them on to God. They work together, which is what Balboa told the monk. But the monk did not find it funny.

22 How dare he find fault with Balboa? Is not Spain as full of torments as the New World? The Spaniards are brought down by smallpox at alarming rates in Seville, in Madrid. Every summer the rich take to the mountains to escape the plague, and in the fall, when they return, aren't their own countrymen lying in the streets feeding the packs of mongrels? Half of all the Spanish babies die. It is not uncommon to see a peasant woman leave her screaming infant on the side of the road, so why come here and beg relief for these savages? Why not go to France, where, one soldier tells Balboa, they butcher the Huguenots[13] and sell their limbs for food in the street? Why rant

[11] **apace:** fast enough to keep up with something.

[12] **epileptic:** caused by epilepsy, a neurological disorder.

[13] **Huguenots:** French Protestants who were persecuted for their faith in the 16th and 17th centuries.

NOTICE & NOTE

ANALYZE PLOT STRUCTURE

Annotate: Mark an example of foreshadowing in paragraph 24.

Analyze: What does this example foreshadow? To what part of the story does it connect?

over the impaling of the Indians when Spaniards—noblemen among them—have suffered the same fate in the name of God? In fact, the Inquisition[14] has been the great educator when it comes to subduing the Indian population.

23 Why take him to task when the world is a violent place?

24 "May your most evil act be visited on you," said the monk. "I curse you."

25 The monk died shortly after that. His threats and bravery were more the result of a deadly fever than the words of a divine message. Did the curse worry Balboa? Perhaps a little. He occasionally revisits a particularly spectacular feat of bloodshed—the time Leoncico tore a chieftain's head from his shoulders—with a pang of concern. But Balboa is a busy man with little time for reflection. When the monk delivered his curse, Balboa was already preparing his troops for the great march to the west. His name had reached Spain, and the king felt his authority threatened.

26 He is the great Balboa.

27 But here, on the slope of the mountain, his name does not seem worth that much. He has to relieve himself and is terrified that some creature—jaguar, snake, spider—will take advantage of his great heaving bareness.

28 "Leoncico," he calls. "At attention."

29 Not that this command means anything to the dog. Leoncico knows "attack," and that is all he needs to know. Leoncico looks up, wags his tail, and lies down, his face smiling into the heat. Balboa climbs onto a boulder. Here, he is exposed to everything, but if that jaguar is still tracking him, he can at least see it coming. He sets his

[14] **the Inquisition:** an investigation by the Roman Catholic Church to identify and punish heretics.

musket down and listens. Nothing. He loosens his belt and is about to lower his pants when he sees it—the flattened glimmer, a shield, the horizon. He fixes his belt and straightens himself. He stares out at the startling bare intrusion, this beautiful nothing beyond the green tangle of trees, the *Mar del Sur*, the glory of Balboa, his gift to Spain.

30 Balboa, having accomplished his goal, luxuriates in this moment of peaceful ignorance. He does not know that his days are numbered, that even after he returns to Darién with his knowledge of the South Sea, even after he has **ceded** the governorship to Pedro Arias Dávila, even after he is promised Dávila's daughter, he has not bought his safety. Dávila will see that as long as Balboa lives he must sleep with one eye open. With the blessing of Spain, Dávila will bring Balboa to trial for treason, and on January 21, 1519, Balboa's head will be severed from his shoulders. His eyes will stay open, his mouth will be slack, and his great head will roll in the dust for everyone—Indians, Spaniards, and dogs—to see.

NOTICE & NOTE

cede
(sēd) *v.* to yield or give away.

ANALYZE THEMATIC DEVELOPMENT

Annotate: Mark details in paragraph 30 that tell you what happens to Balboa.

Analyze: How does the knowledge of what happens affect your understanding of Balboa?

CHECK YOUR UNDERSTANDING

Answer these questions before moving on to the **Analyze the Text** section.

1 What surprises Balboa when he drinks from the mountain stream?

A A jaguar

B An Indian

C A thunderstorm

D A Spaniard hoping to share in his glory

2 Why does Martín Fernández de Enciso dislike Balboa?

F Balboa called him "weak."

G Balboa led a rebellion against him.

H Balboa stole money and property from him.

J Balboa gave the governorship to Pedro Arias Dávila.

3 What eventually happens to Balboa?

A Balboa kills Pedro Arias Dávila.

B Balboa is killed by a wild animal.

C Balboa goes to jail for a violent crime.

D Pedro Arias Dávila executes Balboa for treason.

RESPOND

ANALYZE THE TEXT

Support your responses with evidence from the text. NOTEBOOK

1. **Analyze** The narrator says that Balboa is "dragging the mantle of civilization up the pristine slopes, over the mud, over the leaves" (paragraph 2). What does this image suggest about Balboa and the "civilization" that he is bringing with him to the setting of the New World?
2. **Interpret** After Leoncico surprises Balboa on the mountain, the action of the story is interrupted by a flashback. What do readers learn about Balboa from this flashback? What theme does it suggest about the nature of power?
3. **Analyze** Note the references to, and images of, dogs throughout the story. What message does the author convey through these references?
4. **Analyze** What is revealed by the flash forward at the end of the story? How does this revelation affect the overall meaning of the work?
5. **Notice & Note** Think about the difference between how Balboa regards himself and how he would like to be regarded. Why does the writer include this information about Balboa? How does this affect your understanding of his character?

RESEARCH

Balboa, from Spain, was just one of many European explorers who sailed during the late 1400s and early 1500s. With a partner, research other explorers of this time from the countries listed in the chart. Summarize why they are remembered.

COUNTRY	EXPLORER	NOTABLE ACHIEVEMENT
France		
Spain		
Portugal		

Extend Find another source that mentions Vasco de Balboa. Find three facts about this explorer that were not reflected in the short story. Discuss with your partner whether the facts align with the depiction of Balboa in the story.

RESEARCH TIP

Even credible resources can have bias. When you read a source, make sure to differentiate between the factual information and the source's interpretation of the facts.

CREATE AND PRESENT

Write a Dramatic Monologue Murray's portrayal of Balboa creates a dynamic character whom readers can visualize and almost hear. Write a dramatic monologue from the point of view of this fictional Balboa, expressing what he might have said aloud as he stood on the boulder surveying the Pacific Ocean.

- ❑ Draw upon the text for details about the path Balboa followed to "the edge of the world." Reveal his motives and feelings upon reaching his goal.
- ❑ Include his reflections on what his accomplishment really means, incorporating your ideas about the story's theme.
- ❑ As you compose your monologue, try using end rhymes. Decide on a rhyme scheme, and consult a rhyming dictionary for help.

Go to **Writing Narratives** in the **Writing Studio** for help with using narrative techniques in writing.

Present a Dramatic Monologue Present your monologue to a small group.

- ❑ Mark your monologue with notes indicating where you intend to slow down, speak forcefully or quietly, and pause.
- ❑ Practice several times before presenting to an audience.
- ❑ Remember to speak clearly at an appropriate volume, using eye contact to connect with your audience.

Go to **Giving a Presentation** in the **Speaking and Listening Studio** for help with presenting to others.

RESPOND TO THE ESSENTIAL QUESTION

? What motivates people to explore the unknown?

Gather Information Review your annotations and notes on "Balboa." Then, add relevant information to your Response Log. As you determine which information to include, think about:

- Balboa's character traits
- experiences that influenced Balboa's willingness to explore
- Balboa's motivations for exploring

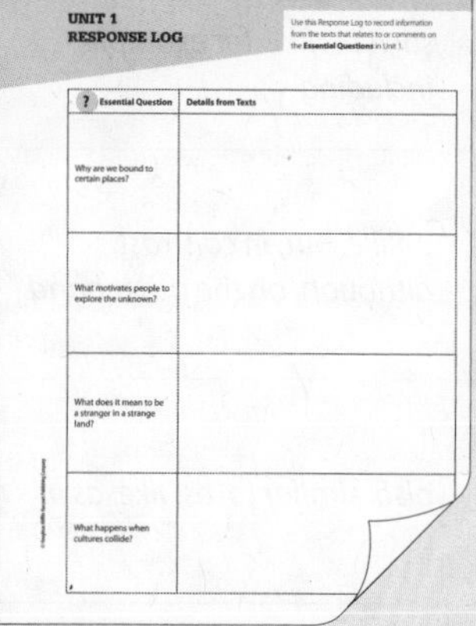

ACADEMIC VOCABULARY

As you write and discuss what you learned from "Balboa," be sure to use the Academic Vocabulary words. Check off each of the words that you use.

- ❑ **adapt**
- ❑ **coherent**
- ❑ **device**
- ❑ **displace**
- ❑ **dynamic**

WORD BANK
- pristine
- supplant
- protrude
- provision
- discord
- distinction
- cede

CRITICAL VOCABULARY

Practice and Apply Answer each question, referring to the meaning of each Critical Vocabulary word in your response.

1. If you **ceded** a toy to your younger brother, would there be **discord?**
2. If both candidates had **pristine** reputations and equal leadership experience, would it be easy to make a **distinction** between them?
3. If children in a family **supplanted** their parents in control of the grocery shopping, how would the family's **provisions** be different?
4. If the lawn has weeds **protruding** from it, is it in **pristine** condition?

VOCABULARY STRATEGY: Context Clues

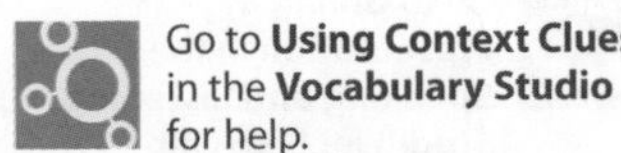

Go to **Using Context Clues** in the **Vocabulary Studio** for help.

The context of a word is the words, phrases, and sentences around it. Looking at the context of an unfamiliar word can help you define it.

> **Balboa had organized the rebellion, supplanted the governor—all of this done with great efficiency and intelligence.**

In this sentence, the word *rebellion* helps you understand that *supplanted* means "to overthrow or replace."

Key words can signal a relationship between the unknown word and others that help define it.

KEY WORDS	CONTEXT CLUES
such as, like, for example, including	The unknown word is followed by examples that illustrate its meaning: *We packed provisions, such as fruit and water.*
unlike, but, in contrast, although, on the other hand	The unknown word is contrasted with a more familiar word or phrase: *The tablecloth was pristine before dinner, but it was covered with stains afterward.*
also, similar to, as, like, as if	The unknown word is compared to a more familiar word or phrase: *The wad of gum protruding from his cheek made him look as if he had the mumps.*
or, that is, which is, in other words	The unknown word is preceded or followed by a restatement of its meaning: *The distinction, or difference, between the identical twins was slight.*

Practice and Apply With a partner, choose three unfamiliar words from the story. Then, to demonstrate your understanding, use context clues to define the unfamiliar words, verify the meanings of the words using a print or digital dictionary, and write original sentences using the words correctly.

LANGUAGE CONVENTIONS: Verb Tenses

Verb tense indicates the time of the action or state of being. An action or state of being can occur in the present, the past, or the future.

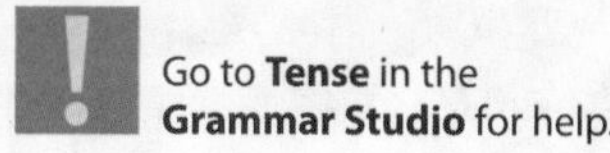
Go to **Tense** in the **Grammar Studio** for help.

VERB TENSES		
TENSE	**USE**	**EXAMPLE**
Present	describe action that is happening at the present time, occurs regularly, or is constant	Balboa stops to take a drink.
Past	describe action that began and ended in the past	Balboa stopped to take a drink.
Future	describe action that will occur	Balboa will stop to take a drink.
Present Perfect	describe action that was completed at an indefinite past time or began in the past and still continues	Balboa has stopped to take a drink.
Past Perfect	describe action in the past that came before another action in the past	Balboa had stopped to take a drink.
Future Perfect	describe action in the future that will be completed before another action in the future	Balboa will have stopped to take a drink.

For the most part, "Balboa" uses present-tense verbs to tell the story. Note the present-tense verbs in this passage from the story:

> **Balboa ascends slowly. His musket is heavy and he would have gladly left it down below, but he doesn't trust his countrymen any more than he trusts the sullen Indians.**

The story also uses past and future tenses to move the story around in time, allowing the author to use flashback to delve into Balboa's memories and flash forward to show how the story ends.

Practice and Apply Identify the verb and its tense in each sentence.

SENTENCE FROM "BALBOA"	VERB	TENSE
But here . . . then he hears a twig snap and the sound of something brushing up against the bushes.		
The sun seemed so much smaller there.		
Dávila will see that as long as Balboa lives he must sleep with one eye open.		

Then, choose a passage in "Balboa" and rewrite it in a different tense. Share this with a partner and discuss how it affects the narrative and the mood or tone.

A DESPERATE TREK ACROSS AMERICA

Article by **Andrés Reséndez**

ESSENTIAL QUESTION:

What does it mean to be a stranger in a strange land?

QUICK START

Most people have experienced failure. But sometimes failure can have unintended benefits. Think of a time when you or someone you know unexpectedly benefited from failure. Discuss your ideas with a partner.

ANALYZE INFORMATIONAL TEXTS

"A Desperate Trek Across America" is an **informational text** that chronicles the efforts of Spanish explorers of North America to recover from disaster. Informational texts may be written for a number of purposes, including:

- to explain or describe a situation or process
- to analyze a situation by explaining causes and effects
- to narrate a sequence of events

Though informational texts are factual, they may also include the author's commentary, including judgments, opinions, or conclusions. The evidence and examples included in the text and the way the text is structured support the author's purpose for writing. As you read, think about the kinds of details the author includes and what they suggest about his purpose.

DETAILS	PURPOSE
What details does the author include about the explorers' situation at the beginning of the text?	
What details does the author include about their efforts to address their problem?	

GENRE ELEMENTS: INFORMATIONAL TEXT

- includes articles, essays, and reference materials
- provides factual information but can include author's commentary, such as judgments, opinions, or conclusions
- may include primary source material for a particular purpose.

ANALYZE AND EVALUATE EVIDENCE

Authors of informational texts that describe historical events may integrate primary source material—the accounts of people who experienced the event—into their writing. In the text you are going to read, the author includes first-hand quotations from Spanish explorers alongside his descriptions and commentary. As you read, think about what these quotations add to the text, how they support the main idea, and how they influence your understanding of events. The primary source material may also provide insight into the writer's purpose.

GET READY

CRITICAL VOCABULARY

straits	**conquistador**	**flotilla**	**posse**
expedition	**interminable**	**unimpeded**	

To see how many Critical Vocabulary words you know, choose the word that is closest in meaning to each numbered phrase.

1. a Spanish warrior ___________
2. an armed band ___________
3. a fleet of water vessels ___________
4. an arduous journey ___________
5. long and drawn out ___________
6. not disrupted ___________
7. a position of difficulty ___________

LANGUAGE CONVENTIONS

Infinitives and Infinitive Phrases An **infinitive** is a verb in its stem form that is used in a sentence as a noun, adjective, or adverb. An **infinitive phrase** is an infinitive plus any modifiers or complements added to the base infinitive.

Infinitive: to take

Infinitive phrase: ordering the captains to take their ships

As you read, notice the writer's use of infinitives and infinitive phrases to describe actions and express ideas.

ANNOTATION MODEL

NOTICE & NOTE

As you read, notice the details that describe the explorers' situation as well as the author's commentary about what is happening. Note quotations from primary sources and what they add to your understanding. In the model, you can see one reader's notes about "A Desperate Trek Across America."

The 250 starving Spanish adventurers dubbed the shallow estuary near their campsite the "Bay of Horses," because every third day they killed yet another draft animal, roasted it, and consumed the flesh. Fifty men had already died of disease, injury, and starvation. What was worse, after having walked the length of Florida without finding gold, those still alive had lost contact with their ships. They were stranded in an alien continent.

details about explorers' condition

"What was worse" gives author's view.

BACKGROUND

From a base in Cuba, conquistadors enriched themselves and the Spanish crown by conquering the Aztec empire. Their success prompted Spain to seek wealth elsewhere in the Americas. In 1527, Álvar Núñez Cabeza de Vaca was second in command of a massive expedition to Florida that included five ships and 600 men. The effort ended disastrously. Two ships sank in a hurricane, and a third of the men perished or deserted. After reaching Florida in the spring of 1528, the party of about 300 men marched overland and raided the Native American settlements they encountered. ***Andrés Reséndez's*** *historical account begins at this point.*

A DESPERATE TREK ACROSS AMERICA

Article by Andrés Reséndez

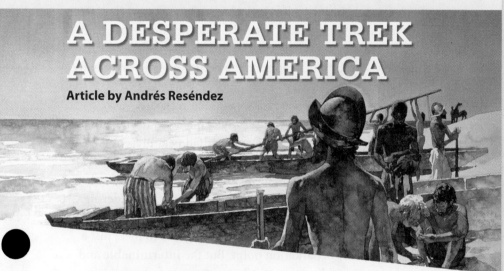

SETTING A PURPOSE

As you read, pay attention to the details that convey the explorers' situation and the efforts they undertook to save themselves.

Notice & Note

Use the side margins to notice and note signposts in the text.

Florida panhandle, Fall 1528

1 The 250 starving Spanish adventurers dubbed the shallow estuary near their campsite the "Bay of Horses," because every third day they killed yet another draft animal, roasted it, and consumed the flesh. Fifty men had already died of disease, injury, and starvation. What was worse, after having walked the length of Florida without finding gold, those still alive had lost contact with their ships. They were stranded in an alien continent.

2 "We were in such **straits** that anything that had some semblance of a solution seemed good to us," wrote Álvar Núñez Cabeza de Vaca, the **expedition's** royal treasurer, in one of the most harrowing[1] survival stories ever told. "I refrain here from telling this at greater length because each one can imagine for himself what could happen in a land so strange."

straits
(strāts) *adj.* a position of difficulty, distress, or extreme need.

expedition
(ĕk´spĭ-dĭsh´ən) *n.* a journey, especially a difficult or hazardous one, undertaken after extensive planning and with a definite objective in mind.

[1] **harrowing:** referring to an experience that is extremely distressing.

NOTICE & NOTE

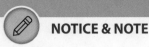

conquistador (kŏng-kē´stə-dôr, kŏn-kwĭs´tə-dôr) *n.* a 16th-century Spanish soldier-explorer who took part in the defeat of the Indian civilizations of Mexico, Central America, or Peru.

interminable (ĭn-tûr´mə-nə-bəl) *adj.* seemingly endless.

ANALYZE AND EVALUATE EVIDENCE

Annotate: Mark the words and phrases in paragraph 6 that come from a primary source.

Infer: What does the information that is included add to your understanding of the explorers' situation?

3 Indeed, Cabeza de Vaca and the other leaders of the ill-fated venture had agreed to a desperate gamble: to trade their most effective weapons against the Indians—horses and firearms—for five makeshift vessels that might or might not be capable of carrying them to safety. Eating the horses gave them time to build the rafts. To make nails and saws, they threw their crossbows,[2] along with stirrups and spurs, into an improvised forge.

4 Like past **conquistadors**, Cabeza de Vaca and his men had relied on their breastplates,[3] horses, and lethal weapons to keep the Indians at bay. Such overwhelming technological advantages meant they often did not even bother to negotiate, instead simply imposing their will. By sacrificing the very tools of their supremacy, they would now have to face the New World fully exposed to its perils and hold on only by their wits.

5 The expedition had unraveled with frightening speed. Just months earlier, the hopeful adventurers had embarked from Cuba in four ships and a brigantine[4] and made landfall near present day Tampa Bay, intending to take possession of Florida in the name of His Most Catholic Majesty.[5] Caught up in the excitement and rush to explore, the commander rashly divided the expedition, ordering the captains to take their ships on an exploration of the coast, while the men and the horses were put ashore. They agreed to meet just a few miles north of the debarkation point. But the **interminable** and confusing coast of Florida prevented the two parties from making contact.

6 With their jury-rigged[6] saws they cut down trees, dragged them to the beach, lashed them together with the tails and manes of their dead horses, and fashioned sails from their tattered shirts. After five or six weeks, they slaughtered their last horse, then dragged the 15-ton rafts into the water. Fifty men crowded aboard each craft, the fifth commanded by Cabeza de Vaca. "And so greatly can necessity prevail," he observed, "that it made us risk going in this manner and placing ourselves in a sea so treacherous, and without any one of us who went having any knowledge of the art of navigation." The rafts floated only a few inches above the waterline; the waves would wash over the men as they traveled.

7 Little did the men on the rafts know that they were embarking on an eight-year adventure that would ultimately take their few survivors across the entire continent. After several weeks, storms separated

[2] **crossbows:** weapons made by fixing a bow crosswise on a wooden base and including grooves on that base to guide the flight of the arrow.

[3] **breastplates:** pieces of armor covering the chest.

[4] **brigantine:** a two-masted sailing ship with square sails on the forward mast and a large mainsail positioned from the front to the back of the ship.

[5] **His Most Catholic Majesty:** honorary title of the king of Spain granted by Pope Alexander VI in 1494.

[6] **jury-rigged:** assembled for temporary use in an improvised way.

NOTICE & NOTE

the **flotilla**. Tormented by extreme hunger and drenched by the splashing of the waves, they were on the brink of death. "The people began to faint in such a manner that when the sun set," Cabeza de Vaca would recall, "all those who came in my raft were fallen on top of one another in it, so close to death that few were conscious." Only the helmsman and Cabeza de Vaca took turns steering the raft: "Two hours into the night, the helmsman told me that I should take charge of the raft, because he was in such condition that he thought he would die that very night." Near dawn, Cabeza de Vaca heard the surf, and later that day they landed.

flotilla
(flō-tĭl´ə) *n.* a fleet of small water craft.

8 While most of the men survived the harrowing month long passage across the Gulf, eventually washing up on the coast of what is now Texas, many more perished of exposure and hunger that winter, some even resorting to cannibalism. Fewer still withstood enslavement at the hands of the natives in the vicinity of Galveston Bay. Ultimately, only four—Cabeza de Vaca, two other Spaniards in commanding positions, and an African slave named Estebanico—would escape their Indian masters after six years of toil. As slaves, Cabeza de Vaca and his companions were forced to cope with native North America on its own terms, bridging two worlds that had remained apart for 12,000 years or more. They lived by their wits, coming to terms with half a dozen native languages and making sense of societies that other Europeans could not even begin to fathom.

LANGUAGE CONVENTIONS

Annotate: Mark the infinitive phrase in the last sentence of paragraph 8.

Analyze: How does this phrase suggest that the explorers are exceptional? Explain.

9 Incredibly, the four castaways used this knowledge to refashion themselves into medicine men. As Cabeza de Vaca would explain it: "we made the sign of the cross over them and blew on them and recited a Pater Noster[7] and an Ave Maria;[8] and then we prayed as best we could to God Our Lord to give them health and inspire them to give us good treatment." In one instance he revived a man who appeared to be dead. At the Indians' insistence, all four survivors performed curing ceremonies. And thus many natives came to believe that these four strange-looking beings were able to manipulate the power of nature.

10 This real or imagined gifts of healing enabled the four survivors to move **unimpeded**, their reputation preceding them wherever they went. Nor were their actions a mere charade to win food and respect. They believed that their curative abilities went somehow much deeper: they came to see their incredible suffering odyssey as a test to which God had subjected them before revealing the true purpose of their existence. They viewed their sufferings as mortifications of the flesh, their beatings and extreme hunger akin to those of flagellants[9]

unimpeded
(ən-im-pē´-dəd) *adj.* not delayed or obstructed in its progress.

[7] **Pater Noster:** a Latin phrase meaning "Our Father" that refers to the Lord's Prayer.

[8] **Ave Maria:** a Latin phrase meaning "Hail Mary" that refers to a Roman Catholic prayer.

[9] **flagellants:** members of a Christian religious sect who publicly beat themselves with whips as an act of religious devotion and discipline.

NOTICE & NOTE

who inflicted torment upon themselves or of monks who fasted nigh unto death.

QUOTED WORDS

Notice & Note: Mark details in paragraph 11 that tell what Cabeza de Vaca does to survive the cold night.

Infer: What does the quotation tell you about Cabeza de Vaca?

11 Once, alone and unable to find his party's camp, Cabeza de Vaca wandered in the woods naked in dread of the approaching chill of night. "But it pleased God that I found a tree aflame, and warmed by its fire I endured the cold that night." For five days he nursed that fire, before finally finding his companions.

12 The four wanderers were no longer mere castaways; they had become explorers once again. Yet theirs was a most peculiar expedition. Four naked and unarmed outsiders were led by hundreds, even thousands, of Indians. They were fed, protected, and passed off as though prized possessions from one indigenous group to the next. They became the first outsiders to behold what would become the American Southwest and northern Mexico, the first non-natives to describe this enormous land and its peoples.

13 By the time the four reemerged from the continental interior and reached the Pacific Coast, they had been so utterly transformed by the experience that fellow Europeans could hardly recognize them. A **posse** of Spanish slavers[10] operating in what is now northwestern Mexico spotted potential prey: 13 Indians walking barefoot and clad in skins. On closer inspection, some of the details did not seem quite right. One was a black man. Could he be an Indian or an African emerging from the heart of the continent? Another member of the party appeared to be a haggard white man with hair hanging down to his waist and a beard reaching to his chest.

posse
(pŏs´ē) *n.* a group of civilians temporarily authorized by officials to assist in pursuing fugitives.

14 When Cabeza de Vaca addressed them in perfect Spanish, the slavers were "so astonished," he wrote, "that they neither talked to me nor managed to ask me anything," but bent themselves on rounding up the Indian escort. But Cabeza de Vaca and his companions would not allow it. No longer did the castaways view their companions as mere chattels,[11] the rightful prize of Christian conquest.

15 Perhaps no one understood their transformation more than the Indians themselves, who were unable to believe that Cabeza de Vaca

[10] **slaver:** one who catches people to enslave them.
[11] **chattels:** enslaved persons.

and his three companions belonged to the same race as the slavers. The Indians had observed, he later wrote, that "we cured the sick, and they [the Spanish slavers] killed those who were well; that we came naked and barefoot, and they went about dressed and on horses and with lances; and that we did not covet anything but rather, everything they gave us we later returned and remained with nothing, and that the others had no other objective but to steal everything they found and did not give anything to anyone."

16 Cabeza de Vaca went back to Spain, attached himself to the court of Charles V, and was able to present his ideas of a humane colonization of the New World. After years of lobbying, he was dispatched to South America, where he attempted to carry out his plans, alas with little success. He spent the last years of his life in his native Andalusia,[12] reminiscing about his adventures in another world.

[12] **Andalusia:** southernmost region of Spain.

NOTICE & NOTE

ANALYZE INFORMATIONAL TEXTS

Annotate: Mark what happens to Cabeza de Vaca in paragraph 16.

Analyze: As a conclusion, what do these examples add to your impression of Cabeza de Vaca?

CHECK YOUR UNDERSTANDING

Answer these questions before moving on to the **Analyze the Text** section.

1 Why do the Spanish adventurers call the estuary near their campsite the "Bay of Horses"?

A There are several herds of horses nearby.

B The surrounding land is shaped like a horse's head.

C They are killing, roasting, and eating their horses.

D The expedition's leader raises and sells horses.

2 Why is the trip by raft so difficult for the Spaniards?

F They face constant storms while traveling the Gulf.

G They do not know how to navigate, and grow weaker.

H They are frequently attacked by Native Americans.

J They have to travel by night for safety.

3 What does Cabeza de Vaca do after returning to Spain the first time?

A He pushes for better treatment of Native Americans.

B He retires and vows never to return to North America again.

C He writes a report glorifying his achievements.

D He argues that Spain should abandon efforts to colonize the Americas.

RESPOND

ANALYZE THE TEXT

Support your responses with evidence from the text. NOTEBOOK

1. **Interpret** The author includes descriptions of "makeshift vessels" manufactured using "jury-rigged" tools. How do these descriptions affect your perception of the situation?
2. **Cite Evidence** In what ways were Cabeza de Vaca and the other survivors "forced to cope with native North America on its own terms"? Cite text evidence in your response.
3. **Draw Conclusions** What is the author's purpose for including information on the survivors' transformation into medicine men?
4. **Analyze** The author concludes that Cabeza de Vaca and the others "had been so utterly transformed" by their experience. What examples and evidence support this conclusion?
5. **Notice & Note** How do the first-hand quotations from Cabeza de Vaca affect your understanding of him? Cite evidence in your response.

RESEARCH

The author writes that the Spaniards benefited greatly from having a technological advantage in carrying out their conquests of Native American empires. With a partner, research the conquest of the Aztec empire to answer these questions.

RESEARCH TIP

Consider using a history textbook to look for answers to the questions. You could check the table of contents or index to see if the conquest of the Aztec empire is covered in the book.

QUESTION	ANSWER
What technological advantages did Cortés and his men have over the Aztecs?	
What role did non-Aztec people play in the conflict between the Spaniards and Aztecs?	
What role did natural causes play in the Spaniards' ability to defeat and rule over Native American peoples who outnumbered them?	

Extend Based on the answers to the questions, compare and contrast Cortés's interactions with Native Americans to those of Cabeza de Vaca. Discuss your thoughts with a partner.

CREATE AND PRESENT

Write an Analytic Response Write a response in which you analyze the author's view of Cabeza de Vaca.

- ❑ Ask yourself whether the writer finds Cabeza de Vaca admirable. Develop a thesis that states your ideas about the writer's view of Cabeza de Vaca.
- ❑ Determine what text evidence you can use to support your thesis.
- ❑ Add original commentary to enhance your ideas.
- ❑ Include at least one quotation from Cabeza de Vaca in your response.

Present a Response Prepare to present your response to a small group of classmates.

- ❑ Practice reading your response. Speak loudly enough to be heard, use appropriate vocabulary, pronounce all words clearly, and place emphasis on the most important points.
- ❑ Present your response to the group. When you are done, ask your listeners if they have any questions and respond to them.
- ❑ Listen to others in the group make their presentations and ask clarifying questions of them.

Go to **Using Textual Evidence** in the **Writing Studio** for help.

Go to **Giving a Presentation: Delivering Your Presentation** in the **Speaking and Listening Studio** for help.

RESPOND TO THE ESSENTIAL QUESTION

What does it mean to be a stranger in a strange land?

Gather Information Review your annotations and notes on "A Desperate Trek Across America." Then add relevant information to your Response Log. As you determine which information to include, think about:

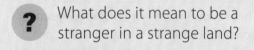

- the situations and experiences the Spaniards encountered
- what they thought about Native American culture and society
- the information and sources the author used in the article

ACADEMIC VOCABULARY

As you write and discuss what you learned from "A Desperate Trek Across America," be sure to use the Academic Vocabulary words. Check off each of the words that you use.

- ❑ **adapt**
- ❑ **coherent**
- ❑ **device**
- ❑ **displace**
- ❑ **dynamic**

CRITICAL VOCABULARY

WORD BANK
straits
expedition
conquistador
interminable
flotilla
unimpeded
posse

Practice and Apply Circle the letter of the best answer to each question. Then, explain your response.

1. Who is mostly likely to undertake an **expedition?**
   a. football players **b.** mountain climbers
2. What is someone who is **unimpeded** not likely to face?
   a. barriers **b.** success
3. Which event is a person most likely to perceive as **interminable?**
   a. boring lecture **b.** exciting movie
4. Which of these individuals is in dire **straits**?
   a. first responder **b.** hurricane victim
5. Who might look to a **posse** for help?
   a. chief of police **b.** criminal
6. Which branch of the armed forces would dispatch a **flotilla?**
   a. army **b.** navy
7. Who relied on **conquistadors?**
   a. king of Spain **b.** president of United States

VOCABULARY STRATEGY: Foreign Words in English

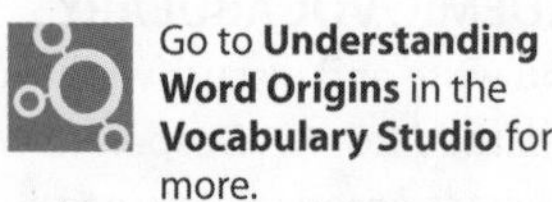
Go to **Understanding Word Origins** in the **Vocabulary Studio** for more.

Many **foreign words and phrases** have come into the English language and kept their original spelling. Some words appear similar to English words or phrases, but to be sure of the meanings, use a dictionary. For example, the word *conquistador* is a form of a Spanish word that means "to conquer." Notice that *conquistador* begins with the same letters as the English word *conquer.* Thinking of clues like this can help you remember the meanings of foreign words and phrases.

Practice and Apply Demonstrate your knowledge of foreign words in English by completing the chart. First, note the language that each word comes from. Then, use each word correctly in a sentence.

FOREIGN WORD	LANGUAGE	SENTENCE
conquistador	Spanish	
posse		
flotilla		

LANGUAGE CONVENTIONS: Infinitives and Infinitive Phrases

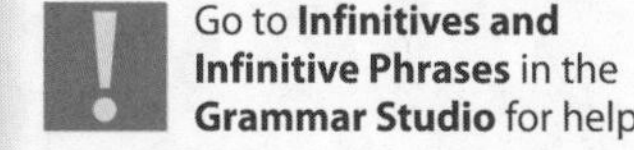

Go to **Infinitives and Infinitive Phrases** in the **Grammar Studio** for help.

Authors use **infinitives** and **infinitive phrases** to meet several functions in their writing. Infinitives can be used as nouns, adverbs, or adjectives. An infinitive is the base form of the verb. It is usually, but not always, signaled by the word *to*. An infinitive phrase opens with the infinitive but includes additional modifiers. Those modifiers can be just one word, as in "She hoped to finish **quickly,**" or it could include multiple words, such as, "She hoped to finish **her chores quickly so she could read her book.**"

- In this example from "A Desperate Trek Across America," an infinitive phrase is used as a noun. It functions in the sentence as a direct object.

  They agreed <u>to meet</u> just a few miles north of the debarkation point.

- In this example from the selection, an infinitive phrase is used as an adjective. It modifies the direct object *time.*

  Eating the horses gave them time <u>to build the rafts</u>.

- In this example from the selection, an infinitive phrase is used as an adverb modifying the verb *threw.*

  <u>To make nails and saws</u>, they threw their crossbows, along with stirrups and spurs, into an improvised forge.

It is generally not desirable to split an infinitive by placing an adverb between the *to* and the base verb form. Thus, "to wait excitedly" is preferred over "to excitedly wait."

Practice and Apply Write three of your own sentences about Cabeza de Vaca's experience using the examples as models. Use a mix of simple infinitives and infinitive phrases. Write one example of each type of function—noun, adjective, and adverb. When you have finished, share your sentences with a partner and compare your use of infinitives and infinitive phrases.

HERE FOLLOW SOME VERSES UPON THE BURNING OF OUR HOUSE, JULY 10th, 1666

Poem by **Anne Bradstreet**

? ESSENTIAL QUESTION:

Why are we bound to certain places?

QUICK START

Have you ever thought about what you value most? Some people especially prize a particular possession. Others may value an idea or feeling instead of a possession. What do you value most? Freewrite your ideas.

ANALYZE VOICE

"Here Follow Some Verses Upon the Burning of Our House, July 10th, 1666" relates the speaker's feelings about losing a home and belongings. Over the course of the poem a distinctive voice emerges. **Voice** refers to the poet's unique use of language that enables a reader to perceive the writer's feelings, attitudes, and personality. To determine a writer's voice, think about:

- **Diction:** What words did the writer choose? What images stand out?
- **Tone:** What is the writer's attitude on the subject?
- **Structure:** How long are lines and stanzas? How does this impact meaning?

To keep track of how the voice changes, look for words and phrases that indicate a shift in the tone of the poem, such as words that suggest a contrast. Think about how the voice can help you identify the poet's purpose for writing. What feelings and beliefs is the poet sharing?

GENRE ELEMENTS: POETRY

- uses diction, tone, and structure to create a distinctive voice
- often uses figurative language and allusions to deepen meaning
- may be written to express a writer's feelings or beliefs

PARAPHRASE

When you **paraphrase** a text, you restate it in your own words, making sure to maintain the meaning and order of the writer's ideas. To paraphrase a poem, you restate each line or sentence in clear and simple prose. Paraphrasing can be especially helpful when you want to clarify the meaning of a difficult section of the poem. For example, when Bradstreet uses **inverted syntax,** or sentence structure in which the expected order of words is reversed, paraphrasing the passage can ensure that you understand it.

A sample paraphrase of the first stanza of Bradstreet's poem appears below. As you read, remember to paraphrase when it can help you comprehend the poem.

POEM	PARAPHRASE
In silent night when rest I took For sorrow near I did not look I wakened was with thund'ring noise And piteous shrieks of dreadful voice. That fearful sound of "Fire!" and "Fire!" Let no man know is my desire.	In the silence of night, I was sleeping and did not expect something bad to happen. I awoke to a loud noise and a voice pitifully shrieking "Fire!" I pray that no person ever hears such a frightening sound. Bradstreet conveys her fear by contrasting the silence and peace of sleep with the terror of waking to cries of "Fire!"

GET READY

ANALYZE ALLUSIONS

An **allusion** is a direct or indirect reference to a person, place, event, or literary work that the poet believes the reader will know. By calling to mind other ideas, stories, or insights, allusions shape the reader's perceptions of events and expand the meaning of the work. Writers frequently make allusions to stories in the Bible because ideas and stories such as the Garden of Eden or David and Goliath are widely known. Bradstreet's Puritan readers would know the Bible well, so they would recognize the allusions in her poems.

In this poem, the phrase "all's vanity" alludes to the book of Ecclesiastes in the Bible, which describes how what we value is meaningless and will vanish. There are also references to the Book of Job, in which a man suffers many losses but stays faithful to God, and to the creation story in the Book of Genesis. By comparing the events in the poem to biblical stories, Bradstreet gives her readers insight into the nature of her loss and recovery. As you read, note how the allusions contribute to the meaning of the poem.

DETAIL FROM POEM	ALLUSION	MEANING
all's vanity	The book of Ecclesiastes	What we value is meaningless and will vanish.

ANNOTATION MODEL

NOTICE & NOTE

As you read, notice words and phrases that develop the voice of the poem. Note when the writer includes allusions and what they add to the poem's meaning. This model shows one reader's notes on the first lines of Bradstreet's poem.

In silent night when rest I took,
For sorrow near I did not look,
I wakened was with thund'ring noise
And piteous shrieks of dreadful voice.
That fearful sound of "Fire!" and "Fire!"
Let no man know is my desire.

The word "sorrow" suggests that what follows will be sad.

Words such as "piteous shrieks," "dreadful voice," and "fearful" all convey emotions of horror.

BACKGROUND

Anne Bradstreet (1612–1672) was one of the first poets in the American colonies and the first woman in the colonies to gain recognition for her work. She had given up a life of wealth in England to follow her father and husband to the wild, unsettled colonies of New England. Much of her poetry focuses on her internal struggle between desiring the pleasures of the world and focusing on the promise of heaven. On the date referenced in the title of this poem, Bradstreet's home was destroyed by a fire.

HERE FOLLOW SOME VERSES UPON THE BURNING OF OUR HOUSE, JULY 10th, 1666

Poem by Anne Bradstreet

SETTING A PURPOSE

As you read, note the details that show how Bradstreet's focus shifts from what she has lost to what she believes is more important.

In silent night when rest I took
For sorrow near I did not look
I wakened was with thund'ring noise
And piteous shrieks of dreadful voice.
That fearful sound of "Fire!" and "Fire!"
Let no man know is my desire.

I, starting up, the light did spy,
And to my God my heart did cry
To strengthen me in my distress
And not to leave me succorless.[1]
Then, coming out, beheld a space
The flame consume my dwelling place.

[1] **succorless** (sŭk´ər-lĭs): without help or relief.

Notice & Note

Use the side margins to notice and note signposts in the text.

ANALYZE VOICE

Annotate: Mark words that suggest a contrast in lines 1–6.

Analyze: What is happening in these lines? How does the diction convey the urgency of the situation?

NOTICE & NOTE

ANALYZE ALLUSIONS

Annotate: Mark the words in lines 13–18 that match the allusion identified in the footnote.

Draw Conclusions: Why do you think the poet includes an allusion to the story of Job?

PARAPHRASE

Annotate: Recall that **inverted syntax** refers to sentence structure in which the expected order of words is reversed. Mark an example of inverted syntax in lines 25–30.

Paraphrase: Create a paraphrase of the example of inverted syntax you marked.

And when I could no longer look,
I blest His name that gave and took,[2]
That laid my goods now in the dust:
Yea, so it was, and so 'twas just.
It was His own, it was not mine,
Far be it that I should repine;[3]

He might of all justly bereft,
But yet sufficient for us left.
When by the ruins oft I past,
My sorrowing eyes aside did cast,
And here and there the places spy
Where oft I sat and long did lie:

Here stood that trunk and there that chest,
There lay that store I counted best.
My pleasant things in ashes lie,
And them behold no more shall I.
Under thy roof no guest shall sit,
Nor at thy table eat a bit.

No pleasant tale shall e'er be told,
Nor things recounted done of old.
No candle e'er shall shine in thee,
Nor bridegroom's voice e'er heard shall be.
In silence ever shalt thou lie;
Adieu, Adieu, all's vanity.[4]

Then straight I 'gin my heart to chide,[5]
And did thy wealth on earth abide?
Didst fix thy hope on mold'ring[6] dust?
The arm of flesh didst make thy trust?
Raise up thy thoughts above the sky
That dunghill mists away may fly.

Thou hast an house on high erect,
Framed by that mighty Architect,
With glory richly furnishéd,[7]
Stands permanent though this be fled.

---

[2] **I . . . took:** an allusion to Job 1:21 in the Bible—"The Lord gave, and the Lord hath taken away; blessed be the name of the Lord."

[3] **repine:** to complain or fret; to long for something.

[4] **all's vanity:** an allusion to Ecclesiastes 1:2 in the Bible—"All is vanity," meaning that all is temporary and meaningless.

[5] **chide:** to scold mildly so as to correct or improve.

[6] **mold'ring:** crumbling, disintegrating, decaying.

[7] **Thou . . . furnishéd:** an allusion to John 14:2–3 in the Bible, where Jesus assures his disciples that, even if they have nothing in this life, there are mansions prepared for them in heaven.

It's purchaséd and paid for too
By Him who hath enough to do.

A price so vast as is unknown
Yet by His gift is made thine own;
There's wealth enough, I need no more,
Farewell, my pelf,[8] farewell my store.
The world no longer let me love,
My hope and treasure lies above.[9]

[8] **pelf:** wealth or riches, especially when dishonestly acquired.

[9] **treasure . . . above:** an allusion to Matthew 13:44–46, which relates how heavenly treasures are safe from thieves and destruction.

ANALYZE VOICE

Annotate: Mark words in the final stanzas that suggest a change in voice.

Compare: How does the poet's choice of words differ at the end of the poem from that of the beginning?

CHECK YOUR UNDERSTANDING

Answer these questions before moving on to the **Analyze the Text** section on the following page.

1 What is the speaker's first response to hearing the "fearful sound" of fire?

A She looked for water.

B She prayed for strength.

C She gathered her belongings.

D She started to scream.

2 The lines *When by the ruins oft I past, / My sorrowing eyes aside did cast* emphasize that the speaker —

F is struggling to let go of her home

G is glad her house burned down

H is watching the house be rebuilt

J no longer wants to have a house

3 What conclusion helps the poet overcome her sorrow?

A Her family is still around her.

B She has started to build anew.

C She knows heaven will be her home.

D She replaces sorrow with anger.

ANALYZE THE TEXT

Support your responses with evidence from the text. NOTEBOOK

1. **Draw Conclusions** Use details from the poem to explain what you learn about the speaker's feelings and beliefs. How does the voice change over the course of the poem?
2. **Interpret** A **metaphor** is a direct comparison of two unlike things that does not use the word *like* or *as.* In lines 43–48, Bradstreet uses a metaphor to make a comparison to something she holds dear. What two things does she compare, and what do they stand for?
3. **Infer** What does the speaker value more than the house? How did this help her accept the loss of her house by fire?
4. **Analyze** A popular verse from the Book of Genesis is "Dust thou art and unto dust shalt thou return." Where in the poem can you find allusions to this verse? How do these allusions relate to the allusion in line 36?
5. **Paraphrase** How would you paraphrase lines 19–20 of the poem: "He might of all justly bereft, / But yet sufficient for left"?

RESEARCH

RESEARCH TIP
In addition to online encyclopedias, information on Anne Bradstreet can also be found on sites about literature and poetry.

Time and place can have a direct impact on a poet's style, the content of the work, and his or her worldview. Research Anne Bradstreet's life and the time period in which she lived. Use what you learn to answer these questions.

QUESTION	ANSWER
What was Anne Bradstreet's life like before she moved to New England?	
How did Bradstreet's Puritan beliefs help her cope with her loss?	
What impact did the Puritan era have on the style and language of the poem?	

Connect Read another well-known poem that contains allusions to biblical stories, such as "Nothing Gold Can Stay" by Robert Frost. With a partner, discuss what the allusion adds to the poem and whether the use of allusion was similar to or different from Bradstreet's allusions. In which poem is the writer's beliefs more evident?

CREATE AND DISCUSS

Write a Poem Write a poem that expresses your thoughts about what matters to you most. Review your notes on the Quick Start activity before you begin.

- ❑ Decide if you want the speaker to be yourself or someone else.
- ❑ Choose examples of memories or feelings you associate with what you have chosen. Use language that evokes those emotions.
- ❑ Include an allusion to something you have read or heard, such as a book or song.

Discuss a Poem Every reader has a unique response to a poem. They may also have a different view of the effectiveness of literary elements. In a small group, discuss your response to "Here Follow Some Verses Upon the Burning of Our House."

- ❑ Think about the events of the poem and how the speaker reacts to them.
- ❑ Talk about how the time period and the poet's beliefs influence her response to losing her house.
- ❑ Discuss how the literary elements in the poem influence your reaction.
- ❑ Make sure everyone gets a chance to participate in the discussion.

Go to **Participating in Collaborative Discussions** in the **Speaking and Listening Studio** for help.

RESPOND TO THE ESSENTIAL QUESTION

Why are we bound to certain places?

Gather Information Review your annotations and notes on "Here Follow Some Verses Upon the Burning of Our House." Then, add relevant information to your Response Log. As you determine what information to include, think about:

- the details the poet includes to describe her house and belongings
- the way the poet reveals her feelings and beliefs
- how the voice changes over the course of the poem

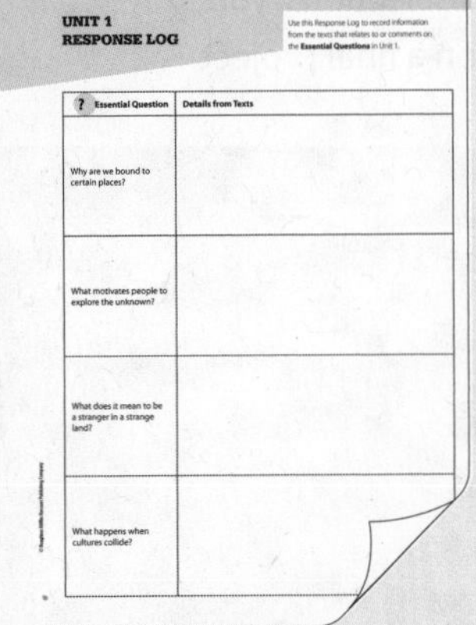

UNIT 1
RESPONSE LOG

Use this Response Log to record information from the texts that relates to or comments on the **Essential Questions** in Unit 1.

? Essential Question	Details from Texts
Why are we bound to certain places?	
What motivates people to explore the unknown?	
What does it mean to be a stranger in a strange land?	
What happens when cultures collide?	

ACADEMIC VOCABULARY

As you write and discuss what you learned from the poem, be sure to use the Academic Vocabulary words. Check off each of the words that you use.

- ❑ **adapt**
- ❑ **coherent**
- ❑ **device**
- ❑ **displace**
- ❑ **dynamic**

HISTORICAL NARRATIVE

from

OF PLYMOUTH PLANTATION

by **William Bradford**

pages 57–61

COMPARE AUTHOR'S PURPOSE

As you read, note how each text describes encounters between British settlers and Native Americans. *Of Plymouth Plantation* is a primary source, or a first-hand account. "Coming of Age in the Dawnland" is a secondary source, an account written after events took place, and it includes information from other sources. Notice how each text presents information about each culture and how groups built relationships with each other. After reading both selections, you will collaborate with a group on a final project.

ESSENTIAL QUESTION:

What happens when cultures collide?

HISTORY WRITING

COMING OF AGE IN THE DAWNLAND

by **Charles C. Mann**

pages 69–75

from Of Plymouth Plantation

QUICK START

Think about what you know about the challenges faced by colonists and Native Americans when they encountered each other. With a partner, share one fact you know about their encounters. Then, share one question you have about the challenges faced by each group.

ANALYZE AUTHOR'S PURPOSE

The **author's purpose** is the reason he or she writes a particular text. This purpose might be to inform, to entertain, to express beliefs or feelings, or to persuade. Some texts seek to achieve more than one of these purposes. To analyze and then evaluate an author's purpose, consider the following.

- A text's **genre** provides clues to the author's overall purpose. *Of Plymouth Plantation* is a historical narrative, a text that tells about real events that happened in the past.
- A text's intended **audience,** or the people intended to read the text, helps suggest the author's reason for writing. *Of Plymouth Plantation,* for example, was intended to be read by future generations.
- A work's **tone,** the author's attitude toward the subject, provides clues about purpose. As you read, note Bradford's vivid descriptions and what they reveal about his feelings about events and people.
- The text's overall **message,** or its central idea, suggests the author's purpose for writing. Note clues about Bradford's message as you read.

GENRE ELEMENTS: HISTORICAL NARRATIVE

- tells a true story about events that happened in the past
- is a narrative text that relates events in chronological order, or the order in which they happened
- may be considered a **primary source** if the author observed the events personally

ANALYZE LANGUAGE

Diction and rhetorical devices are elements of language that help authors shape the perceptions of readers. **Diction** is the writer's choice of words and it may be formal or informal, technical or common, or abstract or concrete. **Rhetorical devices** are techniques a writer uses to communicate ideas and convince readers of their truth. Repetition and allusions are two examples of rhetorical devices, among others.

RHETORICAL DEVICE	DEFINITION
repetition	repeating a word, phrase, or idea
allusion	references to something the author expects will be familiar to readers; for example, references to the Bible for Bradford's audience

As you read *Of Plymouth Plantation,* notice Bradford's diction and his use of repetition and allusion to convey the events he describes. Also, consider how his use of language supports his purpose for writing.

GET READY

CRITICAL VOCABULARY

patent **clave** **calamity** **sundry** **divers**

Use the Critical Vocabulary words to answer the following questions.

1. Which word might be used in a description of a hurricane?
2. What might you display to prove that you own something?
3. Which two Critical Vocabulary words are synonyms for the word *various*?
4. Which word describes an action you might take toward someone next to you if you were startled?

LANGUAGE CONVENTIONS

Active and Passive Voice The voice of a verb tells whether its subject performs or receives the action expressed by the verb.

- If the subject performs the action, the verb is in the **active voice:** *Liam mailed the letter.*
- If the subject receives the action, the verb is in the **passive voice:** *The letter was mailed.*

As you read the excerpt from *Of Plymouth Plantation,* think about when and why Bradford uses active and passive voice and how each use affects your perception of the event or events he describes.

ANNOTATION MODEL

NOTICE & NOTE

As you read, note details that suggest the author's purpose. Here are one reader's notes about *Of Plymouth Plantation.*

The rest of this history (if God give me life and opportunity) I shall, for brevity's sake, handle by way of annals, noting only the heads of principal things, and passages as they fell in order of time, and may seem to be profitable to know or to make use of. And this may be as the Second Book.

"History" and "in order of time" tell me that this is a fact-based account told in chronological order.

Chapter XI

The Remainder of Anno 1620

[The Mayflower Compact]

I shall a little return back, and begin with a combination made by them before they came ashore; being the first foundation of their government in this place.

Bradford believes this record, including the "first foundation of their government," may be "profitable" to his readers. He thinks others might learn from the experiences he will relate.

NOTICE & NOTE

BACKGROUND

Born in England in 1590, **William Bradford** *became involved in the Protestant Reformation while still a boy. He joined the Puritans, reformers who wanted to purify the Church of England and eventually separated from it. With other Puritans, he migrated to Holland in search of religious freedom. He helped organize the journey on the Mayflower in 1620 that brought about 100 people—half of them his fellow "Pilgrims"—to the New World. His* History of Plymouth Plantation, 1620–1647, *describes this journey and provides a glimpse of the settlers' life in what became New England.*

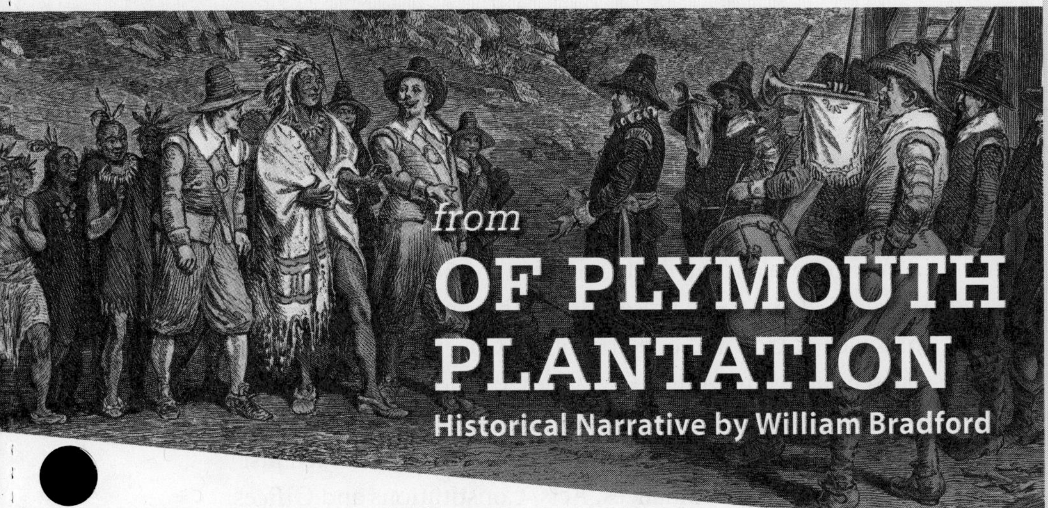

from

OF PLYMOUTH PLANTATION

Historical Narrative by William Bradford

PREPARE TO COMPARE

As you read, pay attention to how the relationship between the colonists and Native Americans changed over time. Note details that help you understand how individuals were able to negotiate a peaceful relationship between the two groups. Identifying these details will help you compare this text with "Coming of Age in the Dawnland."

Notice & Note

Use the side margins to notice and note signposts in the text.

The Second Book

1 The rest of this history (if God give me life and opportunity) I shall, for brevity's sake, handle by way of annals, noting only the heads of principal things, and passages as they fell in order of time, and may seem to be profitable to know or to make use of. And this may be as the Second Book.

Chapter XI

The Remainder of Anno 1620
[The Mayflower Compact]

2 I shall a little return back, and begin with a combination made by them before they came ashore; being the first foundation of their government in this place. Occasioned partly by the

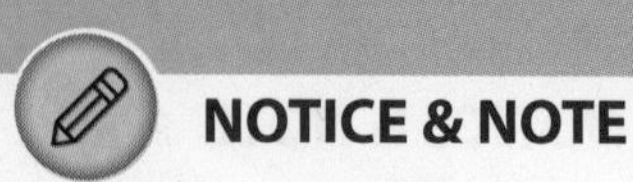

NOTICE & NOTE

patent
(păt´nt) *n.* an official document granting ownership.

ANALYZE AUTHOR'S PURPOSE

Annotate: Mark three phrases in paragraph 4 that suggest a formal tone.

Infer: What can you infer about the author's purpose based on his tone thus far? Cite text evidence in your response.

discontented and mutinous[1] speeches that some of the strangers amongst them had let fall from them in the ship: That when they came ashore they would use their own liberty, for none had power to command them, the **patent** they had being for Virginia and not for New England, which belonged to another government, with which the Virginia Company had nothing to do. And partly that such an act by them done, this their condition considered, might be as firm as any patent, and in some respects more sure.

The form was as followeth:
In the Name of God, Amen.

3 We whose names are underwritten, the loyal subjects of our dread Sovereign Lord King James, by the Grace of God of Great Britain, France, and Ireland King, Defender of the Faith, etc.

4 Having undertaken, for the Glory of God and advancement of the Christian Faith and Honour of our King and Country, a Voyage to plant the First Colony in the Northern Parts of Virginia, do by these presents solemnly and mutually in the presence of God and one of another, Covenant and Combine ourselves together into a Civil Body Politic, for our better ordering and preservation and furtherance of the ends aforesaid; and by virtue hereof to enact, constitute and frame such just and equal Laws, Ordinances, Acts, Constitutions and Offices, from time to time, as shall be thought most meet and convenient for the general good of the Colony, unto which we promise all due submission and obedience. In witness whereof we have hereunder subscribed our names at Cape Cod, the 11th of November, in the year of the reign of our Sovereign Lord King James, of England, France and Ireland the eighteenth, and of Scotland the fifty-fourth. Anno Domini 1620.

5 After this they chose, or rather confirmed, Mr. John Carver (a man godly and well approved amongst them) their Governor for that year. And after they had provided a place for their goods, or common store (which were long in unlading for want of boats, foulness of the winter weather and sickness of divers) and begun some small cottages for their habitation; as time would admit, they met and consulted of laws and orders, both for their civil and military government as the necessity of their condition did require, still adding thereunto as urgent occasion in several times, and as cases did require.

6 In these hard and difficult beginnings they found some discontents and murmurings arise amongst some, and mutinous speeches and carriages in other; but they were soon quelled and overcome by the wisdom, patience, and just and equal carriage

[1] **mutinous:** rebellious.

NOTICE & NOTE

of things, by the Governor and better part, which **clave** faithfully together in the main.

clave
(klāv) *v.* past tense of *cleave:* to cling; to adhere

[The Starving Time]

7 But that which was most sad and lamentable was, that in two or three months' time half of their company died, especially in January and February, being the depth of winter, and wanting houses and other comforts; being infected with the scurvy[2] and other diseases which this long voyage and their inaccommodate condition had brought upon them. So as there died some times two or three of a day in the foresaid time, that of 100 and odd persons, scarce fifty remained. And of these, in the time of most distress, there was but six or seven sound persons who to their great commendations, be it spoken, spared no pains night nor day, but with abundance of toil and hazard of their own health, fetched them wood, made them fires, dressed them meat, made their beds, washed their loathsome[3] clothes, clothed and unclothed them. In a word, did all the homely and necessary offices for them which dainty and queasy stomachs cannot endure to hear named; and all this willingly and cheerfully, without any grudging in the least, showing herein their true love unto their friends and brethren; a rare example and worthy to be remembered. Two of these seven were Mr. William Brewster, their reverend Elder, and Myles Standish, their Captain and military commander, unto whom myself and many others were much beholden in our low and sick condition. And yet the Lord so upheld these persons as in this general **calamity** they were not at all infected either with sickness or lameness. . . .

calamity
(kə-lăm´ĭ-tē) *n.* an event that brings terrible loss or lasting distress.

[Indian Relations]

8 All this while the Indians came skulking about them, and would sometimes show themselves aloof off, but when any approached near them, they would run away; and once they stole away their tools where they had been at work and were gone to dinner. But about the 16th of March, a certain Indian came boldly amongst them and spoke to them in broken English, which they could well understand but marveled at it. At length they understood by discourse with him, that he was not of these parts, but belonged to the eastern parts where some English ships came to fish, with whom he was acquainted and could name **sundry** of them by their names, amongst whom he had got his language. He became profitable to them in acquainting them with many things concerning the state of the country in the east parts where he lived, which was afterwards profitable unto them; as also of the people here, of their names, number and strength, of their situation and distance from this place, and who was chief amongst

ANALYZE LANGUAGE

Annotate: Mark words in paragraph 8 that describe the interaction between colonists and Native Americans.

Evaluate: How does Bradford's diction reflect a change in tone? What does this change reveal about his attitude toward the Native Americans?

sundry
(sŭn´drē) *adj.* various or assorted.

[2] **scurvy:** a disease caused by a lack of vitamin C in the diet.
[3] **loathsome:** offensive or disgusting.

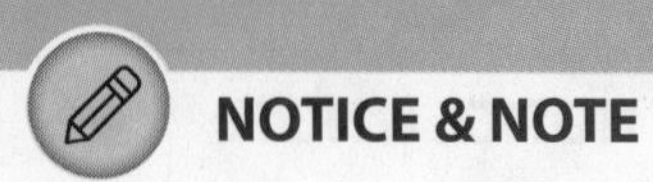

them. His name was Samoset. He told them also of another Indian whose name was Squanto, a native of this place, who had been in England and could speak better English than himself.

9 Being, after some time of entertainment and gifts dismissed, a while after he came again, and five more with him, and they brought again all the tools that were stolen away before, and made way for the coming of their great Sachem,[4] called Massasoit. Who, about four or five days after, came with the chief of his friends and other attendance, with the aforesaid Squanto. With whom, after friendly entertainment and some gifts given him, they made a peace with him (which hath now continued this 24 years) in these terms:

1. That neither he nor any of his should injure or do hurt to any of their people.
2. That if any of his did hurt to any of theirs, he should send the offender, that they might punish him.
3. That if anything were taken away from any of theirs, he should cause it to be restored; and they should do the like to his.
4. If any did unjustly war against him, they would aid him; if any did war against them, he should aid them.
5. He should send to his neighbours confederates[5] to certify them of this, that they might not wrong them, but might be likewise comprised in the conditions of peace.
6. That when their men came to them, they should leave their bows and arrows behind them.

LANGUAGE CONVENTIONS

Annotate: Circle the passive-voice verb in item 3 of the list, and underline the active verbs.

Respond: What is the effect of using the passive voice in this item?

10 After these things he returned to his place called Sowams, some 40 miles from this place, but Squanto continued with them and was their interpreter and was a special instrument sent of God for their good beyond their expectation. He directed them how to set their corn, where to take fish, and to procure other commodities, and was also their pilot to bring them to unknown places for their profit, and never left them till he died. He was a native of this place, and scarce any left alive besides himself. He was carried away with **divers** others by one Hunt, a master of a ship, who thought to sell them for slaves in Spain. But he got away for England and was entertained by a merchant in London, and employed to Newfoundland and other parts, and lastly brought hither into these parts by one Mr. Dermer, a gentleman employed by Sir Ferdinando Gorges and others for discovery and other designs in these parts. . . .

divers
(dī´vərz) *adj.* various; several.

[First Thanksgiving]

11 They began now to gather in the small harvest they had, and to fit up their houses and dwellings against winter, being all well recovered in health and strength and had all things in good plenty. For as

[4] **Sachem:** chief.

[5] **confederates:** allies; persons who share a common purpose.

some were thus employed in affairs abroad, others were exercised in fishing, about cod and bass and other fish, of which they took good store, of which every family had their portion. All the summer there was no want; and now began to come in store of fowl, as winter approached, of which this place did abound when they came first (but afterward decreased by degrees). And besides waterfowl there was great store of wild turkeys, of which they took many, besides venison, etc. Besides they had about a peck a meal a week to a person, or now since harvest, Indian corn to that proportion. Which made many afterwards write so largely of their plenty here to their friends in England, which were not feigned but true reports.[6]

[6] **reports:** Although the specific day of the Plymouth colonists' first Thanksgiving is not known, it occurred in the fall of 1621. For three days, Massasoit and almost a hundred of his men joined the Pilgrims for feasts and games.

NOTICE & NOTE

ANALYZE LANGUAGE

Annotate: Mark two examples of repetition in the final paragraph of the excerpt.

Analyze: What does this repetition emphasize in the description?

CHECK YOUR UNDERSTANDING

Answer these questions before moving on to the **Analyze the Text** section on the following page.

1 Why did the colonists decide to create the *Mayflower Compact*?

A King James required them to sign such a document.

B Some of them were speaking out against King James.

C Their original patent did not extend to establishing a colony in New England.

D They were facing extreme hardship and starvation and wanted to elect a new leader.

2 Why were Squanto and Samoset able to help make peace between the colonists and the Native Americans?

F They spoke English and could help the two groups communicate.

G They showed the colonists what foods to eat to avoid scurvy.

H They brought the colonists food during the winter so they would not starve.

J They planned a three-day festival where both groups could share abundant food.

3 How did Squanto help the colonists prepare for the winter?

A He showed them how to build fires and cook food.

B He showed them how to sew warmer clothing.

C He showed them how to make their homes sturdier.

D He showed them how to grow and find food to store.

RESPOND

ANALYZE THE TEXT

Support your responses with evidence from the text. NOTEBOOK

1. **Analyze** What does the Mayflower Compact explicitly say? What does it suggest through its careful diction, or word choice, and tone?
2. **Evaluate** Paraphrase the terms of the treaty between Massasoit and the Pilgrims (paragraph 9). Then, evaluate the treaty. Is it equally fair to both sides? Explain.
3. **Analyze** Which beliefs most contributed to the colonists' willingness to face hardships together? What passages best reveal those beliefs?
4. **Cite Evidence** Locate and analyze two examples of Bradford's use of biblical allusions or references to God's intervention in events. What purpose might these devices serve in his account?
5. **Synthesize** What is the central idea of the excerpt from *Of Plymouth Plantation?* How does this reflect Bradford's purpose in writing it?

RESEARCH

RESEARCH TIP
To make sure your information is accurate, confirm all facts with at least two credible sources.

Find out more about Native American farming. Do some research on two Native American groups and their agricultural practices. Record your findings in the chart below.

NATIVE AMERICAN GROUP	MAIN CROPS	IMPORTANT FARMING METHODS AND TOOLS

Extend Compare and contrast the groups you researched. How were their farming practices and crops similar? How were they different?

CREATE AND DISCUSS

Write an Informational Text Bradford's account describes how the Native Americans helped the colonists adapt to life in New England. Write a three- or four-paragraph informational text that explains how the colonists and Native Americans confronted challenges together.

- ❑ Include an introduction with a thesis on how Native Americans helped the colonists adapt.
- ❑ Support your thesis with relevant supporting details.
- ❑ Use verbs in both active and passive voice.
- ❑ Sum up your ideas in a conclusion.

Go to **Writing Informative Texts** in the **Writing Studio** for help.

Hold a Group Discussion With a small group, discuss how the relationship between Native Americans and colonists developed over time and what factors caused changes to occur.

- ❑ Review the selection with your group to identify the specific events that sparked change.
- ❑ Then, discuss how each event caused a positive or negative change.
- ❑ Finally, end your discussion by summarizing your group's main ideas.

Go to **Participating in Collaborative Discussions** in the **Speaking and Listening Studio** for help with having a group discussion.

RESPOND TO THE ESSENTIAL QUESTION

What happens when cultures collide?

Gather Information Review your annotations and notes on the excerpt from *Of Plymouth Plantation*. Then, add relevant details to your Response Log. As you determine which information to include, think about:

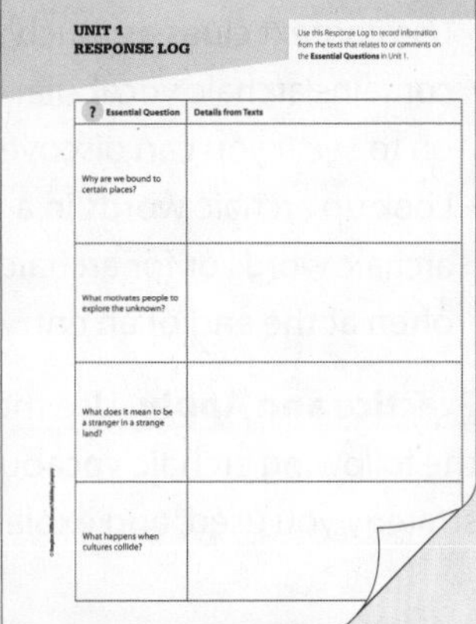

UNIT 1
RESPONSE LOG

Use this Response Log to record information from the texts that relates to or comments on the **Essential Questions** in Unit 1.

? Essential Question	Details from Texts
Why are we bound to certain places?	
What motivates people to explore the unknown?	
What does it mean to be a stranger in a strange land?	
What happens when cultures collide?	

- how the colonists initially viewed the Native Americans
- how and why this view changed
- particular actions that helped change the relationship between the two groups

ACADEMIC VOCABULARY

As you write and discuss what you learned from the historical account, be sure to use the Academic Vocabulary words. Check off each of the words that you use.

- ❑ **adapt**
- ❑ **coherent**
- ❑ **device**
- ❑ **displace**
- ❑ **dynamic**

RESPOND

CRITICAL VOCABULARY

WORD BANK
patent
clave
calamity
sundry
divers

Practice and Apply Mark the italicized alternative that best relates to the Critical Vocabulary word in each sentence. Then, explain your choice.

1. If you and your friends have **divers** opinions about what to eat, is it *easy* or *difficult* to choose a restaurant?
2. Did the *Mayflower* passengers' **patent** *officially* or *unofficially* suggest that they would live in Virginia?
3. Would **sundry** pairs of shoes be *identical* or *different* from each other?
4. If you experienced a **calamity,** would the result be *good* or *bad?*
5. If you **clave** to someone's principles, did you *support* or *oppose* them?

VOCABULARY STRATEGY: Archaic Vocabulary

Of Plymouth Plantation contains many examples of **archaic vocabulary**—words that are no longer commonly used. The Critical Vocabulary word *divers,* for example, was common until the end of the 17th century but has now been almost completely replaced by *diverse.* English usage and vocabulary have changed a great deal over time.

Here are some strategies to help you understand archaic vocabulary:

- Notice if the word is similar to a current, familiar word, and try substituting the current word to make a meaningful sentence.
- Use context clues as much as possible when reading a selection that contains archaic vocabulary. Don't stop at every unfamiliar word, but read on to see if you can discover hints about the word's meaning.
- Look up archaic words in a dictionary. Many dictionaries include notes for archaic words or for archaic meanings of familiar words; this information is often at the end of an entry and is labeled with the word *archaic* or *obsolete.*

Practice and Apply Use the strategies above to determine the meaning of the following archaic vocabulary from *Of Plymouth Plantation.* Identify each strategy you used, and explain how it helped you find the word's meaning.

WORD	MEANING	NOTES ON STRATEGY
aforesaid (paragraph 4)		
thereunto (paragraph 5)		
inaccommodate (paragraph 7)		

LANGUAGE CONVENTIONS:
Active and Passive Voice

The **voice** of a verb tells whether its subject performs or receives the verb's action. If the subject *performs* the action, the verb is in the **active voice.** If the subject *receives* the action, the verb is in the **passive voice.** In Bradford's writing, the colonists or the Native Americans are most often subjects who perform the action. Sometimes, however, the subject of a sentence or clause receives the action.

Consider this example from the narrative, which contains several active voice verbs in succession, emphasizing the praiseworthy work the "six or seven" did when a terrible illness struck:

> **. . . there was but six or seven sound persons who to their great commendations, be it spoken, spared no pains night nor day, but with abundance of toil and hazard of their own health, fetched them wood, made them fires, dressed them meat, made their beds, washed their loathsome clothes, clothed and unclothed them.**

Now consider this example, which contains both active voice and passive voice:

> **He was carried away with divers others by one Hunt, a master of a ship, who thought to sell them for slaves in Spain. But he got away for England and was entertained by a merchant in London. . . .**

This example describes how Squanto managed to learn English through a sequence of events in which he sometimes takes action ("got away") and sometimes has actions done to or for him ("was carried," "was entertained"). Note how the sentence shows a contrast between the way the slaver and the merchant treated Squanto—he was carried away by one but entertained by another. How his fortunes changed!

Practice and Apply Return to the informational text you wrote in response to this selection's Create and Present. First, identify any examples of passive voice and rewrite those sentences in the active voice. Then, choose two examples of active voice and rewrite those sentences in the passive voice. Finally, compare the emphasis and clarity created by the use of each voice. Write your original and revised sentences below.

ORIGINAL SENTENCE	REVISED SENTENCE

Go to **Active Voice and Passive Voice** in the **Grammar Studio** for help.

HISTORY WRITING

COMING OF AGE IN THE DAWNLAND

by **Charles C. Mann**

pages 69–75

COMPARE AUTHOR'S PURPOSE

Now that you've read the excerpt from *Of Plymouth Plantation,* read "Coming of Age in the Dawnland" to explore how this secondary source describes some of the same ideas. As you read, consider the differences between the two texts—one a primary source and one a secondary source—and the unique perspective each one brings to similar subject matter. Consider the author's purpose as you read.

ESSENTIAL QUESTION:

What happens when cultures collide?

HISTORICAL NARRATIVE

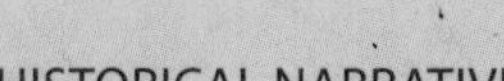

from

OF PLYMOUTH PLANTATION

by **William Bradford**

pages 57–61

Coming of Age in the Dawnland

QUICK START

Pretend you have landed on an unfamiliar island and are approached by an inhabitant. What might happen? What might you do? Think of a few scenarios for your first interaction, and discuss them with your group.

EVALUATE AUTHOR'S PURPOSE

The **author's purpose** is the reason he or she writes a particular text, and this purpose generally is not stated. Instead, readers must **infer** the purpose, or draw a logical conclusion about it, based on text evidence. The purpose might be to inform, to entertain, or to persuade readers to agree with the author.

No matter the purpose, effective writing must have an appealing style. Style elements include **word choice, tone** (the writer's attitude about the topic), and **imagery** (words that appeal to a reader's senses). Use these points to analyze and evaluate "Coming of Age in the Dawnland":

- Think about what the text says. What ideas does the author state directly, and what facts and examples does he include?
- Analyze the author's style. What words and images do you find especially powerful? What tone does the writing convey? What does the text's use of graphics or illustrations suggest?
- Evaluate the text. How well do the elements support Mann's purpose?

GENRE ELEMENTS: HISTORY WRITING

- is a type of nonfiction writing meant to inform readers about a historical person, time, or event
- relies on facts, dates, and verifiable details to support the main ideas
- incorporates quotations from and references to experts and scholars
- uses primary sources to provide authenticity
- may use graphic features, such as maps and photographs

ANALYZE LANGUAGE

To understand a sophisticated text like "Coming of Age in the Dawnland," you must analyze the meanings of words and phrases as the author uses them. These meanings may be literal or nonliteral. The chart provides examples.

TECHNICAL TERMS	FIGURATIVE LANGUAGE	CONNOTATIONS
Mann draws on evidence from social scientists, and some of the language he uses comes from specialized fields of study. Examples are *casus belli* and *tripartite alliance*. Mann also uses some Native American words when no accurate translation is available. He defines some terms in the text; others you must look up in a dictionary.	Words are often used in an imaginative way to make comparisons. A **simile,** for example, compares things using the word *like* or *as*. Mann says an Indian not admitting a loss in a fight was "like failing to resign after losing a major piece in a chess tournament." This simile helps readers grasp an unfamiliar topic by comparing it to a familiar one.	To convey subtle shades of meaning, authors choose words with particular **connotations,** or associated feelings. For example, describing bedtime for a Native American family, Mann uses the words *firelight* and *lullaby*. These words have pleasant connotations that help readers connect with the lives of the people.

GET READY

CRITICAL VOCABULARY

project **settlement** **regimen** **defection** **stoically**

To preview the Critical Vocabulary words, complete the sentences.

1. To __________ is to communicate or put forth an impression or message.
2. When a community experiences __________, it loses members.
3. A __________ is a small community in an area without a large population.
4. A daily __________ is a routine of behavior performed every day.
5. If you endure something __________, you do not show emotion.

LANGUAGE CONVENTIONS

Clauses All clauses contain a subject and a verb. An **independent clause** can stand on its own. However, a **dependent clause** (often called a **subordinate clause**) cannot stand alone as a sentence; it depends on, or is subordinate to, an independent clause. Consider the sentence:

As Tisquantum's later history made clear, he regarded himself first and foremost as a citizen of Patuxet, a shoreline settlement halfway between what is now Boston and the beginning of Cape Cod.

"As Tisquantum's later history made clear" is a dependent clause; it cannot stand on its own. As you read, look for ways Mann uses dependent clauses to add detail, interest, and variety.

ANNOTATION MODEL

NOTICE & NOTE

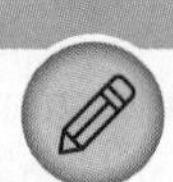

Here are one reader's notes about the author's purpose and language in "Coming of Age in the Dawnland."

Consider Tisquantum, the "friendly Indian" of the textbook. More than likely Tisquantum was not the name he was given at birth. In that part of the Northeast, *tisquantum* referred to rage, especially the rage of *manitou*, the world-suffusing spiritual power at the heart of coastal Indians' religious beliefs. When Tisquantum approached the Pilgrims and identified himself by that sobriquet, it was as if he had stuck out his hand and said, Hello, I'm the Wrath of God. No one would lightly adopt such a name in contemporary Western society. Neither would anyone in seventeenth-century indigenous society. Tisquantum was trying to project something.

The words "friendly Indian" are in quotation marks. Mann wants to call attention to the way Tisquantum is frequently described to students.

Mann explains that the name Tisquantum was chosen to make an impression, even if the Pilgrims didn't understand. Mann's purpose is to dispel myths about Tisquantum and provide a more accurate portrayal.

NOTICE & NOTE

BACKGROUND

In his 2005 book, 1491: New Revelations of the Americas Before Columbus, *science journalist* **Charles C. Mann** *reviews and synthesizes the work of recent scholars who have studied early Native American societies. Christopher Columbus's voyage to the Caribbean in 1492 marked the beginning of contact between native people in the Americas and Europeans. By 1620 Native Americans in coastal New England had been trading on a limited basis with Europeans for about a hundred years. The man named Tisquantum in this excerpt from Mann's book is the person whom William Bradford called Squanto.*

COMING OF AGE IN THE DAWNLAND

History Writing by Charles C. Mann

PREPARE TO COMPARE

As you read, look for ways Mann draws parallels between the daily lives of settlers and Native American people. Notice how the European settlers viewed Native American customs and practices. Think back to Bradford's account in the excerpt from Of Plymouth Plantation, *and look for similar ideas in this text.*

Notice & Note

Use the side margins to notice and note signposts in the text.

1 Consider Tisquantum, the "friendly Indian" of the textbook. More than likely Tisquantum was not the name he was given at birth. In that part of the Northeast, *tisquantum* referred to rage, especially the rage of *manitou*, the world-suffusing spiritual power at the heart of coastal Indians' religious beliefs. When Tisquantum approached the Pilgrims and identified himself by that sobriquet,[1] it was as if he had stuck out his hand and said, Hello, I'm the Wrath of God. No one would lightly adopt such a name in contemporary Western society. Neither would anyone in seventeenth-century indigenous society. Tisquantum was trying to **project** something.

project
(prə-jĕkt´) *v.* to communicate or put forth.

[1] **sobriquet** (sō´brĭ-kā´): nickname.

NOTICE & NOTE

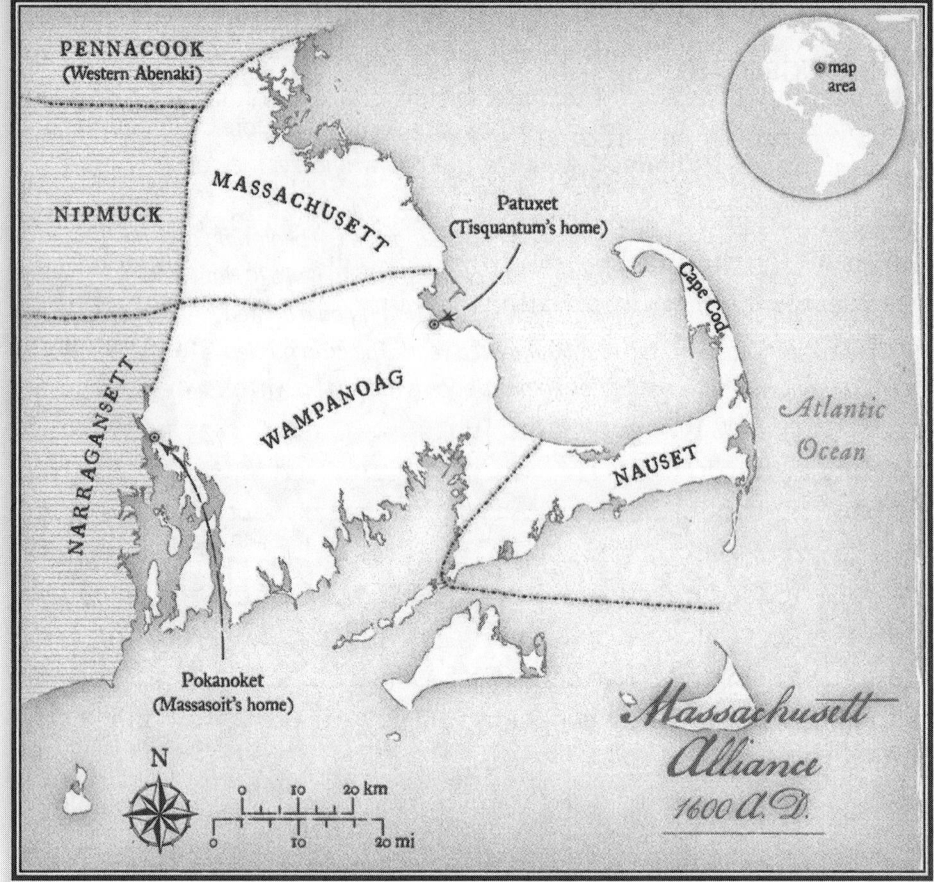

MASSACHUSETT ALLIANCE, 1600 A.D.

EVALUATE AUTHOR'S PURPOSE
Annotate: Mark places on the map that correspond to places mentioned in the text.

Infer: What can you infer about the author's purpose for including this map?

EVALUATE AUTHOR'S PURPOSE
Annotate: Mark words and phrases in paragraph 2 that indicate the author is presenting new or surprising information.

Infer: What can you infer about the author's purpose?

settlement
(sĕt′l-mənt) *n.* a small community in a sparsely populated area.

2 Tisquantum was not an Indian. True, he belonged to that category of people whose ancestors had inhabited the Western Hemisphere for thousands of years. And it is true that I refer to him as an Indian, because the label is useful shorthand; so would his descendants, and for much the same reason. But "Indian" was not a category that Tisquantum himself would have recognized, any more than the inhabitants of the same area today would call themselves "Western Hemisphereans." Still less would Tisquantum have claimed to belong to "Norumbega," the label by which most Europeans then referred to New England. ("New England" was coined only in 1616.) As Tisquantum's later history made clear, he regarded himself first and foremost as a citizen of Patuxet, a shoreline **settlement** halfway between what is now Boston and the beginning of Cape Cod.

3 Patuxet was one of the dozen or so settlements in what is now eastern Massachusetts and Rhode Island that comprised[2] the Wampanoag confederation. In turn, the Wampanoag were part of a tripartite alliance with two other confederations: the Nauset, which comprised some thirty groups on Cape Cod; and the Massachusett, several dozen villages clustered around Massachusetts Bay. All of these people spoke variants of Massachusett, a member of the

[2] **comprised:** made up of.

Algonquian language family, the biggest in eastern North America at the time. (Massachusett thus was the name both of a language and of one of the groups that spoke it.) In Massachusett, the name for the New England shore was the Dawnland, the place where the sun rose. The inhabitants of the Dawnland were the People of the First Light. . . .

4 Tucked into the great sweep of Cape Cod Bay, Patuxet sat on a low rise above a small harbor, jigsawed by sandbars and shallow enough that children could walk from the beach hundreds of yards into the water before the waves went above their heads. To the west, maize hills marched across the sandy hillocks[3] in parallel rows. Beyond the fields, a mile or more away from the sea, rose a forest of oak, chestnut, and hickory, open and park-like, the underbrush kept down by expert annual burning. "Pleasant of air and prospect," as one English visitor described the area, Patuxet had "much plenty both of fish and fowl every day in the year." Runs of spawning Atlantic salmon, shortnose sturgeon, striped bass, and American shad annually filled the harbor. But the most important fish harvest came in late spring, when the herring-like alewives swarmed the fast, shallow stream that cut through the village. So numerous were the fish, and so driven, that when mischievous boys walled off the stream with stones the alewives would leap the barrier—silver bodies gleaming in the sun—and proceed upstream.

5 Tisquantum's childhood *wetu* (home) was formed from arched poles lashed together into a dome that was covered in winter by tightly woven rush mats and in summer by thin sheets of chestnut bark. A fire burned constantly in the center, the smoke venting through a hole in the center of the roof. English visitors did not find this arrangement peculiar; chimneys were just coming into use in Britain, and most homes there, including those of the wealthy, were still heated by fires beneath central roof holes. Nor did the English regard the Dawnland *wetu* as primitive; its multiple layers of mats, which trapped insulating layers of air, were "warmer than our English houses," sighed the colonist William Wood. The *wetu* was less leaky than the typical English wattle-and-daub house, too. Wood did not conceal his admiration for the way Indian mats "deny entrance to any drop of rain, though it come both fierce and long."

6 Around the edge of the house were low beds, sometimes wide enough for a whole family to sprawl on them together; usually raised about a foot from the floor, platform-style; and always piled with mats and furs. Going to sleep in the firelight, young Tisquantum would have stared up at the diddering[4] shadows of the hemp bags and bark boxes hanging from the rafters. Voices would skirl[5] up in the darkness: one person singing a lullaby, then another person,

ANALYZE LANGUAGE

Annotate: Mark words with positive connotations in the first five lines of paragraph 4.

Evaluate: What feeling about Patuxet do these words create?

EVALUATE AUTHOR'S PURPOSE

Annotate: Mark examples in paragraph 5 that describe English reactions to Patuxet homes.

Evaluate: What can you infer about the author's purpose for including these descriptions? How effective are the descriptions?

[3] **hillocks:** small hills.

[4] **diddering:** trembling.

[5] **skirl:** make a high-pitched sound, like bagpipes.

NOTICE & NOTE

The exterior of a *wetu*

EVALUATE AUTHOR'S PURPOSE

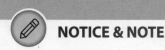

Annotate: Mark a comparison in paragraph 6 of the diets of Patuxet and European citizens.

Infer: What can you infer about the author's purpose in including this comparison?

ANALYZE LANGUAGE

Annotate: Mark words and images in paragraphs 8–9 that have negative connotations.

Analyze: How do these words support the idea that "Tisquantum's regimen was probably tougher than that of his friends"?

until everyone was asleep. In the morning, when he woke, big, egg-shaped pots of corn-and-bean mash would be on the fire, simmering with meat, vegetables, or dried fish to make a slow-cooked dinner stew. Outside the *wetu* he would hear the cheerful thuds of the large mortars and pestles[6] in which women crushed dried maize into *nokake*, a flour-like powder "so sweet, toothsome, and hearty," colonist Gookin wrote, "that an Indian will travel many days with no other but this meal." Although Europeans bemoaned the lack of salt in Indian cuisine, they thought it nourishing. According to one modern reconstruction, Dawnland diets at the time averaged about 2,500 calories a day, better than those usual in famine-racked Europe.

7 Pilgrim writers universally reported that Wampanoag families were close and loving—more so than English families, some thought. Europeans in those days tended to view children as moving straight from infancy to adulthood around the age of seven, and often thereupon sent them out to work. Indian parents, by contrast, regarded the years before puberty as a time of playful development, and kept their offspring close by until marriage. (Jarringly, to the contemporary eye, some Pilgrims interpreted this as sparing the rod.) Boys like Tisquantum explored the countryside, swam in the ponds at the south end of the harbor, and played a kind of soccer with a small leather ball; in the summer and fall they camped out in huts in the fields, weeding the maize and chasing away birds. Archery practice began at age two. By adolescence boys would make a game of shooting at each other and dodging the arrows.

8 The primary goal of Dawnland education was molding character. Men and women were expected to be brave, hardy, honest, and uncomplaining. Chatterboxes and gossips were frowned upon. "He that speaks seldom and opportunely, being as good as his word, is the only man they love," Wood explained. Character formation began early, with family games of tossing naked children into the

[6] **mortars and pestles:** bowl-shaped containers and blunt tools for grinding and crushing.

NOTICE & NOTE 

The interior of a *wetu*

snow. (They were pulled out quickly and placed next to the fire, in a practice reminiscent of Scandinavian saunas.) When Indian boys came of age, they spent an entire winter alone in the forest, equipped only with a bow, a hatchet, and a knife. These methods worked, the awed Wood reported. "Beat them, whip them, pinch them, punch them, if [the Indians] resolve not to flinch for it, they will not."

9 Tisquantum's **regimen** was probably tougher than that of his friends, according to Salisbury, the Smith College historian, for it seems that he was selected to become a *pniese*, a kind of counselor-bodyguard to the sachem. To master the art of ignoring pain, future *pniese* had to subject themselves to such miserable experiences as running barelegged through brambles. And they fasted often, to learn self-discipline. After spending their winter in the woods, *pniese* candidates came back to an additional test: drinking bitter gentian juice until they vomited, repeating this bulimic process over and over until, near fainting, they threw up blood.

regimen
(rĕj´ə-mən) *n.* a system or organized routine of behavior.

10 Patuxet, like its neighboring settlements, was governed by a sachem, who upheld the law, negotiated treaties, controlled foreign contacts, collected tribute, declared war, provided for widows and orphans, and allocated farmland when there were disputes over it. (Dawnlanders lived in a loose scatter, but they knew which family could use which land—"very exact and punctuall," Roger Williams, founder of Rhode Island colony, called Indian care for property lines.) Most of the time, the Patuxet sachem owed fealty[7] to the great sachem in the Wampanoag village to the southwest, and through him to the sachems of the allied confederations of the Nauset in Cape Cod and the Massachusett around Boston. Meanwhile, the Wampanoag were rivals and enemies of the Narragansett and Pequots to the west and the many groups of Abenaki to the north. As a practical matter, sachems had to gain the consent of their people, who could easily move away and join another sachemship. Analogously, the great

LANGUAGE CONVENTIONS

Annotate: Subordinate clauses add details and cannot stand alone as sentences. Underline one subordinate clause in paragraph 10 and circle its subordinating conjunction.

Analyze: Explain the relationship between the subordinate clause and the independent clause. Why do you think Mann used a subordinate clause in this sentence?

[7] **fealty:** obedient loyalty.

NOTICE & NOTE

defection
(dē-fĕkt´shŭn) *n.* the abandonment of one social or political group in favor of another.

sachems had to please or bully the lesser, lest by the **defection** of small communities they lose stature.

11 Sixteenth-century New England housed 100,000 people or more, a figure that was slowly increasing. Most of those people lived in shoreline communities, where rising numbers were beginning to change agriculture from an option to a necessity. These bigger settlements required more centralized administration; natural resources like good land and spawning streams, though not scarce, now needed to be managed. In consequence, boundaries between groups were becoming more formal. Sachems, given more power and more to defend, pushed against each other harder. Political tensions were constant. Coastal and riverine New England, according to the archaeologist and ethnohistorian Peter Thomas, was "an ever-changing collage of personalities, alliances, plots, raids and encounters which involved every Indian [settlement]."

WORD GAPS

Notice & Note: Mark the foreign phrase the author uses in the second sentence of paragraph 12.

Analyze: What clues in the sentence help you figure out the meaning of the phrase? Explain.

12 Armed conflict was frequent but brief and mild by European standards. The *casus belli*[8] was usually the desire to avenge an insult or gain status, not the wish for conquest. Most battles consisted of lightning guerrilla raids by ad hoc companies in the forest: flash of black-and-yellow-striped bows behind trees, hiss and whip of stone-tipped arrows through the air, eruption of angry cries. Attackers slipped away as soon as retribution had been exacted. Losers quickly conceded their loss of status. Doing otherwise would have been like failing to resign after losing a major piece in a chess tournament—a social irritant, a waste of time and resources. Women and children were rarely killed, though they were sometimes abducted and forced to join the winning group. Captured men were often tortured (they were admired, though not necessarily spared, if they endured the pain **stoically**). Now and then, as a sign of victory, slain foes were scalped,

stoically
(stō´ĭk-lē) *adv.* without showing emotion or feeling.

[8] ***casus belli*** (kā´səs bĕl´ī): Latin: cause for war.

Ground maize used to make *nokake*

NOTICE & NOTE

much as British skirmishes with the Irish sometimes finished with a parade of Irish heads on pikes. In especially large clashes, adversaries might meet in the open, as in European battlefields, though the results, Roger Williams noted, were "farre less bloudy, and devouring then the cruell Warres of Europe." Nevertheless, by Tisquantum's time defensive palisades[9] were increasingly common, especially in the river valleys.

13 Inside the settlement was a world of warmth, family, and familiar custom. But the world outside, as Thomas put it, was "a maze of confusing actions and individuals fighting to maintain an existence in the shadow of change."

14 And that was before the Europeans showed up.

[9] **defensive palisades:** fortified walls of tall stakes.

ANALYZE LANGUAGE

Annotate: Mark words in paragraph 13 that describe the contrast between life inside and outside the settlement.

Predict: Given this contrast, what is suggested by the final sentence of the selection?

CHECK YOUR UNDERSTANDING

Answer these questions before moving on to the **Analyze the Text** section on the following page.

1 Why does Mann begin the selection with a discussion of Tisquantum?

A It serves to introduce the topic of Wampanoag culture at Patuxet.

B It gives important details about the way the Wampanoag lived at Patuxet.

C It suggests a reason that the Pilgrims continually failed to understand Wampanoag culture.

D It provides background information on why the Pilgrims traveled from Europe and encountered Wampanoag culture.

2 Why was Patuxet called the Dawnland?

F The Pilgrims called the New England shoreline the Dawnland.

G The Pilgrims called their own settlement in New England the Dawnland.

H In the language of the Wampanoag, the New England shoreline was called the Dawnland.

J In the language of the Wampanoag, the Pilgrim settlement in New England was called the Dawnland.

3 How does Mann characterize life at Patuxet?

A Difficult and harsh

B Peaceful and civilized

C Unorganized and chaotic

D Primitive and violent

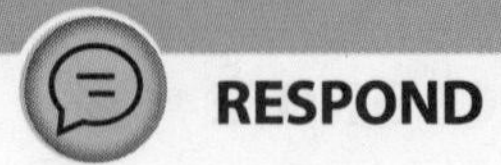

RESPOND

ANALYZE THE TEXT

Support your responses with evidence from the text. NOTEBOOK

1. **Analyze** Note sensory details Mann uses in paragraph 4 to describe life in Patuxet at the end of the 16th century. What is the purpose of these details? What impression of the community does this use of imagery create?
2. **Synthesize** Review instances in which Mann cites evidence from European primary sources from the 17th century. What does word choice and tone in the sources reveal about the opinions of these Europeans?
3. **Draw Conclusions** What central idea about Native American societies in the Dawnland is communicated in this excerpt? Explain.
4. **Evaluate** What do you think was Mann's overall purpose for writing this text? Did he successfully achieve that purpose? Cite reasons and evidence in your answer.
5. **Notice & Note** In paragraph 6, Mann describes *nokake* as "a flour-like powder." What purpose might he want to achieve by comparing a Native American food with one that is commonly known today?

RESEARCH

The selection mentions three confederations that were part of an alliance of Native American groups in the New England area. Research these groups and compare their first interactions with Europeans by completing the chart.

	FIRST CONTACT WITH EUROPEAN COLONISTS
Wampanoag	
Nauset	
Massachusett	

Extend Evaluate the sources you used for your research. List the source in the chart and state whether the source seems biased or objective. Then give reasons for each evaluation. Consider why it is important to use objective sources in your research and writing.

SOURCE	BIASED/OBJECTIVE	REASONS

RESEARCH TIP

Avoid biased sources during most research. These sources present one viewpoint and include websites designed to promote products, opinion sites or publications, and other sites that present the agendas of specific groups.

Rely instead on objective sources, such as those maintained by educational institutions, museums, government offices, and scientific organizations.

CREATE AND DEBATE

Write an Argument This selection presents Mann's view of Native American societies in New England. Evaluate how successfully he achieves his purpose by writing a brief argument.

- ❑ Write a statement that summarizes Mann's purpose for writing.
- ❑ Decide whether he succeeded or failed in achieving that purpose. How well do his word choices, tone, and content support his purpose? Your position on that question will form the claim of your argument.
- ❑ If you think Mann achieved his purpose, cite evidence that supports this claim. If you think he failed, provide reasons for this opinion.
- ❑ Incorporate appropriate dependent clauses to make your writing more specific, interesting, and varied.

Go to **Writing Arguments** in the **Writing Studio** for help.

Share and Debate Use your reasons and evidence to debate a partner with a different point of view.

- ❑ Share your argument's claim, reasons, and supporting evidence.
- ❑ Listen as your partner explains his or her argument.
- ❑ Compose and present counterarguments based on your partner's claims and supporting evidence.

Go to **Analyzing and Evaluating Presentations** in the **Speaking and Listening Studio** for help.

RESPOND TO THE ESSENTIAL QUESTION

What happens when cultures collide?

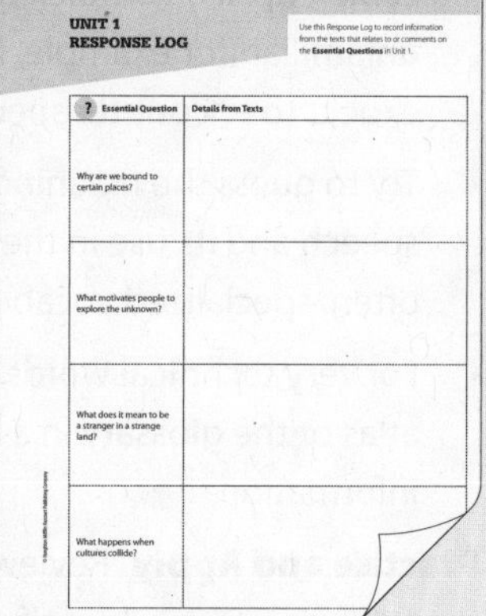

UNIT 1 RESPONSE LOG

Use this Response Log to record information from the texts that relates to or comments on the **Essential Questions** in Unit 1.

? Essential Question	Details from Texts
Why are we bound to certain places?	
What motivates people to explore the unknown?	
What does it mean to be a stranger in a strange land?	
What happens when cultures collide?	

Gather Information Review your annotations and notes on "Coming of Age in the Dawnland." Then add relevant details to your Response Log. As you determine which information to include, think about:

- Mann's descriptions of life at the time
- ideas that Mann conveys about Native American societies
- memorable phrases Mann uses to describe situations

ACADEMIC VOCABULARY

As you write and discuss what you learned from the selection "Coming of Age in the Dawnland," be sure to use the Academic Vocabulary words. Check off each of the words that you use.

- ❑ **adapt**
- ❑ **coherent**
- ❑ **device**
- ❑ **displace**
- ❑ **dynamic**

WORD BANK
project
settlement
regimen
defection
stoically

CRITICAL VOCABULARY

Practice and Apply Use complete sentences to answer each question, showing that you understand the meaning of each Critical Vocabulary word.

1. When a Native American acted **stoically** during torture, what image did she or he hope to **project?**
2. Why would a *sachem* be concerned about the **defection** of a small **settlement?**
3. Why did young Indians have to endure their training **regimen stoically?**

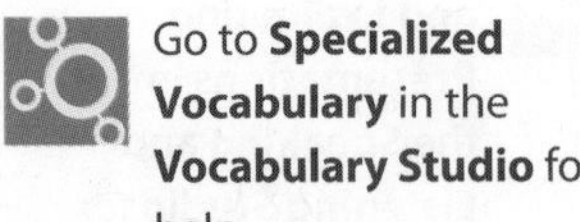

Go to **Specialized Vocabulary** in the **Vocabulary Studio** for help.

VOCABULARY STRATEGY: Specialized Vocabulary

Mann's writing contains language from a variety of sources. For example, he cites an archaeologist and ethnohistorian, recounts observations from Pilgrim writers, uses foreign words and phrases, and even uses some Native American words when there is no accurate or exact English translation. Many of the words he uses are examples of **specialized vocabulary,** or words specific to a particular topic. The Critical Vocabulary word *settlement,* for example, is used in a specialized sense, "a small community in a sparsely populated area." This is an example of a specialized meaning for a word with which you might already be familiar.

The following strategies can help you determine the meaning of specialized vocabulary.

- Look it up. If a complex text is about a specialized topic with which you are unfamiliar (for example, *volcanology,* the study of volcanoes), you should expect to encounter specialized vocabulary that you will need to look up.
- Try to guess the meaning. Use context clues, including the word's part of speech and its use in the sentence, to help determine the meaning. Very often, specialized vocabulary will be defined in the text for readers.
- For very technical words, use a specialized reference work, such as an atlas or the glossary in a book on a specialized topic, to get more specific information.

Practice and Apply Review "Coming of Age in the Dawnland" to find the following terms. Identify context clues for each word's meaning. Then complete the chart.

WORD	CONTEXT CLUES	MEANING
tripartite alliance		
sachem		
ad hoc		

LANGUAGE CONVENTIONS: Dependent (or Subordinate) Clauses

All **clauses** contain a subject and a verb. A **dependent** or **subordinate clause** depends on, or is subordinate to, an independent clause and cannot stand alone. Using dependent clauses skillfully allows Charles Mann to vary the **syntax,** or arrangement of words, of his sentences.

Consider these examples from "Coming of Age in the Dawnland."

> **And it is true that I refer to him as an Indian, because the label is useful shorthand . . .**

> **Although Europeans bemoaned the lack of salt in Indian cuisine, they thought it nourishing.**

In each of these complex sentences, the dependent clause begins with a **subordinating conjunction** (*because* and *although*). The conjunction reveals a relationship between the two clauses. The word *because* indicates a cause-and-effect relationship between two factors. *Although* indicates a concession or exception to the point that Mann makes. Using subordinating conjunctions allows Mann to make nuanced and detailed arguments appropriate to his topic. It also allows him to create a varied rhythm in his prose, making his text more engaging and easier to read.

This chart shows some common subordinating conjunctions and the relationships they signal.

TYPE OF RELATIONSHIP	SUBORDINATING CONJUNCTIONS
Causal (i.e., making something happen)	because, since
Concession/Contrast	although, as, as much as, than, though, while
Place	where, wherever
Purpose	in order that, so that, that
Time	after, as, as long as, as soon as, before, since, until, when, whenever, while

Practice and Apply Look back at the argument you wrote in response to this selection's Create and Debate. Revise your argument by crafting complex sentences to replace some of your simple sentences. Use appropriate subordinating conjunctions to show the relationships between ideas. Vary the placement of dependent clauses at the beginning, the middle, and the end of sentences to create varied sentence structure and a smooth, flowing rhythm.

Go to **Kinds of Clauses** in the **Grammar Studio** for help.

RESPOND

from
OF PLYMOUTH PLANTATION
by William Bradford

Collaborate & Compare

COMPARE AUTHOR'S PURPOSE

Compare Genres Comparing two different genres, or types of writing, on the same topic can help you better understand the topic. William Bradford wrote *Of Plymouth Plantation* from his own personal experience. As an eyewitness account, it is a **primary source** about a crucial time in American history. Charles C. Mann wrote *1491: New Revelations of the Americas Before Columbus* in 2005. As a **secondary source,** it draws on a broad range of sources, both primary sources and other secondary sources, to give a wider perspective of events in the past. Using primary sources, such as diaries, in historical writing helps readers visualize and understand the events and people.

To compare the two authors' purposes, consider each text's audience and tone. How did each author envision the audience? How did each feel about his subject matter? Then, consider the events described in each text. Why did the author choose to include these particular events?

In a small group, complete the chart with the audience, tone, and main events of each text. You will use these to identify and compare the authors' purposes.

	OF PLYMOUTH PLANTATION	"COMING OF AGE IN THE DAWNLAND"
Audience		
Tone		
Main Events		
Author's Purpose		

ANALYZE THE TEXTS

Discuss these questions in your group.

1. **Contrast** How is the historical figure Tisquantum, or Squanto, portrayed in each text?
2. **Compare** How were the European colonists surprised by the Native Americans they encountered in each text?
3. **Infer** How do the main ideas of each selection reflect the author's purpose?
4. **Evaluate** How effectively does each author use the characteristics of its genre—primary versus secondary sources—to support his purpose?

COLLABORATE AND PRESENT

Now, your group can collaborate on a project that compares and evaluates benefits and drawbacks of primary and secondary sources. Follow these steps:

Go to **Giving a Presentation** in the **Speaking and Listening Studio** for help.

1. **Analyze the Selections** With your group, review the selections. Analyze the effectiveness of their elements: their purposes, main ideas, use of evidence, and use of language and tone. Then, determine how effectively each text supports its author's purpose.

	ELEMENTS	EFFECTIVENESS
Primary Source: ***Of Plymouth Plantation***		
Secondary Source: "Coming of Age in the Dawnland"		

2. **Compare Types of Sources** Use your analysis to consider the benefits and drawbacks of primary and secondary sources for learning about history. Record the benefits and drawbacks of each.

	BENEFITS	DRAWBACKS
Primary Source		
Secondary Source		

3. **Present Your Ideas** Work together to present your ideas about the two types of sources. Your presentation should include:
   - definitions and characteristics of primary and secondary sources
   - a comparison of each author's purpose and a claim about how effectively each text met that purpose
   - a statement about the benefits and drawbacks of each type of source for learning about history
   - evidence from the texts to support your ideas
   - relevant images and text to clarify your points and add interest

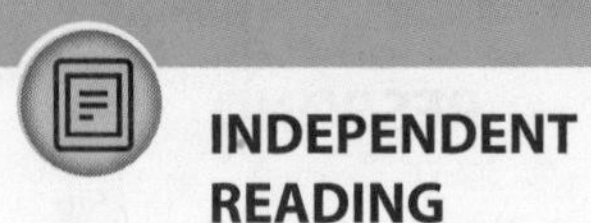

INDEPENDENT READING

? *ESSENTIAL QUESTIONS*

Review the four Essential Questions for this unit on page 1.

Reader's Choice

Setting a Purpose Select one or more of these options from your eBook to continue your exploration of the Essential Questions.

- Read the descriptions to see which text grabs your interest.
- Think about which genres you would like to learn more about.

Notice & Note

In this unit, you practiced noticing and noting the signposts and asking big questions about nonfiction. As you read independently, these signposts and others will aid your understanding. Below are the anchor questions to ask when you read literature and nonfiction.

Reading Literature: Stories, Poems, and Plays	
Signpost	**Anchor Question**
Contrasts and Contradictions	Why did the character act that way?
Aha Moment	How might this change things?
Tough Questions	What does this make me wonder about?
Words of the Wiser	What's the lesson for the character?
Again and Again	Why might the author keep bringing this up?
Memory Moment	Why is this memory important?

Reading Nonfiction: Essays, Articles, and Arguments	
Signpost	**Anchor Question(s)**
Big Questions	What surprised me? What did the author think I already knew? What challenged, changed, or confirmed what I already knew?
Contrasts and Contradictions	What is the difference, and why does it matter?
Extreme or Absolute Language	Why did the author use this language?
Numbers and Stats	Why did the author use these numbers or amounts?
Quoted Words	Why was this person quoted or cited, and what did this add?
Word Gaps	Do I know this word from someplace else? Does it seem like technical talk for this topic? Do clues in the sentence help me understand the word?

You can preview these texts in Unit 1 of your eBook.

Then, check off the text or texts that you select to read on your own.

MEMOIR

☐ ***from* The Way to Rainy Mountain**
N. Scott Momaday

A man visits the grave of his grandmother to reflect on his Native American heritage and connect to his homeland.

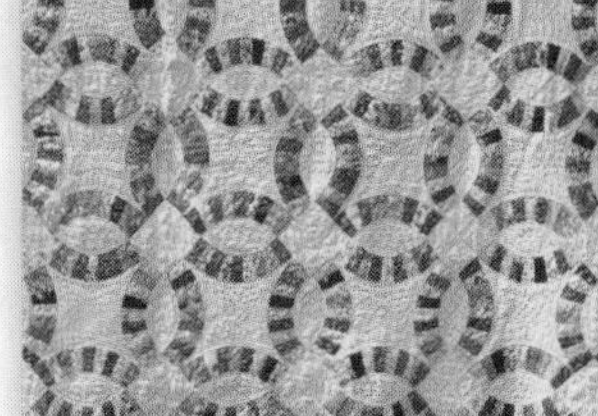

POEM

☐ **To My Dear and Loving Husband**
Anne Bradstreet

A wife speaks eloquently of love and marriage.

HISTORICAL NARRATIVE

☐ ***from* La relación**
Álvar Núñez Cabeza de Vaca

How do Native Americans respond to shipwrecked Spanish explorers who are starving and near death?

HISTORICAL NARRATIVE

☐ ***from* The General History of Virginia**
John Smith

What is the fate of Jamestown when colonist John Smith is taken prisoner by Powhatan?

POEM

☐ **New Orleans**
Joy Harjo

See how a writer resurrects Creek Indian culture in a town where her Creek ancestors were exploited.

Collaborate and Share With a partner, discuss what you learned from at least one of your independent readings.

- Give a brief synopsis or summary of the text.
- Describe any signposts that you noticed in the text and explain what they revealed to you.
- Describe what you most enjoyed or found most challenging about the text. Give specific examples.
- Decide if you would recommend the text to others. Why or why not?

Go to the **Reading Studio** for more resources on **Notice & Note.**

Write a Literary Analysis

Go to the **Writing Studio** for help writing a literary analysis.

In this unit, you have read works about early explorations in America. Andrés Reséndez based his article "A Desperate Trek Across America" on Álvar Núñez Cabeza de Vaca's *La relación,* a first-hand account of the ill-fated Spanish expedition to Florida beginning in 1528. Although Reséndez's narrative article on Cabeza de Vaca's account is not a formal analysis, he uses several techniques which you can apply to the literary analysis you are going to create for your next writing task.

As you write your literary analysis, you can use the notes from your Response Log, which you filled out after reading the texts in this unit.

Writing Prompt

Read the information in the box below.

This is the context for your literary analysis.

> **Reséndez creatively presented a historical narrative that explores the theme of meeting challenges in strange surroundings. Use this theme as a starting point to make your own connections with the literary selection of your choice.**

Think carefully about the following question.

How might this Essential Question relate to other literary selections you have read?

> **What does it mean to be a stranger in a strange land?**

Think about several selections and their possible connections to the theme before you make your final choice.

Write a literary analysis explaining how your chosen selection connects with the idea of being a stranger in a strange land or unfamiliar surroundings.

Be sure to—

Review these points as you write and again when you finish. Make any needed changes.

- ❑ make a clear thesis statement or claim
- ❑ give reasons for your claim in a logical order
- ❑ support your claim with details and evidence from the text
- ❑ quote passages from the text
- ❑ end your analysis with a strong conclusion

1 Plan

Plan your analysis carefully before you start to write. First, note the genre—literary analysis. Then, you need to settle on a particular topic which is reflected in the selection you choose and its Essential Question. For example, if you choose to analyze *La relación,* your topic might be about survival in a strange land. Next, gather ideas for the claim you will make in your thesis statement. What does the author of the literary text seem to convey about your topic? As you consider how you may support your claim, use any background reading or class discussions for ideas. Use the table below to help in your planning.

Literary Analysis Planning Table	
Genre	Literary analysis
Selection	
Possible topics	
Ideas for the thesis statement	
Ideas from background reading	
Ideas from class discussion	

Background Reading Review the notes you have taken in your Response Log that relate to the question, "What does it mean to be a stranger in a strange land?" Texts in this unit provide background reading that will help you formulate the thesis and evidence you will use in your literary analysis.

Go to **Writing Informative Texts: Developing a Topic** for help planning your literary analysis.

Notice & Note

From Reading to Writing

As you plan your literary analysis, apply what you've learned about signposts to your own writing. Remember that writers use common features, called signposts, to help convey their message to readers.

Think how you can incorporate **Quoted Words** into your literary analysis.

Go to the **Reading Studio** for more resources on **Notice & Note.**

Use the notes from your Response Log as you plan your literary analysis.

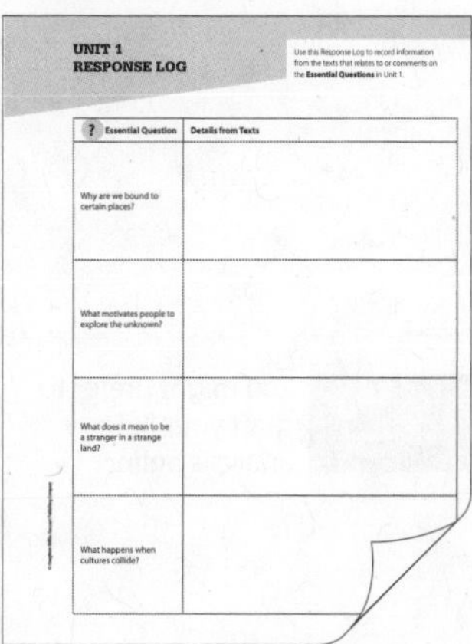

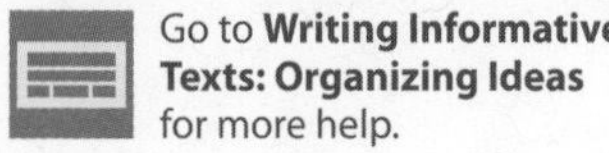

Go to **Writing Informative Texts: Organizing Ideas** for more help.

Organize Your Ideas After you have gathered ideas from your planning activities, you need to organize them in a way that will help you draft your literary analysis. Choose your selection and topic. Next, you need to decide what claim you will make about the selection. Write your claim in a clear thesis statement. List reasons for your claim. Then, find specific evidence in the text that supports your opinion. Use the chart below to assist your organization.

Organizational Plan	
Genre	Literary analysis
Selection	
Topic	
Claim/Thesis Statement	
Reasons	1. 2. 3.
Evidence	

2 Develop a Draft

You might prefer to draft your literary analysis online.

Once you have completed your planning activities, you will be ready to begin drafting your literary analysis. Refer to your Graphic Organizer, your planning chart, and any notes you took as you studied the texts in this unit as a kind of map for you to follow as you write. Using an online writing application makes it easier to make changes or move sentences around later when you are ready to revise your first draft.

Use the Mentor Text

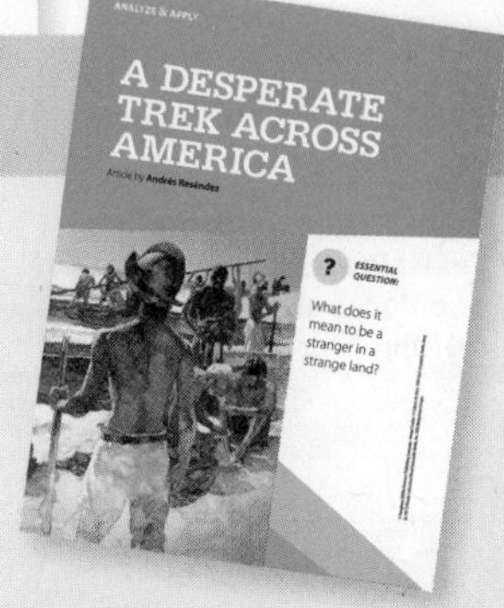

Making a Claim or Thesis Statement

A literary analysis will always contain a claim or thesis statement, usually near the beginning of your essay. The following paragraph from Reséndez's article "A Desperate Trek Across America" contains a thesis statement. Reséndez had already described the adventurers' plight and their initial attempt at survival. They have eaten their horses and used their firearms to build rafts. In the passage below, notice how Reséndez contrasts their previous sense of confidence with their current state.

Like past conquistadors, Cabeza de Vaca and his men had relied on their breastplates, horses, and lethal weapons to keep the Indians at bay. Such overwhelming technological advantages meant they often did not even bother to negotiate. . . . By sacrificing the very tools of their supremacy, they would now have to face the New World fully exposed to its perils and hold on only by their wits.

The last sentence expresses the overall perspective of his article—it is similar to a thesis.

The rest of the author's article shows their struggle to survive only by their wits.

Apply What You've Learned After you've chosen the selection, the topic, and the point you want to make, begin your analysis with a clear thesis statement or claim. Tell your reader which selection you are writing about and what claim you are making. What interesting insight will you be conveying to your reader?

Offering Details and Evidence from the Text

When you analyze a literary selection, it is important to offer specific details and evidence from the text in order to support your thesis. Like Reséndez, you can use direct quotations to strengthen your thesis.

Fifty men crowded aboard each craft, the fifth commanded by Cabeza de Vaca. "And so greatly can necessity prevail," he observed, "that it made us risk going in this manner and placing ourselves in a sea so treacherous, and without any one of us who went having any knowledge of the art of navigation."

Notice that Reséndez directly quotes Cabeza de Vaca to support his idea that the Spaniards were surviving on their wits alone.

Apply What You've Learned When you are giving reasons for your claim, be sure to offer details that will help convince your reader of your point. Try to cite direct evidence from the text whenever you make a main point. Use multiple pieces of evidence when possible.

3 Revise

Go to **Writing Informative Texts: Precise Language and Vocabulary** for help revising your analysis.

On Your Own Once you have written your draft, you'll want to go back and look for ways to improve your literary analysis. As you reread and revise, think about whether you have achieved your purpose. The Revision Guide will help you focus on specific elements to make your writing stronger.

Revision Guide

Ask Yourself	Tips	Revision Techniques
1. Did I state my thesis, or claim, clearly and in an interesting way?	**Highlight** your thesis statement.	If necessary, add a sentence or two to clarify your thesis. **Add** an interesting example or related quotation to hook your reader.
2. Do I have enough reasons to support my thesis?	**List** your reasons.	**Read** your thesis statement aloud, followed by your reasons. Does your argument make sense so far? **Add** another reason if you can.
3. Are my thoughts logically organized?	**Outline** your main ideas and check for the most logical order.	**Reorder** ideas, if needed, so that each idea flows easily to the next one.
4. Did I include sufficient evidence from the text?	**Underline** any specific quotations or examples you used.	**Add** more details from the text to strengthen your claim.
5. Did I prove my point by the end of the analysis?	**Review** the main points and ideas of your analysis.	**Fill** in any noticeable gaps with more relevant details.
6. Is my conclusion strong?	**Highlight** your conclusion.	**Add** a statement that summarizes your ideas.

ACADEMIC VOCABULARY

As you conduct your **peer review,** be sure to use these words.

- ❑ adapt
- ❑ coherent
- ❑ device
- ❑ displace
- ❑ dynamic

With a Partner Once you and your partner have worked through the Revision Guide on your own, exchange analyses and evaluate each other's draft in a **peer review.** Focus on providing revision suggestions for at least three of the items mentioned in the chart. Explain why you think your partner's draft should be revised and make your specific suggestions.

When receiving feedback from your partner, listen attentively and ask questions to make sure you fully understand the revision suggestions.

4 Edit

Once you have written and revised your literary analysis, it is time to edit for some of the finer details. Read through your draft carefully to ensure proper use of standard English conventions. Look for ways to improve your word choice and be sure to correct all spelling and grammatical errors.

Go to **Active and Passive Voice** in the **Grammar Studio** to learn more.

Language Conventions

Active and Passive Voice As you edit, try to liven up your writing with verbs in the active voice as much as possible. Remember, a verb is in the **active voice** when its subject is performing the action. If the subject is the receiver of the action, the verb is in the **passive voice.** Notice that the verb in the following sentence is in the active voice because the subject is performing the action: *Cabeza de Vaca **heard** the surf.* The verb in this next sentence, however, is in the passive voice because the subject is being acted upon: *Four naked and unarmed outsiders **were led** by hundreds . . . of Indians.*

Note Reséndez's use of active and passive voice verbs in the chart. Notice how his frequent use of the active voice makes his narrative vibrant. When he uses the passive voice, he emphasizes what is happening to de Vaca and his men.

Active Voice	Passive Voice
• every third day they killed yet another draft animal	• Cabeza de Vaca and his companions were forced to cope
• they threw their crossbows	• They were fed, protected, and passed off
• they cut down trees, dragged them to the beach, lashed them together	• they had been . . . transformed by the experience

As you edit your literary analysis, find any verbs in the passive voice. Unless you need to emphasize the receiver of an action, or unless the doer is unknown, try to change the passive voice to active.

5 Publish

Finalize your literary analysis and choose a way to share it with your audience. Consider these options:

- Save your analysis as a writing sample to include with your college application.
- Research various literary journals and their guidelines for submission. Choose at least one to which you will submit your paper.

WRITING TASK

Use the scoring guide to evaluate your literary analysis.

Writing Task Scoring Guide: Literary Analysis

	Organization/Progression	Development of Ideas	Use of Language and Conventions
4	• The structure is clearly organized and appropriate. • The analysis includes a strong thesis statement; all ideas are related to the thesis. • Ideas are in logical order and connected with meaningful transitions.	• The development of ideas is effective, with credible and compelling analysis. • The analysis includes sufficient, relevant textual evidence. • The analysis contains thoughtful and engaging content; it demonstrates thorough understanding of the text.	• Word choice is precise and appropriate. • Sentences are strong and varied. • Command of spelling, punctuation, grammar, and usage conventions is strong.
3	• The structure is, for the most part, organized and appropriate. • The analysis includes a clear thesis statement; most ideas are related to the thesis, with only minor lapses in unity or focus. • Ideas are generally in logical order and connected with sufficient transitions.	• The development of ideas is fairly sound, with largely convincing analysis. • The analysis includes sufficient, relevant textual evidence, though at times this needs to be more complete. • The analysis provides thoughtful content; it demonstrates good understanding of the text.	• For the most part, word choice is clear and specific. • Sentences are reasonably varied. • Command of spelling, punctuation, grammar, and usage conventions is adequate.
2	• The structure is evident but is not always appropriate or clear. • The thesis statement is weak or unclear; some irrelevant information affects unity and focus. • Ideas are not always in logical order or connected with sufficient transitions.	• The development of ideas is minimal, with superficial analysis. • The analysis includes textual evidence which is sometimes irrelevant or inaccurate, or underdeveloped ideas. • The analysis reflects little thoughtfulness; it demonstrates limited understanding of the text.	• Word choice is general or imprecise. • Sentences are sometimes awkward. • Command of spelling, punctuation, grammar, and usage conventions is less than adequate.
1	• The structure is inappropriate to the purpose. • The thesis statement is missing, unclear, or illogical; the analysis contains irrelevant information. • The analysis demonstrates a weak progression of ideas; it includes repetition and wordiness, or lacks sufficient transitions.	• The development of ideas is weak, with ineffective analysis. • The analysis includes little if any relevant textual evidence; overall, there is vague development. • The analysis provides a vague or confused response to the text; it demonstrates lack of understanding of the text.	• Word choice is vague or limited. • Sentences are simplistic and awkward. • The writing shows little or no command of spelling, punctuation, grammar, and usage conventions.

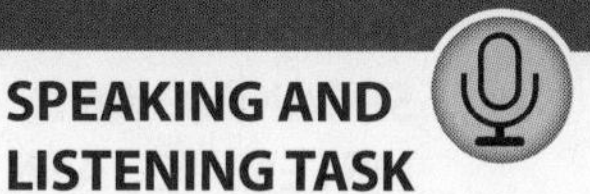

Participate in a Panel Discussion

You will now adapt your literary analysis for presentation to your classmates. You also will listen to their presentations, ask questions to better understand their ideas, and help them improve their work.

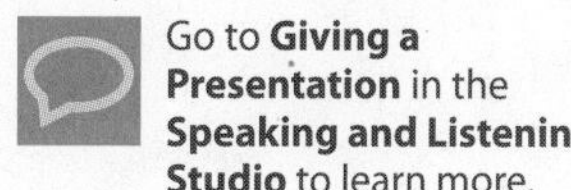

Go to **Giving a Presentation** in the **Speaking and Listening Studio** to learn more.

1 Adapt Your Essay for Presentation

In the chart below, record specific ideas for your presentation, which you will use as part of a panel discussion.

Presentation Planning Chart		
Introduction	Begin with an interesting quotation or anecdote from the literary selection. State your **thesis** and the **title** and **author** of your selection. Clarify its connection to the question: What does it mean to be a stranger in a strange land?	
Major Points	Write main ideas on note cards to aid your memory. Make sure you present them in a logical order.	
Cite Evidence	Include quotations and details from the text to support your claim.	
Hold the Attention of Your Audience	Consider using a visual aid. Charts, photos, or short video clips make effective and memorable presentations. Prepare a handout outlining important ideas.	
Conclusion	Close your presentation with a strong restatement of your thesis and a memorable quote, illustration, or example from your literary selection.	

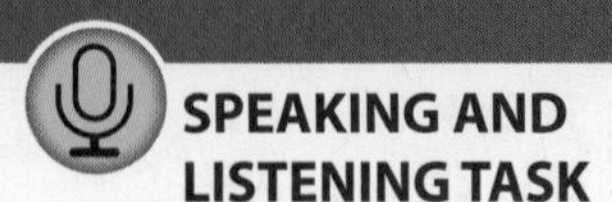

2 Practice with a Partner

Once you've prepared your materials, practice with a partner to improve the following elements of your presentation:

- ❑ **Voice** Enunciate your words clearly and speak slowly and loudly enough so that everyone can hear you. Use your voice to show enthusiasm and emphasis.
- ❑ **Eye Contact** Try to let your eyes rest on each member of the audience at least once.
- ❑ **Facial Expression** Smile, frown, or raise an eyebrow to show your feelings or to emphasize points.
- ❑ **Gestures** Use natural gestures—shrugs, nods, or shakes of your head—to add meaning and interest to your presentation.

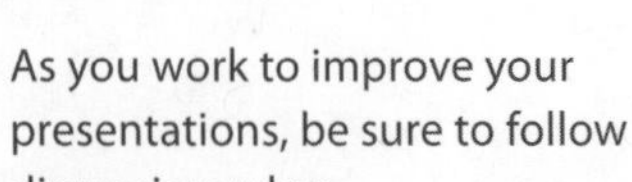

As you work to improve your presentations, be sure to follow discussion rules:

- ❑ **Listen closely to each other.**
- ❑ **Don't interrupt.**
- ❑ **Stay on topic.**
- ❑ **Ask only helpful, relevant questions.**
- ❑ **Provide only clear, thoughtful, and direct answers.**

Provide and Consider Advice for Improvement

As you and your partner practice, take notes and provide helpful advice to each other. Consider ways to revise your presentation to make sure your points are clear and logically sequenced.

3 Hold a Panel Discussion

- Create panels of four or five people.
- The panelists will remain seated in front of the class to make their presentations.
- Choose one person from the class to be the moderator. He or she can open with a comment on the Essential Question that ties the discussion together.
- The moderator will introduce all of the speakers on the panel and then each panelist will present his or her analysis in turn.
- After all the members of the panel have made presentations, the moderator will recognize those audience members who wish to ask questions and the panelists will respond.
- If necessary, remind participants that discourse should be meaningful and respectful throughout the discussion.
- To conclude, the moderator can summarize the discussion.
- To evaluate the experience, audience members can engage in an informal follow-up discussion. Compare the panelists' analyses with the mentor text. How well did Reséndez show what it was like for the explorers and how they adapted to a strange land? How well did each panelist present his or her analysis?

Reflect on the Unit

By completing your literary analysis, you have created a writing product that pulls together and expresses your thoughts about the reading you have done in this unit. Now is a good time to reflect on what you have learned.

Reflect on the Essential Questions

- Review the four Essential Questions. How have your answers to these questions changed in response to the texts you read in this unit?
- What are some examples from the texts you read that show what it means to be a stranger in a strange land?

Reflect on Your Reading

- Which selections were the most interesting or surprising to you?
- From which selection did you learn the most about what it means to be a stranger in a strange land?

Reflect on the Writing Task

- What difficulties did you encounter while working on your literary analysis? How might you avoid them next time?
- What part of the literary analysis was the easiest and hardest to write? Why?
- What improvements did you make to your literary analysis as you were revising?

UNIT 1 SELECTIONS

- **"The World on the Turtle's Back"**
- **"Balboa"**
- **"A Desperate Trek Across America"**
- **"Here Follow Some Verses Upon the Burning of Our House, July 10th, 1666"**
- **from *Of Plymouth Plantation***
- **"Coming of Age in the Dawnland"**

UNIT 2

BUILDING A DEMOCRACY

THE REVOLUTIONARY PERIOD

> "A nation is formed by the willingness of each of us to share the responsibility for upholding the common good."
>
> —Barbara Jordan

Discuss the **Essential Questions** with your whole class or in small groups. As you read Building a Democracy, consider how the selections explore these questions.

ESSENTIAL QUESTION:

What does oppression look like?

Between 1763 and 1775 Parliament imposed a number of regulations and taxes on Britain's American colonies. The colonists reacted with pamphlets and acts of rebellion that eventually led to a declaration of independence and war. Ironically, many of the men who decried British oppression were themselves slaveholders. Even those who weren't saw no hypocrisy in denying women the same rights as men. Why might someone identify oppression in some instances and yet be blind to it in others?

ESSENTIAL QUESTION:

How do we gain our freedom?

It is often necessary to fight to gain freedom. When Britain failed to respond to repeated requests from the colonists, their protests escalated. Britain retaliated by placing Massachusetts under the direct control of a military governor. Clashes between local militias and British soldiers became a war for independence that involved all 13 of Britain's American colonies. Why are people motivated to risk everything for freedom?

ESSENTIAL QUESTION:

How can we share power and build alliances?

After gaining independence from England, the 13 former colonies had to come up with a plan for the future. They knew that they stood a better chance if they could work together, but how? Their first attempt at unification failed because the states did not want to relinquish any authority to a central government. The Constitution, however, provided a balance of power between federal and state governments. How does sharing power make partners stronger?

ESSENTIAL QUESTION:

How do we transform our lives?

Americans had to make the transition from colonists to citizens of a new nation, one that was an experiment in democracy founded on Enlightenment ideals. Generation after generation, Americans have reinvented themselves as they confronted new opportunities and challenges. For more than two centuries, people from many lands have arrived with new customs and ideas. How does this experience change their lives and the lives of those they encounter?

THE REVOLUTIONARY PERIOD

By the 1750s the colonies in North America had already begun to bind themselves together into a confederation. Even then, the colonists still thought of themselves as British subjects, despite a lack of representation in Parliament. The British government, in turn, protected the colonies from Native American and other European threats. After American colonial forces under George Washington tried unsuccessfully to drive the French from the Ohio River valley, Britain sent reinforcements, whom colonists helped support. By the time the French and Indian War ended in 1763, Britain controlled all the land east of the Mississippi River. But when the British tried to recover the costs of the war by taxing the colonists, they rebelled.

As the colonists moved toward independence, they drew on Enlightenment ideals, which questioned previously accepted truths about strongly centralized governments. People began to question traditional authority, eventually leading the colonists to break from Britain's control and embrace democracy. American colonial writers such as Benjamin Franklin, Thomas Paine, and Thomas Jefferson adapted the ideals of the European Enlightenment to their own circumstances. In time, this new philosophy combined with a wave of religious enthusiasm called the Great Awakening. Preachers such as Jonathan Edwards called upon colonists to rededicate themselves to the original Puritan vision of sinless living, hard work, thrift, and responsibility, thus rekindling in the geographically and culturally diverse colonists a desire to be religious and ethical role models for all.

As the colonists began to question their relationship with Great Britain, many gifted minds turned to political writing. Between 1763 and 1783, about two thousand inexpensive pamphlets were published, reaching thousands of people and stirring debate and action. *Common Sense* by Thomas Paine was a key pamphlet that helped move the colonists to revolution. Paine's Enlightenment ideas were combined with the Puritan belief that America was destined to be a model of freedom to the world. Thomas Jefferson also wrote pamphlets, but his great contribution to American government, literature, and the cause of freedom throughout the world is the Declaration of Independence, in which he eloquently articulated the natural law that would govern America. This natural law is

COLLABORATIVE DISCUSSION

In a small group, review the timeline and discuss which literary or historical events had the most impact.

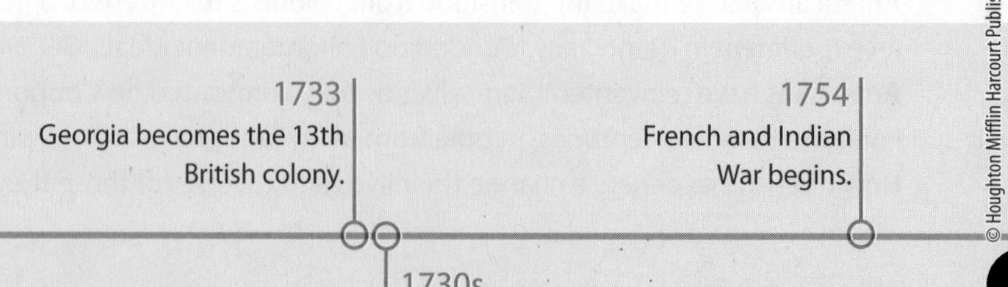
1700
1733
Georgia becomes the 13th British colony.
1730s
Great Awakening begins.
1754
French and Indian War begins.

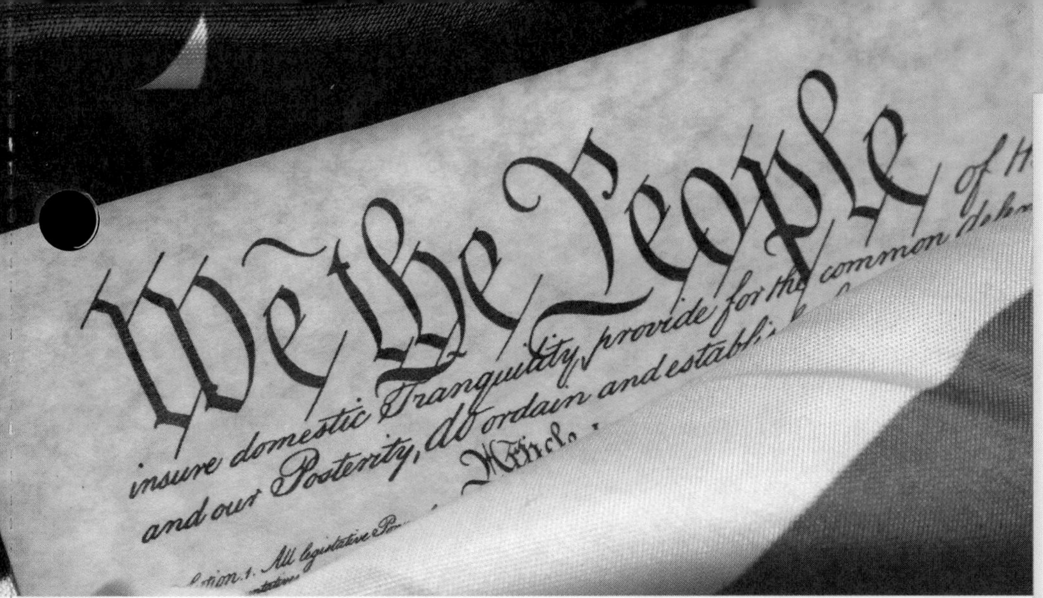
We the People of the
insure domestic Tranquility, provide for the common defen
and our Posterity, do ordain and establish

the idea that people are born with rights and freedoms and that it is the function of government to protect those freedoms.

Jefferson's Declaration marked the beginning of the colonies' independence, but it was the adoption of the Constitution of the United States of America in 1788 that created the lasting framework for an independent government and cemented the historical and literary legacies of its founders. Ideological debates over the scope and nature of federal power raged throughout the republic's early years. For example, in 1803 President Thomas Jefferson stirred controversy by purchasing the vast Louisiana Territory west of the Mississippi River from France, thus doubling the size of the United States. Jefferson, who normally favored a limited federal government, took this bold step even though the Constitution gave him no explicit authority to do so.

During the second half of the 18th century, the religious grip of the Puritans on New England began to relax as a new Yankee secular society emerged. In the early Colonial period, Puritan literary achievements were great, although they decried fiction and drama. As the Puritans saw their spiritual world view challenged by the political views of Enlightenment thinkers, even poetry sometimes examined political and social themes. Among the finest is the work of former slave Phillis Wheatley. In her poems and letters, Wheatley wrote of the "natural rights" of African Americans and pointed out the discrepancy between the colonists' "cry for freedom" and their enslavement of fellow human beings.

RESEARCH
What about this historical period interests you? Choose a topic, event, or person to learn more about. Then, add your own entry to the timeline.

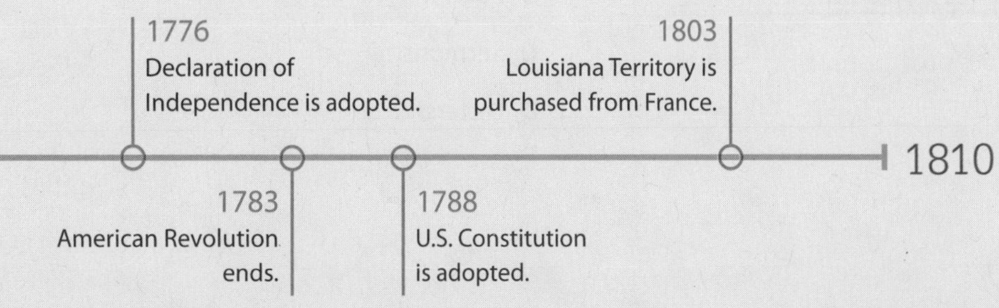
1765
Colonists rebel against the Stamp Act.
1776
Declaration of Independence is adopted.
1783
American Revolution ends.
1788
U.S. Constitution is adopted.
1803
Louisiana Territory is purchased from France.
1810

Another voice calling for the rights of all citizens was Abigail Adams, whose husband John became the nation's second president. In letters written while the couple was apart, Adams encouraged her husband to include the rights of women in the nation's founding documents. Wheatley, Adams, and other women writers joined the Puritans and patriots who came before them to give us an understanding of the dreams and values that shaped our nation. All contributed their voices and ideals to building the metaphorical "city upon a hill" that Puritan preacher John Winthrop first envisioned as a beacon to all in 1630.

CHECK YOUR UNDERSTANDING

Choose the best answer to each question.

1 Why did the American colonists rebel against Britain?

- **A** They didn't want to defend territory Britain had captured from the French.
- **B** They didn't want to pay the costs of the French and Indian War.
- **C** Britain tried to outlaw slavery in the colonies.
- **D** Britain tried to keep Jefferson from buying the Louisiana Territory.

2 What type of publication became the major means of spreading political ideas?

- **F** Books
- **G** Almanacs
- **H** Pamphlets
- **J** Newspapers

3 What kind of writing did the Puritans disapprove of?

- **A** Drama
- **B** Poetry
- **C** Sermons
- **D** Letters

ACADEMIC VOCABULARY

Academic Vocabulary words are words you use when you discuss and write about texts. In this unit, you will learn the following five words:

✔ **contrary** ❑ **founder** ❑ **ideological** ❑ **publication** ❑ **revolution**

Study the Word Network to learn more about the word **contrary.**

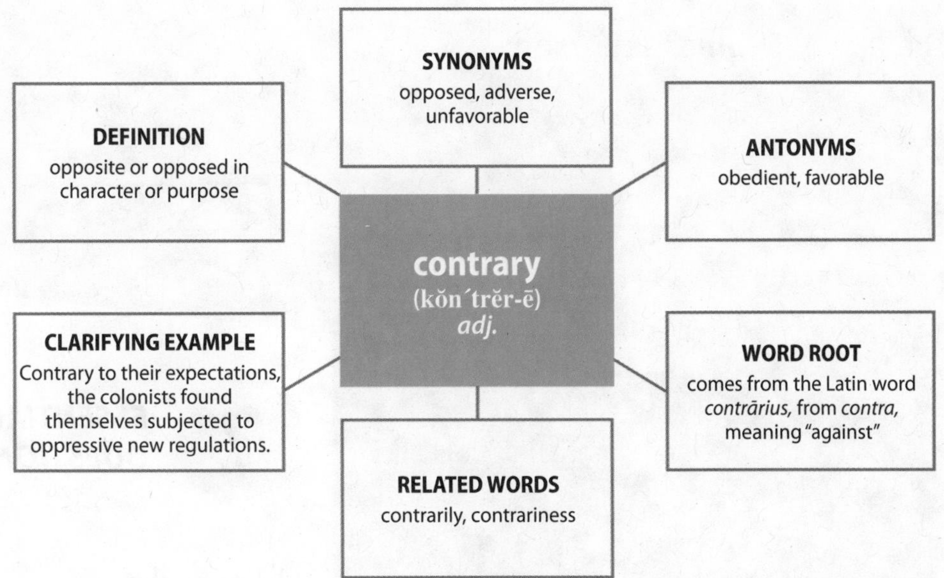

SYNONYMS
opposed, adverse, unfavorable
DEFINITION
opposite or opposed in character or purpose
ANTONYMS
obedient, favorable
contrary
(kŏn´trĕr-ē)
adj.
CLARIFYING EXAMPLE
Contrary to their expectations, the colonists found themselves subjected to oppressive new regulations.
WORD ROOT
comes from the Latin word contrārius, from contra, meaning "against"
RELATED WORDS
contrarily, contrariness

Write and Discuss Discuss your completed Word Network with a partner, making sure to talk through all of the boxes until you both understand the word, its synonyms, antonyms, and related forms. Then, fill out a Word Network for the remaining four words. Use a dictionary or online resource to help you complete the activity.

Go online to access the Word Networks.

RESPOND TO THE ESSENTIAL QUESTIONS

In this unit, you will explore four different **Essential Questions** about 18th-century literature and other related texts. As you read each selection, you will gather your ideas about one of these questions and write about it in the **Response Log** that appears on page R2. At the end of the unit, you will have the opportunity to write a **research report** related to one of the Essential Questions. Filling out the Response Log after you read each text will help you prepare for this writing task.

You can also go online to access the Response Log.

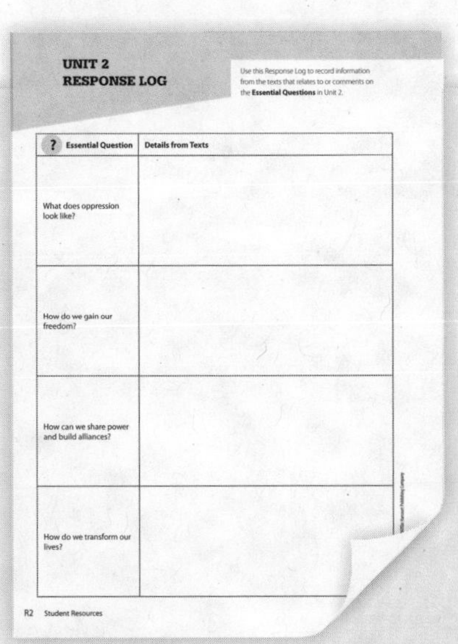

UNIT 2
RESPONSE LOG

Use this Response Log to record information from the texts that relates to or comments on the **Essential Questions** in Unit 2.

? Essential Question	Details from Texts
What does oppression look like?	
How do we gain our freedom?	
How can we share power and build alliances?	
How do we transform our lives?	

R2 Student Resources

THE DECLARATION OF INDEPENDENCE

Public Document by **Thomas Jefferson**

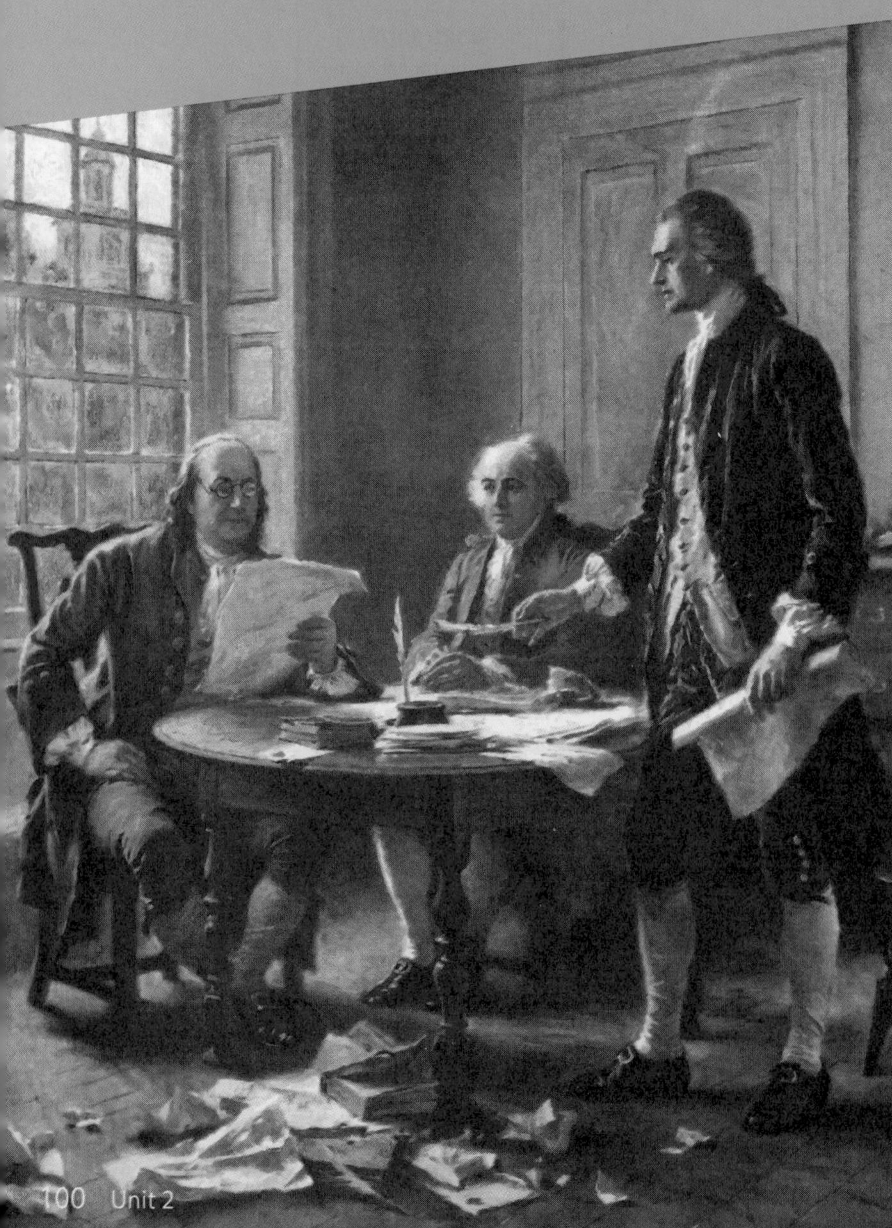

? **ESSENTIAL QUESTION:**

How do we gain our freedom?

QUICK START

The Declaration of Independence represented the views of American patriots on what constituted good government and oppressive government. What are your ideas about good government and bad government?

ANALYZE ARGUMENTATIVE TEXTS

Thomas Jefferson wrote this text to justify to the British the colonies' move toward independence. It is an **argumentative text** with the following characteristics:

- a clear, arguable **thesis,** or central idea
- **reasons** and **evidence** that support the thesis
- logical and emotional **appeals** to the audience
- a convincing **conclusion** that sums up the important ideas
- a **call to action** that encourages the audience to do something

As you read, identify the thesis, types of support, appeals, conclusion, and call to action in the Declaration of Independence.

GENRE ELEMENTS: PUBLIC DOCUMENT

- provides information of public interest or concern
- may include attempts at persuasion using sophisticated language
- includes government documents, speeches, signs, and rules and regulations

ANALYZE TEXT STRUCTURE

The power of the Declaration of Independence comes not just from *what* it says, but also from *how* Jefferson says it. Jefferson's style is reflected in the **structure** of the work. The Declaration can be divided into four sections: a preamble, or forward, that announces the reason for the document; a declaration of people's fundamental rights; the presentation of evidence and responses to **counterarguments,** or claims against Jefferson's proposal; and a conclusion that states the desired action. Jefferson also uses **syntax**—the arrangement of words to express and emphasize ideas. The structure and syntax convey a determined tone and reflect the purpose of his argument.

Use the chart to record key ideas in each section of the text.

PREAMBLE	DECLARATION OF RIGHTS	EVIDENCE	CONCLUSION/CALL TO ACTION

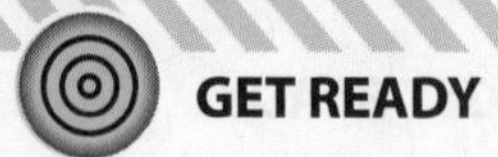

GET READY

CRITICAL VOCABULARY

established **affected** **invested** **abdicated**

To see how many Critical Vocabulary words you already know, use them to complete the sentences.

1. The U.S. Constitution __________ our current form of government.
2. Due to ill health, the king __________ the throne and was succeeded by his oldest child.
3. In a republican government, elected officials are __________ with the authority of office by voters.
4. Representatives of people who would be most __________ by the new law testified about its provisions to the congressional committee.

LANGUAGE CONVENTIONS

Parallel Structure Parallelism, or parallel structure, is the use of similar grammatical constructions to express ideas that are closely related or equal in importance. Constructions may include phrases, clauses, or sentences. Parallel structures are an important element in a writer's syntax. Consider this example from the Declaration of Independence:

> **. . . laying its foundation on such principles, and organizing its powers in such form . . .**

Jefferson uses two phrases with parallel structure. The use of parallel phrases makes it clear that the two actions are of equal importance.

ANNOTATION MODEL

NOTICE & NOTE

As you read, notice how Jefferson presents his ideas. Mark words or phrases that reveal key ideas, present evidence, or move the argument forward. In the model, you can see one reader's notes about the Declaration of Independence.

When, in the course of human events, it becomes necessary for one people to dissolve the political bands which have connected them with another, and to assume, among the powers of the earth, the separate and equal station to which the laws of nature and of nature's God entitle them, a decent respect to the opinions of mankind requires that they should declare the causes which impel them to the separation.

Jefferson states up front what he thinks must happen.

Jefferson will offer reasons for the action he proposes.

BACKGROUND

Thomas Jefferson *(1743–1826) was one of the most accomplished of our nation's founders. He was minister to France after the American Revolution and the third president of the United States. However, more important than his titles was his vision of liberty and self-government, eloquently expressed in the Declaration of Independence. Drafted by Jefferson, the Declaration was debated by the Second Continental Congress and adopted July 4, 1776. The Declaration begins with an assertion of the Enlightenment ideas of "self-evident" truths of liberty and human rights.*

THE DECLARATION OF INDEPENDENCE

Public Document by Thomas Jefferson

SETTING A PURPOSE

As you read, pay attention to the evidence Jefferson uses to support the idea of American independence.

1 When, in the course of human events, it becomes necessary for one people to dissolve the political bands which have connected them with another, and to assume, among the powers of the earth, the separate and equal station to which the laws of nature and of nature's God entitle them, a decent respect to the opinions of mankind requires that they should declare the causes which impel them to the separation.

2 We hold these truths to be self-evident:—That all men are created equal; that they are endowed by their Creator with certain unalienable rights; that among these are life, liberty, and the pursuit of happiness. That, to secure these rights, governments are instituted among men, deriving their just powers from the consent of the governed; that, whenever any form of government becomes destructive of these ends, it is the right of the people to alter or to abolish it, and to institute a new government, laying its foundation on such principles, and organizing its powers in such form, as to them shall seem most likely to effect their safety

Notice & Note

Use the side margins to notice and note signposts in the text.

ANALYZE ARGUMENTATIVE TEXTS

Annotate: Mark words in paragraph 2 that state Jefferson's thesis.

Cite Evidence: What details in paragraph 2 present justification for his thesis? Explain.

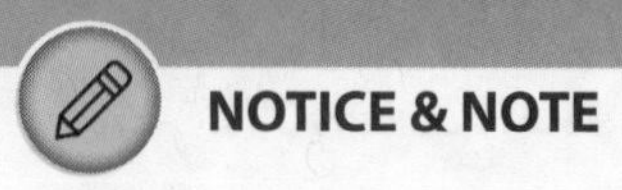

establish
(ĭ-stăb´lĭsh) *v.* to formally set up; institute.

ANALYZE TEXT STRUCTURE
Annotate: Circle the repeated phrase in paragraphs 3–10. Underline the phrases in paragraphs 6 and 7 that give reasons for the King's behavior.

Draw Conclusions: How do the examples of Jefferson's syntax strengthen his argument?

and happiness. Prudence, indeed, will dictate that governments long **established** should not be changed for light and transient causes; and, accordingly, all experience hath shown that mankind are more disposed to suffer, while evils are sufferable, than to right themselves by abolishing the forms to which they are accustomed. But, when a long train of abuses and usurpations, pursuing invariably the same object, evinces a design to reduce them under absolute despotism,[1] it is their right, it is their duty, to throw off such government, and to provide new guards for their future security. Such has been the patient sufferance of these colonies; and such is now the necessity that constrains them to alter their former systems of government. The history of the present King of Great Britain[2] is a history of repeated injuries and usurpations, all having, in direct object, the establishment of an absolute tyranny over these States. To prove this, let facts be submitted to a candid world.

3 He has refused his assent to laws[3] the most wholesome and necessary for the public good.

4 He has forbidden his Governors to pass laws of immediate and pressing importance, unless suspended in their operation till his assent should be obtained; and, when so suspended, he has utterly neglected to attend to them.

5 He has refused to pass other laws for the accommodation of large districts of people, unless these people would relinquish the right of representation in the legislature—a right inestimable to them, and formidable to tyrants only.

6 He has called together legislative bodies at places unusual, uncomfortable, and distant from the depository of their public records, for the sole purpose of fatiguing them into compliance with his measure.

7 He has dissolved representative houses repeatedly, for opposing, with manly firmness, his invasions on the rights of the people.

8 He has refused, for a long time after such dissolutions, to cause others to be elected; whereby the legislative powers, incapable of annihilation, have returned to the people at large for their exercise; the State remaining, in the meantime, exposed to all dangers of invasion from without, and convulsions within.

9 He has endeavored to prevent the population[4] of these States; for that purpose obstructing the laws for the naturalization of foreigners; refusing to pass others to encourage their migration hither, and raising the conditions of new appropriations of lands.

---

[1] **despotism** (dĕs´pə-tĭz əm): government by a ruler with unlimited power.

[2] **the present King of Great Britain:** George III, who reigned from 1760 to 1820.

[3] **refused his assent to laws:** Laws passed in the colonial legislative assemblies needed the king's approval; sometimes it took years for laws to be approved or rejected.

[4] **to prevent the population:** to keep the population from growing.

10 He has obstructed the administration of justice, by refusing his assent to laws for establishing judiciary powers.

11 He has made judges dependent on his will alone for the tenure of their offices,[5] and the amount and payment of their salaries.

12 He has erected a multitude of new offices, and sent hither swarms of officers to harass our people and eat out their substance.[6]

13 He has kept among us, in times of peace, standing armies, without the consent of our legislatures.

14 He has **affected** to render the military independent of, and superior to, the civil power.

affect
(ə-fĕkt´) *v.* to cause or influence.

15 He has combined with others to subject us to a jurisdiction foreign to our constitutions,[7] and unacknowledged by our laws; giving his assent to their acts of pretended legislation:

16 For quartering large bodies of armed troops among us;

17 For protecting them, by a mock trial, from punishment for any murders which they should commit on the inhabitants of these States;

18 For cutting off our trade with all parts of the world;

19 For imposing taxes on us without our consent;

20 For depriving us, in many cases, of the benefits of trial by jury;

21 For transporting us beyond the seas, to be tried for pretended offenses;

22 For abolishing the free system of English laws in a neighboring province,[8] establishing there an arbitrary government, and enlarging its boundaries, so as to render it at once an example and fit instrument for introducing the same absolute rule into these colonies;

23 For taking away our charters, abolishing our most valuable laws, and altering, fundamentally, the forms of our governments;

24 For suspending our own legislatures, and declaring themselves **invested** with power to legislate for us in all cases whatsoever.

25 He has **abdicated** government here, by declaring us out of his protection, and waging war against us.

26 He has plundered our seas, ravaged our coasts, burnt our towns,[9] and destroyed the lives of our people.

27 He is at this time transporting large armies of foreign mercenaries to complete the works of death, desolation, and tyranny, already begun with circumstances of cruelty and perfidy scarcely paralleled in the most barbarous ages, and totally unworthy the head of a civilized nation.

LANGUAGE CONVENTIONS

Annotate: Mark examples of parallelism that Jefferson uses in paragraphs 16–24.

Analyze: How does this structure strengthen Jefferson's argument against the king?

invest
(ĭn-vĕst´) *v.* to grant or endow.

abdicate
(ăb´dĭ-kāt) *v.* to relinquish or cede responsibility for.

[5] **the tenure of their offices:** their job security.

[6] **eat out their substance:** use up their resources.

[7] **subject us . . . our constitutions:** Parliament had passed the Declaratory Act in 1766, stating that the king and Parliament could make laws for the colonies.

[8] **a neighboring province:** the province of Quebec, which at the time extended south to the Ohio River and west to the Mississippi.

[9] **plundered . . . our towns:** American seaports such as Norfolk, Virginia, had already been shelled.

NOTICE & NOTE

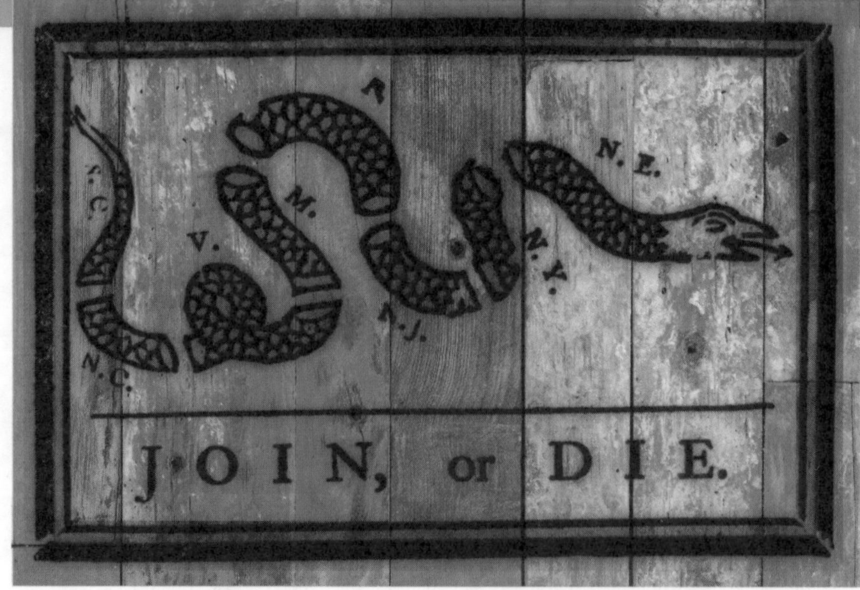

28 He has constrained our fellow citizens, taken captive on the high seas, to bear arms against their country, to become the executioners of their friends and brethren, or to fall themselves by their hands.

29 He has excited domestic insurrection amongst us,[10] and has endeavored to bring on the inhabitants of our frontiers the merciless Indian savages, whose known rule of warfare is an undistinguished destruction of all ages, sexes, and conditions.

ANALYZE TEXT STRUCTURE

Annotate: Mark the sentence in paragraph 30 that describes the response of the colonists to the king's actions.

Infer: How does Jefferson use the colonists' actions to rebut the counterargument that declaring independence is a rash decision?

30 In every stage of these oppressions we have petitioned for redress,[11] in the most humble terms; our repeated petitions have been answered only by repeated injury. A prince whose character is thus marked by every act which may define a tyrant is unfit to be the ruler of a free people.

31 Nor have we been wanting in our attentions to our British brethren. We have warned them, from time to time, of attempts by their legislature to extend an unwarrantable jurisdiction over us. We have reminded them of the circumstances of our emigration and settlement here. We have appealed to their native justice and magnanimity; and we have conjured them, by the ties of our common kindred, to disavow these usurpations, which would inevitably interrupt our connections and correspondence.

32 They, too, have been deaf to the voice of justice and of consanguinity.[12] We must, therefore, acquiesce in the necessity which denounces our separation; and hold them, as we hold the rest of mankind, enemies in war, in peace friends.

33 We, Therefore, the Representatives of the United States of America, in General Congress assembled, appealing to the Supreme Judge of the world for the rectitude[13] of our intentions, do, in the name and by the authority of the good people of these colonies,

[10] **excited . . . amongst us:** Lord Dunmore, the royal governor of Virginia, had encouraged slaves to rise up and rebel against their masters.

[11] **redress:** the correction of a wrong; compensation.

[12] **deaf to . . . consanguinity:** The British have ignored pleas based on their common ancestry with the colonists.

[13] **rectitude:** morally correct behavior or thinking.

NOTICE & NOTE 

solemnly publish and declare, that these United Colonies are, and of right ought to be, Free and Independent States; that they are absolved from all allegiance to the British crown, and that all political connection between them and the state of Great Britain is, and ought to be, totally dissolved; and that, as free and independent states, they have full power to levy war, conclude peace, contract alliances, establish commerce, and to do all other acts and things which independent states may of right do. And, for the support of this declaration, with a firm reliance on the protection of Divine Providence, we mutually pledge to each other our lives, our fortunes, and our sacred honor.

ANALYZE ARGUMENTATIVE TEXTS

Annotate: Mark the call to action in paragraph 33.

Analyze: How does Jefferson's use of "ought" in this call to action relate to his thesis?

CHECK YOUR UNDERSTANDING

Answer these questions before moving on to the **Analyze the Text** section on the following page.

1 On what did Jefferson base his belief that all men are created equal?

A Their rights as British citizens

B The will of the British king

C The laws of nature and God

D Traditions of the colonies

2 What is Jefferson's main argument against remaining connected to Great Britain?

F The colonies are ready to be on their own.

G The British king has been an unjust tyrant.

H The colonists no longer wish to obey British law.

J Other countries expect this of the colonists.

3 What is the conclusion of Jefferson's argument?

A The colonists must separate from Britain.

B The colonists should give Britain another chance.

C Britain had always been good to the colonists.

D Britain should overthrow its king.

RESPOND

ANALYZE THE TEXT

Support your responses with evidence from the text. NOTEBOOK

1. **Analyze** How does the syntax in paragraph 2 add to the persuasiveness of Jefferson's argument? Cite at least two examples in your response.

2. **Analyze** A **logical appeal** is a method of argument based on evidence and reasons. Choose an example of a logical appeal in the Declaration and explain how it supports the thesis.

3. **Evaluate** Jefferson's list of complaints makes up the largest part of his structure. How does this structure contribute to his argument? How does it support his thesis?

4. **Evaluate** In the final paragraph, what tone is created by Jefferson's use of the word *all* several times, as well as the phrase *totally dissolved?*

5. **Draw Conclusions** How does the structure of Jefferson's argument support his purpose? Consider elements such as evidence and a call to action in your response.

RESEARCH

RESEARCH TIP
When researching information about the United States, its history, its government, and its founders, websites that end in .gov are often very useful. Also, a search of "acts leading to American Revolution" will turn up lists of laws to which colonists objected.

The colonists' differences with Great Britain had grown over a long period of time. Research the laws Britain passed in the years before the Declaration of Independence and the colonists' responses. Then, complete the chart.

QUESTION	ANSWER
What did the Stamp Act do?	
What was required by the Quartering Act?	
What did the laws the colonists called the Intolerable Acts do?	

Extend Research another document about colonial relations with Great Britain written at the time, such as Thomas Paine's *Common Sense*. Compare its ideas to those presented in the Declaration of Independence and discuss what the second text adds to your understanding of the historical period.

CREATE AND PRESENT

Write an Argument Write an essay in which you evaluate the effectiveness of Jefferson's argument. Review your notes before you begin.

- ❑ Decide if you think Jefferson successfully supported his thesis, and then defend or challenge his claims.
- ❑ Carefully choose details and examples from the text that support your opinion.
- ❑ Outline your points in a logical structure with smooth transitions.
- ❑ Cite supporting examples and passages accurately.
- ❑ Add rhetorical devices such as repetition and parallelism to strengthen your argument.

Go to **Writing Arguments** in the **Writing Studio** for help.

Present an Argument Imagine you are trying to convince an audience to adopt Jefferson's ideas. Prepare a script of an argument that you will present to the class.

- ❑ Practice your presentation, reading it over a few times so you are comfortable presenting it.
- ❑ Use eye contact with your audience to engage their attention.
- ❑ Use facial expressions and appropriate gestures to emphasize key points.

Go to **Giving a Presentation** in the **Speaking and Listening Studio** for help.

RESPOND TO THE ESSENTIAL QUESTION

How do we gain our freedom?

Gather Information Review your annotations and notes on the Declaration of Independence. Then, add relevant information to your Response Log. As you determine which information to include, think about:

- how Jefferson defines freedom
- why he saw freedom as important
- what the last paragraph suggests about the cost of freedom

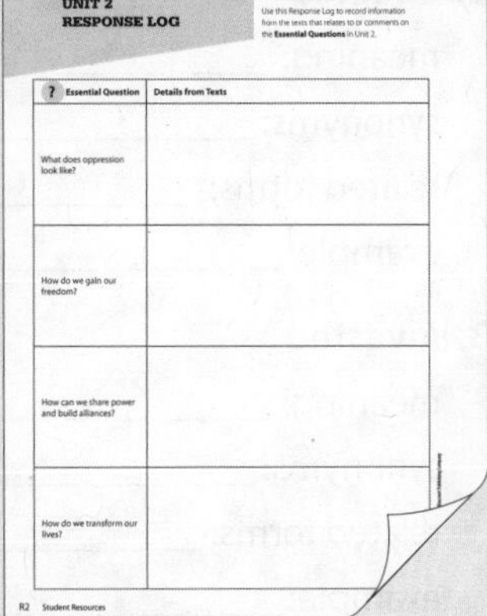

UNIT 2 RESPONSE LOG

Use this Response Log to record information from the texts that relates to or comments on the **Essential Questions** in Unit 2.

? Essential Question	Details from Texts
What does oppression look like?	
How do we gain our freedom?	
How can we share power and build alliances?	
How do we transform our lives?	

R2 Student Resources

ACADEMIC VOCABULARY

As you write and discuss what you learned from the document, be sure to use the Academic Vocabulary words. Check off each of the words that you use.

- ❑ **contrary**
- ❑ **founder**
- ❑ **ideological**
- ❑ **publication**
- ❑ **revolution**

RESPOND

WORD BANK
established
affected
invested
abdicated

CRITICAL VOCABULARY

One way to explore a new word is to use a semantic map, which identifies the definition of the term, related words, examples of the word in use, and synonyms of the word. Study the web below, which provides a semantic map for the word *instituted* from paragraph 2 of the Declaration of Independence.

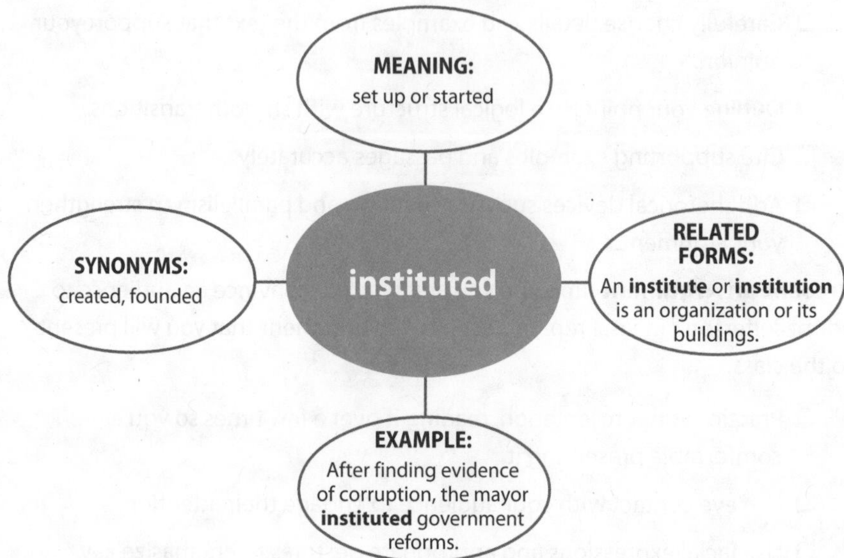
MEANING:
set up or started
SYNONYMS:
created, founded
instituted
RELATED FORMS:
An institute or institution is an organization or its buildings.
EXAMPLE:
After finding evidence of corruption, the mayor instituted government reforms.

Practice and Apply Fill in the blanks to create a semantic map for each Critical Vocabulary word. Use print or online references to check your work.

1. established

meaning: ________________

synonyms: ________________

related forms: ________________

example: ________________

2. affected

meaning: ________________

synonyms: ________________

related forms: ________________

example: ________________

3. invested

meaning: ________________

synonyms: ________________

related forms: ________________

example: ________________

4. abdicated

meaning: ________________

synonyms: ________________

related forms: ________________

example: ________________

VOCABULARY STRATEGY: Domain-Specific Words

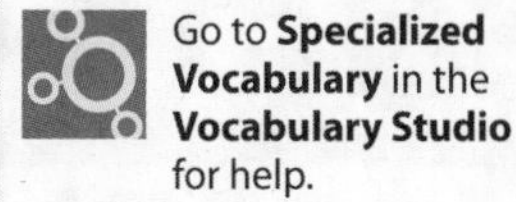

Go to **Specialized Vocabulary** in the **Vocabulary Studio** for help.

In the Declaration of Independence, Jefferson uses the Critical Vocabulary word *abdicated.* This word is more common in works of political science than in other writing. The field of political science, the study of government, has **domain-specific words** that identify types of government or government functions or describe the way a government acts. Context clues, knowledge of Greek and Latin roots, and a dictionary or other reference work can help establish the meaning of a word. Dictionaries also show related forms of the word, such as *legislative, legislature,* and *legislate.*

Practice and Apply Work with a partner to investigate the meaning, **etymology** (word origin), and related forms of these domain-specific words. Use a dictionary or other reference work to help you.

1. sovereign
2. despotism
3. tyranny
4. govern
5. oligarchy
6. republic
7. democracy
8. legislative
9. executive
10. judicial

LANGUAGE CONVENTIONS: Parallel Structure

Jefferson makes frequent use of the rhetorical device of parallelism in the Declaration of Independence. **Parallelism** is the use of similar grammatical constructions to express ideas that are closely related or equal in importance. It helps emphasize important ideas.

The chart shows examples of parallel structure from the Declaration of Independence. Try reading each passage aloud. Note how the parallelism creates rhythm and helps emphasize similarities among related ideas.

STRUCTURE	EXAMPLE
Parallel phrases	He has plundered our seas, ravaged our coasts, burnt our towns, and destroyed the lives of our people.
Parallel clauses or sentences	We have warned them, from time to time, of attempts by their legislature to extend an unwarrantable jurisdiction over us. We have reminded them of the circumstances of our emigration and settlement here. We have appealed to their native justice and magnanimity; and we have conjured them, by the ties of our common kindred, to disavow these usurpations, which would inevitably interrupt our connections and correspondence.

Practice and Apply Review the essay you wrote for your Create and Present activity in which you evaluated Jefferson's ideas. Incorporate parallel structure into your essay by grouping related ideas together using parallel construction.

ANALYZE & APPLY

THOMAS JEFFERSON: THE BEST OF ENEMIES

History Writing by **Ron Chernow**

? ESSENTIAL QUESTION:

How can we share power and build alliances?

QUICK START

Think about a time you had a disagreement with a friend. What happened as a result of the disagreement? Were there any long-term effects on your friendship? Discuss your experience with a partner.

ANALYZE INFORMATIONAL TEXTS

An **informational text** is a nonfiction text that presents fact-based information about a topic. History articles, like Chernow's piece, are a type of informative writing that focuses on important historical figures or events. Although the purpose of a history article is to inform readers, an author usually has a central idea to present about the event or people described. This central idea is contained in the **thesis** of the article, with the **body** of the article providing relevant supporting details and examples. The **conclusion** of the article summarizes important ideas and wraps up the piece in a satisfying way. As you read, identify the thesis, body, and conclusion of the essay.

Authors use organizational patterns to make their main point clear and to connect the supporting details. In this article, Chernow makes use of **chronological order,** which presents events in the order in which they happened. Use the following strategies when analyzing the sequence of events in an informational text.

- Look for words and phrases that identify time such as *in a year* or *three weeks earlier.*
- Look for words that signal order, such as *first* and *then* to see how events are related.

GENRE ELEMENTS: HISTORY WRITING

- presents information about historical events or persons
- includes facts, dates, and information, presented in chronological order
- may employ literary devices to emphasize details and increase engagement

ANALYZE STRUCTURE

The overarching structure of Chernow's article is a point-by-point **comparison and contrast** of Jefferson and Hamilton that shows how and why they became "the best of enemies." In such a structure, a writer discusses a particular point of comparison about both subjects and then moves on to the next point. Chernow uses this structure to make his exposition of complex ideas clear, weaving in narrative elements to make the text more engaging.

Within these basic structural elements, Chernow employs literary devices, syntax, and diction to achieve his purpose.

- His straightforward **syntax,** or arrangement of words, and use of dashes to present information creates a clear, brisk style.
- His precise **diction,** or word choice, communicates a vivid picture of the two men and contributes to the author's tone of admiration for them.
- Chernow also uses **irony**—events that contrast with expectations—to add a lighthearted yet memorable note to his essay.

As you read, notice how Chernow uses structure and style to achieve his purpose.

GET READY

CRITICAL VOCABULARY

tepid **copious** **cardinal** **rudiments** **façade** **anomalous**

To see how many Critical Vocabulary words you already know, decide whether the following statements are true or false.

1. The outline of a story contains the **rudiments** of what it will eventually become.
2. The **cardinal** rule of learning to drive is: Safety first.
3. The **tepid** television ratings led the company to renew the series for a year.
4. The diligent student filled a notebook with **copious** notes.
5. The **façade** of the building shows a spacious and elegant interior.
6. The team of scientists was elated by the **anomalous** results of their experiment.

LANGUAGE CONVENTIONS

Hyphenation Hyphens are punctuation marks that join words to clarify meaning and improve style. Hyphens are often used to attach a prefix to a proper noun or to a date (as in *pre-Revolutionary* or *pre-1776)* or to join multiple adjectives *(He works two part-time jobs to make ends meet.)*. Using hyphenated words can make writing concise and memorable. As you read the article, notice the way the writer uses hyphens.

ANNOTATION MODEL

NOTICE & NOTE

As you read, note how the author compares Hamilton and Jefferson and uses time order words to tell you the sequence of events. In the model, you can see one reader's notes about Chernow's article.

On March 21, 1790, Thomas Jefferson belatedly arrived in New York City to assume his duties as the first Secretary of State after a five-year ministerial stint in Paris. Tall and lanky, with a freckled complexion and auburn hair, Jefferson, 46, was taken aback by the adulation being heaped upon the new Treasury Secretary, Alexander Hamilton, who had streaked to prominence in his absence. Few people knew that Jefferson had authored the Declaration of Independence, ... Instead, the Virginian was eclipsed by the 35-year-old wunderkind from the Caribbean. . . .

author includes time references to events he will describe

compares age, accomplishments, background

BACKGROUND

Ron Chernow *(b. 1949) is an award-winning author of several biographies, including* Alexander Hamilton *(2004) and* Washington: A Life *(2010). In this magazine article from 2004, he explores the ideological differences that brought Thomas Jefferson (1743–1826) and Alexander Hamilton (1755/57–1804) into conflict when both served in President George Washington's first cabinet.*

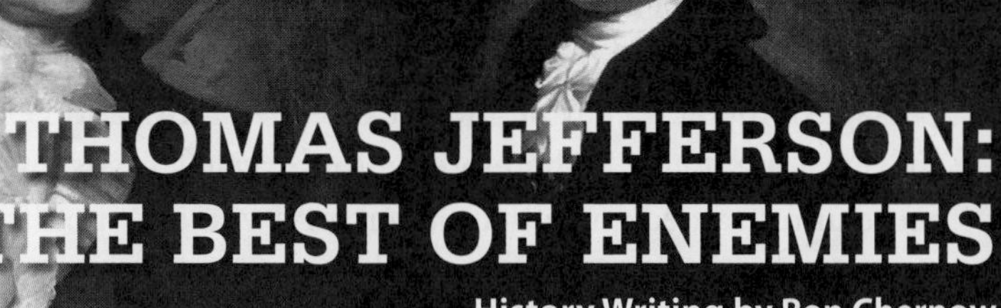

THOMAS JEFFERSON: THE BEST OF ENEMIES

History Writing by Ron Chernow

SETTING A PURPOSE

As you read, look for clues that reveal similarities and differences between Jefferson's and Hamilton's personalities and beliefs.

1 On March 21, 1790, Thomas Jefferson belatedly arrived in New York City to assume his duties as the first Secretary of State after a five-year ministerial stint in Paris. Tall and lanky, with a freckled complexion and auburn hair, Jefferson, 46, was taken aback by the adulation being heaped upon the new Treasury Secretary, Alexander Hamilton, who had streaked to prominence in his absence. Few people knew that Jefferson had authored the Declaration of Independence, which had yet to become holy writ for Americans. Instead, the Virginian was eclipsed by the 35-year-old wunderkind from the Caribbean, who was a lowly artillery captain in New York when Jefferson composed the famous document. Despite his murky background as an illegitimate orphan, the self-invented Hamilton was trim and elegant, carried himself with an erect military bearing and had a mind that worked with dazzling speed. At first, Hamilton and Jefferson socialized on easy terms, with little inkling that they were destined to become mortal foes. But their clash inside

Notice & Note

Use the side margins to notice and note signposts in the text.

ANALYZE INFORMATIONAL TEXTS

Annotate: Mark information in paragraph 1 about the long-term effects of the clash between Jefferson and Hamilton.

Infer: In your own words, state the author's thesis.

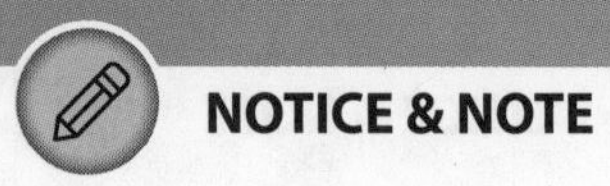

George Washington's first Cabinet proved so fierce that it would spawn the two-party system in America. It also produced two divergent visions of the country's future that divide Americans to the present day.

ANALYZE STRUCTURE

Annotate: Underline words in paragraph 2 that reveal Hamilton's vision of government power. Circle words that tell you about Jefferson's vision.

Analyze: How would you describe the core difference between the men's views? Cite text evidence in your response.

2 For Hamilton, the first Treasury Secretary, the supreme threat to liberty arose from insufficient government power. To avert that, he advocated a vigorous central government marked by a strong President, an independent judiciary and a liberal reading of the Constitution. As the first Secretary of State, Jefferson believed that liberty was jeopardized by concentrated federal power, which he tried to restrict through a narrow construction of the Constitution. He favored states' rights, a central role for Congress and a comparatively weak judiciary.

3 At first glance, Hamilton might seem the more formidable figure in that classic matchup. He took office with an ardent faith in the new national government. He had attended the Constitutional Convention, penned the bulk of the Federalist papers to secure passage of the new charter and spearheaded ratification efforts in New York State. He therefore set to work at Treasury with more unrestrained gusto than Jefferson—who had monitored the Constitutional Convention from his post in Paris—did at State. Jefferson's enthusiasm for the new political order was **tepid** at best, and when Washington crafted the first government in 1789, Jefferson didn't grasp the levers of power with quite the same glee as Hamilton, who had no ideological inhibitions about shoring up federal power.

tepid
(tĕp´ĭd) *adj.* lukewarm; indifferent.

4 Hamilton—brilliant, brash and charming—had the self-reliant reflexes of someone who had always had to live by his wits. His overwhelming intelligence petrified Jefferson and his followers. As an orator, Hamilton could speak extemporaneously for hours on end. As a writer, he could crank out 5,000- or 10,000-word memos overnight. Jefferson never underrated his foe's **copious** talents. At one point, a worried Jefferson confided to his comrade James Madison that Hamilton was a one-man army, "a host[1] within himself."

copious
(kō´pē-əs) *adj.* extensive.

5 Whether in person or on paper, Hamilton served up his opinions promiscuously. He had a true zest for debate and never left anyone guessing where he stood. Jefferson, more than a decade older, had the quiet, courtly manner of a Virginia planter. He was emphatic in his views—Hamilton labeled him "an atheist in religion and a fanatic in politics"—but shrank from open conflict. Jefferson, a diffident speaker, mumbled his way through his rare speeches in a soft, almost inaudible voice and reserved his most scathing strictures for private correspondence.

6 The epic battle between these two Olympian[2] figures began not long after Jefferson came to New York City to assume his State

[1] **host:** an army or large group of troops.

[2] **Olympian:** like a god; one from Mount Olympus.

Department duties in March 1790. By then Hamilton was in the thick of a contentious campaign to retire massive debt inherited from the Revolution. America had suspended principal and interest payments[3] on its obligations, which had traded as low as 15¢ on the dollar. In an audacious scheme to restore public credit, Hamilton planned to pay off that debt at face value, causing the securities to soar from depressed levels. Jefferson and Madison thought the original holders of those securities—many of them war veterans—should profit from that appreciation even if they had already sold their paper to traders at depressed prices. Hamilton thought it would be impractical to track them down. With an eye on future U.S. capital markets, he wanted to enshrine the **cardinal** principle that current owners of securities incurred all profits and losses, even if that meant windfall gains for rapacious speculators who had only recently bought the securities.

ANALYZE INFORMATIONAL TEXTS

Annotate: Mark words in paragraph 6 that show the sequence of events.

Infer: Why does the author include information about the order of events?

cardinal
(kär´dn-əl) *adj.* most important; prime.

7 That skirmish over Hamilton's public credit plan was part of a broader tussle over the U.S.'s economic future. Jefferson was fond of summoning up idyllic scenes of an agrarian America peopled by sturdy yeoman farmers.[4] That poetic vision neglected the underlying reality of large slave plantations in the South. Jefferson was a fine populist on paper but not in everyday life, and his defense of Virginia interests was inextricably bound up with slavery. Hamilton—derided as a pseudo aristocrat, an elitist, a crypto-monarchist[5]—was a passionate abolitionist with a far more expansive economic vision. He conceded that agriculture would persist for decades as an essential component of the economy. But at the same time he wanted to foster the **rudiments** of a modern economy—trade, commerce, banks, stock exchanges, factories and corporations—to enlarge economic opportunity.

rudiment
(ro͞o´də-mənt) *n.* basic form.

8 Hamilton dreamed of a meritocracy, not an aristocracy, while Jefferson retained the landed gentry's disdain for the vulgar realities of trade, commerce and finance. And he was determined to undermine Hamilton's juggernaut.[6]

9 Because we celebrate Jefferson for his sonorous words in the Declaration of Independence—Hamilton never matched Jefferson's gift for writing ringing passages that were at once poetic and inspirational—we sometimes overlook Jefferson's consummate skills as a practicing politician. A master of subtle, artful indirection, he was able to marshal his forces without divulging his generalship. After Hamilton persuaded President Washington to create the Bank of the United States, the country's first central bank, Jefferson was aghast

[3] **principal and interest payments:** the amount borrowed and the fees charged by the lender.
[4] **yeoman farmers:** owners of small independent farms.
[5] **crypto-monarchist:** one who secretly supports government rule by a king.
[6] **juggernaut:** an extremely powerful force.

at what he construed[7] as a breach of the Constitution and a perilous expansion of federal power. Along with Madison, he recruited the poet Philip Freneau to launch an opposition paper called the National Gazette. To subsidize the paper covertly, he hired Freneau as a State Department translator. Hamilton was shocked by such flagrant disloyalty from a member of Washington's Cabinet, especially when Freneau began to mount withering assaults on Hamilton and even Washington. Never one to suffer in silence, Hamilton retaliated in a blizzard of newspaper articles published under Roman pseudonyms. The backbiting between Hamilton and Jefferson grew so acrimonious that Washington had to exhort both men to desist.

10 Instead, the feud worsened. In early 1793, a Virginia Congressman named William Branch Giles began to harry Hamilton with resolutions ordering him to produce, on short deadlines, stupendous amounts of Treasury data. With prodigious bursts of energy, Hamilton complied with those inhuman demands, foiling his opponents. Jefferson then committed an unthinkable act. He secretly drafted a series of anti-Hamilton resolutions for Giles, including one that read, "Resolved, That the Secretary of the Treasury has been guilty of maladministration in the duties of his office and should, in the opinion of Congress, be removed from his office by the President of the United States." The resolution was voted down, and the effort to oust Hamilton stalled. Jefferson left the Cabinet in defeat later that year.

11 Throughout the 1790s, the Hamilton-Jefferson feud continued to fester in both domestic and foreign affairs. Jefferson thought Hamilton was "bewitched" by the British model of governance, while Hamilton considered Jefferson a credulous apologist for the gory excesses of the French Revolution. Descended from French

[7] **construed:** interpreted.

Huguenots[8] on his mother's side, Hamilton was fluent in French and had served as Washington's liaison with the Marquis de Lafayette and other French aristocrats who had rallied to the Continental Army. The French Revolution immediately struck him as a bloody affair, governed by rigid, Utopian thinking. On Oct. 6, 1789, he wrote a remarkable letter to Lafayette, explaining his "foreboding of ill" about the future course of events in Paris. He cited the "vehement character" of the French people and the "reveries" of their "philosophic politicians," who wished to transform human nature. Hamilton believed that Jefferson while in Paris "drank deeply of the French philosophy in religion, in science, in politics." Indeed, more than a decade passed before Jefferson fully realized that the French Revolution wasn't a worthy sequel to the American one so much as a grotesque travesty.[9]

12 If Jefferson and Hamilton define opposite ends of the political spectrum in U.S. history and seem to exist in perpetual conflict, the two men shared certain traits, feeding a mutual cynicism. Each scorned the other as excessively ambitious. In his secret diary, or Anas, Jefferson recorded a story of Hamilton praising Julius Caesar as the greatest man in history. (The tale sounds dubious, as Hamilton invariably used Caesar as shorthand for "an evil tyrant.") Hamilton repaid the favor. In one essay he likened Jefferson to "Caesar coyly refusing the proffered diadem"[10] and rejecting the trappings, but "tenaciously grasping the substance of imperial domination."

13 Similarly, both men hid a potent hedonism[11] behind an intellectual **façade**. For all their outward differences, the two

ANALYZE INFORMATIONAL TEXTS

Annotate: Mark the references to time in paragraph 11.

Analyze: How did the men's view of the French Revolution change over time? Cite text evidence in your response.

façade
(fə-säd´) *n.* false or misleading appearance.

[8] **French Huguenots:** a group of Protestants who were persecuted in Catholic France; many fled to North America.

[9] **travesty:** an unreasonable distortion or parody.

[10] **"Caesar . . . diadem":** In Shakespeare's *Julius Caesar,* the Roman general refuses a crown three times, but republicans believe he really wanted to be named king.

[11] **hedonism:** the belief that personal pleasure is the primary goal in life.

Thomas Jefferson

politicians stumbled into the two great sex scandals of the early Republic. In 1797 a journalist named James T. Callender exposed that Hamilton, while Treasury Secretary and a married man with four children, had entered into a yearlong affair with grifter Maria Reynolds, who was 23 when it began. In a 95-page pamphlet, Hamilton confessed to the affair at what many regarded as inordinate length. He wished to show that the money he had paid to Reynolds' husband James had been for the favor of her company and not for illicit speculation in Treasury securities, as the Jeffersonians had alleged. Forever after, the Jeffersonians tagged Hamilton as "the amorous Treasury Secretary" and mocked his pretensions to superior morality.

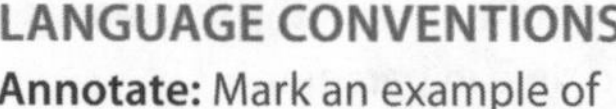

Annotate: Mark an example of hyphenation in paragraph 13.

Evaluate: How does hyphenation help make this sentence more concise?

14 By an extraordinary coincidence, during Jefferson's first term as President, Callender also exposed Jefferson's relationship with Sally Hemings. Callender claimed that "Dusky Sally," a.k.a. the "African Venus," was the President's slave concubine, who had borne him five children. "There is not an individual in the neighborhood of Charlottesville who does not believe the story," Callender wrote, "and not a few who know it." Jefferson never confirmed or denied Callender's story. But the likely truth of the Hemings affair was dramatically bolstered by DNA tests published in 1998, which indicated that a Jefferson male had sired at least one of Hemings' children.

15 The crowning irony of the stormy relations between Hamilton and Jefferson is that Hamilton helped install his longtime foe as President in 1801. Under constitutional rules then in force, the candidate with the majority of electoral votes became President; the runner-up became Vice President. That created an **anomalous** situation in which Jefferson, his party's presumed presidential nominee, tied with Aaron Burr, its presumed vice presidential nominee. It took 36 rounds of voting in the House to decide the election in Jefferson's favor. Faced with the prospect of Burr as President, a man he considered unscrupulous, Hamilton not only

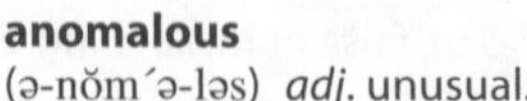
(ə-nŏm′ə-ləs) *adj.* unusual.

NOTICE & NOTE

opted for Jefferson as the lesser of two evils but also was forced into his most measured assessment of the man. Hamilton said he had long suspected that as President, Jefferson would develop a keen taste for the federal power he had deplored in opposition. He recalled that a decade earlier, in Washington's Cabinet, Jefferson had seemed like a man who knew he was destined to inherit an estate—in this case, the presidency—and didn't wish to deplete it. In fact, Jefferson, the strict constructionist, freely exercised the most sweeping powers as President. Nothing in the Constitution, for instance, permitted the Louisiana Purchase[12]. Hamilton noted that with rueful mirth.

CONTRASTS AND CONTRADICTIONS

Notice & Note: Mark a surprising fact that Chernow includes in the concluding paragraph of the article.

Analyze: What contradiction does this fact reveal? Explain.

[12] **Louisiana Purchase:** France's 1803 sale of its territory west of the Mississippi River to the United States.

CHECK YOUR UNDERSTANDING

Answer these questions before moving on to the **Analyze the Text** section on the following page.

1 What event sparked the beginning of the conflict between Hamilton and Jefferson?

A Jefferson came back from France.

B Hamilton arrived from the Caribbean.

C Jefferson wrote the Declaration of Independence.

D Hamilton attended the Constitutional Convention.

2 What is a main difference between the economic visions of America held by Jefferson and Hamilton?

F Jefferson's vision was urban, while Hamilton's was rural.

G Jefferson's vision was modern, while Hamilton's was agrarian.

H Jefferson's vision included slavery, while Hamilton's was abolitionist.

J Jefferson's vision included government controls, while Hamilton favored the aristocracy.

3 How did Hamilton respond to the accusations of illicit speculation?

A He confessed to speculating in Treasury securities.

B He confessed at length to having an extramarital affair.

C He accused Jefferson of having an affair with Sally Hemings.

D He accused the Jeffersonians of lying about his financial dealings.

RESPOND

ANALYZE THE TEXT

Support your responses with evidence from the text. NOTEBOOK

1. **Evaluate** How effectively did Chernow use chronological order and the comparison-and-contrast structure to portray the idea that Hamilton and Jefferson were "destined to become mortal foes"?
2. **Analyze** An author's choice of words, or **diction,** can communicate a great deal about a subject. Reread Chernow's description of Hamilton in paragraphs 4 and 5, paying attention to the adjectives and adverbs. What words best communicate the author's tone toward Hamilton's personality and character?
3. **Cite Evidence** How did Hamilton's and Jefferson's different personal styles affect the ways they carried out their feud?
4. **Analyze** How does Chernow's point-by-point comparison of these two rivals add to the strength of his concluding paragraph?
5. **Notice & Note** Chernow points out that despite the two leaders' conflicts, they shared some common traits. In what ways were Jefferson and Hamilton similar, according to Chernow? How does describing their similarities strengthen the article?

RESEARCH

The article mentions the *Federalist Papers* written by Alexander Hamilton. Research the *Federalist Papers* and answer these questions about them.

QUESTION	ANSWER
Why were the *Federalist Papers* written?	
Who besides Hamilton contributed to the *Federalist Papers?*	
What was Hamilton's position on the Bill of Rights? Why?	

RESEARCH TIP
Quoted or paraphrased ideas from both primary and secondary sources must be attributed to their author using citations in the correct format. Complete these citations as you research and take notes on a topic, so you won't waste time at the end of a research project searching for source information.

Extend Read one of the *Federalist Papers* Hamilton wrote. Summarize Hamilton's argument and then add a paragraph outlining how you think Jefferson would have responded to Hamilton's views.

Go to **Writing Informative Texts** in the **Writing Studio** for help.

CREATE AND PRESENT

Write an Essay Chernow states that the clash between Hamilton and Jefferson "produced two divergent visions of the country's future that divide Americans to the present day."

- ❑ Write an essay that provides a point-by-point comparison of these two visions.
- ❑ Use Chernow's article as a structural model and a source of content.
- ❑ Include a paragraph that explores whether these visions are relevant to Americans today. Use prior knowledge or conduct research to help you build your argument. Correctly cite any sources you use.

Present an Essay Present your essay to the class or a small group.

Go to **Giving a Presentation** in the **Speaking and Listening Studio** for help.

- ❑ Consider adding visuals to your presentation to enhance the audience's understanding.
- ❑ If available, use slide presentation software to create slides to accompany your essay. For example, you may use them to highlight important main ideas and add visual interest.
- ❑ Speak clearly and slowly, making eye contact with your audience as you present your essay.

RESPOND TO THE ESSENTIAL QUESTION

How can we share power and build alliances?

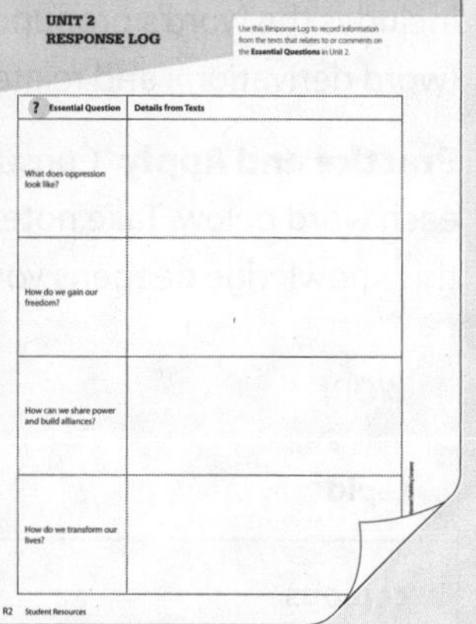

Gather Information Review your annotations and notes on "Thomas Jefferson: The Best of Enemies." Then, add relevant information to your Response Log. As you determine which information to include, think about:

- important accomplishments of Jefferson and Hamilton
- differences between Jefferson and Hamilton
- how conflict between the two men influenced, enhanced, or impeded their ability to achieve their goals

ACADEMIC VOCABULARY

As you write and discuss what you learned from the history article, be sure to use the Academic Vocabulary words. Check off each of the words that you use.

- ❑ **contrary**
- ❑ **founder**
- ❑ **ideological**
- ❑ **publication**
- ❑ **revolution**

RESPOND

CRITICAL VOCABULARY

WORD BANK
tepid **rudiments**
copious **façade**
cardinal **anomalous**

Practice and Apply Circle the letter of the best answer to each question. Then, explain your response.

1. Which of these responses is **tepid?**
   a. a shrug **b.** a shout

2. An **anomalous** answer to a question is most likely to provoke
   a. satisfaction **b.** confusion

3. Which type of print material has a **copious** number of pages?
   a. pamphlet **b.** encyclopedia

4. A **façade** is most similar to which of the following?
   a. a mask **b.** a hat

5. How does a musician learn the **rudiments** of playing an instrument?
   a. practicing **b.** humming

6. Which of the following is a **cardinal** principle of American democracy?
   a. free markets **b.** individual rights

VOCABULARY STRATEGY: Use Print and Digital Resources

Go to **Using Reference Sources** in the **Vocabulary Studio** for help.

Consulting both print and digital reference works, such as college-level dictionaries and thesauruses, can help you clarify and validate your understanding of the **multiple meanings** of words. A dictionary entry includes the word's pronunciation, part of speech, definitions, etymology (word derivation), and related words.

Practice and Apply Consult references to find additional information about each word below. Take notes in the chart. Then, discuss with a partner how this knowledge deepens your understanding of the article by Ron Chernow.

WORD	ADDITIONAL INFORMATION
tepid	
copious	
cardinal	
rudiments	
façade	
anomalous	

LANGUAGE CONVENTIONS: Hyphenation

Go to **Hyphens** in the **Grammar Studio** for more help.

Following the conventions of punctuation is important for clear communication. "Thomas Jefferson: The Best of Enemies" contains several examples of hyphenated words. Using a hyphen joins words into compounds so that their meaning is clear. Using hyphenated words can also be a simple way of expressing an idea. Compare the phrase from the article to the alternative that does not use a hyphen.

Phrase from article:

after a five-year ministerial stint in Paris

Nonhyphenated alternative:

after a ministerial stint of five years in Paris

The hyphenated adjective creates a more succinct text and contributes to a straightforward style. Hyphens have several purposes that are demonstrated in the article.

USES OF HYPHENS	
PURPOSE	**EXAMPLES**
join parts of a compound with *all-*, *ex-*, *self-*, or *-elect*	the self-invented Hamilton the self-reliant reflexes
join numbers to a noun to make an adjective	35-year-old wunderkind the 95-page pamphlet
join a prefix to a proper noun	anti-Hamilton resolutions
join two or more compounds to a single base	5,000- or 10,000-word memos
join a prefix or suffix to a noun	crypto-monarchist runner-up

Some compounds do not use hyphens. They may be open, as in *stock exchange* or *pseudo aristocrat*. They may be closed, as in *courthouse* or *underrated.* Consult a dictionary or style guide if you are unsure whether a compound word should be hyphenated, open, or closed.

Practice and Apply Look back at the essay you wrote comparing Hamilton's and Jefferson's visions of the future. Review your writing to see if you have used hyphenation conventions correctly. See if you can add one or two hyphenated words to give your writing a more concise style or more clarity. Review your edits with a partner and compare your use of hyphens.

MEDIA

AMERICAN EXPERIENCE: ALEXANDER HAMILTON

Video by **PBS**

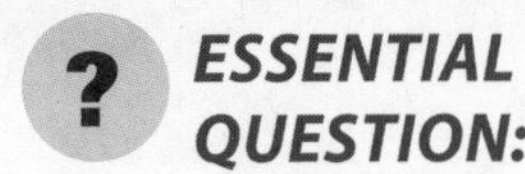

How can we share power and build alliances?

QUICK START

List two facts you know about Alexander Hamilton. Then, list two questions that you have about him. Discuss your questions about him with a partner.

DETERMINE AUTHOR'S PURPOSE

The **purpose,** or intent, of an informational video is often to communicate a message about the subject. To achieve the purpose, the video's creator uses words as well as graphic features and sound elements. In a documentary about a historical person, the purpose is often to explain that person's accomplishments and significance to an audience.

ANALYZE EFFECTIVENESS OF DIGITAL TEXT

Digital texts like videos convey ideas through graphic features and sound elements. You must determine if they are conveyed effectively. **Graphic features** can help viewers clarify their understanding of complex events.

STILLS	Images that are visually motionless, such as illustrations, maps, or photographs.
ANIMATION	Images that appear to move and seem alive are created through drawings, computer graphics, or photographs.
ACTOR PORTRAYALS	Actors playing the roles of historical or fictional people bring the subject matter to life and provide context.

Sound elements are what viewers hear in a video or embedded sound file.

MUSIC	Sounds created by singing, playing instruments, or using computer-generated tones can create a mood.
NARRATION	Narrator voice-overs guide the viewer; the words as well as the vocal quality of the narrator add to the experience.
SOUND EFFECTS	If reenactments or animations are used, sound effects—such as noises that suggest fighting in a war documentary—add realism.

GENRE ELEMENTS: VIDEO

- is created for a specific purpose, usually to convey a message
- targets a particular audience
- includes graphic features and sound elements to convey ideas

BACKGROUND

The PBS American Experience *documentary "Alexander Hamilton" traces Hamilton's life from his tragic childhood to his rise to prominence in the American Revolution and in the founding of the United States. It focuses on Hamilton's unique perspective, intellectual genius, and strong personality. It connects these characteristics to both his remarkable achievements and his demise. The segment of the documentary that you are about to watch explains the influence of Hamilton on the establishment of the central government in the challenging aftermath of the Revolution.*

SETTING A PURPOSE

As you view the video, evaluate how effectively the video uses graphic features and sound elements to achieve its purpose.

To view the video, log in online and select **"AMERICAN EXPERIENCE: ALEXANDER HAMILTON"** from the unit menu.

As needed, pause the video to make notes about what impresses you or about ideas you might want to talk about later. Replay the video so that you can clarify anything you do not understand.

RESPOND

ANALYZE MEDIA

Support your answers with evidence from the video. NOTEBOOK

1. **Analyze** The video states that Hamilton was "almost alone in his determination to change the direction of the country." Explain whether graphic features and sound elements effectively reflect this statement.
2. **Summarize** According to the video, how did Hamilton's childhood in the Caribbean affect his approach to solving the nation's problems?
3. **Evaluate** Overall, what is the purpose of this video segment, and what graphic features and sound elements does the video's creator use to achieve this purpose?
4. **Analyze** How does the video characterize the Confederation Congress in the narrator's voice-over? How does the actor speaking Hamilton's own words show a contrast between the government's present state and Hamilton's dreams for a better government?
5. **Evaluate** According to the historians in the video, what is Hamilton's strategy for putting his ideas forward? How does Hamilton himself portray his actions? How effectively does the video use both Hamilton's own ideas and the ideas of others to create a full picture of a complex person?

RESEARCH

Hamilton was a delegate to the Constitutional Convention. Research this important meeting to find out more and answer the questions in the chart.

QUESTION	ANSWER
Which state did Alexander Hamilton represent at the Convention, and who else were delegates from that state?	
Which state did not send delegates to the Convention? What was the reason?	
Of the 55 men who went to the Convention, how many did not sign the Constitution? What were their reasons?	

RESEARCH TIP

To find credible sources, look for information on a site that tells who created and maintains it. If the site contains no information about those who created it—an "About Us" or similar explanation—you may need to use the name of the group in a search engine in order to discover more about the content creators.

Extend A number of paintings depict the Constitutional Convention. Research and choose two to compare and contrast. What do they have in common, and how do they differ? If you were planning to use one of the paintings as a still in a documentary about the Convention, which one would you choose, and why? Briefly write your ideas and share them with a partner.

CREATE AND PRESENT

Write an Essay Both this video segment and "Thomas Jefferson: The Best of Enemies" explore the contributions of Alexander Hamilton to the founding of the United States. Write an essay comparing and contrasting the two pieces.

- ❑ First, organize your thoughts. Make lists or charts to record the similarities and differences between the two selections.
- ❑ Make sure to compare the content, delivery, purpose, and audience of each.
- ❑ Evaluate the major differences between the video and article formats as well as differences in focus and message.
- ❑ Outline your main points of comparison. Include examples from each source that illustrate those main points.
- ❑ Be sure to begin your essay with a clear thesis statement and to end with a summarizing or concluding statement.

Go to **Writing Informative Texts: Organizing Ideas** in the **Writing Studio** for help.

Present Your Ideas Communicate your ideas as a multimedia presentation.

- ❑ Use slide presentation software to communicate your main ideas.
- ❑ Include text examples from the article and embedded video or still images from the documentary to illustrate your points.
- ❑ Speak clearly and stay focused on your main points as you present your ideas.

Go to **Using Media in a Presentation** in the **Speaking and Listening Studio** for help.

RESPOND TO THE ESSENTIAL QUESTION

How can we share power and build alliances?

Gather Information Review your notes on "American Experience: Alexander Hamilton." Then, add relevant information to your Response Log. As you determine which information to include, think about:

- what made Hamilton unique among early leaders of the country
- how Alexander Hamilton built alliances with others
- his influence on the founding of the United States

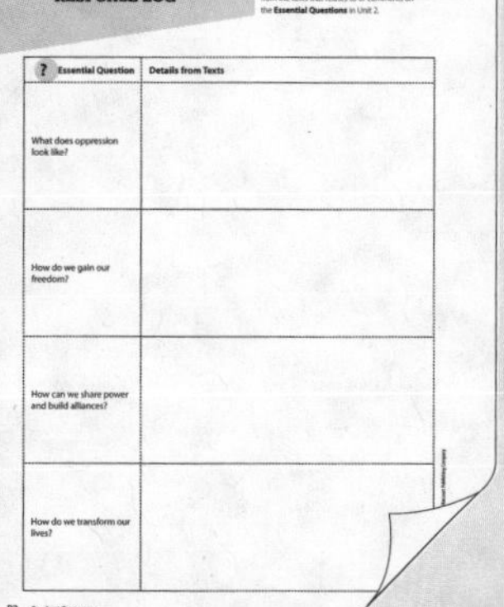

ACADEMIC VOCABULARY

As you write and discuss what you learned from the video, be sure to use the Academic Vocabulary words. Check off each of the words that you use.

- ❑ **contrary**
- ❑ **founder**
- ❑ **ideological**
- ❑ **publication**
- ❑ **revolution**

ANALYZE & APPLY

A SOLDIER FOR THE CROWN

Short story by **Charles Johnson**

? ESSENTIAL QUESTION:

How do we gain our freedom?

QUICK START

Share with a partner a time you or someone you know risked something in hopes of a desirable outcome. Did subsequent events unfold as expected? Was the risk worthwhile?

ANALYZE LITERARY ELEMENTS

Point of view refers to the method an author uses to narrate a story. In a work written in the **first-person point of view,** the narrator is a character in the story and plot events are experienced from the narrator's limited perspective. When a writer uses the **third-person point of view,** the narrator is not a character in the story but an outside observer. A more unusual method of narration is the **second-person point of view,** in which the narrator addresses someone using the pronoun *you.* In "A Soldier for the Crown," the narrator addresses the main character, Alexander Freeman, but often speaks as if he or she has entered the mind of that character.

With the second-person point of view, the reader may not know if the author is addressing a character, the reader, or the self. The reader must piece together information the narrator reveals to understand plot events or characters' behaviors. Point of view can also shape the development of the theme—the underlying message of a story—by affecting how much readers know and when they learn key information.

GENRE ELEMENTS: SHORT STORY

- is told from a particular point of view that impacts the reader's understanding of events
- contains literary elements that influence the development of the plot
- expresses a theme or the author's message

ANALYZE AND EVALUATE PLOT

Plot is the sequence of events in a literary work. Charles Johnson uses literary elements to develop the events surrounding the main character, a gambler named Alexander Freeman, in "A Soldier for the Crown."

- **Suspense** is the excitement or tension that readers feel as they wait to find out how a story ends. The author builds suspense when he introduces the main character as a risk-taker and creates suspense about the story's outcome with statements such as, "But did you win *this* time?"
- **Setting** is the time and place in which events take place. Setting also includes the work's historical context. **Historical context** refers to the conditions and customs during the time period in which events occur. In "A Soldier for the Crown," the writer includes details that tell you the historical context. As you read, think about how the setting influences the events of the plot.
- **Ambiguity** is the uncertainty created when readers can interpret words, phrases, or events in more than one way. The author builds the story by forcing the reader to put together clues about Freeman. As you read, your understanding of these clues may change.

As you read, analyze the writer's use of literary elements and evaluate how they shape the author's portrayal of the plot.

CRITICAL VOCABULARY

capacity **belatedly** **unalienable** **elusive**

To see how many Critical Vocabulary words you understand, restate each sentence using a different word or words for the boldfaced term.

1. She insisted that her rights were **unalienable** and the court must guarantee them.
2. His carelessness and lack of concern for others' feelings were evident in his always apologizing **belatedly.**
3. The solution to the mystery proved **elusive,** despite the detective's hard work.
4. She served in the **capacity** of an interpreter for her parents.

LANGUAGE CONVENTIONS

Subject-Verb Agreement The subject and verb in a clause must agree in number. That means that if the subject is singular, the verb must also be singular. A plural subject requires a plural verb.

The document, dated April 1783, brings a broad smile to your lips.

When a pronoun is the subject of a sentence, the verb also needs to agree in person—first, second, or third—and number. For example: *I am, he is, you are, they are.* As you read, notice how correct subject-verb agreement adds clarity to what is happening in the story.

ANNOTATION MODEL

NOTICE & NOTE

As you read, notice the way the writer uses literary elements to develop the plot. Note examples of the use of point of view and how it links to plot, character, and theme. Mark any other details that stand out to you. In the model, you can see one reader's notes about "A Soldier for the Crown."

Before the war broke out, when you were still a servant in Master William Selby's house, you'd bet on anything—how early spring thaw might come, or if your older brother Titus would beat your cousin Caesar in a wrestling match—and most of the time you won.

What war broke out? Seems like it is in the past.

Second-person point of view reveals character traits.

BACKGROUND

Charles Johnson *(1948–), a writer, philosopher, artist, and educator, has often confronted the effects of race and racism. "Racism is based on our belief in a division between Self and Other, and our tendency to measure ourselves against others," he says. "Sad to say, it is also based on fear." Johnson's work has earned a MacArthur fellowship, the National Book Award for* Middle Passage *(1990), and the American Academy of Arts and Letters Award.*

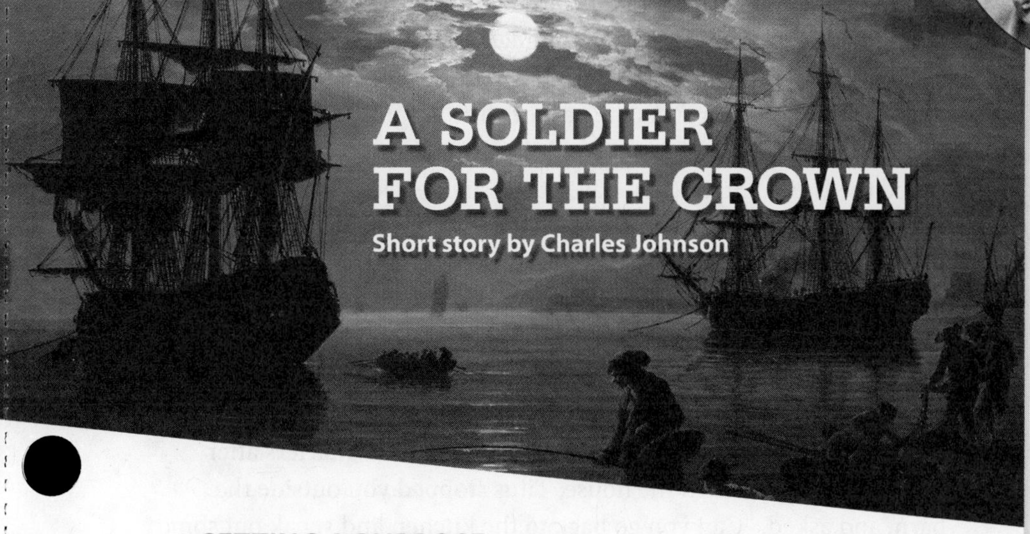

A SOLDIER FOR THE CROWN

Short story by Charles Johnson

SETTING A PURPOSE

As you read, pay attention to the way in which personal circumstance, social standing, and ideological differences affect the meaning of liberty.

1 YOU ALWAYS WERE a gambler.

2 Before the war broke out, when you were still a servant in Master William Selby's house, you'd bet on anything—how early spring thaw might come, or if your older brother Titus would beat your cousin Caesar in a wrestling match—and most of the time you won. There was something about gambling that you could not resist. There was suspense, the feeling that the future was not already written by white hands. Or finished. There was chance, the luck of the draw. In the roll of dice or a card game, there was always—what to call it?— an *openness*, a chance that the outcome would go this way or that. For or against you. Of course, in bondage to Master Selby there were no odds. Whichever way the dice fell or the cards came up, you began and ended your day a slave.

3 But did you win *this* time?

4 Standing by the wooden rail on a ship bound for Nova Scotia, crammed with strangers fleeing the collapse of their colonial world—women and children, whites and blacks, whose names

NOTICE & NOTE

Notice & Note

Use the side margins to notice and note signposts in the text.

ANALYZE AND EVALUATE PLOT

Annotate: Identify statements in paragraph 2 that introduce suspense.

Infer: What do these statements make you wonder about what will happen next?

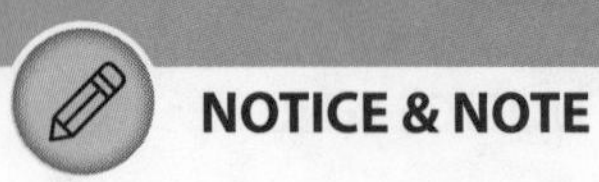

NOTICE & NOTE

ANALYZE LITERARY ELEMENTS

Annotate: Mark the phrase in paragraph 4 that reveals how the narrator thinks the main character feels.

Draw Conclusions: What effect does the second-person narration have?

LANGUAGE CONVENTIONS

Annotate: Read the dialogue in paragraphs 6–12. Mark the contraction with a first-person pronoun. Mark the contraction with the second-person pronoun.

Analyze: How do you know the subjects and verbs agree? How do the person and number of each subject affect the verb?

appear in Brigadier General Samuel Birch's *Book of Negroes*—you pull a long-shanked pipe from your red-tinted coat, pack the bowl with tobacco, and strike a friction match against a nail in your bootheel. You know you are fortunate to be on board. Now that the Continental Army is victorious, blacks who fought for the crown are struggling desperately to leave on His Majesty's ships departing from New York harbor. Even as your boat eased away from the harbor, some leaped from the docks into the water, swimming toward the ship for this last chance to escape slavery. Seeing them, you'd thought, *That might have been me.* But it wasn't; you've always been lucky that way, at taking risks. Running away from bondage. Taking on new identities. Yet you wonder what to call yourself now. A loyalist? A traitor? A man without a country? As the harbor shrinks, growing fainter in the distance, severing you forever from this strange, newly formed nation called the United States, you haven't the slightest idea after years of war which of these names fits, or what the future holds, though on one matter you *are* clear:

5 From the start, you were fighting for no one but yourself.

6 The day after Lieutenant General Sir Henry Clinton promised liberty to all blacks deserting the rebel standard and willing to fight on the side of the British, you learned that Titus and Caesar were planning to flee. In the evening, on your way to the quarters after finishing your duties in the house, Titus stopped you outside the barn, and asked, "Can you go back to the kitchen and sneak out some provisions for us?" Naturally, you'd asked him what for, and he put his fingers to his lips, shushing you. They planned to steal two horses, he said. Then ride to safety behind British lines. "You're leaving?" You were almost speechless with anger. "And you're not taking *me*?"

7 "How can I?" he asked. "You're only fifteen."

8 "What's that got to do with anything? I can fight!"

9 "You ever fired a gun?"

10 "No, but I can learn!"

11 "Once I'm free, and got the papers to prove it, I'll come back."

12 "Titus, if you don't take me, I'll *tell*."

13 For a heartbeat or two, Titus looked as if he might hit you. Grudgingly, he agreed to bring you along, despite your age and his declaration after your parents' deaths that he'd keep you from harm. You did as he requested, returning to the house and filling a sack with food, Master Selby's clothing, even some of the mistress's jewelry that the three of you might barter, then delivered all this to your brother and Caesar in the barn. The three of you left that night on two of the master's best horses, you riding behind Titus, your arms tightly circling his waist until you stopped to make camp in the woods. There, Caesar suggested that it would help if you all changed your names and appearances as much as possible since Master Selby was sure to post your descriptions. Titus said fine, he'd grow a beard and

call himself John Free. Caesar liked that, said, "Then I'll be George Liberty." They waited for you to pick a name, poking sticks at the campfire, sending up sparks into the starless sky. "Give me time," you'd said, changing into buckskin breeches, blue stockings, and a checkered, woolen shirt. "I'll shave my hair off, and I'll think of *some*thing before we get there. I don't want to rush." What you didn't tell them that night was how thrilling, how sweet this business of renaming oneself felt, and that you wanted to toy with a thousand possibilities—each name promising a new nature—turning them over on your tongue, and creating whole histories for each before settling, as you finally did, on "Alexander Freeman" as your new identity.

14 Thus, it was Alexander Freeman, George Liberty, and John Free who rode a few days later, bone weary from travel, into the British camp. You will never forget this sight: scores of black men in British uniforms, with the inscription LIBERTY TO SLAVES on their breasts, bearing arms so naturally one would have thought they were born with a rifle in their hands. Some were cleaning their weapons. Others marched. Still others were relaxing or stabbing their bayonets at sacks suspended from trees or performing any of the thousand chores that kept a regiment well-oiled and ready. When you signed on, the black soldier who wrote down your names didn't question you, though he remarked he thought you didn't look very strong. The three of you were put immediately to work. Harder work, you recall, than anything you'd known working in Master Selby's house, but for the first time in fifteen years you fell to each task eagerly, gambling that the labor purchased a new lease on life.

15 Over the first months, then years of the seesawing war, you, Titus, and Caesar served His Majesty's army in more **capacities** than you had fingers on the hand: as orderlies[1] to the white officers, laborers, cooks, foragers, and as foot soldiers who descended upon farms abandoned by their white owners, burning the enemy's fortifications and plundering plantations for much-needed provisions; as spies slipping in and out of southern towns to gather information; and as caretakers to the dying when smallpox swept through your regiment, weakening and killing hundreds of men. Your brother among them. And it was then you nearly gave up the gamble. You wondered if it might not be best to take your chips off the table. And pray the promise of the Virginia Convention that black runaways to the British side would be pardoned was genuine. And slink back home, your hat in your hand, to Master Selby's farm—if it was still there. Or perhaps you and Caesar might switch sides, deserting to the ranks of General Washington who, pressured for manpower, **belatedly** reversed his opposition to Negroes fighting in the Continental Army. And then there was that magnificent Declaration penned by Jefferson, proclaiming that "We hold these truths to be self-evident, that all

[1] **orderlies:** soldiers who provide assistance to and perform tasks for an officer.

ANALYZE AND EVALUATE PLOT

Annotate: Mark the phrase in paragraph 13 that tells what Titus decided.

Infer: What questions from the beginning of this story are answered by his decision? What new question arises?

capacity
(kə-păs´ĭ-tē) *n.* ability to hold or have something; function or role.

belatedly
(bĭ-lā´tĭd-lē) *adv.* done too late or overdue.

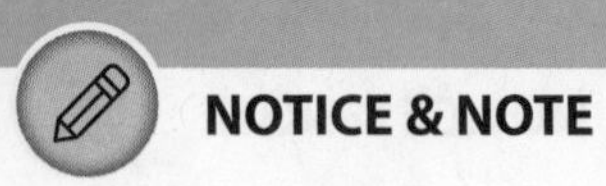

unalienable
(ŭn-āl´yə-nə-bəl) *adj.* impossible to be taken away.

men are created equal, that they are endowed by their Creator with certain **unalienable** Rights, that among these are Life, Liberty and the pursuit of Happiness," words you'd memorized after hearing them. If the Continentals won, would this brave, new republic be so bad?

16 "Alex, those are just *words*," said Caesar. "White folks' words for other white folks."

17 "But without us, the rebels would lose—"

18 "So would the redcoats. Both sides need us, but I don't trust neither one to play fair when this thing is over. They can do that Declaration over. Naw, the words I want to see are on a British pass with my name on it. I'm stayin' put 'til I *see that*."

ANALYZE LITERARY ELEMENTS

Annotate: Mark details in paragraph 19 that refer to Alexander's feelings.

Interpret: What is the effect of the second-person point of view on your understanding of Alexander?

19 Caesar never did. A month later your regiment was routed by the Continental Army. The rebels fired cannons for six hours, shelling the village your side occupied two days before. You found pieces of your cousin strewn everywhere. And you ran. Ran. You lived by your wits in the countryside, stealing what you needed to survive until you reached territory still in British hands, and again found yourself a pawn in the middle of other men's battles—Camden, where your side scattered poorly trained regulars led by General Gates, then liberated slaves who donned their masters' fancy clothing and powdered wigs and followed along behind Gates as his men pressed on; and the disastrous encounter at Guilford Court House, where six hundred redcoats died and Cornwallis was forced to fall back to Wilmington for supplies, then later abandon North Carolina altogether, moving on to Virginia. During your time as a soldier, you saw thousands sacrifice their lives, and no, it wasn't as if you came through with only a scratch. At Camden you took a ball in your right shoulder. Fragments remain there still, making it a little hard for you to sleep on that side or withstand the dull ache in your shoulder on days when the weather is damp. But, miraculously, as the war began to wind down, you were given the **elusive**, long-coveted British pass.

elusive
(ĭ-lo͞o´sĭv) *adj.* difficult to define.

20 On the ship, now traveling north past Augusta, you knock your cold pipe against the railing, shaking dottle from its bowl, then reach into your coat for the scrap of paper that was so difficult to earn. Behind you, other refugees are bedding down for the night, covering themselves and their children with blankets. You wait until one of the hands on deck passes a few feet beyond where you stand, then you unfold the paper with fingers stiffened by the cold. In the yellowish glow of the ship's lantern, tracing the words with your forefinger, shaping your lips silently to form each syllable, you read:

> This is to certify to whomfoever[2] it may concern, that the Bearer hereof . . . Alexander Freeman . . . a Negro, reforted to the Britifh Lines, in confequence of the Proclamations of Sir William Howe, and Sir Henry Clinton, late Commanders

[2] **whomfoever:** In the 1800s, handwritten and printed documents sometimes used the "long s," which looked like an *f* without the crossbar, in place of a lowercase *s*.

in Chief in America; and that the faid Negro has hereby his Excellency Sir Benjamin Hampton's Permiffion to go to Nova-Scotia, or wherever elfe he may think proper . . . By Order of Brigadier General Ruttledge

21 The document, dated April 1783, brings a broad smile to your lips. Once your ship lands, and you find a home, you will frame this precious deed of manumission.[3] At least in this sense, your gamble paid off. And for now you still prefer the adopted name Alexander Freeman to the one given you at birth—Dorothy.

22 Maybe you'll be Dorothy again, later in Nova Scotia. Of course, you'll keep the surname Freeman. And, Lord willing, when it's safe you will let your hair grow out again to its full length, wear dresses, and perhaps start a new family to replace the loved ones you lost during the war.

[3] **deed of manumission:** a document confirming a person's release from slavery.

NOTICE & NOTE

ANALYZE AND EVALUATE PLOT

Annotate: Mark the sentence in paragraph 21 that reveals a surprising truth about the main character.

Infer: Why doesn't the narrator name the main character until the end? What ambiguity about the situation remains?

CHECK YOUR UNDERSTANDING

Answer these questions before moving on to the **Analyze the Text** section.

1 What is Dorothy doing when the story begins?

A Sailing away from New York to freedom

B Fleeing from Master Selby's farm

C Running away from the army after a battle

D Sailing with British troops for a new military campaign

2 Which most likely explains why Titus resists taking Dorothy with him?

F He does not take his promise to protect her seriously.

G He does not want her to slow down their escape.

H He does not think she will be safe because she is young and female.

J He thinks she would be happier staying on Master Selby's farm.

3 How does Dorothy gain the pass granting freedom?

A She takes Caesar's pass after he was killed in battle.

B She earns it through her service in the British army.

C She has to buy the pass from a British soldier.

D The British give passes to all African Americans.

ANALYZE THE TEXT

Support your responses with evidence from the text. NOTEBOOK

1. **Cite Evidence** How does the setting shape the writer's portrayal of the plot? Explain, citing details about the historical context.
2. **Analyze** Why does the conversation between Caesar and Freeman about the Declaration of Independence leave the reader with a sense of ambiguity, but hold greater significance once Freeman's identity is revealed?
3. **Analyze** Why does the writer include Freeman's reaction to Titus's death? How does it build suspense in the story?
4. **Interpret** What effect does the use of the second-person point of view have on the scene in paragraph 13? What idea is the author able to communicate by using this point of view?
5. **Draw Conclusions** The theme is the truth about life that the writer conveys. Theme can be suggested by what happens to the main character and the key events in the plot. What theme can you draw from these literary elements?

RESEARCH

RESEARCH TIP
Narrow search terms by putting phrases like *American Revolution* in quotation marks.

Tens of thousands of loyalists fled the United States after the American Revolution. Research what happened to loyalists during and after the American Revolution. Start by finding answers to these questions.

QUESTION	ANSWER
In what areas were most of the loyalists living?	
How were loyalists treated by the patriots? Why were they treated this way?	
How many loyalists left the United States? Where did they go?	

Connect What perspective on loyalists of the American Revolution does the writer present in the story? How do the answers to the research question support this perspective? What new information is introduced?

CREATE AND DEBATE

Write an Argumentative Essay Write a three- to four-paragraph opinion essay about whether taking risks is worthwhile. Consider whether some risks are worth taking even if they could have serious consequences.

- ❑ In the first paragraph, introduce your opinion about taking risks.
- ❑ Use details from the text as well as real-life examples to support your view on taking risks.
- ❑ Include your own commentary to support your opinion.
- ❑ Include a strong conclusion that restates your opinion and summarizes your reasons.

Go to **Writing Arguments** in the **Writing Studio** for help.

Have a Debate Have a debate about Freeman's "gamble" and if you think that gamble paid off.

- ❑ Divide into two groups: those who agree with Freeman's gamble and those who do not.
- ❑ Find details from the text and think about reasons that support your group's opinion. Consider the options Freeman had before and after her brother died. Also consider the setting and how it affected the characters' choices.
- ❑ Listen closely to the opposing group's ideas and present counterarguments.

RESPOND TO THE ESSENTIAL QUESTION

How do we gain our freedom?

Gather Information Review your annotations and notes on "A Soldier for the Crown." Then, add relevant information to your Response Log. As you determine which information to include, think about:

- why individuals desire freedom
- the social and political factors that determine who is free
- the risks people take to gain freedom

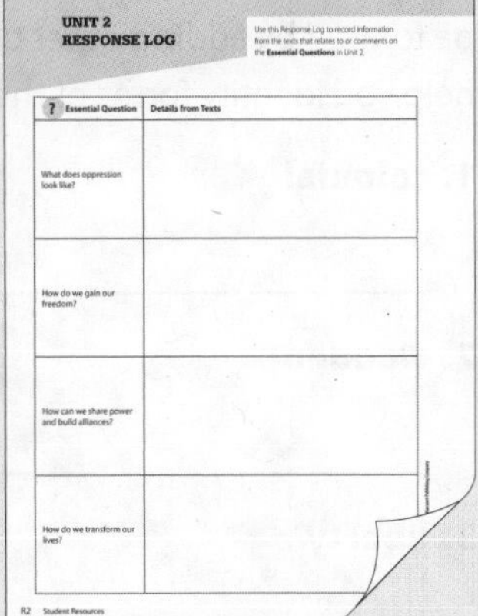

UNIT 2
RESPONSE LOG

Use this Response Log to record information from the texts that relates to or comments on the **Essential Questions** in Unit 2.

? Essential Question	Details from Texts
What does oppression look like?	
How do we gain our freedom?	
How can we share power and build alliances?	
How do we transform our lives?	

R2 Student Resources

ACADEMIC VOCABULARY

As you write and discuss what you learned from "A Soldier for the Crown," be sure to use the Academic Vocabulary words. Check off each of the words that you use.

- ❑ **contrary**
- ❑ **founder**
- ❑ **ideological**
- ❑ **publication**
- ❑ **revolution**

CRITICAL VOCABULARY

WORD BANK
capacity
belatedly
unalienable
elusive

Practice and Apply Show your understanding of the vocabulary words by answering these questions.

1. What do you possess as an individual that is **unalienable?** Explain.
2. Describe a circumstance in which you receive something **belatedly.**
3. When have you tried to grasp something that proved **elusive?** Explain.
4. In what **capacity** might you help out at a local animal shelter?

VOCABULARY STRATEGY: Prefixes and Suffixes

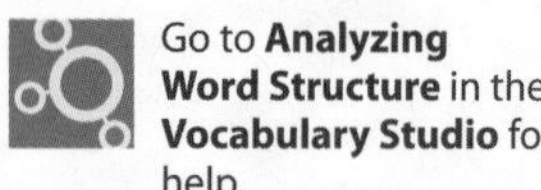

Go to **Analyzing Word Structure** in the **Vocabulary Studio** for help.

The Critical Vocabulary word *unalienable* is an example of a word built by adding the prefix *un-* and the suffix *-able* to the base word *alien.* Adding a prefix to the word changes the word's meaning. Adding a suffix changes the word's part of speech. As the word web shows, other prefixes and suffixes can be added to the base word *alien* with a variety of meanings and parts of speech.

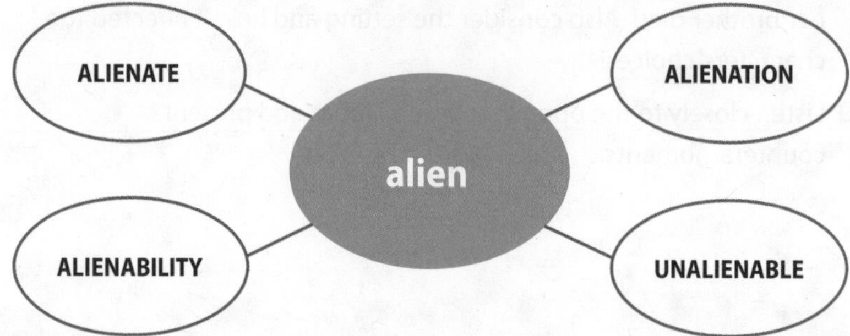

Practice and Apply Each of the following words appears in the selection. For each one, identify the base word and at least three other words that can be formed by adding other prefixes or suffixes. Use print or online sources to help you identify forms of the word.

1. **colonial**

____

2. **wooden**

____

3. **liberty**

____

4. **inscription**

____

LANGUAGE CONVENTIONS:
Subject-Verb Agreement

The rules for **subject-verb agreement** are relatively simple—subjects and verbs should agree in number (singular or plural). When the subject is a pronoun, the verb must also agree in person—first person, second person, or third person.

First-Person Singular	I *ride* a bike to school every day.
Third-Person Singular	She *rides* a bike to school every day.
First-Person Plural	We *ride* our bikes to school together every day.

Compound subjects make subject-verb agreement more complicated. If two single subjects are joined by *and,* the subjects become a plural compound subject and need a plural verb, since both subjects are doing the action. If two subjects are joined by the words *or* or *nor,* they function in the sentence as a singular subject because *either one* is doing the action, but not both.

Plural Compound Subject	Terry **and** Raja *ride* their bikes to school every day.
Singular Compound Subject	Either Terry **or** Raja *rides* a bike to school every day.

If the subject is a **collective noun—**one that refers to several individuals—the verb may be singular or plural, depending on how the noun is used. The subject takes a singular verb if the subject is being viewed as a unit. It takes a plural verb if the focus is on the individual members of the collective group.

As a Unit	The **team** *takes* the bus to the game.
As Individuals	The **team** *take* turns at practice.

Practice and Apply Read the passage from the story that includes the escape from the Selby farm. Write a third-person narrative of what the three characters did to prepare and to flee. Use a mix of singular and compound subjects and choose the correct verb form to show subject-verb agreement.

! Go to **Subject-Verb Agreement** in the **Grammar Studio** for help

from THE AUTOBIOGRAPHY

Autobiography by **Benjamin Franklin**

? ESSENTIAL QUESTION:

How do we transform our lives?

QUICK START

It is said that virtues are the core of our character and that character determines destiny. Do you believe this? Why or why not? With a partner, list virtues you think shape your character and answer these questions.

MONITOR COMPREHENSION

When you **monitor comprehension,** you check your understanding as you read. Monitoring your comprehension can clarify ideas and help you when you are confused. Here are a few ways to monitor comprehension:

- **Reread** slowly and carefully when you face a long sentence or cannot follow the author's sequence of ideas.
- **Ask questions** about what is happening or why the writer shares certain information. This will deepen your understanding of the text.
- **Use background knowledge** to help you make sense of what you read.
- **Read an outside source** that can give you additional information.

In the excerpt from his autobiography, Benjamin Franklin describes his quest for moral perfection. As you read, be sure to monitor your comprehension so you can understand the key ideas and significant events that he conveys.

GENRE ELEMENTS: AUTOBIOGRAPHY

- uses the first-person point of view
- focuses on significant events in author's life
- often includes thoughts about or interpretations of what is happening

EVALUATE PRINT AND GRAPHIC FEATURES

Print and **graphic features** are text and visual tools that present and organize information. Captions, special print like boldface or italics, lists, and subheads are print features that help you understand what you read. Images, charts, and graphs are some of the graphic features that may also help. As you read, consider why Franklin chooses a different print or graphic feature for each part of the project and whether each feature is effective. Use a chart like this to keep track of the print and graphic features and the purpose of each. What information does Franklin organize and share by using them?

PRINT OR GRAPHIC FEATURE	PURPOSE

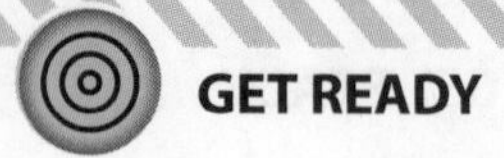

GET READY

CRITICAL VOCABULARY

trifling	affluence	eradicate	artifice
unremitting	contrive	incorrigible	felicity

To see how many Critical Vocabulary words you already know, use them to complete the sentences.

1. He thought sincerity was a better means to an end than ________.
2. Day and night, the pain was ________.
3. If we all work to clean the park, we can ________ litter.
4. The ________ at winning the award was shared by the whole family.
5. The rich furnishings of the house underscored the owners' ________.
6. How did he ________ to build that machine?
7. The little glass toys seemed silly and ________.
8. In trouble again, is he? He is ________.

LANGUAGE CONVENTIONS

Standard English When writing Standard English, writers follow conventions of sentence structure, usage, and punctuation that demonstrate an understanding of the language and audience. However, writers may not always use Standard English. They may include sentence fragments or dialogue that is written in a dialect, often to achieve a particular tone or style. Look for ways Franklin adheres to, and departs from, Standard English usage, and think about why he might be doing so.

ANNOTATION MODEL

NOTICE & NOTE 

As you read, use the side margins to write any notes or questions. Mark any details in the text that stand out to you, including any graphic features. This model shows one student's notes about *The Autobiography.*

As I knew, or thought I knew, what was right and wrong, I did not see why I might not always do the one and avoid the other. But I soon found I had undertaken a task of more difficulty than I had imagined.

He introduces uncertainty here.

What difficulties will he face?

NOTICE & NOTE

BACKGROUND

Benjamin Franklin *(1706–1790) was the oldest of the founders. He was 69 when he was sent as a delegate to the Second Continental Congress where he assisted Thomas Jefferson in drafting the Declaration of Independence. But by that time, he'd already had a remarkable life, finding success as a printer, publisher, scientist, inventor, businessman, philosopher, postmaster, and statesman. He was also a prolific writer, producing volumes of essays, travel journals, newspaper articles, almanacs, speeches, and more. His autobiography, however, was his masterpiece, and it is still popular today.*

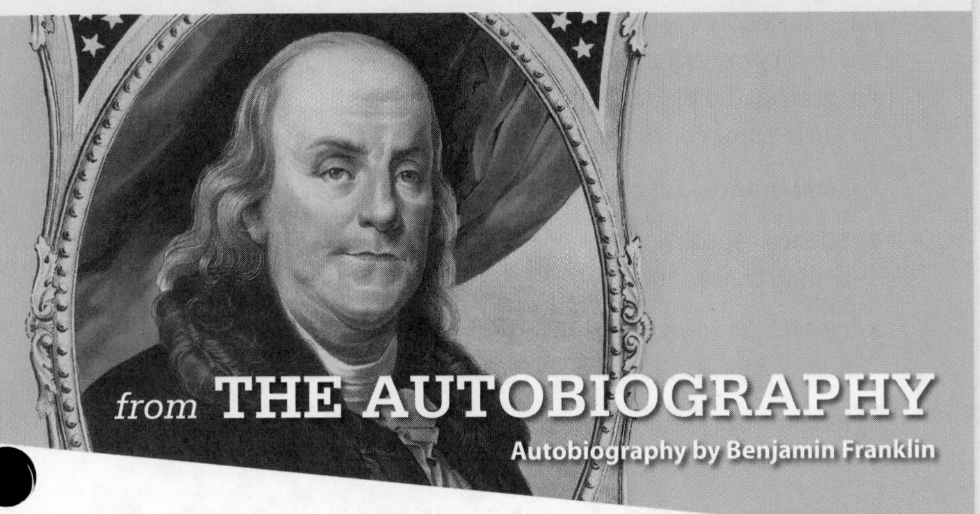

from THE AUTOBIOGRAPHY

Autobiography by Benjamin Franklin

SETTING A PURPOSE

As you read, look for details that reveal Franklin's practical nature, even as he shows his faith in reason, order, and human perfectibility—common ideas in the 18th century.

1 It was about this time I conceived the bold and arduous project of arriving at moral perfection. I wished to live without committing any fault at any time; I would conquer all that either natural inclination, custom, or company might lead me into. As I knew, or thought I knew, what was right and wrong, I did not see why I might not always do the one and avoid the other. But I soon found I had undertaken a task of more difficulty than I had imagined. While my care was employed in guarding against one fault, I was often surprised by another; habit took the advantage of inattention; inclination was sometimes too strong for reason. I concluded, at length, that the mere speculative conviction that it was our interest to be completely virtuous, was not sufficient to prevent our slipping; and that the contrary habits must be broken, and good ones acquired and established, before we can have any dependence on a steady, uniform rectitude of conduct. For this purpose I therefore **contrived** the following method.

Notice & Note

Use the side margins to notice and note signposts in the text.

MONITOR COMPREHENSION

Annotate: Mark the words in the first paragraph that Franklin uses to describe the project.

Analyze: What questions do you have about Franklin's project so far?

contrive
(kən-trīv′) *v.* to plan skillfully; to design.

2 In the various enumerations of the moral virtues I had met with in my reading, I found the catalogue more or less numerous, as different writers included more or fewer ideas under the same name. Temperance, for example, was by some confined to eating and drinking, while by others it was extended to mean the moderating every other pleasure, appetite, inclination, or passion, bodily or mental, even to our avarice and ambition. I proposed to myself, for the sake of clearness, to use rather more names, with fewer ideas annexed to each, than a few names with more ideas; and I included under thirteen names of virtues all that at that time occurred to me as necessary or desirable, and annexed to each a short precept, which fully expressed the extent I gave to its meaning.

EVALUATE PRINT AND GRAPHIC FEATURES
Annotate: Mark where Franklin's list of virtues begins.

Analyze: Why does Franklin organize the virtues in this way?

3 These names of virtues, with their precepts were:

1. **Temperance.** Eat not to dullness; drink not to elevation.
2. **Silence.** Speak not but what may benefit others or yourself; avoid **trifling** conversation.
3. **Order.** Let all your things have their places; let each part of your business have its time.
4. **Resolution.** Resolve to perform what you ought; perform without fail what you resolve.
5. **Frugality.** Make no expense but to do good to others or yourself; *i.e.,* waste nothing.
6. **Industry.** Lose no time; be always employed in something useful; cut off all unnecessary actions.
7. **Sincerity.** Use no hurtful deceit; think innocently and justly; and, if you speak, speak accordingly.
8. **Justice.** Wrong none by doing injuries, or omitting the benefits that are your duty.
9. **Moderation.** Avoid extremes; forbear resenting injuries so much as you think they deserve.
10. **Cleanliness.** Tolerate no uncleanliness in body, clothes, or habitation.
11. **Tranquillity.** Be not disturbed at trifles, or at accidents common or unavoidable.
12. **Chastity.** Rarely use venery but for health or offspring, never to dulness, weakness, or the injury of your own or another's peace or reputation.
13. **Humility.** Imitate Jesus and Socrates.[1]

trifling
(trī´flĭng) *adj.* frivolous; inconsequential.

[1] **Socrates** (sŏk´rə-tēz): Greek philosopher (470?–399 BC) who believed that true knowledge comes through dialogue and systematic questioning of ideas.

4 My intention being to acquire the *habitude* of all these virtues, I judged it would be well not to distract my attention by attempting the whole at once, but to fix it on one of them at a time; and, when I should be master of that, then to proceed to another, and so on, till I should have gone through the thirteen; and, as the previous acquisition of some might facilitate the acquisition of certain others, I arranged them with that view, as they stand above. Temperance first, as it tends to procure that coolness and clearness of head, which is so necessary where constant vigilance was to be kept up, and guard maintained against the **unremitting** attraction of ancient habits, and the force of perpetual temptations. This being acquired and established, Silence would be more easy; and my desire being to gain knowledge at the same time that I improved in virtue, and considering that in conversation it was obtained rather by the use of the ears than of the tongue, and therefore wishing to break a habit I was getting into of prattling, punning, and joking, which only made me acceptable to trifling company, I gave *Silence* the second place. This and the next, *Order,* I expected would allow me more time for attending to my project and my studies. *Resolution,* once become habitual, would keep me firm in my endeavors to obtain all the subsequent virtues; *Frugality* and Industry freeing me from my remaining debt, and producing **affluence** and independence, would make more easy the practice of Sincerity and Justice, etc., etc.

Form of the pages.

TEMPERANCE eat not to dullness; drink not to elevation.							
	S.	M.	T.	W.	T.	F.	S.
T.							
S.	•	•		•		•	
O.	••	•	•		•	•	•
R.			•			•	
F.		•			•		
I.			•	•			
S.							
J.							
M.							
C.							
T.							
C.							
H.							

NOTICE & NOTE

MONITOR COMPREHENSION

Annotate: Mark the sentence in paragraph 4 describing the process Franklin chose.

Paraphrase: Reread the sentence slowly and carefully. Then, describe Franklin's process in your own words.

unremitting
(ŭn rĭ-mĭt´ĭng) *adj.* constant; never stopping.

affluence
(ăf´lo͞o-əns) *n.* wealth.

EVALUATE PRINT AND GRAPHIC FEATURES

Annotate: Mark the area of the chart that shows Franklin succeeded in being temperate for most of the week.

Analyze: Does the information in the chart suggest Franklin will succeed on his project? Explain.

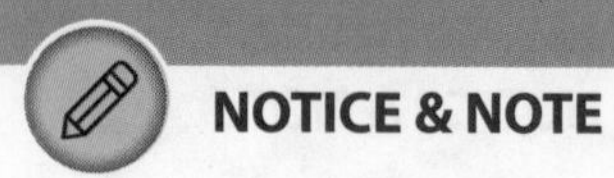

NOTICE & NOTE

Conceiving then, that, agreeably to the advice of Pythagoras in his Golden Verses,[2] daily examination would be necessary, I contrived the following method for conducting that examination.

5 I made a little book, in which I allotted a page for each of the virtues. I ruled each page with red ink, so as to have seven columns, one for each day of the week, marking each column with a letter for the day. I crossed these columns with thirteen red lines, marking the beginning of each line with the first letter of one of the virtues, on which line, and in its proper column, I might mark, by a little black spot, every fault I found upon examination to have been committed respecting that virtue upon that day.

EXTREME OR ABSOLUTE LANGUAGE

Notice & Note: Mark the statement in paragraph 6 that contains extreme or absolute language.

Interpret: Explain whether Franklin is stating an uncompromising position or an exaggeration.

eradicate (ĭ-răd´ĭ-kāt) *v.* tear up by the roots; eliminate.

6 I determined to give a week's strict attention to each of the virtues successively. Thus, in the first week, my great guard was to avoid every[3] the least offense against *Temperance,* leaving the other virtues to their ordinary chance, only marking every evening the faults of the day. Thus, if in the first week I could keep my first line, marked T, clear of spots, I supposed the habit of that virtue so much strengthened, and its opposite weakened, that I might venture extending my attention to include the next, and for the following week keep both lines clear of spots. Proceeding thus to the last, I could go through a course complete in thirteen weeks, and four courses in a year. And like him who, having a garden to weed, does not attempt to **eradicate** all the bad herbs at once, which would exceed his reach and his strength, but works on one of the beds at a time, and, having accomplished the first, proceeds to a second, so I should have, I hoped, the encouraging pleasure of seeing on my pages the progress I made in virtue, by clearing successively my lines of their spots, till in the end, by a number of courses, I should be happy in viewing a clean book, after thirteen weeks' daily examination. . . .

7 The precept of *Order* requiring that *every part of my business should have its allotted time,* one page in my little book contained the following scheme of employment for the twenty-four hours of a natural day.

8 I entered upon the execution of this plan for self-examination, and continued it with occasional intermissions for some time. I was surprised to find myself so much fuller of faults than I had imagined; but I had the satisfaction of seeing them diminish. To avoid the trouble of renewing now and then my little book, which, by scraping out the marks on the paper of old faults to make room for new ones in a new course, became full of holes, I transferred my tables and precepts to the ivory leaves of a memorandum book, on which the lines were drawn with red ink, that made a durable stain, and on

[2] **Pythagoras** (pĭ-thăg´ər-əs)**. . . Golden Verses:** Pythagoras was a Greek philosopher.

[3] **every:** even.

The Morning. *Question.* What good shall I do this day?	5 6 7	Rise, wash, and address *Powerful Goodness!* Contrive day's business, and take the resolution of the day; prosecute the present study, and breakfast.
	8 9 10 11	Work.
Noon.	12 1	Read, or overlook my accounts, and dine.
	2 3 4 5	Work.
Evening. *Question.* What good have I done today?	6 7 8 9	Put things in their places. Supper. Music or diversion, or conversation. Conversation. Examination of the day.
Night.	10 11 12 1 2 3 4	Sleep.

those lines I marked my faults with a black-lead pencil, which marks I could easily wipe out with a wet sponge. After a while I went through one course only in a year, and afterward only one in several years, till at length I omitted them entirely, being employed in voyages and business abroad, with a multiplicity of affairs that interfered; but I always carried my little book with me.

9 My scheme of *Order* gave me the most trouble; and I found that, though it might be practicable where a man's business was such as to leave him the disposition of his time, that of a journeyman printer, for instance, it was not possible to be exactly observed by a master, who must mix with the world, and often receive people of business at their own hours. *Order,* too, with regard to places for things, papers, etc., I found extremely difficult to acquire. I had not been early accustomed to it, and, having an exceeding good memory, I was not so sensible of the inconvenience attending want of method. This article, therefore, cost me so much painful attention, and my faults in it vexed me so much, and I made so little progress in amendment, and had such frequent relapses, that I was almost ready to give up the attempt, and content myself with a faulty character in that respect, like the man

NOTICE & NOTE

EVALUATE PRINT AND GRAPHIC FEATURES

Annotate: Circle the boldface text and underline the sentence fragments Franklin uses in his daily schedule.

Analyze: How do these features help the reader understand why Franklin wrote his book? Are they effective organizers?

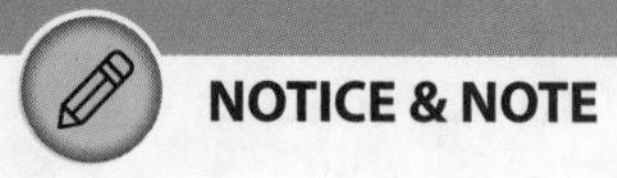

MONITOR COMPREHENSION

Annotate: Mark the phrase in paragraph 9 that tells the kind of ax the man decided was best.

Analyze: How does this story about the ax relate to Franklin's project?

incorrigible
(ĭn-kôr´ĭ-jə-bəl) *adj.* incapable of being reformed or corrected.

LANGUAGE CONVENTIONS

Annotate: Underline a short sentence in paragraph 10. Put brackets around a very long sentence.

Analyze: Explain how Franklin uses sentence variety in this paragraph.

artifice
(är´tə-fĭs) *n.* a clever means to an end.

felicity
(fĭ-lĭs´ĭ-tē) *n.* great happiness.

who, in buying an ax of a smith, my neighbor, desired to have the whole of its surface as bright as the edge. The smith consented to grind it bright for him if he would turn the wheel; he turned, while the smith pressed the broad face of the ax hard and heavily on the stone, which made the turning of it very fatiguing. The man came every now and then from the wheel to see how the work went on, and at length would take his ax as it was, without farther grinding. "No," said the smith, "turn on, turn on; we shall have it bright by-and-by; as yet, it is only speckled." "Yes," says the man, *"but I think I like a speckled ax best."* And I believe this may have been the case with many, who, having, for want of some such means as I employed, found the difficulty of obtaining good and breaking bad habits in other points of vice and virtue, have given up the struggle, and concluded that *"a speckled ax was best;"* for something, that pretended to be reason, was every now and then suggesting to me that such extreme nicety as I exacted of myself might be a kind of foppery in morals,[4] which, if it were known, would make me ridiculous; that a perfect character might be attended with the inconvenience of being envied and hated; and that a benevolent man should allow a few faults in himself, to keep his friends in countenance.

10 In truth, I found myself **incorrigible** with respect to Order; and now I am grown old, and my memory bad, I feel very sensibly the want of it. But, on the whole, though I never arrived at the perfection I had been so ambitious of obtaining, but fell short of it, yet I was, by the endeavor, a better and a happier man than I otherwise should have been if I had not attempted it; as those who aim at perfect writing by imitating the engraved copies, though they never reach the wished-for excellence of those copies, their hand is mended by the endeavor, and is tolerable while it continues fair and legible.

11 It may well be my posterity should be informed that to this little **artifice,** with the blessing of God, their ancestor owed the constant **felicity** of his life, down to his 79th year, in which this is written. What reverses may attend the reminder is in the hand of Providence; but, if they arrive, the reflection on past happiness enjoyed ought to help his bearing them with more resignation. To Temperance he ascribes his long-continued health, and what is still left to him of a good constitution; to Industry and Frugality, the early easiness of his circumstances and acquisition of his fortune, with all that knowledge that enabled him to be a useful citizen, and obtained for him some degree of reputation among the learned; to Sincerity and Justice, the confidence of his country, and the honorable employs it conferred upon him; and to the joint influence of the whole mass of the virtues, even in the imperfect state he was able to acquire them, all that

[4] **foppery in morals:** excessive regard for and concern about one's moral appearance.

evenness of temper, and that cheerfulness in conversation, which makes his company still sought for, and agreeable even to his younger acquaintance. I hope, therefore, that some of my descendants may follow the example and reap the benefit.

CHECK YOUR UNDERSTANDING

Answer these questions before moving on to the **Analyze the Text** section on the following page.

1 What reason did Franklin have for placing *Temperance* first?

A He hoped to achieve the most difficult goal first.

B Mastering it would make the others easier to achieve.

C Since it was mentioned by other writers, it must be most important.

D Temperance was the virtue he valued most.

2 Why did Franklin make a book with a chart for each of the virtues?

F To keep track of how well he was doing

G To share the information with the people he knew

H Because his friend Pythagoras told him to do it

J He preferred thinking in visual terms

3 What did Franklin think of the endeavor, once he realized he would not achieve his original goals?

A He believed the endeavor had been a waste of time and nothing had been gained.

B He decided that his ideas about reason and order were probably wrong.

C He was better and happier than he would have been if he hadn't tried.

D He believed he was a worse man than he had been when he started out.

RESPOND

ANALYZE THE TEXT

Support your responses with evidence from the text. NOTEBOOK

1. **Evaluate** How did the print and graphic features Franklin included help you understand his progress on his project?
2. **Draw Conclusions** How do you think Franklin's ideas about human perfectibility changed as a result of his endeavor? Cite specific details that suggest when his view changed.
3. **Infer** Do you think Franklin's descendants would have benefited from his example, as he hoped they would? Why or why not?
4. **Evaluate** Some critics consider Franklin to be self-righteous and materialistic; others have ridiculed his plan for moral perfection as regimented and superficial. Do you find any evidence for these charges in the excerpt? Explain.
5. **Notice & Note** Franklin's stated goal is "to live without committing any fault at any time." Does Franklin's extreme language convince you that this goal is important? Is this a reasonable expectation? Explain, citing evidence from the text.

RESEARCH

RESEARCH TIP

For information about Franklin and the postal service, check the website of the United States Postal Service. The Franklin Institute is also a good source of information.

Benjamin Franklin was a remarkable, brilliant, and accomplished person. Research his life and identify some of his accomplishments. Use what you learn to answer these questions.

QUESTION	ANSWER
What are two things Benjamin Franklin invented?	
What was Franklin's association with the postal service?	
In what foreign country did Franklin work during the American Revolution, and what job did he have there?	

Extend Find another work written by Benjamin Franklin and compare the virtues and character flaws revealed in that work to those in *The Autobiography.* With a partner, discuss what it would have been like to spend time with the Ben Franklin portrayed in both selections.

CREATE AND DISCUSS

Go to **Developing a Topic** in the **Writing Studio** for help.

Write an Essay Write an autobiographical essay about a time you tried to learn something new or improve existing skills. Review your notes on the Quick Start activity before you begin.

- ❑ Decide which project from your past would make an interesting topic for an autobiographical essay.
- ❑ Be sure to give details about your plans, your efforts, and the outcome of your project.
- ❑ Write a conclusion where you explain what you learned and whether you successfully achieved your goal.

Go to **Participating in Collaborative Discussions** in the **Speaking and Listening Studio** for help.

Discuss Autobiographies In a small group, discuss what you learned about making goals and carrying out plans to meet them. Compare your experience to what you read about Franklin and to what others share.

- ❑ Talk about how reading Franklin's autobiography affected your thinking about planning and achieving goals.
- ❑ Share the types of projects, how you approached them, and what the outcomes were.
- ❑ Discuss any similarities between the projects in the group and even with Franklin's project.
- ❑ Summarize the lessons you learned from your experiences.

RESPOND TO THE ESSENTIAL QUESTION

How do we transform our lives?

Gather Information Review your annotations and notes on this excerpt from *The Autobiography.* Then, add relevant information to your Response Log. As you determine which information to include, think about:

- why we strive for self-improvement
- how to balance the desire for a big change with the need to set realistic goals
- the best way to pursue a goal

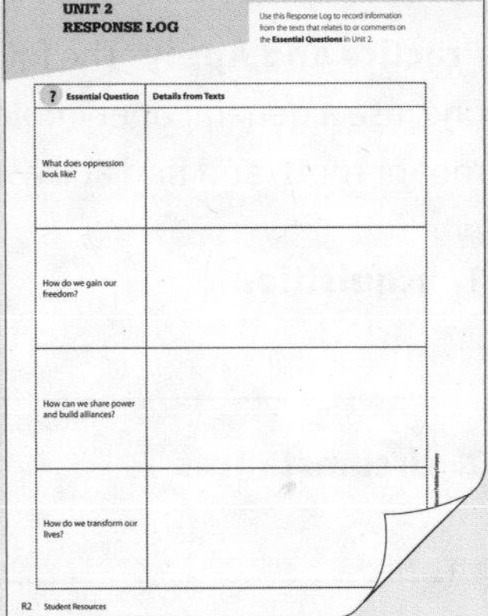

UNIT 2
RESPONSE LOG

Use this Response Log to record information from the texts that relates to or comments on the **Essential Questions** in Unit 2.

? Essential Question	Details from Texts
What does oppression look like?	
How do we gain our freedom?	
How can we share power and build alliances?	
How do we transform our lives?	

R2 Student Resources

ACADEMIC VOCABULARY

As you write and discuss what you learned from *The Autobiography,* be sure to use the Academic Vocabulary words. Check off each of the words that you use.

- ❑ **contrary**
- ❑ **founder**
- ❑ **ideological**
- ❑ **publication**
- ❑ **revolution**

RESPOND

CRITICAL VOCABULARY

WORD BANK

trifling	**eradicate**
unremitting	**incorrigible**
affluence	**artifice**
contrive	**felicity**

Practice and Apply Show your understanding of the vocabulary words by answering these questions.

1. What is a project that requires **unremitting** attention?
2. What news might give you a feeling of **felicity?**
3. What would people wear to display their **affluence?**
4. How would you **eradicate** weeds from a field of grass?
5. Is a **trifling** issue something you should spend much time on?
6. Would you describe a hero or a villain as **incorrigible?**
7. Would someone use **artifice** to perform a magic trick?
8. Why might you **contrive** a way to get the day off?

VOCABULARY STRATEGY: Latin Roots

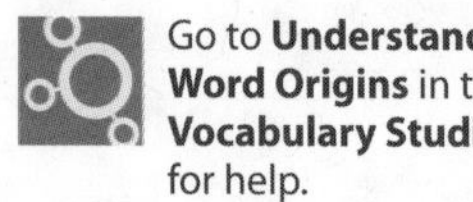

Go to **Understanding Word Origins** in the **Vocabulary Studio** for help.

A **root** is a word part that carries the core meaning of a word. In most cases, roots combine with other word parts to form whole words. Often, these word parts are prefixes or suffixes, but sometimes they are additional roots. Groups of words with the same root are called **word families**.

English has collected words and roots from around the world. Thousands of those roots came into English from Latin. Knowing some of the roots can help you figure out other words in the family. For example, the words *number, numerous,* and *enumeration* are all in one word family with the Latin root *numerus,* meaning "a number or quantity."

Practice and Apply The following words appear in the selection. For each one, use a general or etymological dictionary in print or online to identify the root or roots, and find at least one other word in the same word family.

1. **acquisition**

____

2. **circumstances**

____

3. **conduct**

____

4. **judge**

____

LANGUAGE CONVENTIONS: Standard English

Standard English requires a writer to follow the **conventions** of sentence structure, usage, and punctuation that demonstrate a writer understands the expectations of the audience. Resources called **style guides** provide valuable assistance to writers in identifying departures from those conventions and suggesting ways to improve the text. Some word processing programs come with a grammar and style checker that a writer can use as a tool to check a text for possible errors. These checkers provide context-appropriate suggestions to correct such issues as sentence fragments, lack of subject-verb agreement, or punctuation problems. Print and online style guides explain the rules of Standard English and show examples of correct and incorrect usage to help illustrate those rules.

A style guide can also provide suggestions on how to undertake such tasks as varying sentence structure. It can provide examples of various sentence types, such as these examples from the selection:

Simple sentence: *It was about this time I conceived the bold and arduous project of arriving at moral perfection.*
Compound sentence: *I entered upon the execution of this plan for self-examination, and continued it with occasional intermissions for some time.*
Complex sentence: *As I knew, or thought I knew, what was right and wrong, I did not see why I might not always do the one and avoid the other.*

Practice and Apply Write four or five sentences stating your opinion of Franklin's character and judgment based on the excerpt from *The Autobiography*. Be sure to include a mix of sentence structures to give variety to your writing. Then, check your sentences against a style guide to ensure that you have structured sentences and used punctuation correctly.

Go to **Sentence Structure** in the **Grammar Studio** for help.

POEM

ON BEING BROUGHT FROM AFRICA TO AMERICA

by **Phillis Wheatley**

pages 159–161

ESSENTIAL QUESTION:

What does oppression look like?

COMPARE THEMES

As you read, note sound devices, voice, and key details in each poem to help you identify the poem's theme, or message about life, society, or human nature. Then, think about how the themes of the two poems relate to each other. After you read the poems, you will collaborate with a small group on a final project.

POEM

SYMPATHY

by **Paul Laurence Dunbar**

pages 162–163

QUICK START

What are you grateful for in your life? What do you long for? Write your ideas in the chart.

GRATEFUL FOR	WISH FOR

ANALYZE SPEAKER

A poem's **speaker**, like the narrator of a story, is the voice that "talks" to the reader. Sometimes, the speaker can be identified with the poet; at other times—even if the poem relies on a first-person perspective—the speaker may be a **persona,** a fictional character adopted by the poet. As you read, note clues about the character of each poem's speaker. Note feelings and ideas being expressed, the speaker's use of language, hints about the speaker's experiences, and the speaker's tone.

GENRE ELEMENTS: POETRY

- develops a theme (or multiple themes) in the work
- is more condensed and suggestive than prose
- uses a variety of sound devices to create voice, add emphasis, and convey meaning

ANALYZE THEME

The **theme** of a work is its message about life or human nature. This message may be stated directly, but readers often must **infer,** or make a logical guess, about it. To infer a poem's theme, note details about its speaker, its key ideas, the feelings it expresses, and the poet's use of imagery, language, and voice.

Use the chart to help you keep track of important details and clues that suggest each poem's theme or themes.

"ON BEING BROUGHT FROM AFRICA TO AMERICA"	"SYMPATHY"
Details and Suggested Theme(s)	Details and Suggested Theme(s)

The poems you are about to read give you the opportunity to compare how different texts treat similar themes. As you read the poems, think about the similarities and differences between them.

GET READY

ANALYZE SOUND DEVICES AND VOICE

Poets use a number of different **sound devices**—such as rhyme, rhythm, alliteration, repetition, and meter—to emphasize ideas, add a musical quality, create mood, and reinforce meaning in their poems.

These devices also contribute to the **voice** of a poem, the unique style of the author or speaker. Wheatley and Dunbar use rhyme, rhythm, repetition, and alliteration, among other sound devices, as they develop their distinct voices.

Rhyme is the occurrence of similar or identical sounds at the end of two or more words. Rhyme that occurs within a single line of poetry, such as *suite, heat,* and *complete* is called **internal rhyme.** Rhyme that appears at the end of a set of lines is called **end rhyme.**

Rhythm refers to the "beat" of a poem and is created by the pattern of stressed and unstressed syllables. **Meter** is the repetition of a regular rhythmic unit in a line.

Repetition is a poetic device in which a sound, word, phrase, or line is repeated to emphasize the importance of an idea, as well as to create an appealing rhythm.

Alliteration is the repetition of consonant sounds at the beginnings of words, placing emphasis on those words, their sounds, and their meanings.

As you read, notice the way that the two poets use each of these sound devices to create their unique voices, draw attention to important ideas, convey meaning, and help suggest theme.

ANNOTATION MODEL

NOTICE & NOTE

As you read, notice the use of sound devices and how these develop the voice and the theme of each poem. In the example below, you can see one reader's notes on "Sympathy."

I know what the caged bird feels, alas!
When the sun is bright on the upland slopes;
When the wind stirs soft through the springing grass,
And the river flows like a stream of glass;
When the first bird sings and the first bud opes,

The phrase "alas!" in the first line expresses the speaker's sorrow.

Repetition of "When the" draws attention to details about springtime, emphasizing the longings a caged bird might feel.

BACKGROUND

***Phillis Wheatley** was the first African American to publish a book of poetry. Born in West Africa, probably in 1753, she was enslaved in 1761 and brought to Boston. There she was purchased by a local merchant, John Wheatley. He named the little girl Phillis, and she became the personal assistant of his wife, Susannah. Phillis learned to read and write English very quickly, and the Wheatley family tutored her in Latin, Greek, English literature, and the classics. Wheatley was quickly recognized as a prodigy, and respect for her talents grew. She published her first poem at age 13 in 1767. The poem was about two men who nearly drowned at sea, and it was printed in the* Newport Mercury.

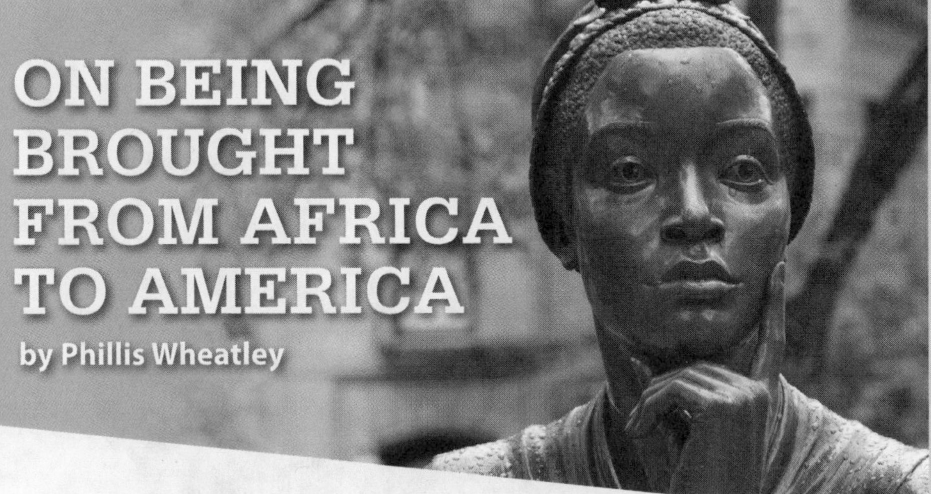

ON BEING BROUGHT FROM AFRICA TO AMERICA

by Phillis Wheatley

Wheatley went on to publish a number of other poems, increasing her fame, and by 1770 her work was known throughout the colonies.

In 1773, Wheatley published her first and only book of verse, Poems on Various Subjects, Religious and Moral. *To prove she was the actual author of the book, 17 men who lived in Boston, including John Hancock, had to verify that Wheatley wrote the poems. Their assertions appear in the preface of the book.*

Poems on Various Subjects *is considered a landmark achievement in U.S. history. With its publication, Wheatley became the first African American and first U.S. slave to publish a book of poems. She also became the third American woman to do so.*

Phillis was given her freedom after Susannah Wheatley's death in 1774. In 1778, she married John Peters. They had three children together—all died in infancy. The couple fell into extreme poverty, and Phillis was forced to work as a maid. Phillis Wheatley died in her early 30s in 1784.

NOTICE & NOTE

Notice & Note

Use the side margins to notice and note signposts in the text.

ANALYZE THEME

Annotate: Mark the words or phrases in the poem that help develop the theme.

Interpret: What do these words and phrases suggest about the speaker's view of life in the Colonies?

PREPARE TO COMPARE

As you read, note how each of the following literary elements helps convey the theme of the poem and communicate information about the speaker's circumstances, thoughts, feelings, and character.

- *rhyme and rhythm*
- *alliteration*
- *word choice*
- *voice*

'Twas mercy brought me from my *Pagan* land,
Taught my benighted[1] soul to understand
That there's a God, that there's a *Saviour* too:
Once I redemption neither sought nor knew.

[1] **benighted:** ignorant.

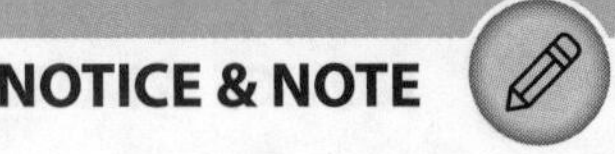

Some view our sable[2] race with scornful eye,
"Their colour is a diabolic die."[3]
Remember, *Christians, Negroes*, black as *Cain*,
May be refin'd, and join th' angelic train.

---

[2] **sable:** dark brown or black.

[3] **diabolic die:** an evil or devilish coloring agent (dye).

ANALYZE SOUND DEVICES AND VOICE

Annotate: In lines 7 and 8, mark the end rhymes and the phrases in which they appear.

Evaluate: What contrast does the rhyme help emphasize? Why is this contrast significant?

CHECK YOUR UNDERSTANDING

Answer these questions about "On Being Brought from Africa to America" before moving on to the next selection.

1 A theme of "On Being Brought from Africa to America" is —

A freedom rests on the ability to read

B all people need understanding

C bigotry toward African Americans is morally wrong

D being brought to America from Africa was an act of oppression

2 Who is the speaker in the poem?

F An enslaved woman in America

G A free woman of color in America

H A Christian slave owner

J The friend of a Pagan slave

3 Which phrase reveals the speaker's attitude about going to America?

A *'Twas mercy brought me*

B *redemption neither sought nor knew*

C *our sable race*

D *May be refin'd*

4 How would you characterize the voice in "On Being Brought from Africa to America"?

F Angry

G Grateful

H Disturbed

J Indifferent

NOTICE & NOTE

BACKGROUND

Paul Laurence Dunbar *was born in Ohio in 1872, the son of former slaves. He was the only African American student in his high school class, and he published poems in the school newspaper, eventually becoming the editor. He self-published his first collection of poems titled* Oak and Ivy *in 1893. Dunbar was one of the premier African American poets in the United States. Dunbar continued publishing poetry and other writing until his death at age 33 in 1906.*

SYMPATHY

by Paul Laurence Dunbar

PREPARE TO COMPARE

As you read, look for how the author uses the following devices to convey the theme of the poem.

- *repetition and rhyme*
- *imagery and sensory detail*
- *alliteration*
- *voice*

Notice & Note

Use the side margins to notice and note signposts in the text.

ANALYZE SOUND DEVICES AND VOICE

Annotate: In stanzas 1 and 2, mark the phrase that is repeated.

Evaluate: How does the repetition of this phrase create a distinct poetic voice? Explain.

I know what the caged bird feels, alas!
    When the sun is bright on the upland slopes;
When the wind stirs soft through the springing grass,
And the river flows like a stream of glass;
    When the first bird sings and the first bud opes[1],
And the faint perfume from its chalice steals—
I know what the caged bird feels!

[1] **ope:** *v.* open.

I know why the caged bird beats his wing
Till its blood is red on the cruel bars;
For he must fly back to his perch and cling
When he fain[2] would be on the bough a-swing;
And a pain still throbs in the old, old scars
And they pulse again with a keener sting—
I know why he beats his wing!

I know why the caged bird sings, ah me,
When his wing is bruised and his bosom sore,—
When he beats his bars and he would be free;
It is not a carol of joy or glee,
But a prayer that he sends from his heart's deep core,
But a plea, that upward to Heaven he flings—
I know why the caged bird sings!

[2] **fain:** *adv.* happily, gladly.

ANALYZE THEME

Annotate: In lines 18–20, mark the words and phrases that refer to the bird's song.

Contrast: What two ways of interpreting the bird's song are noted by the speaker? How does the difference between these two help develop the theme?

CHECK YOUR UNDERSTANDING

Answer these questions about "Sympathy" before moving on to the **Analyze the Texts** section on the following page.

1 Which action stirs feelings in the caged bird?

A When it is caged

B When it hears the first bird sing

C When it feels pain from old scars

D When it prays

2 Which line in "Sympathy" describes what the bird wants to do?

F *When the sun is bright on the upland slopes;*

G *For he must fly back to his perch and cling*

H *When he fain would be on the bough a-swing;*

J *But a plea, that upward to Heaven he flings—*

3 Which line in the poem most directly refers to the conditions of slavery?

A *When the wind stirs soft through the springing grass,*

B *For he must fly back to his perch and cling*

C *It is not a carol of joy or glee,*

D *And a pain still throbs in the old, old scars*

RESPOND

ANALYZE THE TEXTS

Support your responses with evidence from the texts. NOTEBOOK

1. **Interpret** Reread lines 5–6 of "On Being Brought from Africa to America." What do these lines tell you about the speaker's experience? How do these lines help develop the theme?

2. **Interpret** Reread lines 1–7 of "Sympathy." How would you describe the voice in this stanza? Cite text evidence to support your response.

3. **Analyze** How would you describe the rhyme scheme of the stanzas in the poem "Sympathy"? What words are emphasized through Dunbar's use of alliteration? What is the effect of each sound device?

4. **Contrast** What effect does the contrast between the imagery in the first stanza and the second stanza of "Sympathy" have? How does this contrast help develop the poem's theme?

5. **Connect** Think about the themes expressed by each poem. Which theme resonates with you the most? State the theme, and explain your response using details from the poem.

RESEARCH

RESEARCH TIP

If you use an Internet search to conduct your research, be sure to use reliable sources for the information you find. Look for sources authored or reviewed by experts on Dunbar's life and poetry.

Conduct research and answer the following questions to learn more about Paul Laurence Dunbar.

QUESTION	ANSWER
What other genres did Dunbar write in? Cite at least three examples.	
What well-known abolitionist did Dunbar write a poem about?	
What well-known book did a line from Dunbar's "Sympathy" give its title to?	

Extend In what ways did Paul Laurence Dunbar influence African American writers who came after him? Write a paragraph that describes Dunbar's influence and legacy.

CREATE AND PRESENT

Write a Prose Adaptation Choose the poem you like best, and write a prose adaptation that contains the same themes and supporting details as the poem.

- ❑ Give your story a title, and include elements of a short story, such as plot, character, narrator, and details about setting.
- ❑ Use the language and style appropriate for a short story.

Present a Theme Board With your group, present a theme board listing the major themes of "On Being Brought from Africa to America" and "Sympathy."

- ❑ Create three headings by writing the name of the first poem on the left side of the board, the phrase "Common Themes" at the center, and the name of the second poem on the right.
- ❑ Identify possible themes in the first poem, and list those themes below its title. Do the same thing for the second poem.
- ❑ Next, add text quotes and evidence from the poems for each theme.
- ❑ Then, determine the common themes of the two poems. Write those themes below "Common Themes" at the board's center.
- ❑ Finally, as a group, present your board to the class, explaining why you chose both the common and individual themes for each poem.

Go to **Writing Narratives** in the **Writing Studio** for help.

Go to **Participating in Collaborative Discussions** in the **Speaking and Listening Studio** for help.

RESPOND TO THE ESSENTIAL QUESTION

What does oppression look like?

Gather Information Review your annotations and notes on "On Being Brought from Africa to America" and "Sympathy." Then, add relevant details to your Response Log. As you determine which information to include, think about:

- what the theme of each poem suggests about oppression
- what mechanisms of oppression are suggested by each poem
- the imagery the writers use in their descriptions of oppression

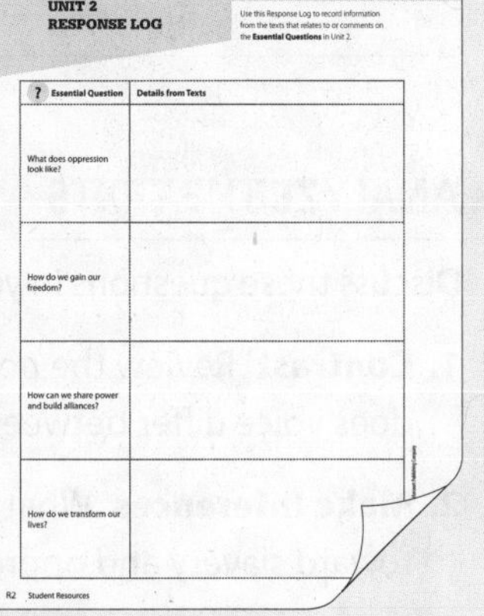

UNIT 2 RESPONSE LOG

Use this Response Log to record information from the texts that relates to or comments on the **Essential Questions** in Unit 2.

? Essential Question	Details from Texts
What does oppression look like?	
How do we gain our freedom?	
How can we share power and build alliances?	
How do we transform our lives?	

R2 Student Resources

ACADEMIC VOCABULARY

As you write and discuss what you learned from the poems, be sure to use the Academic Vocabulary words. Check off each of the words that you use.

- ❑ **contrary**
- ❑ **founder**
- ❑ **ideological**
- ❑ **publication**
- ❑ **revolution**

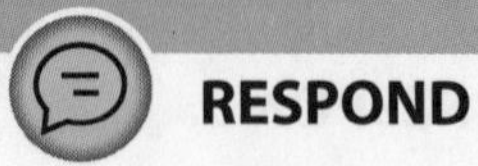

Collaborate & Compare

COMPARE THEMES

ON BEING BROUGHT FROM AFRICA TO AMERICA
by Phillis Wheatley

Both "On Being Brought from Africa to America" and "Sympathy" deal with the issues of slavery and oppression, although they address the topics in very different ways. Each has a specific **theme,** or message about life, society, and human nature that the poet develops over the course of the poem.

You can evaluate important details to determine the theme of a poem. You can also infer a theme based on the speaker's voice and point of view, and on sound devices. As you examine the poems to determine theme(s), consider:

- **Important details**—What information is provided by each poem's speaker?
- **Voice and point of view**—Who is speaking? What does the speaker feel, want, or believe?
- **Sound devices**—Does the poet use rhyme, repetition, or other sound devices to convey important information? What do the devices suggest?

With your group, complete the chart with details from both poems.

	"ON BEING BROUGHT FROM AFRICA TO AMERICA"	"SYMPATHY"
Important Details		
Voice and Point of View		
Sound Devices		

ANALYZE THE TEXTS

Discuss these questions in your group.

1. **Contrast** Review the notes you made on voice in the chart. In what ways does voice differ between the two poems? Explain.
2. **Make Inferences** What inference(s) can you make about the attitude toward slavery and oppression expressed by each poem?
3. **Evaluate** Both poems rhyme. Which poem's rhyme scheme did you find to be the most engaging? Explain why.
4. **Interpret** What role does religion or religious faith play in each poem? Cite evidence from the poems in your discussion.

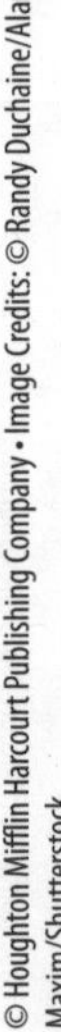

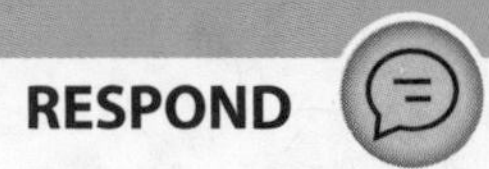

COLLABORATE AND PRESENT

Go to **Giving a Presentation** in the **Speaking and Listening Studio** for help.

Now, your group can continue exploring the ideas expressed in the poems by analyzing and comparing their themes. You can use information from the earlier Create and Present activity, if you desire. Follow these steps:

1. **Determine the important details** With your group, review your chart and determine which details are most important. Decide how you want to present your analysis of the poems' themes using text evidence.
2. **Create theme statements** Decide as a group what the theme or themes are in each poem. You can use a chart to organize your ideas.

DETAIL FROM "ON BEING BROUGHT FROM AFRICA TO AMERICA"	DETAIL FROM "ON BEING BROUGHT FROM AFRICA TO AMERICA"	THEME
DETAIL FROM "SYMPATHY"	**DETAIL FROM "SYMPATHY"**	**THEME**

3. **Compare themes** Discuss with your group similarities and differences in the themes of the poems. Listen actively to members of your group, and ask each other to clarify any points that aren't clear. Doing this will strengthen what your group presents to the class.
4. **Present to the class** Now it's time to present your ideas to the class. Make sure your statement of each poem's theme(s) is clear and understandable. Discuss similarities and differences in the themes you have identified, ask for and answer questions from the class, and respond politely to any disagreements.

LETTER

LETTER TO JOHN ADAMS

by **Abigail Adams**

pages 171–173

COMPARE VOICE AND TONE

As you read, look for details that convey the voice, or distinct personality, of each author. Also pay attention to the tone, or attitude of each author toward her subject. Consider similarities and differences in voice and tone as the two authors address similar issues at different times in history. After you read both works, you will collaborate with a small group on a final project.

ESSENTIAL QUESTION:

How can we share power and build alliances?

ESSAY

from

LEAN IN

by **Sheryl Sandberg**

pages 181–185

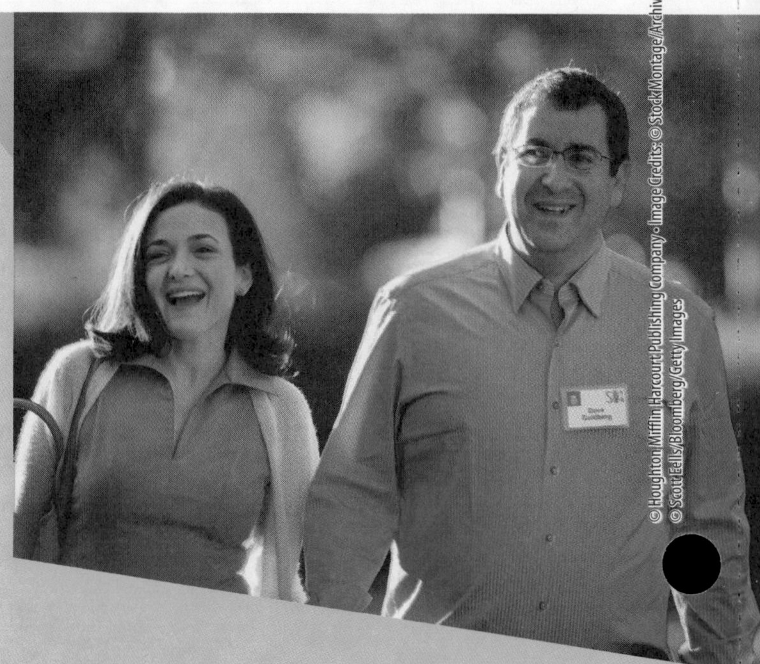

Letter to John Adams

QUICK START

How do you communicate with the people you know and love? Does how you communicate change in different circumstances? With a group, discuss how major events might affect how we communicate with others.

ANALYZE AUTHOR'S PURPOSE

An **author's purpose** is the reason he or she writes a text. Authors might write to persuade, inform, explain, express thoughts or feelings, motivate, or entertain. Most authors have more than one purpose for writing. For example, a writer may want to inform readers about an important topic, but he or she may also want to persuade readers to agree with certain ideas or values. You can determine an author's purpose by **making inferences,** or logical guesses, based on the use of key details, word choice, and tone in the text.

An author's purpose may depend on her particular audience. Abigail Adams has more than one purpose for writing to her husband, John. She was an important advisor, so she focused on issues of the day, but she was also his wife and shared news about their children.

As you read, look for clues to Abigail Adams's purposes for writing a letter to her husband. Use a chart like this to record details from the text and her purpose for including them.

ADAMS'S TEXT	INFERENCE ABOUT PURPOSE

GENRE ELEMENTS: LETTER

- is addressed to a specific person or group
- may have a formal or informal tone, depending on writer's purpose
- may convey personal information, share opinions, or make requests

ANALYZE LANGUAGE: Voice and Tone

An author's **voice** is his or her unique use of language, which allows the reader to "hear" a human personality in the writing. The elements of style that determine a writer's voice include syntax, diction, and tone.

Diction is a writer's choice of words. Diction includes both vocabulary (words) and **syntax** (arrangement of words). Diction can be formal or informal, common or technical, abstract or concrete. Diction can also reveal an author's **tone,** or attitude toward a subject.

As you read this letter, think about how the diction and syntax help communicate Adams's thoughts and her attitude toward the issues of freedom and liberty.

GET READY

CRITICAL VOCABULARY

deprive **tyrannical** **impunity** **abhor**

To see how many Critical Vocabulary words you already know, write the correct word after each definition.

1. exemption from punishment, penalty, or harm: __________
2. to keep from possessing or enjoying; deny: __________
3. to regard with horror or loathing; detest: __________
4. despotic and oppressive: __________

LANGUAGE CONVENTIONS

Formal English Today, formal English is used almost exclusively in formal situations, such as in legal documents and in speeches. However, you may notice that the language in a fairly informal piece of writing, such as a letter, composed in the past seems formal relative to writing today. Notice the formal language and complex syntax in the passage below.

> **I have sometimes been ready to think that the passion for Liberty cannot be Eaquelly Strong in the Breasts of those who have been accustomed to deprive their fellow Creatures of theirs.**

It was customary to capitalize nouns in certain categories, such as concrete objects, and nouns that the writer considered important. As you read, note Adams's use of formal English in the text and its effect on voice and tone.

ANNOTATION MODEL

NOTICE & NOTE

As you read, look for details that suggest Adams's purpose for writing a letter to her husband. Notice phrases that convey the writer's voice and suggest her tone. Here are one reader's notes about Abigail Adams's letter.

I wish you would ever write me a Letter half as long as I write you; and tell me if you may where your Fleet are gone? What sort of Defence Virginia can make against our common Enemy? Whether it is so situated as to make an able Defence?	Her husband doesn't write as often as she'd like. Her tone seems urgent. She repeats "Defence" and also capitalizes it. She must be greatly concerned about military matters.

BACKGROUND

***Abigail Adams** was educated by her parents and grandparents since public education for women was limited. Access to her family's library grounded her in the classics, history, government, law, and philosophy. Married in 1764 to future U.S. President John Adams, Abigail had four children by the time John was sent to the Second Continental Congress in 1774. After that, John was absent more than he was at home. Abigail cared for the farm and the children, and she began the correspondence that would continue for the rest of her life. Her letters reflect life at the time but are also filled with her passion for politics and her intense patriotism.*

LETTER TO JOHN ADAMS

Letter by Abigail Adams

PREPARE TO COMPARE

As you read, make note of what Abigail Adams says about the treatment of women and how her tone supports what she says. This will help you compare her letter to the essay from Lean In *which follows.*

Abigail Adams to John Adams

Braintree March 31 1776

1 I wish you would ever write me a Letter half as long as I write you; and tell me if you may where your Fleet are gone? What sort of Defence Virginia can make against our common Enemy?[1] Whether it is so situated as to make an able Defence? Are not the Gentery Lords and the common people vassals,[2] are they not like the uncivilized Natives Brittain represents us to be? I hope their Riffel Men who have shewen themselves very savage and even Blood thirsty; are not a specimen of the Generality of the people. I am willing to allow the Colony great merrit for having

[1] **common Enemy:** Great Britain; Virginia and Massachusetts were the oldest colonies, and both were influential, but their cultures were very different. Adams is wondering here if Virginia will be helpful if the colonies break with Britain.

[2] **vassal** (vă´səl): a subordinate or dependent.

NOTICE & NOTE

Notice & Note

Use the side margins to notice and note signposts in the text.

ANALYZE VOICE AND TONE

Annotate: Mark the four question marks in the opening sentences of the letter.

Infer: How does the series of questions help establish the voice and tone of the letter?

NOTICE & NOTE

deprive
(dĭ-prīv´) *v.* to keep from possessing or enjoying; deny.

QUOTED WORDS

Notice & Note: Mark the "christian principal" that Adams, the daughter of a minister, refers to in paragraph 1.

Analyze: What does this reveal about her attitude toward slavery in the colony?

tyrannical
(tĭ-răn´ĭ-kəl): *adj.* characteristic of a tyrant or tyranny; despotic and oppressive.

impunity
(ĭm-pyōō´nĭ-tē): *n.* exemption from punishment, penalty, or harm.

abhor
(ăb-hôr´): *v.* to regard with horror or loathing; detest.

ANALYZE AUTHOR'S PURPOSE

Annotate: In paragraph 3, mark phrases describing the nature of men, according to Adams.

Draw Conclusions: What might her purpose for using these phrases be?

LANGUAGE CONVENTIONS

Annotate: Mark each "title" Adams refers to in paragraph 3.

Analyze: What effect does her choice of these words have on her tone?

produced a Washington but they have been shamefully duped by a Dunmore.[3] I have sometimes been ready to think that the passion for Liberty cannot be Eaquelly Strong in the Breasts of those who have been accustomed to **deprive** their fellow Creatures of theirs.[4] Of this I am certain that it is not founded upon that generous and christian principal of doing to others as we would that others should do unto us. . . .

2 I long to hear that you have declared an independancy—and by the way in the new Code of Laws which I suppose it will be necessary for you to make I desire you would Remember the Ladies, and be more generous and favourable to them than your ancestors. Do not put such unlimited power into the hands of the Husbands. Remember all Men would be tyrants if they could. If perticuliar care and attention is not paid to the Laidies we are determined to foment[5] a Rebelion, and will not hold ourselves bound by any Laws in which we have no voice, or Representation.

3 That your Sex are Naturally **Tyrannical** is a Truth so thoroughly established as to admit of no dispute, but such of you as wish to be happy willingly give up the harsh title of Master for the more tender and endearing one of Friend. Why then, not put it out of the power of the vicious and the Lawless to use us with cruelty and indignity with **impunity**. Men of Sense in all Ages **abhor** those customs which treat us only as the vassals of your Sex. Regard us then as Beings placed by providence under your protection and in immitation of the Supreme Being make use of that power only for our happiness.

---

[3] **Dunmore:** Lord Dunmore was the last British governor of Virginia. In April 1775, in reaction to events in Boston, Dunmore had all the gunpowder in Williamsburg confiscated. Then, in November 1775, he offered freedom to any slaves or indentured servants who would leave and join the British to fight the colonists.

[4] **I have sometimes . . . of theirs:** Adams is referring to slavery, which was common in Virginia. She questioned whether those who denied slaves freedom would not really have a passion for freedom.

[5] **foment** (fō-mĕnt´): to arouse or incite.

CHECK YOUR UNDERSTANDING

Answer these questions before moving on to the **Analyze the Text** section on the following page.

1 What is the complaint with which Abigail Adams begins the letter?

A Her husband's letters are too short.

B Her husband is in Philadelphia.

C Her husband is going to Virginia.

D Her husband is with the Fleet.

2 Why does Abigail Adams think Virginia might not be passionate about liberty?

F It is a new colony.

G It allows slavery.

H Washington lives there.

J There are no rifles.

3 What does Abigail Adams predict will happen if no laws protect women?

A Men will start becoming tyrannical.

B Men will imitate the supreme being.

C Men will give up the title of master.

D Women will incite a revolt of their own.

RESPOND

ANALYZE THE TEXT

Support your responses with evidence from the text. NOTEBOOK

1. **Summarize** What is Abigail Adams trying to determine in the first paragraph?
2. **Analyze** How does the writer's use of diction help establish both her voice and tone of the letter? Cite examples of words that convey Adams's tone.
3. **Cite Evidence** What details suggest that Abigail Adams may have a low opinion of Virginians as a whole? How does including this information support her purpose?
4. **Draw Conclusions** What can you determine about the relationship between John and Abigail Adams based on what she writes about men? Why do you think she includes this information?
5. **Evaluate** Do you think Abigail Adams does a good job of presenting her case for the need to pass laws that protect women? Support your response with evidence from the text.

RESEARCH

The influence and importance of the Adams family in America's early history was profound. Find at least one interesting fact about or quotation from each family member listed. Note how this fact or quote reveals the person's influence.

RESEARCH TIP
Organizations that focus on the American Revolution, such as the Colonial Williamsburg Foundation, are excellent sources of information on the people and events from the founding of the United States.

FAMILY MEMBER	INTERESTING INFORMATION	INFLUENCE
John Adams		
Abigail Adams		
Samuel Adams		
John Quincy Adams		

Extend Explain why her relationships with John Adams and John Quincy Adams put Abigail Adams in a remarkable position to influence the country during this important period of time.

CREATE AND DISCUSS

Write a Letter Write a letter to a historical figure you have studied who lived during the American Revolution.

- ❑ Decide on a person to whom you would like to write.
- ❑ Relate details about events with which you are familiar.
- ❑ Write in a formal style that is appropriate for the time period. Review "Letter to John Adams" for examples and inspiration.
- ❑ Encourage the person you are writing to to take some sort of action.
- ❑ Discuss anything else appropriate about life at that time.

Go to **Writing Informative Texts** in the **Writing Studio** for help with formal style.

Discuss with a Small Group Discuss why you think letters were so important at the time of the American Revolution. Compare your experience communicating with others with communication during Abigail Adams's day.

- ❑ Talk about how personal letters like Abigail Adams's can make history come to life.
- ❑ Discuss what information we get from letters that we may not get from secondary sources such as history articles.
- ❑ Read part of the letter you wrote and share what it was like writing your Revolutionary War letter.
- ❑ Discuss why you think letters have been so valued through the years.

Go to **Participating in Collaborative Discussions** in the **Speaking and Listening Studio** for help.

RESPOND TO THE ESSENTIAL QUESTION

How can we share power and build alliances?

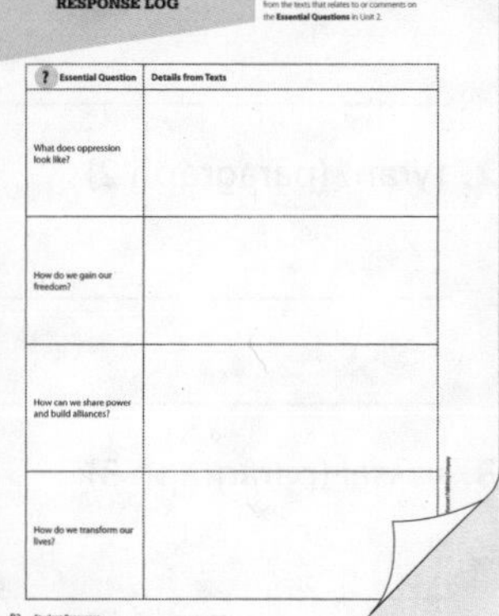

Gather Information Review your annotations and notes on "Letter to John Adams." Then, add relevant information to your Response Log. As you determine which information to include, think about:

- the issues Adams raises in the letter
- Adams's attitude toward the circumstances of women at the time
- how Adams addresses building alliances and sharing power

ACADEMIC VOCABULARY

As you write and discuss what you learned from the letter, be sure to use the Academic Vocabulary words. Check off each of the words that you use.

- ❑ **contrary**
- ❑ **founder**
- ❑ **ideological**
- ❑ **publication**
- ❑ **revolution**

RESPOND

WORD BANK
deprive
tyrannical
impunity
abhor

CRITICAL VOCABULARY

Practice and Apply In the spaces provided, write the Critical Vocabulary word that best fits the sentence.

1. The Declaration of Independence accused King George of __________ behavior.
2. Law-abiding citizens generally __________ violence and lawlessness.
3. Some criminals seem to believe they can break laws with __________.
4. The laws being passed would __________ people of their rights.

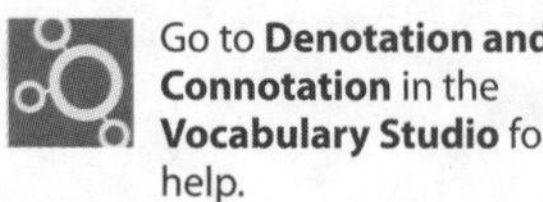

Go to **Denotation and Connotation** in the **Vocabulary Studio** for help.

VOCABULARY STRATEGY: Evaluate Nuances in Meaning

In choosing to use the Critical Vocabulary word *impunity* in this letter, Abigail Adams was conscious not only of the word's **denotation,** or dictionary definition, but also of its **connotations** and **nuances**—its emotional connections and subtle shades of meaning and tone. The dictionary definition of *impunity* is "exemption from punishment, penalty, or harm," but the word's nuances, its shades of meaning, suggest an avoidance of a deserved penalty. The overall tone of the letter, the context in which *impunity* is used, and its nuances make the word's negative connotation clear.

Practice and Apply Write the denotation, or definition for each of the following words from Abigail Adams's letter. Then, note each word's nuances and state whether the connotation is negative or positive; finally, explain how you can tell.

1. duped (paragraph 1)

____

____

2. tyrant (paragraph 2)

____

____

3. vassal (paragraph 3)

____

____

LANGUAGE CONVENTIONS: Formal English

Formal English combines **diction,** or word choice, with **syntax,** or the arrangement of words within sentences, closing adhering to the rules of grammar. In some cases, the topic or field dictates the style, requiring specific language and syntax—for example, in a legal document.

Abigail Adams used formal English because that is how educated people wrote in the 1700s. Although the letter is to her husband, her diction and syntax are formal. For example, in this sentence, while acknowledging that her husband is among those who happily treat women well, she pleads for laws that will protect women from those who are "Lawless."

> **That your Sex are Naturally Tyrannical is a Truth so thoroughly established as to admit of no dispute, but such of you as wish to be happy willingly give up the harsh title of Master for the more tender and endearing one of Friend.**

Today, although more casual forms of style are widely accepted, it is important to know how to write formally. For example, a letter to a potential employer, a report to a manager, or an essay produced for a college professor require use of formal English.

Practice and Apply Write a brief summary of "Letter to John Adams." Use formal, contemporary language, choosing words wisely, forming sentences carefully, and observing all rules of grammar.

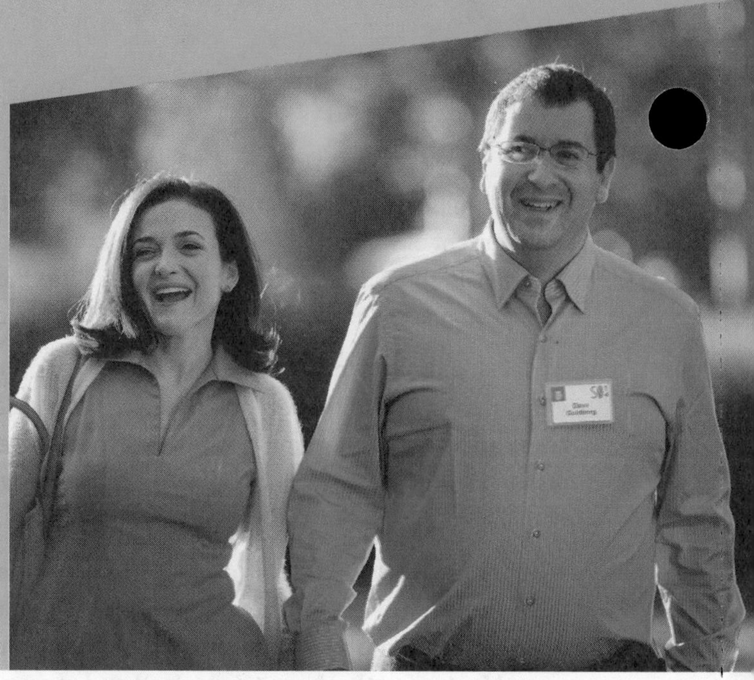

ESSAY

from

LEAN IN

by **Sheryl Sandberg**

pages 181–185

COMPARE VOICE AND TONE

Now that you've read "Letter to John Adams," read this excerpt from Sheryl Sandberg's *Lean In* and consider how her voice, tone, and concerns compare to those of Abigail Adams. As you read, think about how the ideas of *Lean In* might apply to you, either now or in the future. After you have finished, you will collaborate with a small group on a final project that involves an analysis of both texts.

ESSENTIAL QUESTION:

How can we share power and build alliances?

LETTER

LETTER TO JOHN ADAMS

by **Abigail Adams**

pages 171–173

from Lean In

QUICK START

Sometimes it is hard to know what you really want—and harder to know what it might take to get it. Think of one or two goals you have for when you graduate high school. Then, list things that you would be willing to do or to give up to gain those goals. Share and discuss your list with a partner.

ANALYZE AUTHOR'S PURPOSE

An **author's purpose** is the reason he or she writes a text. The overall purpose might be to entertain, to inform, to describe, to express an idea or feeling, or to persuade. The purpose can also be a combination of these—to inform and persuade, for example. Purpose is related to both the text's **message,** the main idea the author wants to convey, and its intended **audience,** the readers the author wants to influence or affect. Authors support their purposes by adjusting tone and style to suit their audiences. As you read, think about Sandberg's purpose, the audience she addresses, and her style and tone.

ANALYZE LANGUAGE: Voice and Tone

Sandberg's **voice,** or writing personality, differs greatly from that of Abigail Adams. Because her subject matter targets a different audience, Sandberg's **tone,** or attitude, differs, as well. Voice and tone are communicated by **diction,** or word choice, and **syntax,** or how sentences are formed. Sandberg's diction and syntax are more modern and less formal than Adams's. As you read the essay from *Lean In,* use the chart to track some of the words or phrases Sandberg uses that Adams would not. Think about what these words reveal about Sandberg, her message, her tone, and her purpose.

WORD OR PHRASE	WHAT IT REVEALS
in sync	informal, modern, tech oriented

As you read this essay, think about how the diction and syntax help communicate the personality and attitudes of Sheryl Sandberg.

GENRE ELEMENTS: ESSAY

- is a short work of nonfiction on a single subject
- may use informal language
- can be autobiographical

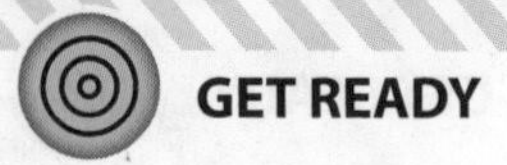

GET READY

CRITICAL VOCABULARY

demurred **watershed** **internalize** **parity**

To see how many Critical Vocabulary words you already know, use them to complete the sentences.

1. All teams should __________ the ideals of good sportsmanship.
2. Finally getting a good pitcher was a __________ in the team's season.
3. In some countries, women cannot dream of achieving __________ with men.
4. She really didn't want to do it, so she __________.

LANGUAGE CONVENTIONS

Contested Usage The English language continually grows and changes, and over time grammatical rules relax or alter. The new usage often breaks with long-standing practices and tends to make writing less formal. The style of *Lean In* is informal, as is common in many essays. Most rules are carefully observed, but some of Sandberg's usage is contested. One rule of grammar she breaks with some regularity is "Don't begin a sentence with a conjunction."

> **But it does help to tell ourselves to fight our fears at every stage of our lives.**

As you read, keep an eye out for places where Sandberg uses conjunctions at the beginning of sentences, and note any other informal usage you see.

ANNOTATION MODEL

NOTICE & NOTE

As you read, note how Sandberg uses diction and syntax to express energy and emotion in the essay. Mark interesting passages and note how they contribute to the tone of the essay or convey the author's voice. In the model, you can see one reader's notes about *Lean In*.

I headed to my first day of work as chief operating officer of a small company called Facebook. As I pulled out of my driveway, I remember feeling excited. I also felt a little nervous . . . a little anxious . . . okay, maybe even a little scared about this new challenge. It wasn't anything specific that concerned me.

The choice of words "excited," "nervous," "anxious," and "scared" makes the tone edgy—energy mixed with fear.

Use of ". . ." adds pauses, a sense of thoughtfulness.

BACKGROUND

Sheryl Sandberg *(1969–) Brilliant and motivated, with degrees in economics and business from Harvard, Sandberg became chief of staff in the U.S. Treasury Department, then vice president at Google, and in 2008, chief operating officer at Facebook.* Lean In *became her philosophy, book title, and also the name of an organization founded by Sandberg. Critics pointed out that her methods worked but came at a cost. That didn't slow Sandberg down. By 2014 she was a billionaire. In 2015 Sandberg's husband died suddenly, and Sandberg began to rethink some of her goals. Today, she is still with Facebook, but also helps women dealing with grief.*

from LEAN IN

Essay by Sheryl Sandberg

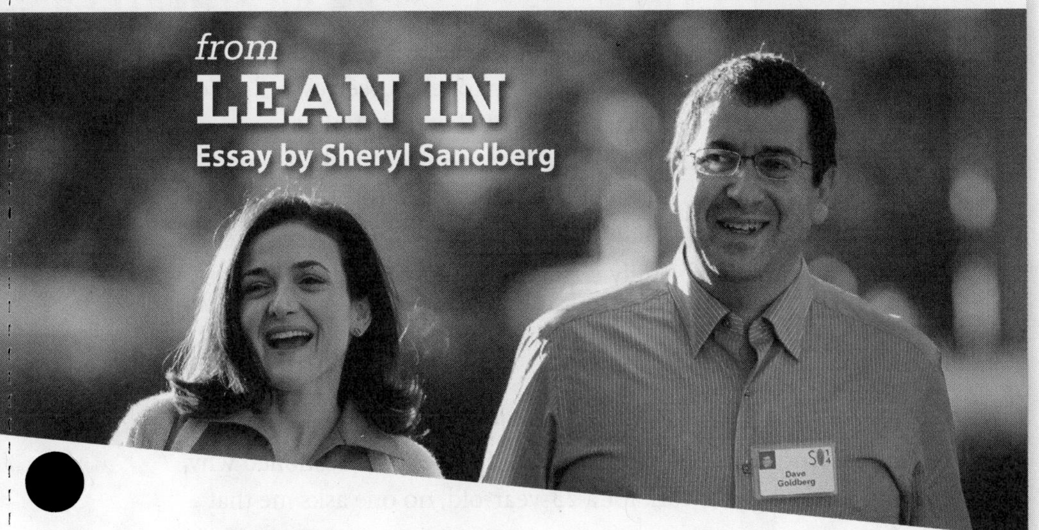

PREPARE TO COMPARE

As you read, pay attention to both the style and content of the essay. Note details describing Sandberg's ideals for work and relationships.

1 On March 24, 2008, I headed to my first day of work as chief operating officer of a small company called Facebook. As I pulled out of my driveway, I remember feeling excited. I also felt a little nervous . . . a little anxious . . . okay, maybe even a little scared about this new challenge. It wasn't anything specific that concerned me. I knew the tech business well after spending more than six years at Google. I had shared many dinners with CEO[1] Mark Zuckerberg before he offered me the job, and I knew we were in sync about the importance of Facebook's mission. My fear was more the general anxiety you feel over the risks associated with a new job and the worry that you won't succeed.

2 I parked my car and went up to an industrial, open-plan office space. My desk faced Mark's and was near the very popular Rainbow Room, which was crammed with couches and video games. At the time, the office walls were bare. Today, those walls are filled with posters that reflect the company's philosophy

[1] **CEO:** chief executive officer, the highest-ranking executive at a company.

Notice & Note

Use the side margins to notice and note signposts in the text.

ANALYZE VOICE

Annotate: Mark elements in paragraph 1 that help establish Sandberg's voice.

Analyze: What can you tell about the author from this paragraph? Explain.

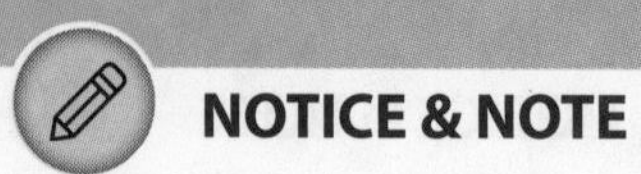

ANALYZE AUTHOR'S PURPOSE

Annotate: In paragraph 2, mark the question that Sandberg refers to in paragraph 3.

Predict: Why do you think she says it has "special significance for women"? What does this suggest about her purpose?

LANGUAGE CONVENTIONS

Annotate: Sentence fragments lack a subject, predicate or both. Mark the sentence fragments in paragraph 3.

Skill: What is the function of this contested usage in Sandberg's writing? How does it impact your understanding?

demurred
(dĭ-mûrd´) *v.* disagreed or refused to accept a request or suggestion.

and encourage employees to take risks. "Proceed and be bold," declares one. "Move fast and break things," advises another. But the one that would have helped me on that first morning doesn't make a statement; it asks a question: "What would you do if you weren't afraid?"

3 This question speaks to everyone, but I think it has special significance for women. Fear is at the root of so many of the barriers that women face. Fear of not being liked. Fear of making the wrong decision. Fear of drawing negative attention. Fear of overreaching. Fear of being judged. Fear of failure. And for those who want to have children, the fear that we can't be both good employees and good mothers.

4 I know it's pointless to tell someone to be fearless. I regularly fail to convince even myself. But it does help to tell ourselves to fight our fears at every stage of our lives. In school, don't be afraid to raise your hand. When you are attending a meeting, don't be afraid to sit at the table. Don't be afraid to offer your opinion. Don't be afraid of waiting to find a life partner who will support you in achieving your dreams. And don't be afraid to be fully engaged in your career, even as you plan to have a family. By fighting these fears, women can pursue professional success and personal fulfillment—and freely choose one or the other . . . or both.

5 Five years ago, I dove into my new Facebook job as fearlessly as I could. And although at the time a lot of people questioned why I would want to go to work for a 23-year-old, no one asks me that question anymore.

6 It's your turn now. Please ask yourself: *What would I do if I weren't afraid?* And then go do it.

SUCCESS SECRET 1: SIT AT THE TABLE

7 A few years ago, I hosted a meeting for Treasury Secretary Tim Geithner at Facebook. We invited 15 executives from across Silicon Valley[2] for breakfast and a discussion about the economy. Secretary Geithner arrived with four members of his staff, two senior and two more junior, and we all gathered in our one nice conference room. After the usual milling around, I encouraged everyone to take a seat. Our invited guests, mostly men, sat down at the large conference table. Secretary Geithner's team, all women, took their food last and sat in chairs off to the side of the room. I motioned for the women to come sit at the table, waving them over publicly so they would feel welcomed. They **demurred** and remained in their seats.

8 The four women had every right to be at this meeting, but because of their seating choice, they seemed like spectators rather than participants. I knew I had to say something. So after the meeting, I pulled them aside to talk. I pointed out that they should

[2] **Silicon Valley:** The location in California of many of the large tech companies. So named because silicon is the element from which computer chips are made.

NOTICE & NOTE

have sat at the table even without an invitation, but when publicly welcomed, they most certainly should have joined. At first, they seemed surprised, then they agreed.

9 It was a **watershed** moment for me. A moment when I witnessed an internal barrier altering women's behavior. A moment when I realized that in addition to facing institutional obstacles, women face a battle from within. We consistently underestimate ourselves. Multiple studies in multiple industries show that women often judge their own performance as worse than it actually is, while men judge their own performance as better than it actually is.

watershed (wô´tər-shĕd) *n.* a turning point, a crucial dividing line.

10 We hold ourselves back in ways both big and small, by lacking self-confidence, by not raising our hands, and by pulling back when we should be leaning in. We **internalize** the negative messages we get throughout our lives—the messages that say it's wrong to be outspoken, aggressive, or more powerful than men. We lower our own expectations of what we can achieve. We continue to do the majority of the housework and childcare. We compromise our career goals to make room for partners and children who may not even exist yet. Compared to our male colleagues, fewer of us aspire to senior positions.

internalize (ĭn-tûr´nə-līz) *v.* to make something, such as an idea or value, an important part of the kind of person you are.

11 Internal obstacles are rarely discussed and often underplayed. Throughout my life, I was told over and over about inequalities in the workplace and how hard it would be to have a career and a family. I rarely, however, heard anything about the ways I might hold myself back. These internal obstacles deserve a lot more attention because they are under our control. We cannot change what we are unaware of, and once we are aware, we cannot help but change.

ANALYZE TONE

Annotate: Mark in paragraph 11 the two examples of "internal obstacles."

Infer: The essay starts out bright and breezy, but the tone changes here. What is the relationship between the topic and the tone?

12 I know that in order to continue to grow and challenge myself, I have to believe in my own abilities. I still face situations that I fear are beyond my qualifications. And I still sometimes find myself spoken over and discounted while men sitting next to me are not. But now I know how to take a deep breath and keep my hand up. I have learned to sit at the table.

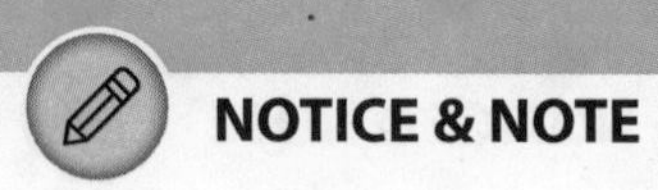

NOTICE & NOTE

SUCCESS SECRET 2: MAKE YOUR PARTNER A REAL PARTNER

13 I truly believe that the single most important career decision that a woman makes is whether she will have a life partner and who that partner is. A woman who can find someone who is willing to share the burdens—and joys—of home life will go further in her work life. I don't know of a single woman in a leadership position whose life partner is not fully—and I mean fully—supportive of her career. No exceptions. And contrary to the popular notion that only unmarried women can make it to the top, the majority of the most successful female business leaders have partners.

14 In the last thirty years, women have made more progress in the workforce than in the home. When a husband and wife both work full-time, the mother does 40 percent more childcare and about 30 percent more housework than the father. So while men are taking on more household responsibilities, this increase is happening very slowly, and we are still far from **parity**. . . .

parity
(păr´ĭ-tē) *n.* equality, being equivalent.

15 This has to change. Just as we need to encourage women to lean in to their careers, we need to encourage men to lean in to their families. If we expect and allow them to do more, they will do more. And everyone will benefit.

ANALYZE AUTHOR'S PURPOSE

Annotate: Mark the sentence in paragraph 15 that signals a change in purpose from the first part of the essay.

Analyze: Explain the change. Why does Sandberg shift her purpose?

16 When husbands do more housework, wives are less depressed, marital conflicts decrease, and satisfaction rises. When women work outside the home and share breadwinning duties, couples are more likely to stay together. In fact, the risk of divorce reduces by about half when a wife earns half the income and a husband does half the housework. For men, participating in child rearing fosters the development of patience, empathy, and adaptability, characteristics that benefit them in all their relationships. For women, earning money increases their decision-making ability in the home, protects them in case of divorce, and can be important security in later years, as women often outlive their husbands. . . .

17 I could not do what I do without my husband, Dave. Still, like all marriages, ours is a work in progress. Dave and I have had our share of bumps on our path to achieving a roughly 50/50 split. After a lot of effort and seemingly endless discussion, we are truly partners.

ANALYZE VOICE

Annotate: Mark words in paragraph 17 that show that Sandberg's voice has become more personal and autobiographical.

Draw Conclusions: How do these words reveal her personality? How does her life affect her ideas?

18 The good news is that men in younger generations appear more eager to be real partners than previous generations did. A survey that asked participants to rate the importance of various job characteristics found that men in their 40s most frequently selected "work that challenges me" as very important, while men in their 20s and 30s most frequently selected having a job with a schedule that "allows me to spend time with my family." If these trends hold as this group ages, this could signal a promising shift toward greater equality.

19 Wonderful, sensitive men of all ages are out there. And the more that women value kindness and support in their boyfriends, the more men will demonstrate it.

So, when looking for a life partner, my advice to women is date all of them: the bad boys, the cool boys, the commitmentphobic boys, the crazy boys. But do not marry them. . . . When it comes time to settle down, find someone who wants an equal partner. Someone who thinks women should be smart, opinionated, and ambitious. Someone who values fairness and expects or, even better, wants to do his share in the home. And at the start of a romance, even though it may be tempting for you to show a more classic girlfriend-y side by cooking meals and taking care of errands, hold yourself back from doing this too much. If a relationship begins in an unequal place, it is likely to get more unbalanced if and when children are added to the equation. Instead, use the beginning of a relationship to establish the bar for the division of labor.

NOTICE & NOTE 

ANALYZE AUTHOR'S PURPOSE

Annotate: Mark Sheryl Sandberg's advice.

Infer: Why do you think she gives this advice? How does it support her overall purpose?

CHECK YOUR UNDERSTANDING

Answer these questions before moving on to the **Analyze the Text** section on the following page.

1 Why is Sandberg nervous when she starts at Facebook?

A It was such a small company at the time.

B She worried that she might not succeed.

C She didn't know anything about technology.

D She had never met Mark Zuckerberg before.

2 Sandberg thinks women could do better in business —

F if they had more education

G if they cared about business

H if they didn't give in to fear

J if they knew Mark Zuckerberg

3 For Sandberg, relationships are an important part of success —

A because the right partner will be fully supportive

B because the wrong partner will lead to divorce

C because you can't get ahead if you're not married

D because you can't get ahead if you are married

RESPOND

ANALYZE THE TEXT

Support your responses with evidence from the text. NOTEBOOK

1. **Summarize** In two or three sentences, summarize what the essay suggests could help women succeed in business. How does the summary help you identify Sandberg's message, audience, and purpose?
2. **Interpret** In paragraph 4, Sandberg writes that it is pointless to tell someone to be fearless. Explain what you think she means by this. How does this belief reveal her tone?
3. **Draw Conclusions** In paragraph 9, why does Sandberg describe the events from paragraph 8 as a "watershed moment"? How does this reveal her purpose?
4. **Evaluate** Do you think Sandberg makes a good case for a life partner being the biggest decision for a woman's career? Is it really bigger than education, interests, talent, or career choice? Explain.
5. **Connect** What aspects of Sandberg's essay do you think might relate to you and your choices or career interests? Use details from the text to support your response.

RESEARCH

RESEARCH TIP
Start by searching for Sheryl Sandberg by name. Then, in addition to searching by name, add other terms, such as *Facebook, Google, billionaire, Harvard, husband,* or *family* to bring up articles more specific to what you're trying to find.

Find newspaper and magazine articles about Sandberg. As you read, pick one or two topics, such as her career, her education, her relationships, or her family background, and look deeper into that topic. Consider how these aspects of her life might have affected her ideas. Keep track of your sources and the information you find in a chart like the one shown.

SOURCE/URL	FACT OR INSIGHT	POSSIBLE IMPACT

Connect Think about what you learned about Sandberg from the articles you selected. Did anything you learned conflict with what you learned about Sandberg in *Lean In*? Discuss your ideas with a partner.

CREATE AND DEBATE

Write an Essay Write an autobiographical essay about something you have accomplished, something you have learned, or a relationship you value.

- ❏ Identify the accomplishment, lesson, or relationship.
- ❏ Share an anecdote that relates to the point you want to make.
- ❏ Include insights about anything that helped you reach your goal or build a relationship.
- ❏ Offer a suggestion for someone who might be interested in doing the same things.

Go to **Writing Narratives** in the **Writing Studio** for help with writing an essay.

Hold a Debate Not everyone agrees with Sandberg's approach to life. In a small group, talk about the pros and cons of some of Sandberg's ideas. Volunteer for a position you'd like to argue for or against, and then create a team with other students.

- ❏ Narrow the topic to some of Sandberg's ideas that can be debated in a reasonable amount of time.
- ❏ Use information from the essay, articles you've read, or your own experience.
- ❏ Outline the points you want to make for or against the selected issue or idea and state your position clearly.
- ❏ Hold a debate, listening carefully to the ideas of others and responding appropriately.

Go to **Analyzing and Evaluating Presentations** in the **Speaking and Listening Studio** for help with holding a debate.

RESPOND TO THE ESSENTIAL QUESTION

How can we share power and build alliances?

Gather Information Review your annotations and notes on *Lean In*. Then, add relevant information to your Response Log. As you determine which information to include, think about:

- advice that Sandberg offers
- Sandberg's purpose for writing
- Sandberg's ideas about success

ACADEMIC VOCABULARY

As you write and discuss what you learned from the essay, be sure to use the Academic Vocabulary words. Check off each of the words that you use.

- ❏ **contrary**
- ❏ **founder**
- ❏ **ideological**
- ❏ **publication**
- ❏ **revolution**

CRITICAL VOCABULARY

WORD BANK
demurred
watershed
internalize
parity

Practice and Apply Mark the letter of the best answer to each question. Then, explain your response.

1. A **watershed** event is more likely to be
a. boring **b.** life-changing

2. People who achieve **parity** could be said to be
a. subordinate **b.** equal

3. Someone who **demurred** when given a suggestion will have said
a. yes **b.** no

4. If a person **internalizes** certain ideals, those ideals
a. become part of the person **b.** are rejected by the person

VOCABULARY STRATEGY: Analyze Meanings of Idioms

Go to the **Idioms, Slang, and Figurative Language section of Context Clues** in the **Vocabulary Studio** for more about idioms.

An **idiom** is a common figure of speech whose meaning is different from the literal meaning of its words. For example, *throw in the towel* comes from boxing, but it can be used in any situation where someone wants to quit. Idioms are more likely to appear in informal writing, and they often have nuanced meanings. For example, the idiom *throw in the towel* means "quit," but the connotation is quitting during a fight, probably that one cannot win.

Practice and Apply In her informal essay, Sandberg uses the following idioms. After each word or phrase, write the non-idiomatic definition of each word in the idiom. Then, write what the idiom means. Finally, explain any nuanced meanings or connotations of the idiom.

1. watershed moment

2. in sync

3. milling around

LANGUAGE CONVENTIONS: Contested Usage

Some of the rules of grammar and usage have actually been contested, or deliberately broken, for decades. Contested usage is common in informal writing but is rarely accepted in formal writing. When breaking the rules, it is important to make certain that the writing is still clear and understandable, and it is best to break the rules only to create an effect or make a point.

One rule that Sandberg breaks frequently is the rule against beginning a sentence with a conjunction. In her essay, the conjunctions *And* and *But* begin several sentences. Her approach lends a chatty, personable tone to her writing, and it invites the reader in, making her advice more compelling.

> **And don't be afraid to be fully engaged in your career, even as you plan to have a family.**

Another rule that Sandberg breaks is the rule against using fragments. Complete sentences have a subject and a verb. However, Sandberg uses fragments for emphasis. Her use of fragments and repetition creates a rhythm and draws attention to her point—the number of things people fear.

> **Fear of making the wrong decision. Fear of drawing negative attention. Fear of overreaching. Fear of being judged. Fear of failure.**

Another common rule, though Sandberg does not break it in this essay, is the rule against ending sentences with prepositions. In informal writing, abiding by the rule can create awkward sentences. For example, "That is something I will not put up with" sounds much less awkward than "That is something up with which I will not put."

Practice and Apply Write two or three sentences that employ contested usage. Then rewrite them employing the rules of formal English. With a partner, discuss which sentences sound better and where each type of sentence might be appropriate.

RESPOND

Collaborate & Compare

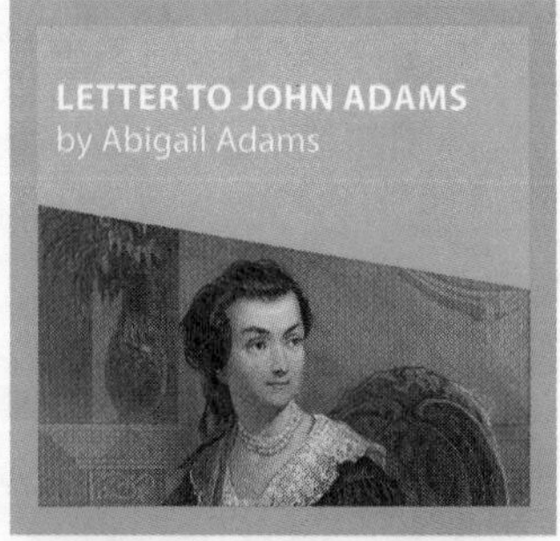
LETTER TO JOHN ADAMS
by Abigail Adams

from
LEAN IN
by Sheryl Sandberg

COMPARE VOICE AND TONE

"Letter to John Adams" and *Lean In* were written two centuries apart and under very different circumstances. You may have noticed differences in the voice and tone of each selection. However, there are some similarities between the texts as well. Review your annotations and notes to find similarities and differences in voice and tone in the two works.

In a small group, discuss how the voice and tone in these two works compare. Then, work together to complete the chart with examples from each text that illustrate tone or voice. In the third column, note if you think the examples are similar or different.

	"LETTER TO JOHN ADAMS"	*LEAN IN*	COMMENTS
Tone			
Voice			

ANALYZE THE TEXTS

Discuss these questions in your group.

1. **Infer** Do you think the two women would agree on what makes an ideal marriage? Explain using examples from each text.
2. **Synthesize** How do Adams's comments about the approaching revolution suggest that she would have appreciated Sandberg's advice on pursuing success?
3. **Compare** Though the two writers have different styles, they have energy and passion in common. Use evidence from the texts—such as details related to style or tone—that demonstrate their energy and passion.
4. **Evaluate** What do these two works suggest about how involved the writers want to be in the world around them?

COLLABORATE AND PRESENT

Now, your group can continue exploring the ideas in these texts by collaborating to create an imagined dialogue between the two authors.

1. **Decide on topics** Discuss what each writer might want to know about the other one's life and concerns. For example, Adams might be glad to hear that slavery has ended, while Sandberg might be delighted to talk about the founding freedoms of the country.

2. **Conduct research** Find out more about each woman and the people in her life that would be of interest to the other writer. Combine this information with text taken from their writing to create an imagined discussion about freedom and relationships. You can alter the original text to make it feel more like part of a dialogue.

3. **Develop and combine ideas** You can use a chart like this to identify ideas, events, quotations, and concerns of the two individuals. Then, in the bottom box, combine the ideas and quotations to create a dialogue. Write enough dialogue that everyone in your group will have a few lines to read.

Abigail Adams	Sheryl Sandberg

↓

Dialogue

4. **Present to the class** Decide who will read which lines of dialogue. Prepare a statement explaining what your dialogue hopes to accomplish and share it with the class. Make sure your listeners know who each speaker represents during the dialogue. Once everyone has had a chance to read his or her part, ask for input from the class. Ask for suggestions about other topics the two women might discuss, were they given the opportunity.

Go to **Giving a Presentation** in the **Speaking and Listening Studio** for help.

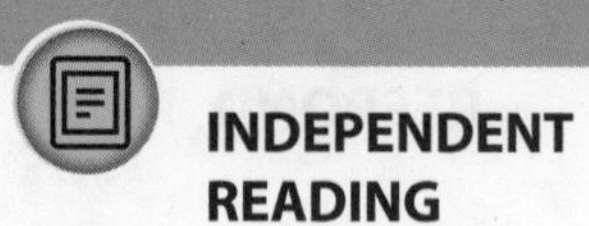

INDEPENDENT READING

Reader's Choice

? ***ESSENTIAL QUESTIONS***

Review the four Essential Questions for this unit on page 95.

Setting a Purpose Select one or more of these options from your eBook to continue your exploration of the Essential Questions.

- Read the descriptions to see which text grabs your interest.
- Think about which genres you enjoy reading.

Notice & Note

In this unit, you practiced noticing and noting the signposts and asking big questions about nonfiction. As you read independently, these signposts and others will aid your understanding. Below are the anchor questions to ask when you read literature and nonfiction.

Reading Literature: Stories, Poems, and Plays	
Signpost	**Anchor Question**
Contrasts and Contradictions	Why did the character act that way?
Aha Moment	How might this change things?
Tough Questions	What does this make me wonder about?
Words of the Wiser	What's the lesson for the character?
Again and Again	Why might the author keep bringing this up?
Memory Moment	Why is this memory important?

Reading Nonfiction: Essays, Articles, and Arguments	
Signpost	**Anchor Question(s)**
Big Questions	What surprised me? What did the author think I already knew? What challenged, changed, or confirmed what I already knew?
Contrasts and Contradictions	What is the difference, and why does it matter?
Extreme or Absolute Language	Why did the author use this language?
Numbers and Stats	Why did the author use these numbers or amounts?
Quoted Words	Why was this person quoted or cited, and what did this add?
Word Gaps	Do I know this word from someplace else? Does it seem like technical talk for this topic? Do clues in the sentence help me understand the word?

You can preview these texts in Unit 2 of your eBook.

Then, check off the text or texts that you select to read on your own.

SPEECH

Speech to the Virginia Convention
Patrick Henry

Discover the context for Henry's famous quotation, "Give me liberty or give me death!"

PUBLIC DOCUMENT

***from* The United States Constitution: The Bill of Rights**

What rights did the founders believe were essential for the protection of citizens?

APHORISMS

***from* Poor Richard's Almanack**
Benjamin Franklin

Discover some of Benjamin Franklin's wittier sayings about human nature.

HISTORY WRITING

Abigail Adams' Last Act of Defiance
Woody Holton

Learn how the wife of John Adams defied the patriarchal property laws of her time.

POEM

Democracy
Langston Hughes

How does a poet express his passionate plea for freedom?

Collaborate and Share With a partner, discuss what you learned from at least one of your independent readings.

- Give a brief synopsis or summary of the text.
- Describe any signposts that you noticed in the text and explain what they revealed to you.
- Describe what you most enjoyed or found most challenging about the text. Give specific examples.
- Decide if you would recommend the text to others. Why or why not?

Go to the **Reading Studio** for more resources on **Notice & Note.**

Write a Research Report

Go to the **Writing Studio** for help writing a research report.

This unit focuses on what it takes to build and maintain a democracy, and how this relates to sharing power and building alliances among people and groups. For this writing task, you will write a research report—a type of informational writing grounded securely in careful research of a topic. Reports synthesize information from multiple relevant and credible primary and secondary sources. For an example of a well-written informational text you can use as a mentor text, review the article "Thomas Jefferson: The Best of Enemies."

As you write your research report, you can use the notes from your Response Log, which you filled out after reading the texts in this unit.

Writing Prompt

Read the information in the box below.

This is the topic or context for your research report.

> **The founding of the United States involved forming and documenting systems and shared fundamental principles.**

Think carefully about the following question.

How might this Essential Question relate to a research report?

> **How can we share power and build alliances?**

Mark words that will help you begin your research.

Write a research report exploring how the founding documents, systems, or fundamental principles facilitate shared power and constructive alliances in our democracy.

Be sure to—

Review these points as you write and again when you finish. Make any needed changes.

- ❑ provide an introduction that catches the reader's attention, clearly states the topic, and includes a clear controlling idea or thesis statement
- ❑ support main ideas with evidence from sources
- ❑ examine sources you use for credibility, bias, and accuracy
- ❑ cite sources of any quoted text and ideas that are not your own
- ❑ organize information in a logical way
- ❑ connect related ideas effectively
- ❑ use appropriate word choice
- ❑ end by summarizing ideas or drawing an overall conclusion

1 Plan

Before you start writing, you need to plan your report. First, consider your topic. Choose a topic that is not too narrow and not too broad. For example, you might compare other founding fathers or foundational documents, or you might explore the historical context that led to the creation of a foundational document. Remember to focus on how the founding documents, systems, or fundamental principles relate to our ability to share power and form alliances. Once you have a topic, formulate a research question. A good research question cannot be answered in a single word and should be open-ended. Next, find sources that will help you answer your research question. These should include primary and secondary sources, in either print or digital formats. Look for sources that are relevant and credible. Use the table below to assist you in planning your draft.

Research Report Planning Table	
Topic	
Research Question(s)	
Possible Sources	

Background Reading Review the notes you have taken in your Response Log that relate to the question, "How can we share power and build alliances?" Texts in this unit provide background reading that will help you formulate questions for your research. They also provide models of text structures and text features that will help you organize your report.

Go to **Writing Informative Texts: Developing a Topic** for help planning your research report.

Notice & Note

From Reading to Writing

As you plan your research report, apply what you've learned about signposts to your own writing. Remember that writers use common features, called signposts, to help convey their message to readers.

Think how you can incorporate **Signposts** into your essay.

Go to the **Reading Studio** for more resources on **Notice & Note.**

Use the notes from your Response Log as you plan your research report.

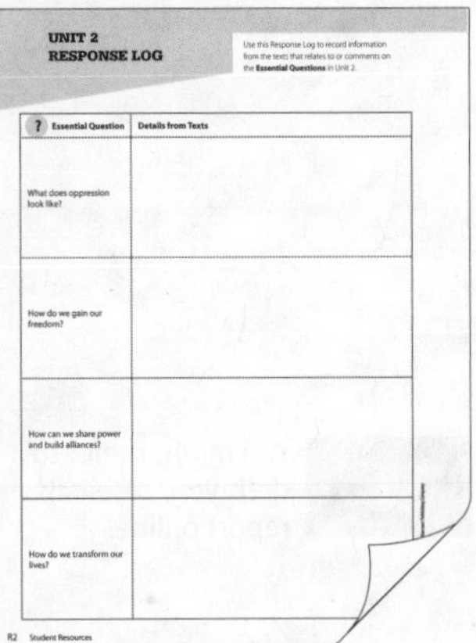

Go to **Writing Informative Texts: Organizing Ideas** for help organizing your ideas.

Organize Your Ideas After you have gathered ideas from your planning activities, you need to organize them in a way that will help you draft your research report. Identify the controlling idea, or thesis statement, which you will state in your introduction. A thesis is a succinct expression about your topic and research question that introduces the claim or main idea you intend to support with additional details, facts, and text evidence. You can use the chart below to map out the organizational structure of your report.

Thesis:

Main Idea/Point of Comparison 1:	Main Idea/Point of Comparison 2:	Main Idea/Point of Comparison 3:
Supporting Details	Supporting Details	Supporting Details

2 Develop a Draft

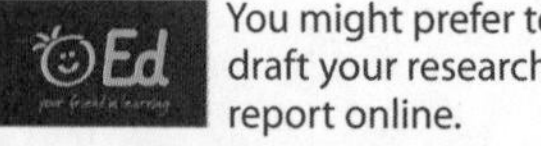

You might prefer to draft your research report online.

Once you have completed your planning activities, you will be ready to begin drafting your research report. Refer to your graphic organizers as well as any notes you took as you studied the texts in this unit. These will provide a kind of map for you to follow as you write. Using a word processor or online writing application makes it easier to make changes or move sentences around later when you are ready to revise your first draft.

THOMAS JEFFERSON: THE BEST OF ENEMIES

Use the Mentor Text

Author's Craft

A strong introduction is essential for capturing the reader's attention. In addition to your controlling idea or thesis statement, your introduction should include something that gets your reader interested in reading your report. Note how the writer begins in the middle of an action and immediately introduces the two "enemies" mentioned in the title of the article, "Thomas Jefferson: The Best of Enemies."

On March 21, 1790, Thomas Jefferson belatedly arrived in New York City to assume his duties as the first Secretary of State after a five-year ministerial stint in Paris. Tall and lanky, with a freckled complexion and auburn hair, Jefferson, 46, was taken aback by the adulation being heaped upon the new Treasury Secretary, Alexander Hamilton, who had streaked to prominence in his absence.

The writer begins with Jefferson in motion—the reader can almost see him arriving in busy New York and being confused as to why this young upstart was getting so much attention.

Apply What You've Learned To capture your reader's attention and to make sure your topic is clear, consider plunging straight into a description of an event that is a significant moment in the development of a document or in the life of a historical person, or that is a turning point in some other way.

Genre Characteristics

Often a text about a historical person or event will use a combination of chronological order and another structure, such as cause and effect or compare and contrast. Chronological order invites the reader to see history as a narrative. Whatever structure is used, main ideas need supporting details and examples. Notice how the author of "Thomas Jefferson: The Best of Enemies" uses chronological order within an overall compare and contrast structure.

Instead, the feud worsened. In early 1793, a Virginia Congressman named William Branch Giles began to harry Hamilton . . . With prodigious bursts of energy, Hamilton complied with those inhuman demands, foiling his opponents. Jefferson then committed an unthinkable act.

The author uses chronological structure in this passage, even though the overall article is compare and contrast. Words like "In early 1793" and "then" signal chronological order.

Apply What You've Learned In your plan, choose where you can use a secondary text structure to enhance your support for a main idea.

WRITING TASK

3 Revise

Go to **Writing Informative Texts: Precise Language and Vocabulary** for help revising your report.

On Your Own Once you have written your draft, you'll want to go back and look for ways to improve your research report. As you reread and revise, think about whether you have achieved your purpose. The Revision Guide will help you focus on specific elements to make your writing stronger.

Revision Guide

Ask Yourself	Tips	Revision Techniques
1. Does my introduction engage the reader and contain a thesis statement that clearly identifies the topic?	**Highlight** sentences that get the audience interested. **Underline** your thesis statement.	**Add** vivid language and details to interest the reader. **Reword** your thesis statement to **clarify** the topic.
2. Do I present relevant text evidence to support my thesis statement and central ideas?	**Highlight** each central idea. **Underline** evidence that supports each idea and **note** evidence that seems weak.	**Add** evidence for any idea that is not supported. **Change** evidence that does not offer strong support.
3. Is my report logically organized with smooth transitions linking ideas and evidence?	**Note** major sections that reflect your organization. **Underline** each transitional word or phrase.	**Reorder** paragraphs if needed. **Add** transitions to **clarify** relationships between ideas.
4. Do I use formal, precise language and maintain an objective tone throughout?	**Highlight** slang and informal language. **Underline** instances of biased perspective.	**Reword** text to avoid informal language. **Replace** sentences that express an attitude or opinion.
5. Does my conclusion follow logically from the ideas I present?	**Note** where the conclusion summarizes your ideas.	**Add** a closing statement if needed to sum up the information your report presents.

ACADEMIC VOCABULARY

As you conduct your **peer review,** be sure to use these words.

- ❑ **contrary**
- ❑ **founder**
- ❑ **ideological**
- ❑ **publication**
- ❑ **revolution**

With a Partner Once you and your partner have worked through the Revision Guide on your own, exchange papers and evaluate each other's draft in a **peer review.** Focus on providing revision suggestions for at least three of the items mentioned in the chart. Explain why you think your partner's draft should be revised and what your specific suggestions are.

When receiving feedback from your partner, listen attentively and ask questions to make sure you fully understand the revision suggestions.

4 Edit

Once you have addressed the organization, development, and flow of ideas in your research report, you can look to improve the finer points of your draft. Edit for the proper use of standard English conventions and make sure to correct any misspellings or grammatical errors.

Go to **Dashes, Parentheses, and Brackets** lesson in the **Grammar Studio** to learn more.

Language Conventions

Dashes An em dash—the long dash you often see used in the middle of sentences—allows writers to make ideas in a long sentence clear, especially when there are already other punctuation marks in the sentence.

- Em dashes can be used in pairs, the same way we use parentheses.
- An em dash can also be used alone, to emphasize a word or short phrase at the end of a sentence.

The chart contains examples of em dash pairs from "Thomas Jefferson: The Best of Enemies."

from "Thomas Jefferson: The Best of Enemies"	Use of Em Dashes
He therefore set to work at Treasury with more unrestrained gusto than Jefferson—who had monitored the Constitutional Convention from his post in Paris—did at State.	This set of dashes gives additional information about something that happened previously but is relevant to the point.
Hamilton—brilliant, brash and charming—had the self-reliant reflexes of someone who had always had to live by his wits.	This set of dashes sets off a description of Hamilton.
He was emphatic in his views—Hamilton labeled him "an atheist in religion and a fanatic in politics"— but shrank from open conflict.	This set of dashes sets off a quotation from a primary document that helps support the author's point.

5 Publish

Finalize your research report and choose a way to share it with your audience. Consider these options:

- Present your report as a podcast.
- Post your report as a blog on a classroom or school website.

WRITING TASK

Use the scoring guide to evaluate your research report.

Writing Task Scoring Guide: Research Report

	Organization/ Progression	Development of Ideas	Use of Language and Conventions
4	• The organization is effective and logical throughout the report. • Transition words and phrases effectively link related ideas and evidence.	• The introduction engages the reader's attention and includes a thesis statement that clearly identifies the topic. • The topic is strongly developed with relevant facts, concrete details, interesting quotations, and examples from the texts. • The concluding section capably follows from and supports the ideas presented.	• The writing reflects a formal style and an objective, knowledgeable tone. • Language is vivid and precise. • Sentence structures vary and have a rhythmic flow. • Spelling, capitalization, and punctuation are correct. Grammar and usage are correct. • Quotations and citations are properly formatted.
3	• The organization is confusing in a few places. • Transitions are needed in a few places to link related ideas and evidence.	• The introduction could do more to attract the reader's curiosity; the thesis statement identifies a topic. • One or two key points could use additional support in the form of relevant facts, concrete details, quotations, and examples from the texts. • The concluding section mostly follows from and supports the ideas presented.	• The style is inconsistent in a few places, and the tone is subjective at times. • Vague language is used in a few places. • Sentence structures vary somewhat. • Some spelling, capitalization, and punctuation mistakes occur. Some grammatical and usage errors are repeated in the report. • Some errors are found in quotation and citation format.
2	• The organization is confusing in some places and often doesn't follow a pattern. • More transition words and phrases are needed throughout to link ideas and evidence.	• The introduction provides some information about a topic but does not include a thesis statement. • Most key points need additional support in the form of relevant facts, concrete details, quotations, and examples from the texts. • The concluding section is confusing and does not follow from the ideas presented.	• The style is too informal; the tone conveys subjectivity and a lack of understanding of the topic. • Vague, general language is used in many places. • Sentence structures barely vary, and some fragments or run-on sentences are present. • Spelling, capitalization, and punctuation are often incorrect but do not make reading the report difficult. Grammar and usage are incorrect in many places, but the writer's ideas are still clear. • Many errors are found in quotation and citation format.
1	• A logical organization is not used; information is presented randomly. • Transitions are not used, making the essay difficult to understand.	• The appropriate elements of an introduction are missing. • Facts, details, quotations, and examples from the texts are missing. • The report lacks an identifiable concluding section.	• The style and tone are inappropriate for the report. • Language is too vague or general to convey the information. • Repetitive sentence structure, fragments, and run-on sentences make the writing difficult to follow. • Spelling, capitalization, and punctuation are incorrect throughout. Grammatical and usage errors change the meaning of the writer's ideas. • Many errors are found in quotation and citation format.

Present a Research Report

You will now adapt your research report for presentation to your classmates. You also will listen to their presentations, ask questions to better understand their ideas, and help them improve their work.

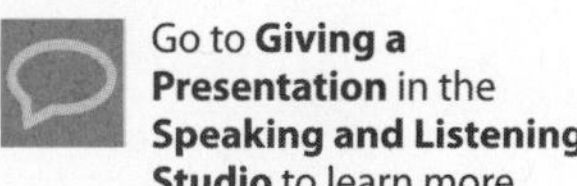
Go to **Giving a Presentation** in the **Speaking and Listening Studio** to learn more.

1 Adapt Your Report for Presentation

Review your research report and use the chart below to guide you as you adapt your report and create a script and presentation materials.

Presentation Planning Chart		
Title and Introduction	How will you revise your title and introduction to capture the listener's attention? Is there a more concise way to state your controlling idea or thesis?	
Audience	What information will your audience already know? What information can you exclude? What should you add?	
Effective Language and Organization	Which parts of your research report should be simplified? Where can you add transitions to help your listeners follow your train of thought?	
Visuals	What images or graphics would help clarify ideas or add interest? What text should appear on screen?	

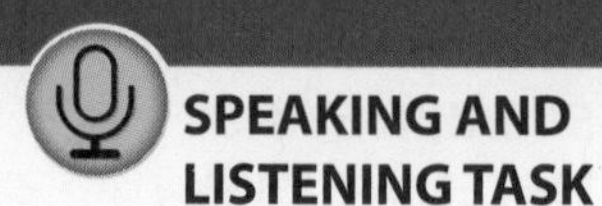

2 Practice with a Partner or Group

Once you've completed your draft, practice with a partner or group to improve both the presentation and your delivery.

As you work to improve your presentations, be sure to follow discussion rules:

- ❑ **listen closely to each other**
- ❑ **don't interrupt**
- ❑ **stay on topic**
- ❑ **ask only helpful, relevant questions**
- ❑ **provide only clear, thoughtful, and direct answers**

Practice Effective Verbal Techniques

- ❑ **Enunciation** Replace words that you stumble over, and rearrange sentences so that your delivery is smooth.
- ❑ **Voice Modulation and Pitch** Use your voice to display enthusiasm and emphasis.
- ❑ **Speaking Rate** Speak slowly enough that listeners understand you. Pause now and then to let them consider important points.
- ❑ **Volume** Remember that listeners at the back of the room need to hear you.

Practice Effective Nonverbal Techniques

- ❑ **Eye Contact** Try to let your eyes rest on each member of the audience at least once.
- ❑ **Facial Expression** Smile, frown, or raise an eyebrow to show your feelings or to emphasize points.
- ❑ **Gestures** Stand tall and relaxed, and use natural gestures—shrugs, nods, or shakes of your head—to add meaning and interest to your presentation.

Provide and Consider Advice for Improvement

As a listener, pay close attention. Take notes about ways that presenters can improve their presentations and more effectively use verbal and nonverbal techniques. Paraphrase and summarize each presenter's key ideas and main points to confirm your understanding, and ask questions to clarify any confusing ideas.

As a presenter, listen closely to questions and consider ways to revise your presentation to make sure your points are clear and logically sequenced. Remember to ask for suggestions about how you might change onscreen text or images to make your presentation clearer and more interesting.

3 Deliver Your Presentation

Use the advice you received during practice to make final changes to your presentation. Then, using effective verbal and nonverbal techniques, present it to your classmates.

Reflect on the Unit

By completing your research report, you have created a writing product that pulls together and expresses your thoughts about the reading you have done in this unit. Now is a good time to reflect on what you have learned.

Reflect on the Essential Questions

- Review the four Essential Questions on page 95. How have your answers to these questions changed in response to the texts you read in this unit?
- What are some examples from the texts you read that show how people share power and build alliances?

Reflect on Your Reading

- Which selections were the most interesting or surprising to you?
- From which selection did you learn the most about how people share power and build alliances?

Reflect on the Writing Task

- What difficulties did you encounter while working on your research report? How might you avoid them next time?
- What part of the research report was the easiest and hardest to write? Why?
- What improvements did you make to your research report as you were revising?

UNIT 2 SELECTIONS

- **The Declaration of Independence**
- **"Thomas Jefferson: The Best of Enemies"**
- ***American Experience*: "Alexander Hamilton"**
- **"A Soldier for the Crown"**
- **from *The Autobiography***
- **"On Being Brought from Africa to America"**
- **"Sympathy"**
- **Letter to John Adams**
- **from *Lean In***

UNIT 3

THE INDIVIDUAL AND SOCIETY

LITERATURE OF THE AMERICAN RENAISSANCE

“Trust thyself: every heart vibrates to that iron string.”

—Ralph Waldo Emerson

Discuss the **Essential Questions** with your whole class or in small groups. As you read The Individual and Society, consider how the selections explore these questions.

? *ESSENTIAL QUESTION:*

In what ways do we seek to remain true to ourselves?

The transcendentalists broke with the Puritan tradition, which emphasized rigid obedience to the laws of society. Transcendentalism exalted the dignity of the individual and stressed the ideals of optimism, freedom, and self-reliance. The notion of the authentic self has become part of the national consciousness. This desire to be ourselves guides us in everything we do. How can we live our lives authentically in a world where so much seems to be false?

? *ESSENTIAL QUESTION:*

How do we relate to the world around us?

In the early 19th century, the Romantics reacted to the negative effects of industrialization—the commercialism, hectic pace, and lack of conscience—by turning to nature and to the self for simplicity, truth, and beauty. In today's world, technological advances are constantly changing the way we do everything, especially the ways we interact with others. How do we make sense of a world in which change seems to be the only constant?

? *ESSENTIAL QUESTION:*

What do we secretly fear?

Fear is a natural response to danger, either real or imagined. Without fear, we would not be able to protect ourselves from real threats. Many people fear the unknown or have seemingly irrational fears. Edgar Allan Poe and other Gothic writers were able to make fear exciting, and modern masters of horror, such as Stephen King and director John Carpenter, continue to use fear to entertain. Are your secret fears real or imagined?

? *ESSENTIAL QUESTION:*

When should we stop and reflect on our lives?

Reflecting on your life can help you learn from your mistakes, give you great ideas, and help you put things in perspective. Some people only pause to reflect during major milestones in their lives. People who frequently take time to reflect tend to be happier than those who don't. How might regularly thinking about your life, either in a journal or simply as you go about your day, help you?

LITERATURE OF THE AMERICAN RENAISSANCE

In 1812 tensions between the United States and Great Britain erupted in a two-year war. The War of 1812 is sometimes referred to as the second war for American independence. Victory in the war cemented the reality of independence and brought great changes to life in the United States, including a new spirit of nationalism. Written after the Battle of Baltimore in 1814, the American national anthem is just one manifestation of that spirit.

Because the war interrupted trade, Americans had to produce many of the goods they had imported in the past. This period marked the beginning of the Industrial Revolution in the United States, as the country shifted from its largely agrarian economy to become an industrial powerhouse. The growth of the factory system brought many people from farms into cities, where they worked long hours for low wages, often under harsh conditions.

Westward Expansion American settlers in search of new farmland and opportunities had been moving west since the late 1700s. This often led to direct conflict with Native American groups living on these lands. In 1830 the United States Congress passed the Indian Removal Act, forcing Native Americans to relocate west of the Mississippi River. Those who resisted were often brutally pushed off their lands.

By mid-century, Americans began to fully embrace the idea of "manifest destiny"—the belief that the United States was destined to expand to the Pacific Ocean and into Mexican Territory. The United States' annexation of Texas in 1845 sparked the Mexican-American War. Through the Treaty of Guadalupe Hidalgo, which ended the war, and later land purchases, the United States established the current borders of the "lower" 48 states.

Nationalism vs. Sectionalism As new territories achieved statehood, the northern and southern states wrangled over the balance between free and slave states. Economic interests also threatened American unity. Tariffs on manufactured goods from Britain forced southerners to buy more expensive northern-manufactured goods. From the South's point of view, the North was getting rich at the South's expense. Sectionalism, or the placing of the interests of one's own region ahead of the nation as a whole, began to take hold.

COLLABORATIVE DISCUSSION

Which events covered above illustrate the new spirit of nationalism in the United States? How did they contribute to nationalism?

1810

1812–14
War of 1812 reaffirms U.S. independence from Great Britain.

1822
Factories built in Lowell, Massachusetts, made it one of the country's largest industrial cities.

1825
Erie Canal links the Great Lakes with the Hudson River.

1830
Congress passes the Indian Removal Act.

Romantics and Transcendentalists American writers of this period were influenced by European romanticism but soon adapted it to their own culture. Ralph Waldo Emerson, a New England writer, led a group focused on transcendentalism. The term *transcendentalism* came from Immanuel Kant, a German philosopher who wrote about "transcendent forms" of knowledge that exist beyond reason and experience. Emerson gave this European philosophy a uniquely American spin, saying that every individual is capable of discovering higher truth through his or her own intuition.

A major target for the transcendentalists' criticism was their Puritan heritage, with its emphasis on material prosperity and rigid obedience to the laws of society. The transcendentalists disliked the commercial side of American life and the hectic pace of the Industrial Revolution. Instead, they stressed spiritual well-being, achieved through intellectual activity and a close relationship to nature. Emerson's friend Henry David Thoreau put his beliefs into practice by building a small cabin on Walden Pond and living there for two years, writing and studying nature.

In 1842 Emerson called for the emergence of a poet worthy of the new America—a fresh voice with limitless passion and originality. Two such poets were Walt Whitman and Emily Dickinson. Both wrote poetry that broke with the traditional conventions of poetic form and content. In this way they followed the transcendentalist ideals of individuals discovering the truth through intuition and following their own beliefs.

RESEARCH
What about this historical period interests you? Choose a topic, event, or person to learn more about. Then, add your own entry to the timeline.

1837
John Deere develops a steel plow for the western prairies.

1844
Samuel B. Morse transmits the first successful telegraph message.

1846–48
Mexican-American War expands the western territory of the United States.

1848
Discovery of gold in California leads to the first gold rush.

1850

Dark Romantics Not all American Romantics were optimistic or had faith in the innate goodness of humankind. Edgar Allan Poe and Nathaniel Hawthorne have been called "dark" or "brooding" Romantics or "anti-transcendentalists." Their stories are characterized by a probing of the inner lives of their characters—an examination of the complex and often mysterious forces that motivate human behavior. Their stories are romantic, however, in their emphasis on emotion, nature, the individual, and the unusual. Both Poe and Hawthorne used elements that are common in Gothic fiction, such as grotesque characters, bizarre situations, and violent events, in order to explore the unknown.

CHECK YOUR UNDERSTANDING

Choose the best answer to each question.

1 Which of the following was a threat to nationalism in the United States?

A The War of 1812

B The Indian Removal Act

C The Mexican-American War

D Sectionalism

2 What is "manifest destiny"?

F The shift from an agrarian to an industrial economy

G The official act of removing Native Americans from their homelands

H The belief that the United States was meant to expand to the Pacific Ocean

J The balance of power between free and slave states

3 Which of the following is a characteristic of transcendentalism?

A An emphasis on material prosperity

B Rigid obedience to the laws of society

C The belief that individuals can discover higher truths through intuition

D An examination of the complex forces that motivate human behavior

ACADEMIC VOCABULARY

Academic Vocabulary words are words you use when you discuss and write about texts. In this unit, you will learn the following five words:

☑ **analogy** ❑ **denote** ❑ **quote** ❑ **topic** ❑ **unique**

Study the Word Network to learn more about the word **analogy.**

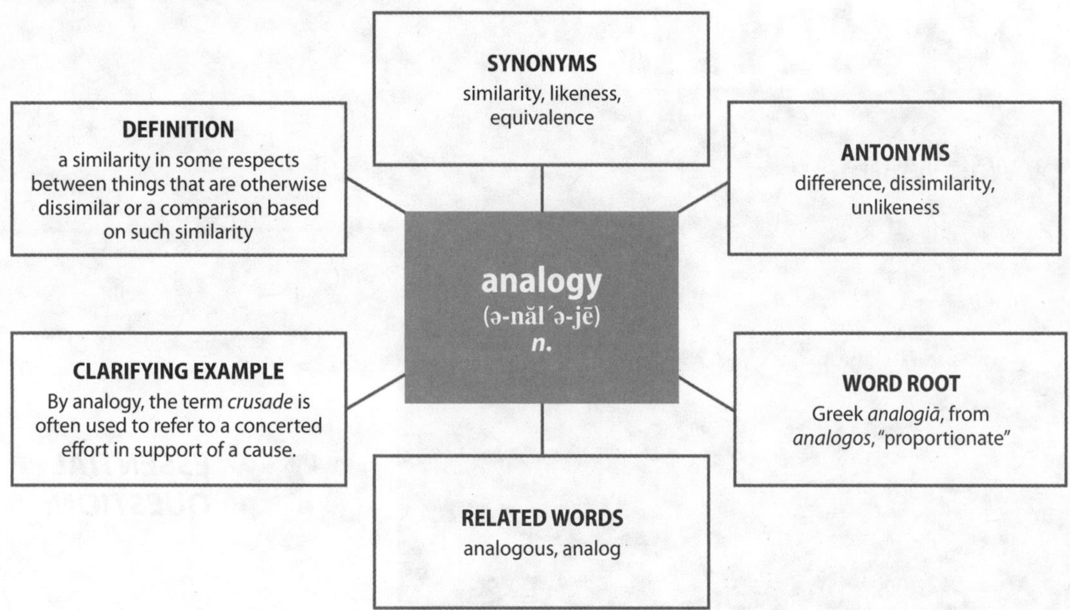
SYNONYMS
similarity, likeness, equivalence
DEFINITION
a similarity in some respects between things that are otherwise dissimilar or a comparison based on such similarity
ANTONYMS
difference, dissimilarity, unlikeness
analogy
(ə-năl´ə-jē)
n.
CLARIFYING EXAMPLE
By analogy, the term crusade is often used to refer to a concerted effort in support of a cause.
WORD ROOT
Greek analogiā, from analogos, "proportionate"
RELATED WORDS
analogous, analog

Write and Discuss Discuss your completed Word Network with a partner, making sure to talk through all of the boxes until you both understand the word, its synonyms, antonyms, and related forms. Then, fill out a Word Network for the remaining four words. Use a dictionary or online resource to help you complete the activity.

Go online to access the Word Networks.

RESPOND TO THE ESSENTIAL QUESTIONS

In this unit, you will explore four different **Essential Questions** about the individual and society. As you read each selection, you will gather your ideas about one of these questions and write about it in the **Response Log** that appears on page R3. At the end of the unit, you will have the opportunity to write an **explanatory essay** related to one of the Essential Questions. Filling out the Response Log after you read each text will help you prepare for this writing task.

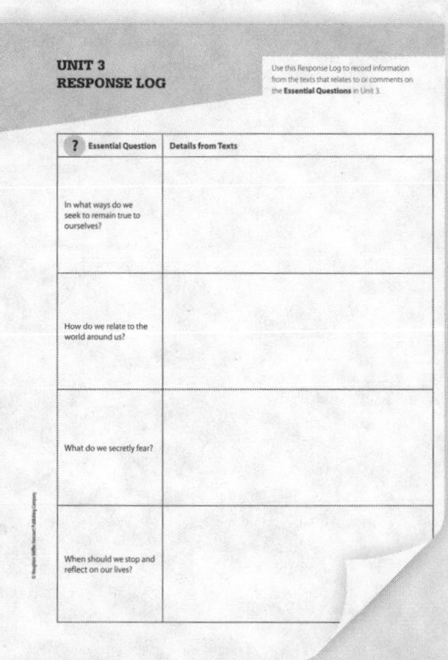
UNIT 3
RESPONSE LOG
Essential Question
Details from Texts
In what ways do we seek to remain true to ourselves?
How do we relate to the world around us?
What do we secretly fear?
When should we stop and reflect on our lives?

You can also go online to access the Response Log.

from SONG OF MYSELF

Poem by **Walt Whitman**

? ESSENTIAL QUESTION:

In what ways do we seek to remain true to ourselves?

QUICK START

You have been asked to mentor students to help them consider a career path. Discuss with a partner the ways in which you could help other students answer questions such as, "What should you ask yourself when thinking about a job or career?" and "How do you know whether a career path is right for you?".

ANALYZE POETRY

"Song of Myself" is written in **free verse.** Poems written in free verse do not have regular patterns of rhyme and rhythm and may not have conventional stanzas. Because it uses varied line lengths and does not rhyme, free verse poetry often has a **rhythm,** or pattern of stressed and unstressed sounds, that is closer to that of everyday speech.

The **speaker** is the voice that is talking in a poem. In free verse, the speaker may be the poet, or a fictional character or narrator. The speaker may even change throughout the poem. As you read "Song of Myself," use a chart like this to help you analyze the relationships between the different elements of free verse poetry.

MY QUESTIONS	EVIDENCE FROM THE POEM
What characteristics of free verse are in the poems?	
Who is the speaker? How do I know?	
How is the identity of the speaker related to the free verse writing style?	

GENRE ELEMENTS: FREE VERSE

- does not have regular patterns of rhyme and rhythm
- uses uneven, unrhymed lines and stanzas that sound like everyday speech
- includes elements of traditional poetry like imagery and sound devices

GET READY

ANALYZE THEME AND STRUCTURE

The **theme** or themes of a poem are the underlying message or messages that a poet wants to convey. The poet will not state the theme directly. It is up to you to infer it based on details in the text.

In the selections of "Song of Myself" that you are about to read, Whitman uses language, structure, and literary devices to communicate his themes. As you read, consider how the following elements impact your understanding of the poems and the themes they express.

ELEMENTS	HOW THEY REVEAL THEMES
Free verse	Look for words that stand out because of the poet's manipulation of lines, repeated words and phrases that create rhythm and heighten emotion in key places, and lists of people, things, or attributes that create rhythm and evoke imagery.
Imagery	Think about the types of images created by sensory language and why the poet wants readers to "see" these pictures.
Figures of speech	Comparisons in the form of similes and metaphors tell readers how the poet wants them to view certain ideas.
Symbols	A person, place, or thing that has meaning beyond itself is often central to the poem's meaning.
Direct statements	Sometimes the poet expresses ideas directly.

ANNOTATION MODEL

NOTICE & NOTE

As you read, note the themes the poet develops and the elements he uses to convey those themes. Pay attention to what the speaker reveals and how the structure of the poem helps convey meaning. This model shows one reader's notes about the beginning of "Song of Myself."

I celebrate myself, and sing myself,
And what I assume you shall assume,
For every atom belonging to me as good belongs to you.

The speaker stresses the idea of individuality by repeating the pronouns "I" and "myself." He also uses the pronoun "you," connecting himself to the audience of humankind.

BACKGROUND

Walt Whitman *(1819–1892) was not born into a prosperous family. The son of a house builder and one of nine children, he grew up in rural Long Island and Brooklyn, New York. Although he was a voracious reader, he did not have much formal education, and at age twelve began work as a printer. In his younger years, he showed little indication of literary promise, moving from job to job and working at various times as an office boy, a typesetter, a school teacher, and a carpenter.*

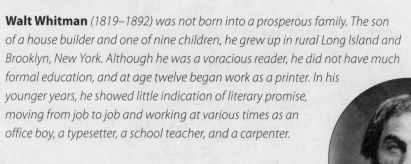

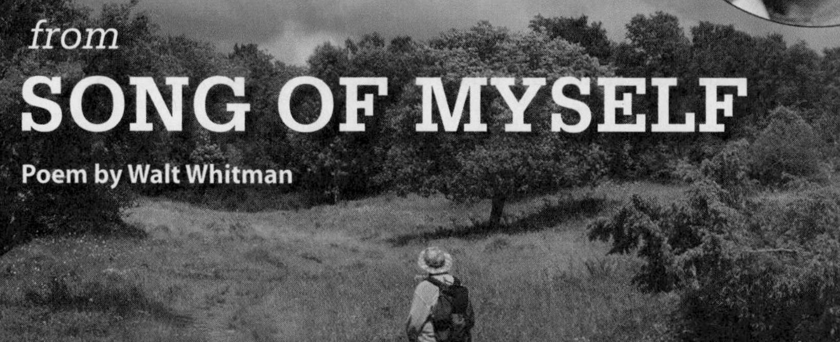

from

SONG OF MYSELF

Poem by Walt Whitman

In the 1840s, Whitman published poems, short stories, and even a novel, but they were fairly conventional efforts that did not stand out from the other literature of the day. Whitman had yet to find the inspiration that would unlock his voice as a writer. He soon found it in the writings of poet and philosopher Ralph Waldo Emerson. After reading Emerson's work, Whitman realized that he could celebrate all aspects of nature and humanity by using spiritual language.

In the early 1850s, Whitman quit his job as a journalist and devoted himself to writing his collection of poems entitled Leaves of Grass. *He printed the volume in 1855. It soon ignited a flurry of reaction from readers because of its content and form, both of which were considered revolutionary. Many early readers scorned his efforts, and the book was so controversial that many of the original 800 copies were thrown away. Undeterred, Whitman continued working on the book for the rest of his life—revising or rearranging existing poems and adding new poems. The ninth and final edition, published in 1892, contained nearly 400 poems.*

Whitman celebrated all aspects of American life—the unique and the commonplace, the beautiful and the ugly. Rejecting the rigidity of earlier poetic conventions, Whitman's poetry captures the vitality, optimism, and voice of America in a style that reflects the freedom and vastness of his beloved country. Today, Leaves of Grass *is widely regarded as one of the most influential books of poetry in American literature.*

NOTICE & NOTE

Notice & Note

Use the side margins to notice and note signposts in the text.

ANALYZE POETRY

Annotate: Mark words and phrases that stand out to you in lines 6 and 7.

Analyze: How does the speaker express a relationship to the wider world in these lines?

ANALYZE THEME AND STRUCTURE

Annotate: Mark examples of metaphor in lines 3–11.

Analyze: How do these metaphors give structure to the poem? What theme do they suggest?

SETTING A PURPOSE

As you read, pay attention to Whitman's unique poetic style and how he uses the elements of a poem to develop a theme.

1 I celebrate myself, and sing myself

I celebrate myself, and sing myself,
And what I assume you shall assume,[1]
For every atom belonging to me as good belongs to you.

I loaf and invite my soul,
I lean and loaf at my ease observing a spear of summer grass.

My tongue, every atom of my blood, form'd from this soil, this air,
Born here of parents born here from parents the same, and their parents the same,
I, now thirty-seven years old in perfect health begin,
Hoping to cease not till death.

Creeds and schools in abeyance,[2]
Retiring back a while sufficed at what they are, but never forgotten,
I harbor for good or bad, I permit to speak at every hazard,
Nature without check with original energy.

6 A child said *What is the grass?*

A child said *What is the grass?* fetching it to me with full hands;
How could I answer the child? I do not know what it is any more than he.

I guess it must be the flag of my disposition, out of hopeful green stuff woven.

Or I guess it is the handkerchief of the Lord,
A scented gift and remembrancer designedly dropt,
Bearing the owner's name someway in the corners, that we may see and remark, and say *Whose?*

Or I guess the grass is itself a child, the produced babe of the vegetation.

---

[1] **assume:** Here, the word *assume* means "take on."

[2] **abeyance:** temporary suspension; inactivity.

Or I guess it is a uniform hieroglyphic,[1]
And it means, Sprouting alike in broad zones and narrow zones,
Growing among black folks as among white,
Kanuck, Tuckahoe, Congressman, Cuff,[2] I give them the same,
I receive them the same.

And now it seems to me the beautiful uncut hair of graves.

Tenderly will I use you curling grass,
It may be you transpire from the breasts of young men,
It may be if I had known them I would have loved them,
It may be you are from old people, or from offspring taken soon out
of their mothers' laps,
And here you are the mothers' laps.

The grass is very dark to be from the white heads of old mothers,
Darker than the colorless beards of old men,
Dark to come from under the faint red roofs of mouths.

O I perceive after all so many uttering tongues,
And I perceive they do not come from the roofs of mouths for
nothing.

I wish I could translate the hints about the dead young men and
women,
And the hints about old men and mothers, and the offspring taken
soon out of their laps.

What do you think has become of the young and old men?
And what do you think has become of the women and children?

They are alive and well somewhere,
The smallest sprout shows there is really no death,
And if ever there was it led forward life, and does not wait at the
end to arrest it,
And ceas'd the moment life appear'd.

All goes onward and outward, nothing collapses,
And to die is different from what any one supposed, and luckier.

ANALYZE THEME AND STRUCTURE

Annotate: In lines 27–32, mark places where the poet expresses his thoughts directly.

Cite Evidence: How do these ideas relate to each other and to Whitman's theme(s)?

[1] **hieroglyphic:** picture symbol used in a writing system to represent sounds or words.

[2] **Kanuck, Tuckahoe, . . .Cuff:** *Kanuck, Tuckahoe,* and *Cuff* are slang terms, now considered offensive, for a French Canadian, an inhabitant of the Virginia lowlands, and an African American, respectively.

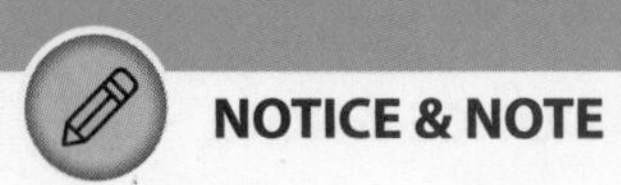

NOTICE & NOTE

from 33 I understand the large hearts of heroes

I understand the large hearts of heroes,
The courage of present times and all times,
How the skipper saw the crowded and rudderless wreck of the steam-ship, and Death chasing it up and down the storm,
How he knuckled tight and gave not back an inch, and was faithful of days and faithful of nights,
And chalk'd in large letters on a board, *Be of good cheer, we will not desert you*;
How he follow'd with them and tack'd with them three days and would not give it up,
How he saved the drifting company at last,
How the lank loose-gown'd women look'd when boated from the side of their prepared graves,
How the silent old-faced infants and the lifted sick, and the sharp-lipp'd unshaved men;
All this I swallow, it tastes good, I like it well, it becomes mine,
I am the man, I suffer'd, I was there.

The disdain and calmness of martyrs,
The mother of old, condemn'd for a witch, burnt with dry wood, her children gazing on,
The hounded slave that flags in the race, leans by the fence, blowing, cover'd with sweat,
The twinges that sting like needles his legs and neck, the murderous buckshot and the bullets,
All these I feel or am.

I am the hounded slave, I wince at the bite of the dogs,
Hell and despair are upon me, crack and again crack the marksmen,
I clutch the rails of the fence, my gore dribs, thinn'd with the ooze of my skin,
I fall on the weeds and stones,
The riders spur their unwilling horses, haul close,
Taunt my dizzy ears and beat me violently over the head with whip-stocks.

Agonies are one of my changes of garments,
I do not ask the wounded person how he feels, I myself become the wounded person,
My hurts turn livid upon me as I lean on a cane and observe.

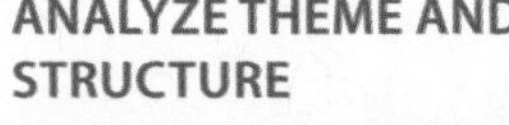

ANALYZE THEME AND STRUCTURE

Annotate: Mark sensory words and phrases in lines 17–22.

Analyze: How does Whitman's use of vivid imagery develop his theme in this section of the poem?

NOTICE & NOTE

I am the mash'd fireman with breast-bone broken,
Tumbling walls buried me in their debris,
Heat and smoke I inspired,[1] I heard the yelling shouts of my comrades,
I heard the distant click of their picks and shovels,
They have clear'd the beams away, they tenderly lift me forth.

I lie in the night air in my red shirt, the pervading hush is for my sake,
Painless after all I lie exhausted but not so unhappy,
White and beautiful are the faces around me, the heads are bared of their fire-caps,
The kneeling crowd fades with the light of the torches.

Distant and dead resuscitate,
They show as the dial or move as the hands of me, I am the clock myself.

I am an old artillerist, I tell of my fort's bombardment,
I am there again.

Again the long roll of the drummers,
Again the attacking cannon, mortars,
Again to my listening ears the cannon responsive.

I take part, I see and hear the whole,
The cries, curses, roar, the plaudits for well-aim'd shots,
The ambulanza slowly passing trailing its red drip,
Workmen searching after damages, making indispensable repairs,
The fall of grenades through the rent roof, the fan-shaped explosion,
The whizz of limbs, heads, stone, wood, iron, high in the air.

Again gurgles the mouth of my dying general, he furiously waves with his hand,
He gasps through the clot *Mind not me—mind—the entrenchments.*

[1] **inspired:** breathed in.

ANALYZE POETRY

Annotate: Mark each place in "I understand the large hearts of heroes" where the speaker's persona changes or seems to change.

Connect: How does Whitman use stanzas to convey a change in the speaker's persona?

ANALYZE THEME AND STRUCTURE

Annotate: In lines 1–3, circle descriptive or action words associated with the spotted hawk. Underline descriptive or action words associated with the speaker.

Draw Conclusions: Why does the speaker compare himself to the hawk?

52 The spotted hawk swoops by

The spotted hawk swoops by and accuses me, he complains
of my gab and my loitering.

I too am not a bit tamed, I too am untranslatable,
I sound my barbaric yawp[1] over the roofs of the world.

The last scud[2] of day holds back for me,
It flings my likeness after the rest and true as any on the
shadow'd wilds,
It coaxes me to the vapor and the dusk.

I depart as air, I shake my white locks at the runaway sun,
I effuse[3] my flesh in eddies,[4] and drift it in lacy jags.

---

[1] **yawp:** a loud, harsh cry.
[2] **scud:** windblown mist and low clouds.
[3] **effuse:** spread out.
[4] **eddies:** small whirlwinds.

I bequeath myself to the dirt to grow from the grass I love,
If you want me again look for me under your boot-soles.

You will hardly know who I am or what I mean,
But I shall be good health to you nevertheless,
And filter and fiber your blood.

Failing to fetch me at first keep encouraged,
Missing me one place search another,
I stop somewhere waiting for you.

CHECK YOUR UNDERSTANDING

Answer these questions before moving on to the **Analyze the Text** section on the following page.

1 Which line best supports the idea that the speaker feels connected and relates to all of humankind?

A *My tongue, every atom of my blood, form'd from this soil, this air* (from "I celebrate myself . . ." line 6)

B *I do not ask the wounded person how he feels, I myself become the wounded person* (from "I understand . . ." line 24)

C *I sound my barbaric yawp over the roofs of the world* (from "The spotted hawk . . ." line 3)

D *I stop somewhere waiting for you* (from "The spotted hawk . . ." line 16)

2 According to the speaker in "I understand the large hearts of heroes," what is the common characteristic shared by all heroes?

F Heroes show deep love for all of humanity.

G Heroes are willing to die for their cause.

H Heroes are able to act despite pain.

J Heroes demonstrate courage.

3 Which symbol does the speaker most closely associate with his own spirit?

A The grass (from "A child said . . .")

B The child (from "A child said . . .")

C The slave (from "I understand . . .")

D The hawk (from "The spotted hawk . . .")

ANALYZE THE TEXT

Support your responses with evidence from the text. NOTEBOOK

1. **Analyze** "I celebrate myself . . ." is the first section of Whitman's poem "Song of Myself." In what ways does this section serve as an introduction to the themes and poetic vision described in these excerpts?
2. **Compare** How do the sections "I celebrate myself . . ." and "I understand the large hearts . . ." communicate Whitman's vision of a bond that unites all humanity?
3. **Infer** What does the grass symbolize in the section "A child said . . ."? How does this symbol relate to the deeper meaning of the poem?
4. **Interpret** Compare the themes of "A child said . . ." and "The spotted hawk swoops by." What insight do they share?
5. **Analyze** Think of Whitman's topics and the ideas he expresses in his poetry. Why is free verse the best form of poetry for him to use? Explain.

RESEARCH

RESEARCH TIP

When you use a search engine, add more terms to a broad topic to get more relevant results. For example, when searching for the preface to *Leaves of Grass*, including the word *preface* will bring better results than searching the book title only.

Walt Whitman has been described as a democratic and inclusive poet. He once described Americans as having "the fullest poetical nature." In the 1855 preface to *Leaves of Grass,* Walt Whitman outlines his vision of the American poet and describes what he or she should write about. With a partner, read the preface and use what you learn to answer these questions.

QUESTION	ANSWER
In the paragraph starting with "The American poets are to enclose . . . ," how would you paraphrase some of the characteristics Whitman lists?	
Find the passage beginning with "This is what you shall do: . . . " Whitman lists many things a poet should do. Which of them reflect inclusive or democratic attitudes?	
How are Whitman's views about America and the role of the poet reflected in the portions of "Song of Myself" that you have read?	

Extend Find another poem by Whitman that reflects his ideas about America. Discuss with your partner how the poem enhances or clarifies your understanding of Whitman's ideas.

CREATE AND DEBATE

Write an Argument Whitman has been accused of being an "egoist," or overly focused on himself, by some readers of his poetry. Use your reading of the selections from "Song of Myself" to write a three- or four-paragraph argument either supporting or refuting this claim.

- ❑ Write an introduction that introduces the claim of egoism and your position about the claim.
- ❑ Develop your argument in the body paragraph(s), using textual examples from "Song of Myself" to support your position.
- ❑ Anticipate and address any counterarguments to strengthen your argument.
- ❑ Conclude by summarizing your views on Walt Whitman and egoism.

Go to **Writing Arguments** in the **Writing Studio** for help.

Debate a Position With a small group of classmates who took your same position in the argument, prepare to defend that position in a class debate.

- ❑ Share your ideas and supporting examples with your group members.
- ❑ As a group, select key, well-supported claims that you will present in the debate.
- ❑ Anticipate the claims that the opposing side will make, and prepare rebuttal statements.
- ❑ Engage your audience by speaking clearly and using appropriate eye contact and volume.
- ❑ Always show respect in your interactions with the opposing side.

Go to **Analyzing and Evaluating Presentations** in the **Speaking and Listening Studio** for more on holding a debate.

RESPOND TO THE ESSENTIAL QUESTION

In what ways do we seek to remain true to ourselves?

Gather Information Review your annotations and notes on "Song of Myself." Then, add relevant information to your Response Log. As you determine which information to include, think about:

- what it means to be true to oneself
- how the individual is related to society as a whole
- the importance of personal identity

ACADEMIC VOCABULARY

As you write and discuss what you learned from the poem, be sure to use the Academic Vocabulary words. Check off each of the words that you use.

- ❑ **analogy**
- ❑ **denote**
- ❑ **quote**
- ❑ **topic**
- ❑ **unique**

MY FRIEND WALT WHITMAN

Essay by **Mary Oliver**

? ESSENTIAL QUESTION:

How do we relate to the world around us?

QUICK START

In this essay, the author examines her life in relationship to the inspiration she got from the poetry of Walt Whitman. What inspires you? It may be a piece of writing, someone you know, or something else entirely. Discuss your ideas with the class.

ANALYZE ESSAYS

An **essay** is a short work of nonfiction on a single subject. Essays can be written for many purposes: to inform, persuade, express an idea or feelings, or entertain. An essay can be formal or informal. This essay is informal—it uses the first person and has a conversational tone.

Essays include a **thesis statement** that expresses the writer's main idea. The author may then use quotations, examples, and personal experiences to support the thesis. The organizational design of an essay often supports the writer's purpose, which in this case is to express her feelings about Whitman and poetry. As you read, look for the thesis statement and think about the essay's organizational design.

GENRE ELEMENTS: ESSAY

- includes a thesis statement to identify writer's argument or purpose
- offers details or evidence to support the thesis
- has a conclusion that restates the thesis and summarizes the evidence

ANALYZE DEVELOPMENT OF KEY IDEAS

When reading an essay, it is important to analyze the development of key ideas. Writers **develop key ideas** by including a variety of evidence—such as facts, quotations, examples, statistics, or personal experiences. To analyze key ideas, think about how the details support the author's thesis and purpose.

One way that Oliver supports her ideas is to cite quotations from Walt Whitman's work. She also relates her own personal experiences. Take notes to keep track of the significant details and how they support your understanding of the writer's important ideas. As you list the details, you can begin to infer which ideas are key to the essay.

TYPE OF EVIDENCE	DETAILS FROM TEXT	HOW IT SUPPORTS KEY IDEA
Quotations by Whitman		
Personal Experiences		

GET READY

CRITICAL VOCABULARY

inclination estrangement delinquent bravado metaphysical

To see how many Critical Vocabulary words you already know, write the correct word after each definition.

1. Something that is immaterial or supernatural is __________.
   a. metaphysical b. delinquent

2. If you have a tendency to act a certain way, you have __________.
   a. bravado b. an inclination

3. When you feel a sense of alienation, you feel __________.
   a. estrangement b. metaphysical

4. If you show bravery or defiance, you show __________.
   a. bravado b. estrangement

5. When you ignore laws or duties, you __________.
   a. are delinquent b. feel an inclination

LANGUAGE CONVENTIONS

Informal Style Informal writing is more like spoken language than formal writing is. It observes many of the same rules as formal style, but it is more casual. Contractions, idioms, and common phrases are often used in informal essays. Notice how Oliver uses the common phrase *of course* in her essay.

> **I never met any of my friends, of course, in a usual way—they were strangers, and lived only in their writings.**

As you read "My Friend Walt Whitman," look for ways in which the writing seems conversational rather than formal.

ANNOTATION MODEL

NOTICE & NOTE

As you read, think about how Mary Oliver develops key ideas in her essay. In the model, you can see one reader's notes about "My Friend Walt Whitman."

My town was no more or less congenial to the fact of poetry than any other small town in America—I make no special case of a solitary childhood. Estrangement from the mainstream of that time and place was an unavoidable precondition, no doubt, to the life I was choosing from among all the lives possible to me.	Poetry was not part of her life. She feels out of place. She had other options; what influenced her to make this choice?

BACKGROUND

__Mary Oliver__ (b. 1935) was born in Maple Heights, Ohio. Her first book of poetry, No Voyage and Other Poems, *was published in the United Kingdom in 1963, when Oliver was 28. Oliver's life choice may have been influenced by Walt Whitman, but another major early influence was poet Edna St. Vincent Millay. Oliver is a prolific poet and has won numerous honors, including the Pulitzer Prize and National Book Award. Her poetry is known for its focus on the natural world and her effort to explore both the beauty and difficulty of nature. Oliver rarely grants interviews, saying she wants people to discover her through her writing.*

MY FRIEND WALT WHITMAN

Essay by Mary Oliver

SETTING A PURPOSE

As you read, pay attention to how Oliver develops key ideas in this essay. Who are her friends, why are they important, and what impact have they had on her life?

1 In Ohio, in the 1950s, I had a few friends who kept me sane, alert, and loyal to my own best and wildest **inclinations.** My town was no more or less congenial to the fact of poetry than any other small town in America—I make no special case of a solitary childhood. **Estrangement** from the mainstream of that time and place was an unavoidable precondition, no doubt, to the life I was choosing from among all the lives possible to me.

2 I never met any of my friends, of course, in a usual way—they were strangers, and lived only in their writings. But if they were only shadow-companions, still they were constant, and powerful, and amazing. That is, they said amazing things, and for me it changed the world.

This hour I tell things in confidence,
I might not tell everybody but I will tell you.[1]

[1] All text in italics, including italic text that is not set apart from the main text, is from Walt Whitman's poem "Song of Myself."

Notice & Note

Use the side margins to notice and note signposts in the text.

inclination
(ĭn-klə-nā´shən) *n.* a characteristic disposition or tendency to act in a certain way; a propensity.

estrangement
(ĭ-strānj´mənt) *n.* the condition of being detached or withdrawn; alienation.

ANALYZE ESSAYS

Annotate: In paragraph 2, mark Oliver's thesis statement.

Analyze: What unusual claim does Oliver make about her "friends"?

NOTICE & NOTE

QUOTED WORDS

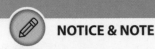

Notice & Note: Mark the Walt Whitman quotes on this page.

Analyze: What is unique about the way Oliver organizes her essay? How does this organization support her purpose?

delinquent
(dĭ-lĭng´kwənt) *adj.* failing to do what law or duty requires.

LANGUAGE CONVENTIONS

Annotate: Mark the informal phrase in the first sentence of paragraph 5.

Analyze: How does this phrase affect the essay and how the reader might react to it?

bravado
(brə-vä´dō) *n.* a show of bravery or defiance, often in order to make a false impression or mislead someone.

metaphysical
(mĕt-ə-fĭz´ĭ-kəl) *adj.* based on speculative or abstract reasoning.

3 Whitman was the brother I did not have. I did have an uncle, whom I loved, but he killed himself one rainy fall day; Whitman remained, perhaps more avuncular[2] for the loss of the other. He was the gypsy boy my sister and I went off with into the far fields beyond the town, with our pony, to gather strawberries. The boy from Romania[3] moved away; Whitman shone on in the twilight of my room, which was growing busy with books, and notebooks, and muddy boots, and my grandfather's old Underwood typewriter.

My voice goes after what my eyes cannot reach,
With the twirl of my tongue I encompass worlds and volumes of worlds.

4 When the high school I went to experienced a crisis of **delinquent** student behavior, my response was to start out for school every morning but to turn most mornings into the woods instead, with a knapsack of books. Always Whitman's was among them. My truancy was extreme, and my parents were warned that I might not graduate. For whatever reason, they let me continue to go my own way. It was an odd blessing, but a blessing all the same. Down by the creek, or in the wide pastures I could still find on the other side of the deep woods, I spent my time with my friend: my brother, my uncle, my best teacher.

The moth and the fisheggs are in their place,
The suns I see and the suns I cannot see are in their place,
The palpable is in its place and the impalpable is in its place.

5 Thus Whitman's poems stood before me like a model of delivery when I began to write poems myself: I mean the oceanic power and rumble that travels through a Whitman poem—the incantatory[4] syntax, the boundless affirmation. In those years, truth was elusive—as was my own faith that I could recognize and contain it. Whitman kept me from the swamps of a worse uncertainty, and I lived many hours within the lit circle of his certainty, and his **bravado.** *Unscrew the locks from the doors! Unscrew the doors themselves from their jambs!* And there was the passion which he invested in the poems. The **metaphysical** curiosity! The oracular[5] tenderness with which he viewed the world—its roughness, its differences, the stars, the spider—nothing was outside the range of his interest. I reveled in the specificity of his words. And his faith—that kept my spirit buoyant surely, though his faith was without a name that I ever heard of.

[2] **avuncular:** of or having to do with an uncle.

[3] **boy from Romania:** This phrase refers to the gypsy in the previous sentence. The gypsies, also called Romani, are one of the largest minority groups in Romania.

[4] **incantatory:** in the manner of a verbal charm or spell.

[5] **oracular:** resembling or characteristic of an oracle; solemnly prophetic.

Do you guess I have some intricate purpose? Well I have . . . for the April rain has, and the mica on the side of a rock has.

6 But first and foremost, I learned from Whitman that the poem is a temple—or a green field—a place to enter, and in which to feel. Only in a secondary way is it an intellectual thing—an artifact, a moment of seemly and robust wordiness—wonderful as that part of it is. I learned that the poem was made not just to exist, but to speak—to be company. It was everything that was needed, when everything was needed. I remember the delicate, rumpled way into the woods, and the weight of the books in my pack. I remember the rambling, and the loafing—the wonderful days when, with Whitman, *I tucked my trowser-ends in my boots and went and had a good time.*

NOTICE & NOTE

ANALYZE DEVELOPMENT OF KEY IDEAS

Annotate: In paragraph 6, mark what Oliver learned from Whitman.

Analyze: How does this sentence develop a key idea expressed in the thesis statement?

CHECK YOUR UNDERSTANDING

Answer these questions before moving on to the **Analyze the Text** section on the following page.

1 How did Oliver think of Whitman?

A As her uncle or Romanian cousin

B As the brother she didn't have

C As a somewhat interesting poet

D As a poet she was forced to read

2 What triggered Oliver's truancy?

F Students in her class displayed delinquent behavior.

G Her parents did not believe in the school.

H The school stopped teaching writing.

J She was meeting her friend and goofing off.

3 What does Oliver mean when she writes that "the poem is a temple"?

A Writing is a religious experience for her.

B Whitman wrote religious poetry.

C It allows her to explore her emotions.

D She prefers traditional forms of poetry.

RESPOND

ANALYZE THE TEXT

Support your responses with evidence from the text. NOTEBOOK

1. **Interpret** In the first paragraph, Oliver writes that she makes "no special case of a solitary childhood." What do you think she means by this? Why do you think she includes this information?
2. **Analyze** How does Oliver support the idea that Whitman was her friend? Cite evidence from the text in your response.
3. **Infer** Oliver does not directly state her purpose for writing. It is up to you to infer it based on details in the text. What is Oliver's main purpose for writing? Cite text evidence in your response.
4. **Evaluate** How do the quotations from Whitman create an organizational design for the essay? How does this organizational design support Oliver's ideas?
5. **Notice & Note** The poem quoted throughout the essay is Walt Whitman's "Song of Myself." How does the title of this poem and the use of quotations support the main idea of Oliver's essay?

RESEARCH

RESEARCH TIP
Use both Oliver's name and the title of the poem to easily find the works specified.

Find and read the poems "Sleeping in the Forest," "Why I Wake Early," and "Song of the Builders" by Mary Oliver. Think about the essay you just read, and note in the chart below the parallels or connections you find between Oliver's poems and what you read in the essay. The parallels can be themes, phrases, words, or ideas.

POEM	PARALLELS AND CONNECTIONS
"Sleeping in the Forest"	
"Why I Wake Early"	
"Song of the Builders"	

Extend Mary Oliver is famous for poetry that focuses on nature. What general view of nature does Oliver express in her writing? In a small group, discuss Oliver's view on the natural world. Cite evidence from the essay and at least one of the poems in your discussion.

CREATE AND DISCUSS

Write an Essay Write an essay about an author whom you admire or whose work you enjoy. Focus on why you think the author's work is important and/or influential.

- ❑ Work on crafting a good thesis statement—what you are going to claim about the author.
- ❑ Include information about the author and quotes from his or her work. The quotes should support your thesis.
- ❑ Include a conclusion that summarizes your thesis statement.

Discuss with a Small Group Discuss the impact of literature on our lives. Use your essay as the basis of your contribution to the discussion. To prepare for the discussion, you may want to think about the following questions:

- ❑ What are the different kinds of literature we read and why are they important?
- ❑ How do movies sometimes revise or change literature?
- ❑ What can we experience by reading various types of literature?

Go to **Writing Informative Texts** in the **Writing Studio** for help with writing essays.

Go to **Participating in Collaborative Discussions** in the **Speaking and Listening Studio** for help.

RESPOND TO THE ESSENTIAL QUESTION

How do we relate to the world around us?

Gather Information Review your annotations and notes on "My Friend Walt Whitman." Then, add relevant information to your Response Log. As you determine which information to include, think about:

- the impact reading Walt Whitman had on the writer
- how the quotes from Walt Whitman's work help develop the main idea
- the effect of the author's use of personal anecdotes

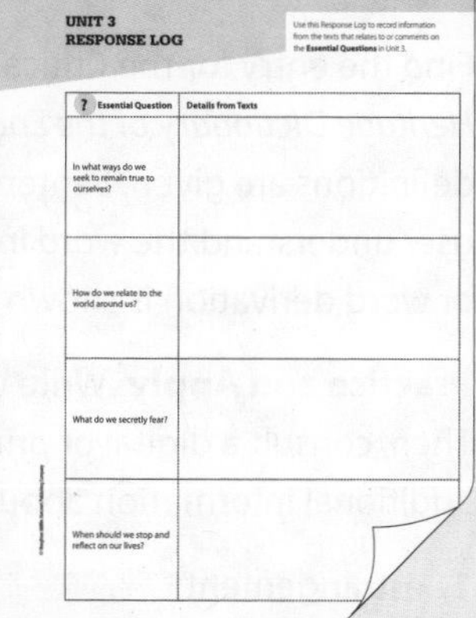

UNIT 3 RESPONSE LOG

Use this Response Log to record information from the texts that relates to or comments on the **Essential Questions** in Unit 3.

? Essential Question	Details from Texts
In what ways do we seek to remain true to ourselves?	
How do we relate to the world around us?	
What do we secretly fear?	
When should we stop and reflect on our lives?	

ACADEMIC VOCABULARY

As you write and discuss what you learned from the essay, be sure to use the Academic Vocabulary words. Check off each of the words that you use.

- ❑ **analogy**
- ❑ **denote**
- ❑ **quote**
- ❑ **topic**
- ❑ **unique**

RESPOND

CRITICAL VOCABULARY

WORD BANK
inclination
estrangement
delinquent
bravado
metaphysical

Practice and Apply Circle the letter of the best answer to each question. Then, explain your response.

1. An example of **delinquent** behavior is —
   a. doing homework **b.** not doing chores

2. **Bravado** is more likely to result in —
   a. standing your ground **b.** running away

3. An interest in the **metaphysical** might draw one to —
   a. philosophy **b.** engineering

4. Which of the following might lead to **estrangement**?
   a. working with someone **b.** arguing with someone

5. Which is an example of an **inclination** of an organized person?
   a. being on time **b.** being spontaneous

VOCABULARY STRATEGY: Use Print and Digital Resources

Go to **Using Reference Sources** in the **Vocabulary Studio** for help with using digital and print resources.

Digital and print resources, such as online and print dictionaries, can provide additional information about unfamiliar words and help you verify the meaning of a word. Using print and digital resources is especially important when the context isn't enough to determine the word's meaning, when a word has multiple meanings, or when the word is archaic, or no longer used.

Find the entry for the Critical Vocabulary word *inclination* in the *American Heritage Dictionary of the English Language.* Notice that a number of definitions are given. Sentences using the word are also included to help the user understand the word in context. In many entries, the word's etymology or word derivation is shown in brackets. Related words are also shown.

Practice and Apply Write what you think each word listed below means. Then, consult a digital or print dictionary to confirm the meaning and find additional information about each word.

1. estrangement: ______

2. bravado: ______

3. metaphysical: ______

LANGUAGE CONVENTIONS:
Informal Style

Authors choose what style they will use based on their purpose for writing. Formal language is used for academic or business settings. Informal language is often used in personal essays, so it sounds more conversational, as if the author is talking to the reader. Informal language often includes slang, idioms, or colloquial phrases. Contractions appear regularly in informal writing. The writer may occasionally address the reader directly, using the second-person *you*. Oliver uses many aspects of informal style.

- Her sentences are long and sound as if they are part of a conversation.

  The boy from Romania moved away; Whitman shone on in the twilight of my room, which was growing busy with books, and notebooks, and muddy boots, and my grandfather's old Underwood typewriter.

- Here, Oliver interjects information in the middle of the sentence.

  Only in a secondary way is it an intellectual thing—an artifact, a moment of seemly and robust wordiness—wonderful as that part of it is.

- She begins a sentence with a conjunction.

  And there was the passion which he invested in the poems.

- She shows empathy for the reader and adds clarification in a relatable way.

  That is, they said amazing things, and for me it changed the world.

Practice and Apply Write a paragraph about Mary Oliver, Walt Whitman, or any other writer you admire, using an informal style. As you write, think about how you would talk to someone about the subject you've chosen. Remember that the writing still has to be clear, but it can be friendly and conversational.

POEMS BY EMILY DICKINSON

? **ESSENTIAL QUESTION:**

In what ways do we seek to remain true to ourselves?

QUICK START

Emily Dickinson cherished her independence. Do you always feel free to just be you or can you be influenced by others? Think about whether it is easy or difficult to stand up for what you believe in. Share your ideas with the class.

ANALYZE THEME AND STRUCTURE

The **theme** of a poem is its underlying message—the point the poet wants to make about life. Most often, a reader has to infer the theme from details in the poem. In addition to her language, Dickinson uses elements of **structure** to convey important ideas and suggest themes. You can use the following structural elements to help you determine the theme.

- **Stanzas** Groups of lines make up the "paragraphs" of a poem. Each stanza may express a key idea that develops the theme.
- **Dashes** Dickinson uses the dash (—) in a variety of ways, including denoting an interruption or abrupt shift in thought, for emphasis, or to denote uncertainty or indecision. Think about how dashes can affect your interpretation of the theme.
- **Rhyme scheme** Rhyme is the occurrence of identical or similar sounds at the ends of words. In addition to being a sound device, rhyming words can serve to emphasize important ideas and concepts.

As you read, notice how Dickinson uses structure as well as language to develop the themes of her poems.

GENRE ELEMENTS: POETRY

- is arranged in verse, or lines, and stanzas
- uses figurative language to convey ideas
- often has patterns of meter and rhyme

ANALYZE FIGURATIVE LANGUAGE

Figurative language is language that communicates ideas beyond the literal meaning of words. Dickinson uses figurative language to add engagement to her poems and convey important ideas. Study the types of figurative language in the chart. Then, add an example of each type of figurative language from Dickinson's poems.

FIGURATIVE LANGUAGE	DEFINITION	EXAMPLE
Metaphor	a comparison of two unlike things that have something in common	
Simile	a comparison using the words *like* or *as* of two unlike things that have something in common	
Personification	the giving of human qualities to an object, animal, idea, or abstract concept	

ANALYZE SOUND DEVICES

In addition to the rich imagery they contain, Dickinson's poems are distinctive for the way they sound. Dickinson uses these sound devices in her poetry.

- **Meter and rhythm** The basic unit of meter is a **foot,** which contains one stressed and at least one unstressed syllable. This pattern of stressed and unstressed syllables creates a rhythm that may emphasize ideas, reinforce subject matter, and bring out the musical quality of language in the poem.
- **Rhyme scheme** Rhyme scheme refers to the pattern of end rhyme in a poem. Poets use patterns of sounds that are alike or similar to create a certain aesthetic quality. When the sounds are similar rather than the same, this is called **slant rhyme.**
- **Repetition** Repetition is a technique in which a sound, word, phrase, or line is repeated for emphasis or unity. Repetition often helps to reinforce meaning and create an appealing rhythm.
- **Punctuation and line breaks** When reading a poem aloud, punctuation can tell you when a pause occurs. These pauses can signify an interruption in thought or a shift in thinking. Dickinson uses line breaks in unusual ways. For example:

  The Soul selects her own Society—
  Then—shuts the Door—
  To her divine Majority—
  Present no more—

Both the line break and the dash at the end of the second line insert a break where there would not be one naturally. The pause this creates emphasizes the finality of the phrase "shuts the Door." Her verse is also unusual for the time in the way that it slows down, speeds up, pauses dramatically, and sometimes trails off.

As you read, note Dickinson's use of sound devices and how they affect your understanding of the poems.

ANNOTATION MODEL

NOTICE & NOTE

As you read, notice Dickinson's use of sound devices and figurative language. Note details that suggest the theme of each poem. Here are one reader's notes on the beginning of one poem by Dickinson.

The Soul selects her own Society—	Personification: the soul performs an action
Then—shuts the Door—	
To her divine Majority—	These dashes are jarring.
Present no more—	

BACKGROUND

Emily Dickinson *(1830–1886) was not known as a poet during her lifetime. After her death, her sister discovered some 1,800 poems in her home, written mostly between 1858 and 1865. Dickinson spent her entire life in and around Amherst, Massachusetts. Although formal schooling was unusual for girls at the time, Dickinson attended school, including Amherst Academy and Mount Holyoke Female Seminary. She occupied her time reading and writing letters as well as singing, gardening, and taking walks in nature. In her youth, she was very social, attending numerous church activities and cultivating a number of close friendships.*

POEMS BY EMILY DICKINSON

According to letters she wrote to her brother Austin, Dickinson increasingly sensed a difference between herself and others, writing in one letter, "What makes a few of us so different from others? It's a question I often ask myself." As she grew older, Dickinson retreated from public life, growing more and more reclusive. In her later years, she mostly interacted with the outside world through reading and writing, corresponding through letters with a few close friends. During her most productive years, she occupied a bedroom in the family home in Amherst. Letters from this time suggest a troubled romantic attachment that was the source of her creative drive.

Dickinson first took an interest in writing poetry in her teens, and by the time she was 35 she had composed more than 1,100 poems in her concise lyrical style, capturing her astute observations on love, nature, art, grief, pain, and joy. She did share a small portion of these poems with select friends and family. A few of her poems were published in newspapers, but only anonymously and apparently without her consent.

Emily Dickinson died at age 55. When the first volume of her poems was published in 1890, it won great critical and public acclaim, and she is now considered one of the greatest American poets.

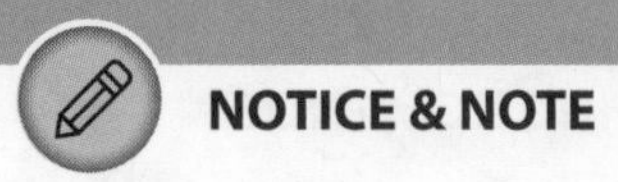

NOTICE & NOTE

Notice & Note

Use the side margins to notice and note signposts in the text.

ANALYZE SOUND DEVICES

Annotate: Mark the repeated word in the second stanza.

Interpret: What is the effect of repeating this word?

ANALYZE FIGURATIVE LANGUAGE

Annotate: Mark the simile in lines 11–12.

Analyze: What two things are being compared? What theme about the soul does this image suggest?

SETTING A PURPOSE

As you read Dickinson's poems, pay attention to the various ways she uses punctuation and line breaks, especially dashes, to create meaning and the concrete images she uses to represent abstract ideas.

The Soul selects her own Society

The Soul selects her own Society—
Then—shuts the Door—
To her divine Majority—
Present no more—

Unmoved—she notes the Chariots—pausing—
At her low Gate—
Unmoved—an Emperor be kneeling
Upon her Mat—

I've known her—from an ample nation—
Choose One—
Then—close the Valves of her attention—
Like Stone—

Illustration of Emily Dickinson's home.

Because I could not stop for Death

Because I could not stop for Death—
He kindly stopped for me—
The Carriage held but just Ourselves—
And Immortality.

We slowly drove—He knew no haste
And I had put away
My labor and my leisure too,
For His Civility—

We passed the School, where Children strove
At Recess—in the Ring—
We passed the Fields of Gazing Grain—
We passed the Setting Sun—

Or rather—He passed Us—
The Dews drew quivering and chill—
For only Gossamer,[1] my Gown—
My Tippet—only Tulle[2]—

We paused before a House that seemed
A Swelling of the Ground—
The Roof was scarcely visible—
The Cornice[3]—in the Ground—

Since then—'tis Centuries—and yet
Feels shorter than the Day
I first surmised the Horses' Heads
Were toward Eternity—

---

[1] **Gossamer:** thin, soft material.

[2] **Tippet . . . Tulle:** shawl made of fine netting.

[3] **Cornice:** molding at the top of a building.

NOTICE & NOTE

ANALYZE FIGURATIVE LANGUAGE

Annotate: In the first three stanzas, mark examples of personification.

Analyze: How does the personification of death affect the meaning of the poem?

ANALYZE THEME AND STRUCTURE

Annotate: Mark the word in the fourth stanza that signifies a shift in thinking.

Analyze: How does the speaker's perception of what is happening change in this stanza? Explain.

NOTICE & NOTE

ANALYZE THEME AND STRUCTURE

Annotate: In line 3, mark the words that come between dashes.

Interpret: What is the function of the dashes in line 3?

Much Madness is divinest Sense

Much Madness is divinest Sense—
To a discerning Eye—
Much Sense—the starkest Madness—
'Tis the Majority
In this, as All, prevail—
Assent—and you are sane—
Demur—you're straightway dangerous—
And handled with a Chain—

Tell all the Truth but tell it slant

Tell all the Truth but tell it slant—
Success in Circuit[4] lies
Too bright for our infirm Delight
The Truth's superb surprise
As Lightning to the Children eased
With explanation kind
The Truth must dazzle gradually
Or every man be blind—

[4] **Circuit:** indirect path.

ANALYZE FIGURATIVE LANGUAGE

Annotate: In lines 4–8, mark the simile.

Interpret: Using this simile, what does the speaker tell us about truth?

CHECK YOUR UNDERSTANDING

Answer these questions before moving on to the **Analyze the Text** section on the following page.

1 What is the theme of "The Soul selects her own Society"?

A It's wrong not to be open to making new friends.

B You shouldn't give up if someone refuses to talk to you.

C The speaker blames herself for her loneliness.

D People only reveal their innermost thoughts and feelings to a very few friends.

2 In the fifth stanza of "Because I could not stop for Death," what is the speaker describing?

F An underground chapel

G Her own grave

H Her own fallen-down house

J The house of the person they are visiting

3 Which of the following is an example of personification?

A *I've known her—from an ample nation—*

B *In this, as All, prevail—*

C *The Truth must dazzle gradually*

D *The Roof was scarcely visible—*

ANALYZE THE TEXT

Support your responses with evidence from the text. NOTEBOOK

1. **Interpret** Consider the sound devices Dickinson uses in "The Soul selects her own Society," such as repetition and rhyme. How do these sound devices support the important ideas in the poem?
2. **Interpret** An **extended metaphor** is a metaphor that is developed through several lines or sometimes an entire poem. What is the extended metaphor in "Because I could not stop for Death"? How does this impact the meaning of the poem?
3. **Analyze** A **paradox** is a statement that seems to contradict itself while suggesting an important truth. What paradox do you find in "Much Madness is divinest Sense"? What does this paradox suggest about the theme of the poem?
4. **Evaluate** In "Tell all the Truth but tell it slant," what are the different ways the speaker says the truth may be told? What theme about truth does she express through these ideas?
5. **Interpret** Dickinson uses dashes freely in her poems. How do the dashes affect the way you read the poem? How do they help clarify the meaning that she conveys?

RESEARCH

Although Emily Dickinson was reclusive for much of her life, she did maintain a lively correspondence with family members and friends. Do some research to find an example of Dickinson's letter writing. Then, answer the questions in the chart below.

QUESTION	ANSWER
To whom did Dickinson address her letter?	
What is the subject of the letter?	
What insight about Dickinson's life did you gain from reading the letter?	

RESEARCH TIP

If you enter *Emily Dickinson* or *Emily Dickinson writer,* you will likely get responses related to poetry. Be sure to enter search terms that are specific to ensure you receive information about her letters.

Extend Excerpts from Dickinson's letters were included in the Tony Award–winning one-woman play *The Belle of Amherst,* starring Julie Harris. Recordings of the show are available on the Internet. Look up a scene from the show. Then, summarize the scene to the class. Be sure to include any new insights on Dickinson that you gained from watching the scene.

CREATE AND DISCUSS

Write a Poem Create a poem that uses concrete images to describe one of these abstract ideas: friendship, adolescence, anger, or summer. As you write your poem:

- ❏ Include at least one example of figurative language. When creating your metaphors and similes, try to use imagery and descriptive language to create comparisons that a reader would not expect.
- ❏ Use sound devices such as rhyme or repetition to convey meaning.
- ❏ Express a theme about the idea you choose.

Go to **Writing as a Process** in the **Writing Studio** for help.

Discuss Poems Form groups or pairs with other students who wrote about the same idea that you did. Compare your poems with others in your group.

- ❏ Identify similarities and differences between the images in the poems.
- ❏ Evaluate the themes that each poem expresses.
- ❏ Discuss any ideas that the group found surprising.

Go to **Participating in Collaborative Discussions** in the **Speaking and Listening Studio** for help.

RESPOND TO THE ESSENTIAL QUESTION

? In what ways do we seek to remain true to ourselves?

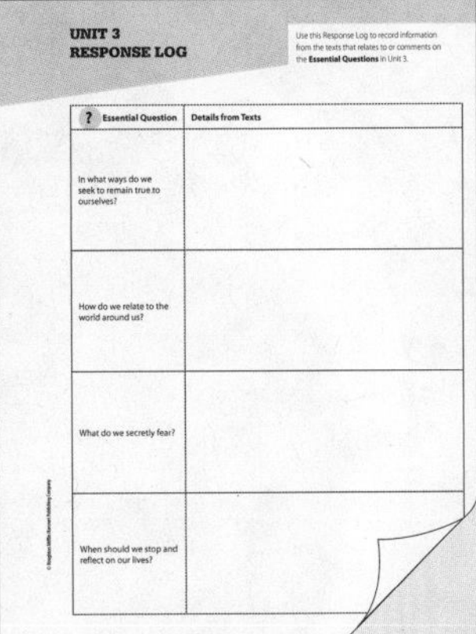

UNIT 3 RESPONSE LOG

Use this Response Log to record information from the texts that relates to or comments on the **Essential Questions** in Unit 3.

? Essential Question	Details from Texts
In what ways do we seek to remain true to ourselves?	
How do we relate to the world around us?	
What do we secretly fear?	
When should we stop and reflect on our lives?	

Gather Information Review your annotations and notes on the poems by Emily Dickinson. Then, add relevant information to your Response Log. As you determine which information to include, think about:

- why people sometimes want to be alone
- how valuable other people's opinions are to us
- the benefits of thinking differently from the crowd

ACADEMIC VOCABULARY

As you write and discuss what you learned from the poem, be sure to use the Academic Vocabulary words. Check off each of the words that you use.

- ❏ **analogy**
- ❏ **denote**
- ❏ **quote**
- ❏ **topic**
- ❏ **unique**

IN THE SEASON OF CHANGE

Poem by **Teresa Palomo Acosta**

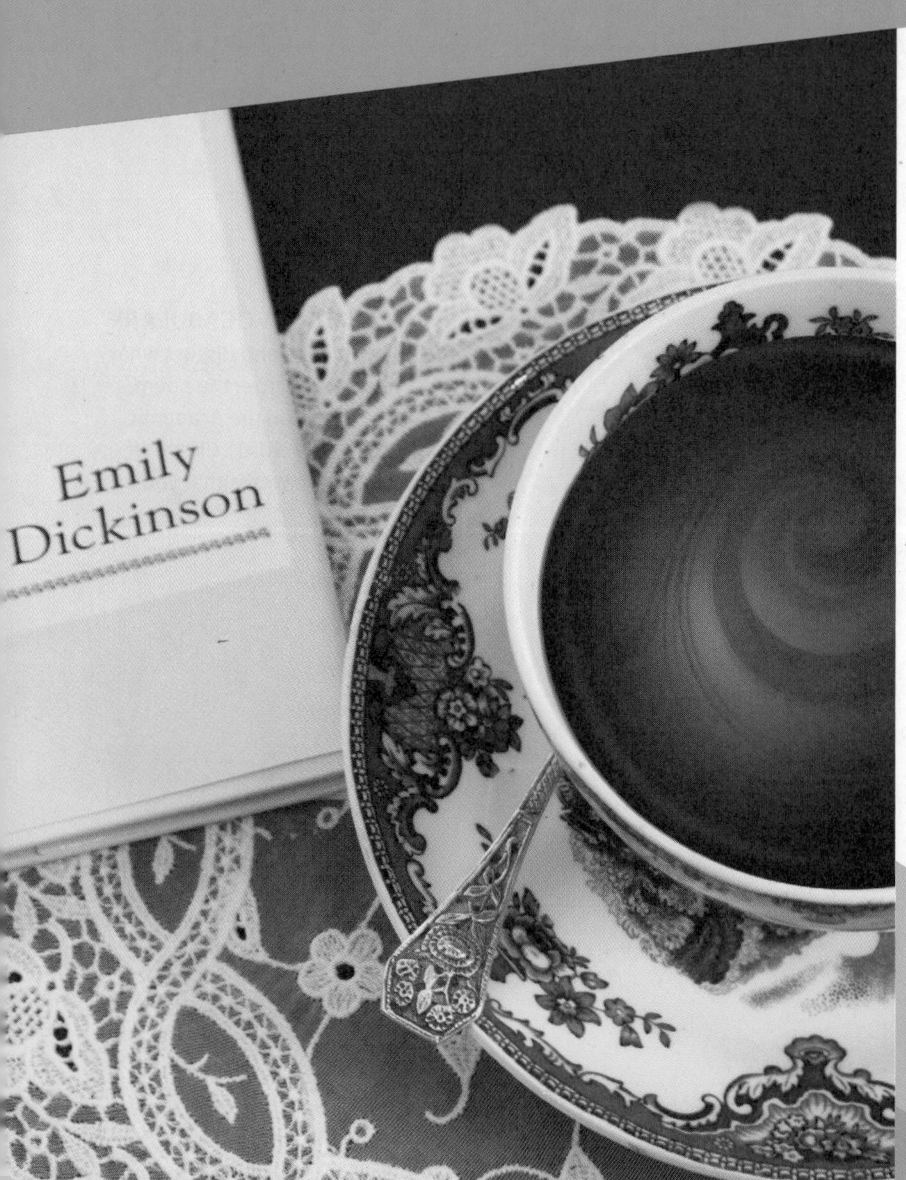

? ***ESSENTIAL QUESTION:***

How do we relate to the world around us?

QUICK START

Have you ever felt a connection to a well-known person? If you could share a meal with this person, what would you ask him or her? Write three questions you would ask. Then, role-play this encounter with a classmate.

ANALYZE SOUND DEVICES

"In the Season of Change" is an example of **free verse.** Free verse is poetry that does not have the regular meter or rhyming patterns of traditional poetry. Instead, free verse uses the natural rhythm of everyday speech. This poem also includes **sound devices** to contribute to the structure, rhythm, and meaning of the work. You will find the following sound devices in the poem:

- **Alliteration:** repetition of consonant sounds at the beginning of words
- **Assonance:** repetition of vowel sounds in nearby words
- **Consonance:** repetition of consonants within or at the end of a word

As you read, note examples of alliteration, assonance, and consonance in the chart. Think about the effect these sound devices have on the poem.

GENRE ELEMENTS: FREE VERSE

- does not have regular meter or rhyme patterns
- flows like natural speech
- lines can break within or flow across stanzas
- uses imagery and sound devices to evoke emotions or draw connections

SOUND DEVICE	EXAMPLES
Alliteration	
Assonance	
Consonance	

ANALYZE LINES AND STANZAS

In all poetry, **lines** are the core unit of a poem. **Line breaks** occur where a line of poetry ends. A line break can come at the end of a thought or sentence, but sometimes poets choose to break in the middle of a thought for effect. **Stanzas** are the groups of lines that form a unit of thought in a poem. When determining the meaning of a poem, consider the key ideas contained in each stanza. As you read, think about the effect line breaks have on the meaning of poem and consider the impact each stanza has on the message the writer expresses.

GET READY

ANALYZE IMAGERY

All poets use language to help them convey **themes,** or messages about life. Many of them convey themes through **imagery,** or vivid language that appeals to the senses. Imagery infuses a poem with meaning and allows readers to connect with similar emotions or experiences they've had. In "In the Season of Change," Teresa Palomo Acosta uses imagery to create a link with Emily Dickinson across time and cultures. In addition, she pairs Spanish terms with English terms—great-grandmothers/*bisabuelas*, rhubarb pie/*cafecito*, chatting/*chismeando*—to represent her heritage and emphasize both the similarities and the differences between her world and Dickinson's.

As you read "In the Season of Change," write down examples of imagery you find and note the senses they appeal to.

SENSE	IMAGERY
Sight	
Sound	
Smell	
Touch	
Taste	

ANNOTATION MODEL

NOTICE & NOTE

As you read, note the author's use of sound devices and the impact they have on meaning. Note the writer's use of imagery and the way she uses lines and stanzas to convey meaning. The model below shows one reader's notes for the first stanza of "In the Season of Change."

If E. Dickinson and I had been friends,
we would have each owned a treasure chest
filled with doilies for laying under our silverware,
for showing off atop our china cabinets.
For softening the scars in the 300-year-old dining room tables
we would have inherited
from our great-grandmothers.

Consonance—words with the "n" sound

The poet's descriptions help me picture the furniture.

BACKGROUND

Teresa Palomo Acosta *(b. 1949) was born in McGregor, Texas, to Mexican parents who had migrated to Texas during the Great Depression. Acosta earned a degree in ethnic studies at the University of Texas and then a master's degree at the Columbia University School of Journalism. She went on to become a leading voice of multiculturalism in the United States. She says her writing helps her retell stories about herself and about the Chicana experience. Acosta is also the coauthor of* Las Tejanas: 300 Years of History, *a history of women of Spanish-Mexican origin in Texas.*

IN THE SEASON OF CHANGE

Poem by Teresa Palomo Acosta

SETTING A PURPOSE

As you read, note the details that suggest a sense of longing, and think about what the poet longs for.

If E. Dickinson and I had been friends,
we would have each owned a treasure chest
filled with doilies for laying under our silverware,
for showing off atop our china cabinets.
For softening the scars in the 300-year-old dining room tables
we would have inherited
from our great-grandmothers.

But our bisabuelas[1] never met,
exchanged glances or
sat next to each other in church.
And I only discovered E. Dickinson
in the few pages she was allowed
to enter in my high school literature texts.

[1] **bisabuelas** (bēs-ä-bwā´läs): great-grandmothers.

Notice & Note

Use the side margins to notice and note signposts in the text.

ANALYZE IMAGERY

Annotate: In the first and second stanzas, mark images that appeal to the senses.

Analyze: How does the poet use the images to describe her relationship to Emily Dickinson?

NOTICE & NOTE

ANALYZE LINES AND STANZAS

Annotate: Use brackets to mark each sentence in lines 14–21.

Infer: How does the line length reflect the ideas expressed in the stanza?

ANALYZE SOUND DEVICES

Annotate: Mark the alliteration in lines 22–28.

Analyze: How does the alliteration serve to unify the lines in the stanza? What is the connection between the stanza and line 29?

Only years later did
I finally pore over her words,
believing that
her songs held
my name inscribed within.
And that they might fill the air
with the ancient signs of kinship
that women can choose to pass along.

And thus left on our own,
E. Dickinson and I
sat down at the same table,
savoring her rhubarb pie and my cafecito[2]
chatting and chismeando[3]
and trading secrets
despite decrees demanding silence between us:

women from separate corners of the room.

---

[2] **cafecito** (kä-fā-sē´tô): little cup of coffee.

[3] **chismeando** (chēs-mā-än´dô): gossiping.

CHECK YOUR UNDERSTANDING

Answer these questions before moving on to the **Analyze the Text** section on the following page.

1 Which of the following phrases from the poem is an example of assonance?

A *a treasure chest*

B *high school literature texts*

C *they might fill the air*

D *despite decrees demanding*

2 How does the poet discover Dickinson?

F The poet's grandmother introduces her.

G She finds a few Dickinson poems in her literature book.

H Her high school teacher spent a lot of time teaching Dickinson.

J She found a book of Dickinson's poems in a china cabinet.

3 What do the lines <u>her songs held</u> / <u>my name inscribed within</u> mean?

A Dickinson had known someone with the poet's name.

B Someone had written in the poet's literature book.

C The poet felt a strong kinship with Dickinson.

D The poet put her name in the book to show it was hers.

ANALYZE THE TEXT

Support your responses with evidence from the text. NOTEBOOK

1. **Infer** Why does the poet think that she and Dickinson could become friends?
2. **Analyze** How do the poem's stanzas give a structure to the poem? How does the structure support the poem's message?
3. **Evaluate** Think about the Spanish terms Acosta includes. What is the effect of using this imagery in the poem?
4. **Interpret** Poets may use sound devices to emphasize important ideas. What idea does Acosta emphasize by saying that she and Dickinson are sharing secrets "despite decrees demanding silence between [them]"?
5. **Connect** How do the lines "And thus left on our own, / E. Dickinson and I / sat down at the same table" help communicate the poem's theme?

RESEARCH

RESEARCH TIP

If you find a reliable online source, check the webpage of the source for links to other sources and or related materials.

Acosta coauthored a book on *Las Tejanas*—women in Texas who are descended from the original Spanish-speaking settlers of Texas and northern Mexico. However, there is some debate in Texas as to who qualifies as a *Tejana/Tejano* and who is *Criollo* or Mexican American. Research the meanings of these terms to find out more about these groups. Complete the chart below.

GROUP	CHARACTERISTICS
Tejano/Tejana	
Criollo	
Mexican American	

Extend Find another poem by Acosta in which she shares something of her Hispanic heritage. How does the second poem help expand the reader's view of Acosta and her life?

CREATE AND PRESENT

Write a Poem Write a free verse poem in which you imagine a meeting with someone you admire. Review your response to the Quick Start activity before you begin.

- ❑ Decide on where your meeting will take place. Incorporate details about the place into your poem.
- ❑ Think carefully about how word choice and structure can help you convey your thoughts and feelings in the poem.
- ❑ Use sound devices, such as alliteration, assonance, and consonance, to make your poem more interesting and memorable.

Go to **Writing as a Process** in the **Writing Studio** for help.

Present a Poem Poetry lends itself to reading aloud. In small groups, share the poems you have written.

- ❑ Practice reading your poem aloud several times so that it flows naturally.
- ❑ Think of your presentation as somewhere between music and acting so you can get the most out of the sound and emotion of the poem.
- ❑ Use your voice to emphasize the imagery, sound, and the structure of the stanzas to draw listeners' attention to important ideas in your poem.

Go to **Giving a Presentation: Delivering Your Presentation** in the **Speaking and Listening Studio** for help.

RESPOND TO THE ESSENTIAL QUESTION

How do we relate to the world around us?

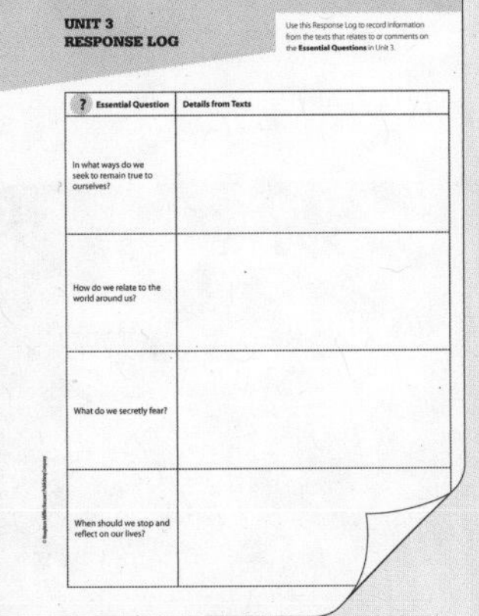

UNIT 3 RESPONSE LOG

Use this Response Log to record information from the texts that relates to or comments on the **Essential Questions** in Unit 3.

? Essential Question	Details from Texts
In what ways do we seek to remain true to ourselves?	
How do we relate to the world around us?	
What do we secretly fear?	
When should we stop and reflect on our lives?	

Gather Information Review your annotations and notes on "In the Season of Change." Then, add relevant information to your Response Log. As you determine which information to include, think about:

- how writing can be a way of connecting with the world around us
- how word choice, structure, and elements of poetry communicate emotions in a poem
- how writing, including poetry, can help us relate to people and see the world through different eyes

ACADEMIC VOCABULARY

As you write and discuss what you learned from the poem, be sure to use the Academic Vocabulary words. Check off each of the words that you use.

- ❑ **analogy**
- ❑ **denote**
- ❑ **quote**
- ❑ **topic**
- ❑ **unique**

ESSAY

from

WALDEN

by **Henry David Thoreau**

pages 253–257

COMPARE MAIN IDEAS

In the 19th century, Henry David Thoreau espoused the view that divinity was found in nature. The contemporary writer Richard Louv believes that humanity's essential connection to nature has been lost. As you read, consider what each author believes people gain from interacting with nature.

ESSENTIAL QUESTION:

When should we stop and reflect on our lives?

INFORMATIONAL TEXT

from

LAST CHILD IN THE WOODS

by **Richard Louv**

pages 258–261

QUICK START

Humans have a complicated relationship with nature. Think of a positive experience and a negative experience you have had in a natural setting. Why were these experiences memorable? Discuss your thoughts with a partner.

SUMMARIZE

One way to identify a text's key ideas is to write an objective summary of it. When you **summarize**, you restate the central ideas in your own words. A summary is much shorter than the original text and includes only the most important supporting details. Use these strategies to summarize the texts.

- Skim titles, headings, and other text features to predict the key ideas.
- See if a topic sentence, usually at the beginning or end of a paragraph, explicitly states the paragraph's key idea.
- Infer a central idea from the details contained in a paragraph.
- If you are struggling, summarize individual paragraphs or sections first.

GENRE ELEMENTS: INFORMATIONAL TEXTS AND ESSAYS

- clearly convey key ideas
- contain details that support key ideas
- use elements of author's craft including literary devices and figures of speech

ANALYZE AUTHOR'S CRAFT

Author's craft refers to how an author expresses his or her ideas. Author's craft can make ideas more compelling and make a text more engaging. Two aspects of author's craft are literary devices and figures of speech.

ELEMENTS OF AUTHOR'S CRAFT	
Literary Devices: Language structures that produce a special effect or convey additional meaning to a text	**Rhetorical question** A question that requires no reply **Repetition** To repeat a sound, word, or phrase for emphasis or unity **Irony** A contrast between appearances and reality **Verbal irony** A contrast between what is said and what is meant
Figures of Speech: Language that communicates ideas beyond the literal meaning of the words used	**Simile** A comparison between two things, using *like* or *as* **Metaphor** A direct comparison that does not use *like* or *as* **Hyperbole** An exaggeration of the truth for emphasis or humorous effect **Personification** To give human traits to objects, animals, or ideas

As you read the texts, notice how each writer employs elements of author's craft to help readers understand the ideas he wants to communicate. Think about how these elements shape your perception of ideas.

GET READY

WORD BANK

superfluous
abstraction
unfathomed
codify
perturbation
remunerative
polarity
configuration

CRITICAL VOCABULARY

Circle the synonym for each Critical Vocabulary word.

1. abstraction
   a. fact b. idea
2. codify
   a. order b. allow
3. configuration
   a. formation b. option
4. perturbation
   a. destruction b. disturbance
5. polarity
   a. convergence b. difference
6. remunerative
   a. paying b. unpaid
7. superfluous
   a. essential b. extra
8. unfathomed
   a. constrained b. vast

LANGUAGE CONVENTIONS

Rhetorical Questions Questions that are asked to make a point and without the expectation of an actual reply are called rhetorical questions. Note the example of a rhetorical question from *Walden* below.

Why should we live with such hurry and waste of life?

In this case, Thoreau does not want readers to answer the question; he wants them to ponder what he has written and see things from his point of view. Note the use of rhetorical questions and why an author includes them.

ANNOTATION MODEL

NOTICE & NOTE

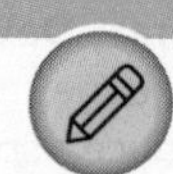

As you read, notice each author's key ideas and elements of author's craft that enhance their writing. Note any details that support the writer's key ideas. In the model, you can see one reader's notes about the essay from *Walden*.

I wanted to live deep and suck out all the marrow of life, to live so sturdily and Spartan-like as to put to rout all that was not life, to cut a broad swath and shave close, to drive life into a corner, and reduce it to its lowest terms, and, if it proved to be mean, why then to get the whole and genuine meanness of it, and publish its meanness to the world; or if it were sublime, to know it by experience, and be able to give a true account of it in my next excursion.

This is a strong statement and conveys an important idea: enthusiasm for life!

"Spartan-like" compares the way Thoreau wants to live—like a soldier. He uses more war imagery—describing an act of aggression.

BACKGROUND

Henry David Thoreau *(1817–1862) of Concord, Massachusetts, was a transcendentalist like his friend and mentor Ralph Waldo Emerson. After graduating from Harvard College and teaching school for a few years, Thoreau decided to become a nature poet. In 1845 he began his two-year experiment living in a cabin that he built in the woods near Walden Pond on property owned by Emerson.* Walden *(1854) is a collection of 18 essays based on his experiences. Thoreau's most famous essay, "Civil Disobedience" (1849), defends the right of an individual to follow his conscience rather than obey unjust laws.*

from

WALDEN

Essay by Henry David Thoreau

PREPARE TO COMPARE

As you read, note observations about "modern" life and the connection between humans and nature. You will compare these ideas with those of Richard Louv in the selection from Last Child in the Woods.

Notice & Note

Use the side margins to notice and note signposts in the text.

from Where I Lived, and What I Lived For

1 When first I took up my abode in the woods, that is, began to spend my nights as well as days there, which, by accident, was on Independence day, or the fourth of July, 1845, my house was not finished for winter, but was merely a defense against the rain, without plastering or chimney, the walls being of rough weather-stained boards, with wide chinks, which made it cool at night. The upright white hewn studs and freshly planed door and window casings gave it a clean and airy look, especially in the morning, when its timbers were saturated with dew, so that I fancied that by noon some sweet gum would exude from them. . . .

2 I was seated by the shore of a small pond, about a mile and a half south of the village of Concord and somewhat higher

SUMMARIZE

Annotate: Mark the title of this section of the essay.

Interpret: What is the most important idea the writer expresses in paragraph 1? How does the title help you predict this idea?

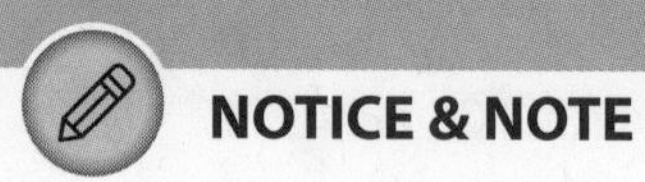

NOTICE & NOTE

ANALYZE AUTHOR'S CRAFT
Annotate: Mark an example of personification and an example of a simile in paragraph 2.

Analyze: How does this figurative language support a key idea in the paragraph?

superfluous
(so͝o-pûr´flo͞o-əs) *adj.* unnecessary.

than it, in the midst of an extensive wood between that town and Lincoln, and about two miles south of that our only field known to fame, Concord Battle Ground; but I was so low in the woods that the opposite shore, half a mile off, like the rest, covered with wood, was my most distant horizon. For the first week, whenever I looked out on the pond it impressed me like a tarn[1] high up on the side of a mountain, its bottom far above the surface of other lakes, and, as the sun arose, I saw it throwing off its nightly clothing of mist, and here and there, by degrees, its soft ripples or its smooth reflecting surface was revealed, while the mists, like ghosts, were stealthily withdrawing in every direction into the woods, as at the breaking up of some nocturnal conventicle.[2] The very dew seemed to hang upon the trees later into the day than usual, as on the sides of mountains. . . .

3 I went to the woods because I wished to live deliberately, to front only the essential facts of life, and see if I could not learn what it had to teach, and not, when I came to die, discover that I had not lived. I did not wish to live what was not life, living is so dear; nor did I wish to practice resignation, unless it was quite necessary. I wanted to live deep and suck out all the marrow of life, to live so sturdily and Spartan-like[3] as to put to rout all that was not life, to cut a broad swath and shave close, to drive life into a corner, and reduce it to its lowest terms, and, if it proved to be mean, why then to get the whole and genuine meanness of it, and publish its meanness to the world; or if it were sublime, to know it by experience, and be able to give a true account of it in my next excursion. For most men, it appears to me, are in a strange uncertainty about it, whether it is of the devil or of God, and have *somewhat hastily* concluded that it is the chief end of man here to "glorify God and enjoy him forever."

4 Still we live meanly, like ants; though the fable tells us that we were long ago changed into men; like pygmies we fight with cranes; it is error upon error, and clout upon clout, and our best virtue has for its occasion a **superfluous** and evitable[4] wretchedness. Our life is frittered away by detail. An honest man has hardly need to count more than his ten fingers, or in extreme cases he may add his ten toes, and lump the rest. Simplicity, simplicity, simplicity! I say, let your affairs be as two or three, and not a hundred or a thousand; instead of a million count half a dozen, and keep your accounts on your thumbnail. In the midst of this chopping sea of civilized life, such are the clouds and storms and quicksands and thousand-and-one items to be allowed for, that a man has to live, if he would not founder and go to the bottom and not make his port at all, by dead reckoning, and he must be a great calculator indeed who succeeds. Simplify, simplify. Instead of three meals a day, if it be necessary eat but one; instead of a hundred dishes, five; and reduce other things in proportion. . . .

[1] **tarn:** a small mountain lake or pool.
[2] **conventicle:** a secret or unlawful religious meeting.
[3] **Spartan-like:** in a simple and disciplined way, like the inhabitants of the ancient city-state of Sparta.
[4] **evitable:** avoidable.

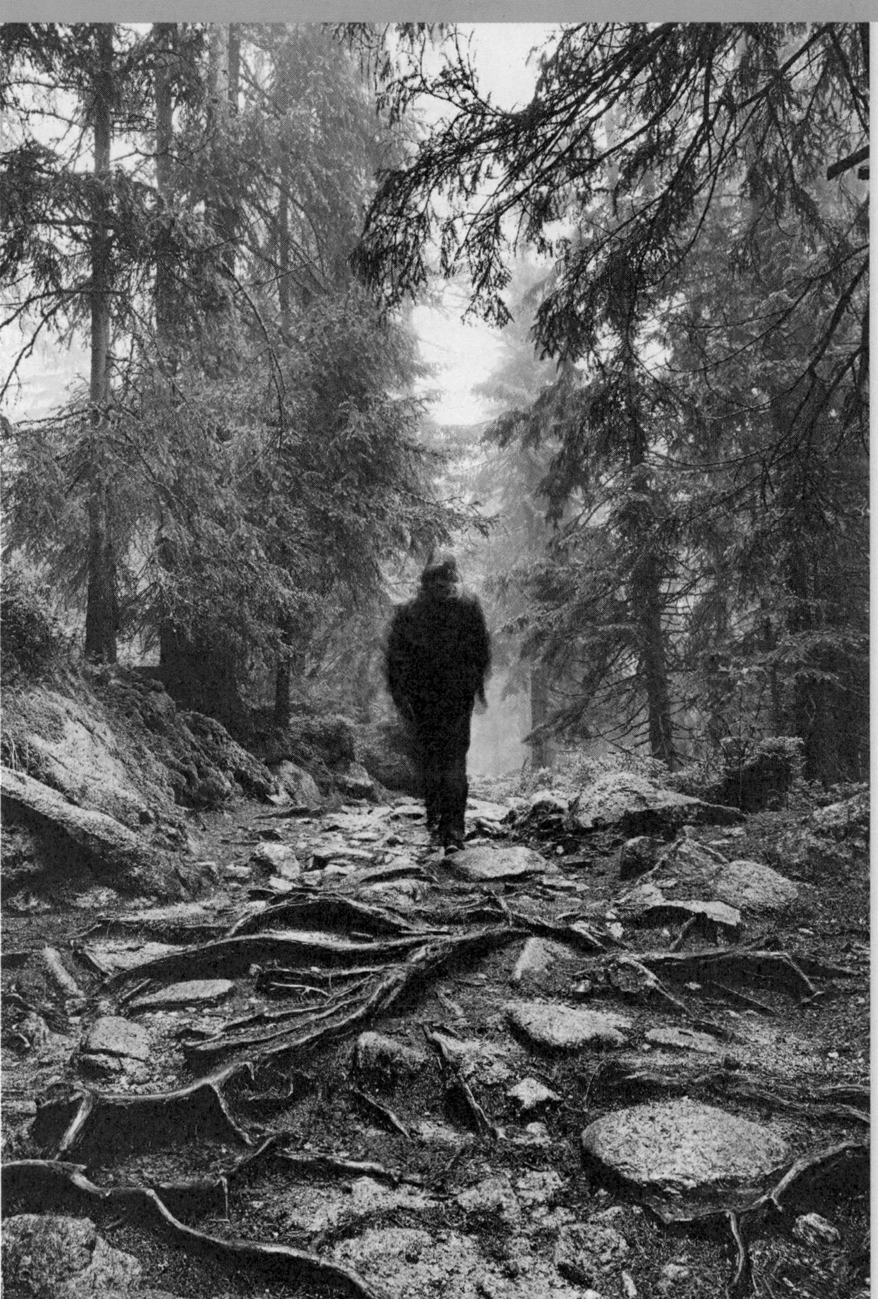

5 Why should we live with such hurry and waste of life? We are determined to be starved before we are hungry. Men say that a stitch in time saves nine, and so they take a thousand stitches today to save nine to-morrow. As for *work*, we haven't any of any consequence. We have the Saint Vitus' dance,[5] and cannot possibly keep our heads still. If I should only give a few pulls at the parish bell-rope, as for a fire, that is, without setting the bell, there is hardly a man on his farm in the outskirts of Concord, notwithstanding that press of engagements which was his excuse so many times this morning, nor a boy, nor a woman, I might almost say, but would forsake all and follow that

LANGUAGE CONVENTIONS

Annotate: Mark the rhetorical question in paragraph 5.

Analyze: What point is Thoreau making by asking this question?

[5] **Saint Vitus' dance:** a disorder of the nervous system, characterized by rapid, jerky, involuntary movements.

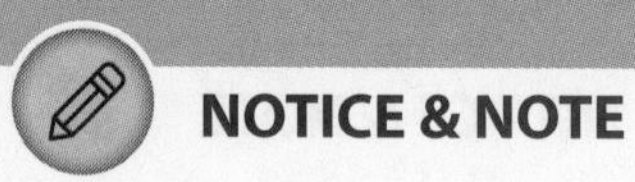

ANALYZE AUTHOR'S CRAFT

Annotate: Mark an example of hyperbole in paragraph 5.

Analyze: What is Thoreau exaggerating in this sentence? What effect does this exaggeration have on the reader? What does this use of hyperbole reveal about Thoreau's purpose?

unfathomed
(ŭn-făth´əmd) *adj.* located at the deepest place.

perturbation
(pûr-tər-bā´shən) *n.* disturbance or agitation.

SUMMARIZE

Annotate: Mark the last sentence of the selection.

Interpret: What does Thoreau mean when he says "the richest vein is somewhere hereabouts"? What key idea does this statement convey?

sound, not mainly to save property from the flames, but, if we will confess the truth, much more to see it burn, since burn it must, and we, be it known, did not set it on fire,—or to see it put out, and have a hand in it, if that is done as handsomely; yes, even if it were the parish church itself. Hardly a man takes a half hour's nap after dinner, but when he wakes he holds up his head and asks, "What's the news?" as if the rest of mankind had stood his sentinels. Some give directions to be waked every half hour, doubtless for no other purpose; and then, to pay for it, they tell what they have dreamed. After a night's sleep the news is as indispensable as the breakfast. "Pray tell me any thing new that has happened to a man any where on this globe,"—and he reads it over his coffee and rolls, that a man has had his eyes gouged out this morning on the Wachito River; never dreaming the while that he lives in the dark **unfathomed** mammoth cave of this world, and has but the rudiment of an eye himself.

6 For my part, I could easily do without the post-office. I think that there are very few important communications made through it. To speak critically, I never received more than one or two letters in my life—I wrote this some years ago—that were worth the postage. The penny-post is, commonly, an institution through which you seriously offer a man that penny for his thoughts which is so often safely offered in jest. And I am sure that I never read any memorable news in a newspaper. If we read of one man robbed, or murdered, or killed by accident, or one house burned, or one vessel wrecked, or one steamboat blown up, or one cow run over on the Western Railroad, or one mad dog killed, or one lot of grasshoppers in the winter,—we never need read of another. One is enough. . . .

7 Let us spend one day as deliberately as Nature, and not be thrown off the track by every nutshell and mosquito's wing that falls on the rails. Let us rise early and fast, or break fast, gently and without **perturbation;** let company come and let company go, let the bells ring and the children cry,— determined to make a day of it. . . .

8 Time is but the stream I go a-fishing in. I drink at it; but while I drink I see the sandy bottom and detect how shallow it is. Its thin current slides away, but eternity remains. I would drink deeper; fish in the sky, whose bottom is pebbly with stars. I cannot count one. I know not the first letter of the alphabet. I have always been regretting that I was not as wise as the day I was born. The intellect is a cleaver; it discerns and rifts its way into the secret of things. I do not wish to be any more busy with my hands than is necessary. My head is hands and feet. I feel all my best faculties concentrated in it. My instinct tells me that my head is an organ for burrowing, as some creatures use their snout and fore-paws, and with it I would mine and burrow my way through these hills. I think that the richest vein is somewhere hereabouts; so by the divining rod and thin rising vapors I judge; and here I will begin to mine.

CHECK YOUR UNDERSTANDING

Answer these questions about *Walden* before moving on to the next selection.

1 Where does Thoreau live during the time described in this essay?

A In the village of Concord

B In the small town of Lincoln

C In a field not far from Lincoln

D In the woods not far from Concord

2 What is Thoreau's main purpose for living there?

F To escape modern life

G To learn what is essential about life

H To be more devoted to God and glorify Him

J To become more like an animal than like a human

3 What are Thoreau's main complaints about human society?

A It is dull and full of empty relationships.

B It is shallow and full of terrifying cruelty.

C It is violent and full of appalling suffering.

D It is rushed and full of meaningless distractions.

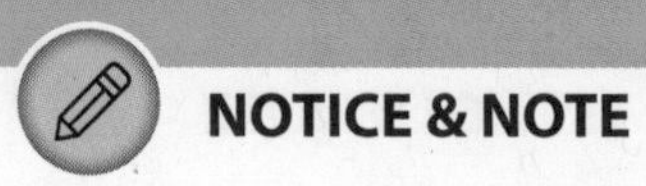

NOTICE & NOTE

BACKGROUND

Journalist **Richard Louv** *(b. 1949) is an active writer and speaker about the importance of reconnecting children to nature. He cofounded the Children & Nature Network, an organization whose vision is a "world in which all children play, learn and grow with nature in their everyday lives." He published the book* Last Child in the Woods: Saving Our Children from Nature-Deficit Disorder *in 2005, and received the Audubon Medal in 2008 for his work.*

from

LAST CHILD IN THE WOODS

Informational Text by Richard Louv

PREPARE TO COMPARE

As you read the excerpt from Last Child in the Woods, *consider how Richard Louv's ideas on nature relate to Thoreau's.*

Notice & Note

Use the side margins to notice and note signposts in the text.

1 One evening when my boys were younger, Matthew, then ten, looked at me from across a restaurant table and said quite seriously, "Dad, how come it was more fun when you were a kid?"

2 I asked what he meant.

3 "Well, you're always talking about your woods and tree houses, and how you used to ride that horse down near the swamp." At first, I thought he was irritated with me. I had, in fact, been telling him what it was like to use string and pieces of liver to catch crawdads in a creek, something I'd be hard-pressed to find a child doing these days. Like many parents, I do tend to romanticize my own childhood—and, I fear, too readily discount my children's experiences of play and adventure. But my son was serious; he felt he had missed out on something important.

SUMMARIZE

Annotate: Mark sentences and phrases in paragraph 4 that contrast the author's childhood and the lives of children today.

Compare: What main idea does this comparison communicate?

4 He was right. Americans around my age, baby boomers or older, enjoyed a kind of free, natural play that seems, in the era of kid pagers, instant messaging, and video games, like a quaint artifact. Within the space of a few decades, the way children understand and experience nature has changed radically. The **polarity** of the relationship has reversed. Today, kids are aware of the global threats

polarity (pō-lăr´ĭ-tē) *n.* separation to opposite sides.

to the environment—but their physical contact, their intimacy with nature, is fading. That's exactly the opposite of how it was when I was a child.

5 As a boy, I was unaware that my woods were ecologically connected with any other forests. Nobody in the 1950s talked about acid rain or holes in the ozone layer or global warming. But I knew my woods and my fields; I knew every bend in the creek and dip in the beaten dirt paths. I wandered those woods even in my dreams. A kid today can likely tell you about the Amazon rain forest—but not about the last time he or she explored the woods in solitude, or lay in a field listening to the wind and watching the clouds move.

6 The shift in our relationship to the natural world is startling, even in settings that one would assume are devoted to nature. Not that long ago, summer camp was a place where you camped, hiked in the woods, learned about plants and animals, or told firelight stories about ghosts or mountain lions. As likely as not today, "summer camp" is a weight-loss camp, or a computer camp. For a new generation, nature is more **abstraction** than reality. Increasingly, nature is something to watch, to consume, to wear—to ignore. A recent television ad depicts a four-wheel-drive SUV racing along a breathtakingly beautiful mountain stream—while in the backseat two children watch a movie on a flip-down video screen, oblivious to the landscape and water beyond the windows.

7 A century ago, the historian Frederick Jackson Turner announced that the American frontier had ended. His thesis has been discussed and debated ever since. Today, a similar and more important line is being crossed.

8 Our society is teaching young people to avoid direct experience in nature. That lesson is delivered in schools, families, even organizations devoted to the outdoors, and **codified** into the legal and regulatory structures of many of our communities. Our institutions, urban/suburban design, and cultural attitudes unconsciously associate nature with doom—while disassociating[1] the outdoors from joy and solitude. Well-meaning public-school systems, media, and parents are effectively scaring children straight out of the woods and fields. In the patent-or-perish environment of higher education, we see the death of natural history as the more hands-on disciplines, such as zoology, give way to more theoretical and **remunerative** microbiology and genetic engineering. Rapidly advancing technologies are blurring the lines between humans, other animals, and machines. The postmodern notion that reality is only a construct—that we are what we program—suggests limitless human possibilities; but as the young spend less and less of their lives in natural surroundings, their senses narrow, physiologically and psychologically, and this reduces the richness of human experience.

9 Yet, at the very moment that the bond is breaking between the young and the natural world, a growing body of research links our

NOTICE & NOTE

ANALYZE AUTHOR'S CRAFT

Annotate: Mark an example of irony in paragraph 6.

Interpret: What point does Louv make through the use of irony?

abstraction
(ăb-străk´shən) *n.* something that is not part of the concrete, material world.

codify
(kŏd´ĭ-fī) *v.* to arrange or systematize.

remunerative
(rĭ-myo͞o´nər-ə-tĭv) *adj.* yielding suitable recompense, profitable.

[1] **disassociating** (dĭs-ə-sō´sē-āt-ĭng): remove from association.

NOTICE & NOTE

SUMMARIZE

Annotate: Mark two significant details about the research that the author cites in paragraph 9.

Analyze: How do these details support the author's key idea that children ought to reconnect with nature?

configuration
(kən-fĭg-yə-rā´shən) *n.* arrangement of parts or elements.

mental, physical, and spiritual health directly to our association with nature—in positive ways. Several of these studies suggest that thoughtful exposure of youngsters to nature can even be a powerful form of therapy for attention-deficit disorders and other maladies. As one scientist puts it, we can now assume that just as children need good nutrition and adequate sleep, they may very well need contact with nature.

10 Reducing that deficit[2]—healing the broken bond between our young and nature—is in our self-interest, not only because aesthetics or justice demands it, but also because our mental, physical, and spiritual health depends upon it. The health of the earth is at stake as well. How the young respond to nature, and how they raise their own children, will shape the **configurations** and conditions of our cities, homes—our daily lives. . . .

11 . . . I am encouraged to find that many people now of college age—those who belong to the first generation to grow up in a largely de-natured environment—have tasted just enough nature to intuitively understand what they have missed. This yearning is a source of power. These young people resist the rapid slide from the

[2] **deficit** (dĕf´ĭ-sĭt): inadequacy or insufficiency.

NOTICE & NOTE

real to the virtual, from the mountains to the Matrix. They do not intend to be the last children in the woods.

12 My sons may yet experience what author Bill McKibben has called "the end of nature," the final sadness of a world where there is no escaping man. But there is another possibility: not the end of nature, but the rebirth of wonder and even joy. Jackson's obituary for the American frontier was only partly accurate: one frontier did disappear, but a second one followed, in which Americans romanticized, exploited, protected, and destroyed nature. Now that frontier—which existed in the family farm, the woods at the end of the road, the national parks, and in our hearts—is itself disappearing or changing beyond recognition. But, as before, one relationship with nature can evolve into another. . . .

SUMMARIZE

Annotate: In paragraph 12, mark a sentence that summarizes Louv's final thought to his readers.

Analyze: How does this final thought help to conclude the essay?

CHECK YOUR UNDERSTANDING

Answer these questions before moving on to the **Analyze the Texts** section on the following page.

1 What event caused Louv to begin thinking about how children relate to nature?

A The birth of his child

B A conversation with his child

C Taking his child on a camping trip

D Looking at his child's science textbook

2 What was Louv's childhood like?

F Playing outside and going fishing

G Going to camp and studying nature

H Wandering the streets of his small town

J Playing video games and being with friends

3 What is the main thing Louv thinks people ought to do?

A Clean up the environment.

B Give children books about nature.

C Help children reconnect with nature.

D Work to make the world a better place.

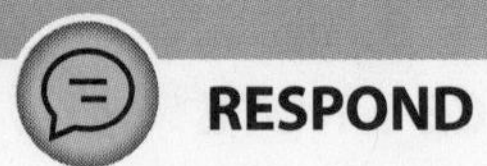

ANALYZE THE TEXTS

Support your responses with evidence from the texts. NOTEBOOK

1. **Summarize** How does Thoreau describe his reasons for moving to the woods in the excerpt from *Walden*? How do these reasons relate to his purpose in writing *Walden*?

2. **Analyze** What is the metaphor that Thoreau uses to describe civilized life in paragraph 4? What meaning does he convey through this figure of speech?

3. **Interpret** What does Thoreau mean by saying we should not be "thrown off the track" in paragraph 7 of the excerpt from *Walden*?

4. **Analyze** How does Louv use contrasts—such as *death* and *rebirth, broken* and *healing*—to develop his essay's main ideas in the excerpt from *Last Child in the Woods*?

5. **Evaluate** Louv includes both scientific evidence and his own personal experiences in *Last Child in the Woods*. Which of the details best support his ideas about the relationship between humanity and nature? Cite text evidence in your response.

RESEARCH

RESEARCH TIP

Narrowing the topic for Internet searches will help you find relevant sources. Using "Frederick Jackson Turner frontier" or "Frederick Jackson Turner biography" will give better results than "Frederick Jackson Turner."

The essay excerpt from *Last Child in the Woods* makes a reference to historian Frederick Jackson Turner and his thesis that the American frontier had ended. Do some research to complete the chart below with details about Turner and his theory.

BIOGRAPHICAL DETAILS ABOUT TURNER	MAJOR WRITINGS	OPINION ON THE AMERICAN FRONTIER

CREATE AND PRESENT

Go to **Conducting Research** in the **Writing Studio** for help.

Write an Essay Transcendentalism emphasized living a simple life and celebrating the truth found in nature, emotion, and imagination. How does the excerpt from *Walden* reflect these key aspects of transcendentalism? In your opinion, does the excerpt from *Last Child in the Woods* contain any transcendentalist ideas? Write an essay to describe your findings.

- ❑ Do any research you need to better understand transcendentalism.
- ❑ Describe the transcendentalist ideas in the two excerpts.
- ❑ Include text evidence to support your response.
- ❑ Close by stating your opinion on the value of these ideas today.

Present an Essay Present your essay to the class or a small group.

Go to **Giving a Presentation: Delivering Your Presentation** in the **Speaking and Listening Studio** for help.

- ❑ Consider adding visuals to your presentation.
- ❑ Practice several times before presenting to an audience.
- ❑ Speak clearly and slowly, making eye contact with your audience as you present your essay.

RESPOND TO THE ESSENTIAL QUESTION

When should we stop and reflect on our lives?

Gather Information Review your annotations and notes on the excerpts from *Walden* and *Last Child in the Woods*. Think about how each author reflects on his life experiences and views them as beneficial. Consider how experiencing nature relates to this reflection. Then, add relevant details to your Response Log.

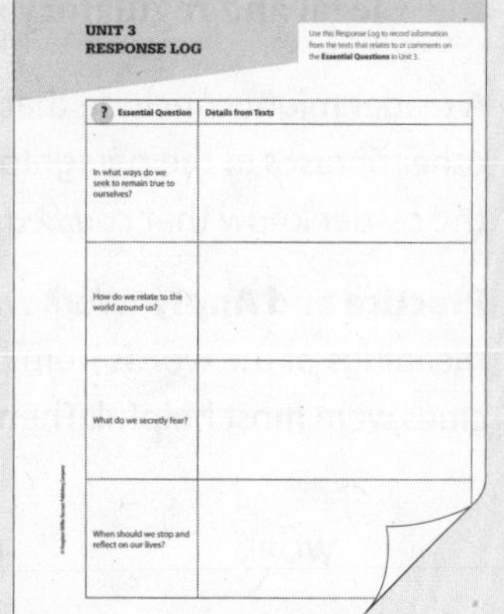

UNIT 3
RESPONSE LOG

Use this Response Log to record information from the texts that relates to or comments on the **Essential Questions** in Unit 3.

? Essential Question	Details from Texts
In what ways do we seek to remain true to ourselves?	
How do we relate to the world around us?	
What do we secretly fear?	
When should we stop and reflect on our lives?	

ACADEMIC VOCABULARY

As you write and discuss what you learned from the two excerpts, be sure to use the Academic Vocabulary words. Check off each of the words that you use.

- ❑ **analogy**
- ❑ **denote**
- ❑ **quote**
- ❑ **topic**
- ❑ **unique**

RESPOND

CRITICAL VOCABULARY

WORD BANK
superfluous **abstraction**
unfathomed **codify**
perturbation **remunerative**
polarity **configuration**

Practice and Apply Use your understanding of the Critical Vocabulary words to answer each question.

1. If Walden Pond was **unfathomed,** was it deep or shallow?
2. Many people experience **perturbation** when listening to the news. Does it make them upset or happy?
3. Thoreau found the post office **superfluous.** Did he think it was necessary or unnecessary?
4. Louv notes that nature has become an **abstraction** for children. Does this mean it is learned by experience or as a concept?
5. Both essayists suggest nature is **remunerative.** Does this mean it harms or benefits them?

VOCABULARY STRATEGY: Draw Conclusions about Word Meanings

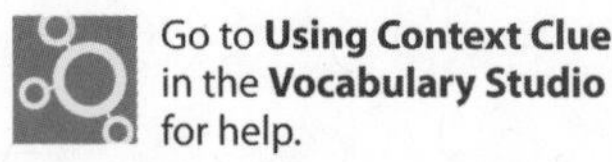
Go to **Using Context Clues** in the **Vocabulary Studio** for help.

Using **context clues**—nearby words, phrases, and sentences—can help you draw conclusions about the meanings of unfamiliar words. Consider the context in *Walden* for the Critical Vocabulary word *perturbation*:

> **Let us rise early and fast, or break fast, gently and without perturbation . . .**

The word *without* signals a contrast between *gently* and *perturbation*. You can guess that *perturbation* means "agitation or uneasiness." Sometimes you have to look at a wider context to find clues to a word's meaning.

The word *codified* appears in this sentence from *Last Child in the Woods*:

> **That lesson is delivered in schools, families, even organizations devoted to the outdoors, and codified into the legal and regulatory structures of many of our communities.**

A reader might conclude that *codified* means "written" or "added." However, other phrases in the paragraph, such as "legal and regulatory structures" let the reader know that *codified* means to be organized and systematized.

Practice and Apply Work with a partner to use context to determine the meanings of the words from *Last Child in the Woods*. Record which context clues were most helpful. Then, check your definitions by using a dictionary.

WORD	CONTEXT CLUES	MEANING
maladies		
ecologically		

LANGUAGE CONVENTIONS:
Rhetorical Questions

Questions that are asked to make a point without the expectation of a reply are called **rhetorical questions.** Rhetorical questions require that readers pause and reflect on some aspect of a writer's argument or claim. However, the writer either does not expect an answer to the question, or may choose to answer it in the course of making a point. Often, rhetorical questions suggest that the writer's view is obvious or common sense. In some instances, a rhetorical question serves as a transition from one topic to another.

Because *Walden* reflects on Thoreau's experiment with living simply and the lessons he learned from the experiment, these questions also suggest the kinds of questions that Thoreau may have asked himself while living alone in the woods.

Practice and Apply Review the essay you wrote in the Create and Present activity. Revise the essay so that it includes at least two rhetorical questions. For example, consider introducing one of your main ideas in the form of a question. Write your revision to the paragraph in the space below.

Collaborate & Compare

from
LAST CHILD IN THE WOODS
by Richard Louv

COMPARE MAIN IDEAS

Both *Walden* and *Last Child in the Woods* are about the human relationship with nature. Even though the texts are from very different historical and social contexts, they discuss some of the same issues. Using examples from the works, complete the chart below with:

- main ideas about the effects of technology on people
- main ideas about the benefits of nature for people
- important images and details that relate to main ideas
- important comparisons that relate to main ideas

	from WALDEN	*from* LAST CHILD IN THE WOODS
Effects of Technology		
Benefits of Nature		
Important Images and Details		
Important Comparisons		

ANALYZE THE TEXTS

Discuss these questions in your group.

1. **Compare** With your group, review the images and details that you cited in your chart. In what ways are the images similar? In what ways are they different? Explain.
2. **Infer** Both essays describe the effects progress and technology have on human beings. According to each, what should be the attitude of people toward technology and toward nature? Cite text evidence in your discussion.
3. **Evaluate** Would you characterize the diction of each excerpt as formal or informal? In what other ways does the diction affect the tone of each piece? How does each author's diction reflect the purpose of each essay? Which author most effectively uses diction to achieve his purpose?
4. **Analyze** Authors can structure their essays in a variety of ways. Compare how Thoreau and Louv construct their arguments to best serve their purpose. For example, did they look at cause and effect or did they compare and contrast elements? Which author had the more effective organizational structure?

COLLABORATE AND PRESENT

Now, your group can continue exploring the ideas in these texts by identifying and comparing their main ideas. Follow these steps:

1. **Decide on the most important ideas** With your group, review your chart to identify the most important ideas from each essay. Identify points you agree on, and resolve any disagreements through a discussion based on evidence from the texts.

2. **Compare main ideas** Compare the main ideas of the two essays. Listen actively to the members of your group and ask them to clarify any points you do not understand. Include similarities and differences in the chart.

Go to **Giving a Presentation** in the **Speaking and Listening Studio** for help.

SIMILARITIES	DIFFERENCES

3. **Synthesize information** Think about what insights you may have gained by reading these two texts in tandem. What connections did you make between the two pieces? What new understanding about nature and humanity's connection to it emerged from your reading? Record your ideas and any supporting details.

4. **Present to the class** Now it is time to present your ideas. Be sure to include a summary of the main ideas of each essay as well as a comparison of those ideas. Consider what new insights you may have learned by synthesizing the information from the two texts. You may adapt the charts you created or prepare other visuals to help convey information to the class.

SHORT STORY

THE MINISTER'S BLACK VEIL

by **Nathaniel Hawthorne**

pages 271–285

COMPARE THEMES

As you read these two short stories, consider how Hawthorne and Poe explored the darker side of Romanticism. Hawthorne examined the psychological effects that sin and guilt have on human life. Poe explored human psychology through first-person narrators who were involved in physical and mental torture.

? ESSENTIAL QUESTION:

What do we secretly fear?

SHORT STORY

THE PIT AND THE PENDULUM

by **Edgar Allan Poe**

pages 293–307

The Minister's Black Veil

QUICK START

How do you react in situations where you feel unsure? Discuss your ideas with a partner.

ANALYZE LITERARY ELEMENTS

In the early 1800s, Romanticism was a major literary movement reflecting a belief that the divine is embodied in nature and people are essentially good. Some American Romantics disagreed, feeling that these views did not account for the presence of suffering in the world and the conflict between good and evil. These **Dark Romantics** did share with other Romantics an interest in the spiritual world; however, they also sought to explore the darker mysteries of human existence.

To do so, Hawthorne and other authors used **literary elements**—character, setting, plot, and theme—to explore their ideas. The plot of a short story can arise not only from a character's **motivations,** or reasons for a character's behavior, but also from the setting of the story. In some stories, like Hawthorne's, the social context of the setting actively influences plot events and a character's actions. For example, in Puritan society, the meetinghouse was the central community gathering place for all religious and civil events. Congregation members sat according to social status and gender with the oldest and most distinguished sitting toward the front. Men and women, even from the same family, sat on opposite sides. This sin-obsessed community provides social context for "The Minister's Black Veil," and can help you understand plot events, character motivations, and the themes that emerge. As you read, notice the way these literary elements relate and impact your understanding.

GENRE ELEMENTS: SHORT STORY

- contains literary elements such as plot, character, and setting, that relate and interact
- uses suspense to maintain readers' interest as the plot is revealed
- may center on a symbol that is central to the story's meaning

ANALYZE STRUCTURE

The **structure** of a story is how the writer organizes and develops the plot. In "The Minister's Black Veil," Hawthorne uses suspense and ambiguity to advance the plot.

- **Suspense** is the tension created by the plot that leaves readers wondering what will happen next and how the central conflict will be resolved.
- **Ambiguity** is the uncertainty created when an author leaves elements of the text open to the reader's interpretation. Ambiguity often surrounds a **symbol—**an object that has a concrete meaning but also stands for something else—as symbols can have complex associations.

The black veil worn by one of the main characters is a central symbol in the story. As you read, note descriptions of the black veil, as well as the way other characters react to and comment on it. What meaning does Hawthorne attempt to convey through the symbol?

GET READY

CRITICAL VOCABULARY

Choose the best definition of each Critical Vocabulary word.

emblem **pathos** **ostentatious** **obstinacy** **plausibility** **mitigate**

1. Her explanation for being late lacked all **plausibility.**
   a. believability b. responsibility c. contrition

2. Nevertheless, she stuck to that explanation with great **obstinacy.**
   a. conviction b. stubbornness c. smugness

3. The **pathos** of the tale left the audience deeply moved.
   a. humor b. sadness c. outrage

4. Each product bore the **emblem** of the manufacturer.
   a. label b. address c. identifying mark

5. A sincere apology might serve to **mitigate** your punishment.
   a. intensify b. lessen c. eliminate

6. The **ostentatious** furnishings were a failed attempt to impress visitors.
   a. rich b. valuable c. pretentious

LANGUAGE CONVENTIONS

Appositives and Appositive Phrases Nouns that identify or rename another noun or a pronoun are called appositives. Appositives are single words; appositive phrases include modifiers of the appositive. An appositive comes immediately after the noun or pronoun to make the connection between the two clear, as in the example "My brother Mychal." As you read, note the author's use of appositives to provide information on the characters.

ANNOTATION MODEL

NOTICE & NOTE

As you read, note how the author uses details to signal the importance of the minister to the townspeople. Here are one reader's notes on "The Minister's Black Veil."

"But what has the good Parson Hooper got upon his face?" cried the sexton in astonishment.

seems like something is terribly wrong

All within hearing immediately turned about, and beheld the semblance of Mr. Hooper, pacing slowly his meditative way toward the meetinghouse. With one accord they started, expressing more wonder than if some strange minister were coming to dust the cushions of Mr. Hooper's pulpit.

Suspense! Character reactions make me wonder what the matter is. Will the writer tell us?

NOTICE & NOTE

BACKGROUND

Nathaniel Hawthorne *(1804–1864) was born in Salem, Massachusetts. By the time he left for Bowdoin College in 1821, Hawthorne knew he wanted to write. After graduation, he lived alone for 12 years, dedicated to building his career. By 1842, he had achieved some success. When times were tough, Hawthorne had friends set him up with government jobs, whose dull routines choked his imagination and limited his time to write. Hawthorne, however, never stopped writing, often exploring the influence of Puritan beliefs on New England society. Today he is most celebrated for his short stories and for* The Scarlet Letter *(1850).*

THE MINISTER'S BLACK VEIL

Short Story by Nathaniel Hawthorne

PREPARE TO COMPARE

*The **theme** is the central message of a work of literature. Think about how a writer develops theme through the introduction and development of characters and the building of plot.*

Notice & Note

Use the side margins to notice and note signposts in the text.

1 The sexton stood in the porch of Milford meetinghouse, pulling lustily at the bell rope. The old people of the village came stooping along the street. Children, with bright faces, tripped merrily beside their parents, or mimicked a graver gait, in the conscious dignity of their Sunday clothes. Spruce[1] bachelors looked sidelong at the pretty maidens, and fancied that the Sabbath sunshine made them prettier than on weekdays. When the throng had mostly streamed into the porch, the sexton began to toll the bell, keeping his eye on the Reverend Mr. Hooper's door. The first glimpse of the clergyman's figure was the signal for the bell to cease its summons.

2 "But what has good Parson Hooper got upon his face?" cried the sexton in astonishment.

ANALYZE STRUCTURE

Annotate: Mark the word in paragraph 2 that shows something unusual has occurred.

Analyze: How does this word choice build suspense in the story?

[1] **Spruce:** neat and clean.

ANALYZE STRUCTURE
Annotate: Mark the words in paragraph 6 that describe what is on Mr. Hooper's face.

Interpret: What is the purpose of a veil? What are possible symbolic meanings of the black color?

ANALYZE LITERARY ELEMENTS
Annotate: Mark the phrases in paragraph 10 that tell you the reaction of the members of the congregation.

Infer: What can you infer about the minister's role in Puritan society from these reactions?

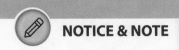

3 All within hearing immediately turned about, and beheld the semblance[2] of Mr. Hooper, pacing slowly his meditative way towards the meetinghouse. With one accord they started, expressing more wonder than if some strange minister were coming to dust the cushions of Mr. Hooper's pulpit.

4 "Are you sure it is our parson?" inquired Goodman[3] Gray of the sexton.

5 "Of a certainty it is good Mr. Hooper," replied the sexton. "He was to have exchanged pulpits with Parson Shute of Westbury; but Parson Shute sent to excuse himself yesterday, being to preach a funeral sermon."

6 The cause of so much amazement may appear sufficiently slight. Mr. Hooper, a gentlemanly person about thirty, though still a bachelor, was dressed with due clerical neatness, as if a careful wife had starched his band, and brushed the weekly dust from his Sunday's garb. There was but one thing remarkable in his appearance. Swathed about his forehead, and hanging down over his face, so low as to be shaken by his breath, Mr. Hooper had on a black veil. On a nearer view, it seemed to consist of two folds of crape,[4] which entirely concealed his features, except the mouth and chin, but probably did not intercept his sight, farther than to give a darkened aspect to all living and inanimate things. With this gloomy shade before him, good Mr. Hooper walked onward, at a slow and quiet pace, stooping somewhat and looking on the ground, as is customary with abstracted[5] men, yet nodding kindly to those of his parishioners who still waited on the meetinghouse steps. But so wonder-struck were they that his greeting hardly met with a return.

7 "I can't really feel as if good Mr. Hooper's face was behind that piece of crape," said the sexton.

8 "I don't like it," muttered an old woman, as she hobbled into the meetinghouse. "He has changed himself into something awful, only by hiding his face."

9 "Our parson has gone mad!" cried Goodman Gray, following him across the threshold.

10 A rumor of some unaccountable phenomenon had preceded Mr. Hooper into the meetinghouse, and set all the congregation astir. Few could refrain from twisting their heads towards the door; many stood upright, and turned directly about; while several little boys clambered upon the seats, and came down again with a terrible racket. There was a general bustle, a rustling of the women's gowns and shuffling of the men's feet, greatly at variance[6] with that hushed repose which should attend the entrance of the minister. But Mr. Hooper appeared not to notice the perturbation of his people. He entered with an almost noiseless step, bent his head mildly to the pews on each side,

[2] **semblance:** appearance.
[3] **Goodman:** a title used by Puritans that was equivalent to *mister*.
[4] **crape:** a black, silky fabric worn as a sign of mourning.
[5] **abstracted:** absent-minded; preoccupied.
[6] **at variance:** contrasting.

and bowed as he passed his oldest parishioner, a white-haired great-grandsire, who occupied an armchair in the centre of the aisle. It was strange to observe how slowly this venerable man became conscious of something singular in the appearance of his pastor. He seemed not fully to partake of the prevailing wonder till Mr. Hooper had ascended the stairs, and showed himself in the pulpit, face-to-face with his congregation, except for the black veil. That mysterious **emblem** was never once withdrawn. It shook with his measured breath as he gave out the psalm; it threw its obscurity between him and the holy page, as he read the Scriptures; and while he prayed, the veil lay heavily on his uplifted countenance. Did he seek to hide from the dread Being whom he was addressing?

emblem
(ĕm´bləm) *n.* an identifying mark or symbol.

11 Such was the effect of this simple piece of crape, that more than one woman of delicate nerves was forced to leave the meetinghouse. Yet perhaps the pale-faced congregation was almost as fearful a sight to the minister as his black veil to them.

12 Mr. Hooper had the reputation of a good preacher, but not an energetic one: he strove to win his people heavenward by mild persuasive influences, rather than to drive them thither by the thunders of the Word. The sermon which he now delivered was marked by the same characteristics of style and manner as the general series of his pulpit oratory. But there was something, either in the sentiment of the discourse itself, or in the imagination of the auditors, which made it greatly the most powerful effort that they had ever heard from their pastor's lips. It was tinged, rather more darkly than

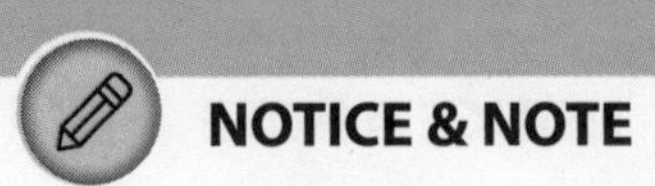

usual, with the gentle gloom of Mr. Hooper's temperament. The subject had reference to secret sin, and those sad mysteries which we hide from our nearest and dearest, and would fain conceal from our own consciousness, even forgetting that the Omniscient[7] can detect them. A subtle power was breathed into his words. Each member of the congregation, the most innocent girl, and the man of hardened breast, felt as if the preacher had crept upon them, behind his awful veil, and discovered their hoarded iniquity[8] of deed or thought. Many spread their clasped hands on their bosoms. There was nothing terrible in what Mr. Hooper said; at least, no violence; and yet, with every tremor of his melancholy voice, the hearers quaked. An unsought **pathos** came hand in hand with awe. So sensible were the audience of some unwonted attribute in their minister, that they longed for a breath of wind to blow aside the veil, almost believing that a stranger's visage would be discovered, though the form, gesture and voice were those of Mr. Hooper.

pathos
(pă´thŏs) *n.* something that evokes pity or sympathy.

13 At the close of the services, the people hurried out with indecorous[9] confusion, eager to communicate their pent-up amazement, and conscious of lighter spirits the moment they lost sight of the black veil. Some gathered in little circles, huddled closely together, with their mouths all whispering in the centre; some went homeward alone, wrapped in silent meditation; some talked loudly, and profaned[10] the Sabbath day with **ostentatious** laughter. A few shook their sagacious heads, intimating[11] that they could penetrate the mystery; while one or two affirmed that there was no mystery at all, but only that Mr. Hooper's eyes were so weakened by the midnight lamp as to require a shade. After a brief interval, forth came good Mr. Hooper also, in the rear of his flock. Turning his veiled face from one group to another, he paid due reverence to the hoary[12] heads, saluted the middle-aged with kind dignity, as their friend and spiritual guide, greeted the young with mingled authority and love, and laid his hands on the little children's heads to bless them. Such was always his custom on the Sabbath day. Strange and bewildered looks repaid him for his courtesy. None, as on former occasions, aspired to the honor of walking by their pastor's side. Old Squire Saunders, doubtless by an accidental lapse of memory, neglected to invite Mr. Hooper to his table, where the good clergyman had been wont[13] to bless the food almost every Sunday since his settlement. He returned, therefore, to the parsonage, and at the moment of closing the door, was observed to look back upon the people, all of whom had their eyes fixed upon the minister. A sad smile gleamed

ostentatious
(ŏs-tĕn-tā´shəs) *adj.* conspicuous and vulgar.

CONTRASTS AND CONTRADICTIONS

Notice & Note: Mark the words in paragraph 13 that show a surprising reaction by the minister.

Analyze: How does this reaction add suspense to the situation?

[7] **the Omniscient:** God; literally, the all-knowing.
[8] **iniquity:** sinfulness.
[9] **indecorous:** undignified; inappropriate.
[10] **profaned:** desecrated; treated irreverently.
[11] **intimating:** revealing.
[12] **hoary:** gray or white due to age.
[13] **wont:** habit.

NOTICE & NOTE

faintly from beneath the black veil, and flickered about his mouth, glimmering as he disappeared.

14 "How strange," said a lady, "that a simple black veil, such as any woman might wear on her bonnet, should become such a terrible thing on Mr. Hooper's face!"

15 "Something must surely be amiss with Mr. Hooper's intellects," observed her husband, the physician of the village. "But the strangest part of the affair is the effect of this vagary,[14] even on a sober-minded man like myself. The black veil, though it covers only our pastor's face, throws its influence over his whole person, and makes him ghost-like from head to foot. Do you not feel it so?"

16 "Truly do I," replied the lady; "and I would not be alone with him for the world. I wonder he is not afraid to be alone with himself!"

17 "Men sometimes are so," said her husband.

18 The afternoon service was attended with similar circumstances. At its conclusion, the bell tolled for the funeral of a young lady. The relatives and friends were assembled in the house, and the more distant acquaintances stood about the door, speaking of the good qualities of the deceased, when their talk was interrupted by the appearance of Mr. Hooper, still covered with his black veil. It was now an appropriate emblem. The clergyman stepped into the room where the corpse was laid, and bent over the coffin, to take a last farewell of his deceased parishioner. As he stooped, the veil hung straight down from his forehead so that, if her eyelids had not been closed forever,

[14]**vagary:** oddity.

ANALYZE LITERARY ELEMENTS

Annotate: Mark the words and phrases in paragraph 18 that are spooky or disturbing.

Synthesize: How does this description reflect what you know about Dark Romanticism?

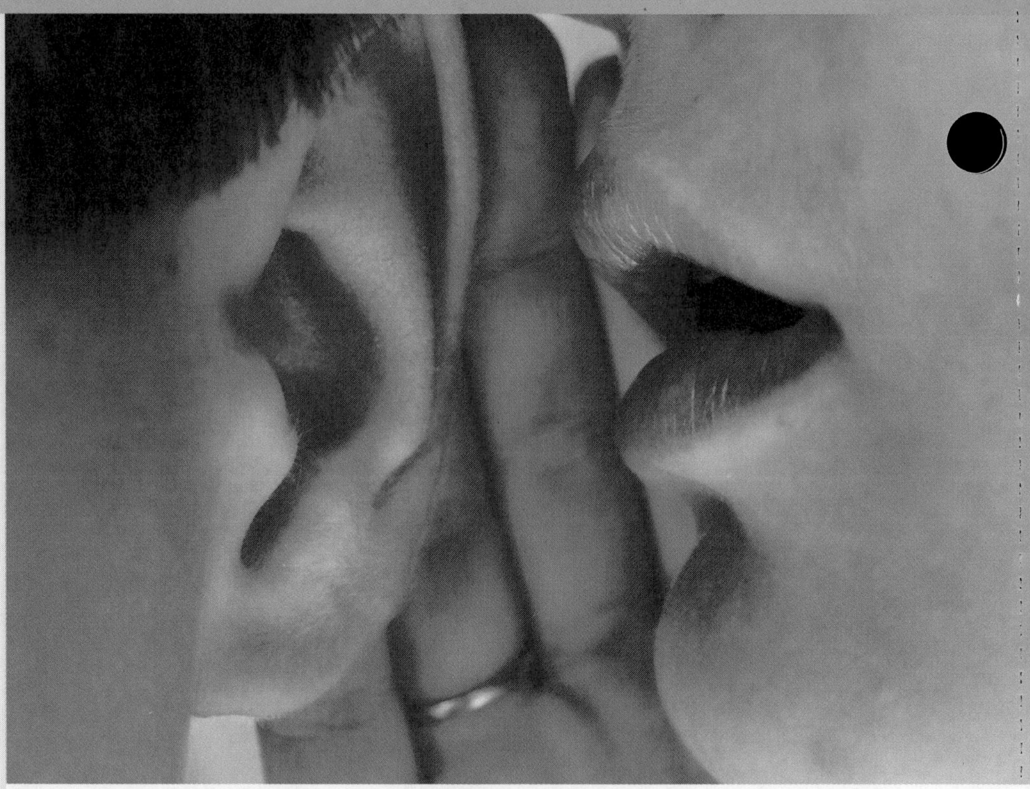

the dead maiden might have seen his face. Could Mr. Hooper be fearful of her glance, that he so hastily caught back the black veil? A person, who watched the interview between the dead and the living, scrupled[15] not to affirm that, at the instant when the clergyman's features were disclosed, the corpse had slightly shuddered, rustling the shroud[16] and muslin cap, though the countenance retained the composure of death. A superstitious old woman was the only witness of this prodigy. From the coffin, Mr. Hooper passed into the chamber of the mourners, and thence to the head of the staircase, to make the funeral prayer. It was a tender and heart-dissolving prayer, full of sorrow, yet so imbued with celestial[17] hopes, that the music of the heavenly harp, swept by the fingers of the dead, seemed faintly to be heard among the saddest accents of the minister. The people trembled, though they but darkly understood him, when he prayed that they, and himself, and all of mortal race might be ready, as he trusted this young maiden had been, for the dreadful hour that should snatch the veil from their faces. The bearers went heavily forth, and the mourners followed, saddening all the street, with the dead before them, and Mr. Hooper in his black veil behind.

19 "Why do you look back?" said one in the procession to his partner.

20 "I had a fancy," replied she, "that the minister and the maiden's spirit were walking hand in hand."

---

[15] **scrupled:** was reluctant.
[16] **shroud:** a cloth in which people were wrapped before burial.
[17] **celestial:** relating to heaven.

21 "And so had I, at the same moment," said the other. That night, the handsomest couple in Milford village were to be joined in wedlock. Though reckoned a melancholy man, Mr. Hooper had a placid cheerfulness for such occasions, which often excited a sympathetic smile, where livelier merriment would have been thrown away. There was no quality of his disposition which made him more beloved than this. The company at the wedding awaited his arrival with impatience, trusting that the strange awe, which had gathered over him throughout the day, would now be dispelled. But such was not the result. When Mr. Hooper came, the first thing that their eyes rested on was the same horrible black veil, which had added deeper gloom to the funeral, and could portend nothing but evil to the wedding. Such was its immediate effect on the guests, that a cloud seemed to have rolled duskily from beneath the black crape, and dimmed the light of the candles. The bridal pair stood up before the minister. But the bride's cold fingers quivered in the tremulous[18] hand of the bridegroom, and her death-like paleness caused a whisper that the maiden who had been buried a few hours before was come from her grave to be married. If ever another wedding were so dismal, it was that famous one where they tolled the wedding knell.[19] After performing the ceremony, Mr. Hooper raised a glass of wine to his lips, wishing happiness to the new-married couple, in a strain of mild pleasantry that ought to have brightened the features of the guests, like a cheerful gleam from the hearth. At that instant, catching a glimpse of his figure in the looking glass, the black veil involved his own spirit in the horror with which it overwhelmed all others. His frame shuddered—his lips grew white—he spilt the untasted wine upon the carpet—and rushed forth into the darkness. For the Earth, too, had on her Black Veil.

22 The next day, the whole village of Milford talked of little else than Parson Hooper's black veil. That, and the mystery concealed behind it, supplied a topic for discussion between acquaintances meeting in the street, and good women gossiping at their open windows. It was the first item of news that the tavern keeper told to his guests. The children babbled of it on their way to school. One imitative little imp covered his face with an old black handkerchief, thereby so affrighting his playmates that the panic seized himself, and he well-nigh lost his wits by his own waggery.[20]

23 It was remarkable that, of all the busybodies and impertinent people in the parish, not one ventured to put the plain question to Mr. Hooper, wherefore he did this thing. Hitherto, whenever there appeared the slightest call for such interference, he had never lacked advisers, nor shown himself averse to be guided by their judgment. If he erred at all, it was by so painful a degree of self-distrust that

ANALYZE STRUCTURE

Annotate: Mark the words in paragraph 21 that describe the minister's reaction to his own image.

Synthesize: How does this reaction intensify the suspense in the story?

[18] **tremulous:** trembling.

[19] **If ever . . . wedding knell:** In Hawthorne's "The Wedding Knell," funeral bells ring during a wedding ceremony.

[20] **waggery:** silly humor.

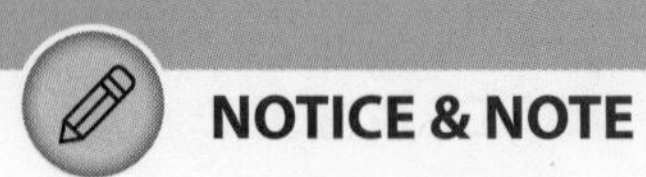

even the mildest censure[21] would lead him to consider an indifferent action as a crime. Yet, though so well acquainted with this amiable weakness, no individual among his parishioners chose to make the black veil a subject of friendly remonstrance.[22] There was a feeling of dread, neither plainly confessed nor carefully concealed, which caused each to shift the responsibility upon another, till at length it was found expedient to send a deputation to the church, in order to deal with Mr. Hooper about the mystery, before it should grow into a scandal. Never did an embassy so ill discharge its duties. The minister received them with friendly courtesy, but became silent, after they were seated, leaving to his visitors the whole burden of introducing their important business. The topic, it might be supposed, was obvious enough. There was the black veil, swathed round Mr. Hooper's forehead, and concealing every feature above his placid mouth, on which, at times, they could perceive the glimmering of a melancholy smile. But that piece of crape, to their imagination, seemed to hang down before his heart, the symbol of a fearful secret between him and them. Were the veil but cast aside, they might speak freely of it, but not till then. Thus they sat a considerable time, speechless, confused, and shrinking uneasily from Mr. Hooper's eye, which they felt to be fixed upon them with an invisible glance. Finally, the deputies returned abashed to their constituents, pronouncing the matter too weighty to be handled, except by a council of the churches, if, indeed, it might not require a general synod.[23]

ANALYZE STRUCTURE
Annotate: Mark the sentence in paragraph 24 that describes the fiancée's upcoming question to the minister.

Predict: How does the information in this paragraph build suspense in the story?

24 But there was one person in the village unappalled by the awe with which the black veil had impressed all beside herself. When the deputies returned without an explanation, or even venturing to demand one, she, with the calm energy of her character, determined to chase away the strange cloud that appeared to be settling round Mr. Hooper, every moment more darkly than before. As his plighted wife,[24] it should be her privilege to know what the black veil concealed. At the minister's first visit, therefore, she entered upon the subject, with a direct simplicity, which made the task easier both for him and her. After he had seated himself, she fixed her eyes steadfastly upon the veil, but could discern nothing of the dreadful gloom that had so overawed the multitude: it was but a double fold of crape, hanging down from his forehead to his mouth, and slightly stirring with his breath.

25 "No," said she aloud, and smiling, "there is nothing terrible in this piece of crape except that it hides a face which I am always glad to look upon. Come, good sir, let the sun shine from behind the cloud. First lay aside your black veil: then tell me why you put it on."

26 Mr. Hooper's smile glimmered faintly.

[21] **censure:** disapproval or criticism.
[22] **remonstrance:** protest.
[23] **synod:** an assembly or court of church officials.
[24] **plighted wife:** fiancée.

27 "There is an hour to come," said he, "when all of us shall cast aside our veils. Take it not amiss, beloved friend, if I wear this piece of crape till then."

28 "Your words are a mystery too," returned the young lady. "Take away the veil from them, at least."

29 "Elizabeth, I will," said he, "so far as my vow may suffer me. Know, then, this veil is a type and a symbol, and I am bound to wear it ever, both in light and darkness, in solitude and before the gaze of multitudes, and as with strangers, so with my familiar friends. No mortal eye will see it withdrawn. This dismal shade must separate me from the world: even you, Elizabeth, can never come behind it!"

30 "What grievous affliction hath befallen you," she earnestly inquired, "that you should thus darken your eyes forever?"

31 "If it be a sign of mourning," replied Mr. Hooper, "I, perhaps, like most other mortals, have sorrows dark enough to be typified by a black veil."

32 "But what if the world will not believe that it is the type of an innocent sorrow?" urged Elizabeth. "Beloved and respected as you are, there may be whispers that you hide your face under the consciousness of secret sin. For the sake of your holy office, do away this scandal!"

33 The color rose into her cheeks, as she intimated the nature of the rumors that were already abroad in the village. But Mr. Hooper's mildness did not forsake him. He even smiled again—that same sad smile, which always appeared like a faint glimmering of light proceeding from the obscurity beneath the veil.

34 "If I hide my face for sorrow, there is cause enough," he merely replied; "and if I cover it for secret sin, what mortal might not do the same?"

35 And with this gentle but unconquerable **obstinacy** did he resist all her entreaties. At length Elizabeth sat silent. For a few moments she appeared lost in thought, considering, probably, what new methods might be tried to withdraw her lover from so dark a fantasy, which, if it had no other meaning, was perhaps a symptom of mental disease. Though of a firmer character than his own, the tears rolled down her cheeks. But, in an instant, as it were, a new feeling took the place of sorrow: her eyes were fixed insensibly on the black veil, when, like a sudden twilight in the air, its terrors fell around her. She arose, and stood trembling before him.

36 "And do you feel it then at last?" said he mournfully.

37 She made no reply, but covered her eyes with her hand, and turned to leave the room. He rushed forward and caught her arm.

38 "Have patience with me, Elizabeth!" cried he passionately. "Do not desert me, though this veil must be between us here on earth. Be mine, and hereafter there shall be no veil over my face, no darkness

ANALYZE LITERARY ELEMENTS

Annotate: Mark the phrases in paragraphs 31 and 34 that the minister uses to comment on his condition.

Analyze: What do these passages suggest about Hawthorne's theme?

obstinacy
(ŏb´stə-nə-sē) *n.* stubbornness.

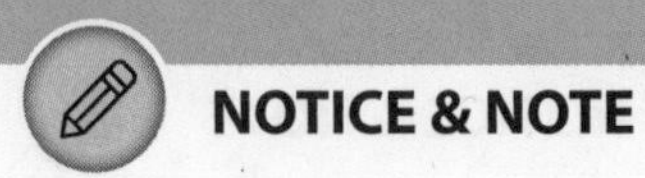

between our souls! It is but a mortal veil—it is not for eternity! Oh! you know not how lonely I am, and how frightened to be alone behind my black veil. Do not leave me in this miserable obscurity forever!"

39 "Lift the veil but once, and look me in the face," said she.

40 "Never! It cannot be!" replied Mr. Hooper.

41 "Then, farewell!" said Elizabeth.

42 She withdrew her arm from his grasp and slowly departed, pausing at the door to give one long, shuddering gaze that seemed almost to penetrate the mystery of the black veil. But even amid his grief, Mr. Hooper smiled to think that only a material emblem had separated him from happiness, though the horrors which it shadowed forth must be drawn darkly between the fondest of lovers.

ANALYZE STRUCTURE

Annotate: Mark the sentences in paragraph 43 that describe Mr. Hooper's inner life beneath the veil.

Analyze: How does the ambiguity over why Mr. Hooper wears the veil affect the meaning of the story?

43 From that time no attempts were made to remove Mr. Hooper's black veil or, by a direct appeal, to discover the secret which it was supposed to hide. By persons who claimed a superiority to popular prejudice, it was reckoned merely an eccentric whim, such as often mingles with the sober actions of men otherwise rational, and tinges them all with its own semblance of insanity. But with the multitude, good Mr. Hooper was irreparably a bugbear.[25] He could not walk the streets with any peace of mind, so conscious was he that the gentle and timid would turn aside to avoid him, and that others would make it a point of hardihood to throw themselves in his way. The impertinence of the latter class compelled him to give up his customary walk, at sunset, to the burial ground, for when he leaned pensively over the gate, there would always be faces behind the gravestones, peeping at his black veil. A fable went the rounds that the stare of the dead people drove him thence. It grieved him to the very depth of his kind heart to observe how the children fled from his approach, breaking up their merriest sports, while his melancholy figure was yet afar off. Their instinctive dread caused him to feel, more strongly than aught else, that a preternatural[26] horror was interwoven with the threads of the black crape. In truth, his own antipathy to the veil was known to be so great that he never willingly passed before a mirror, nor stooped to drink at a still fountain, lest, in its peaceful bosom, he should be affrighted by himself. This was what gave **plausibility** to the whispers that Mr. Hooper's conscience tortured him for some great crime too horrible to be entirely concealed, or otherwise than so obscurely intimated. Thus, from beneath the black veil there rolled a cloud into the sunshine, an ambiguity of sin or sorrow, which enveloped the poor minister, so that love or sympathy could never reach him. It was said that ghost and fiend consorted with him there. With self-shudderings and outward terrors, he walked continually in its shadow, groping darkly

plausibility (plô-zə-bəl´ĭ-tē) *n.* likelihood; believability.

[25]**bugbear:** source of irrational fear.

[26]**preternatural:** inexplicable, supernatural.

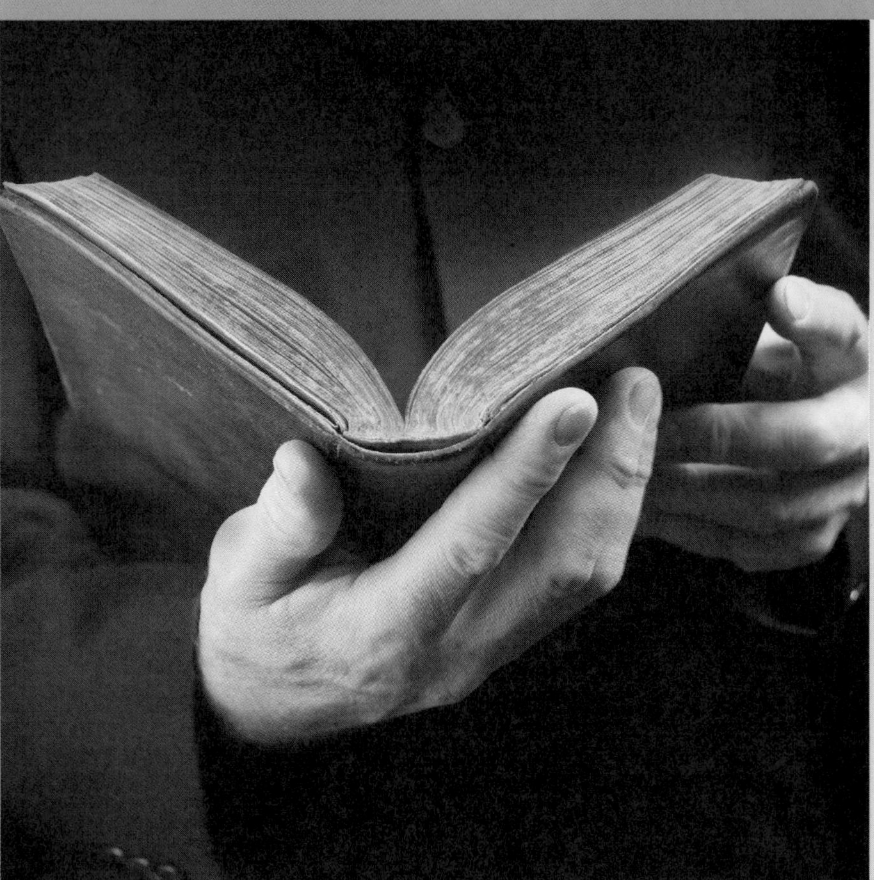

within his own soul, or gazing through a medium that saddened the whole world. Even the lawless wind, it was believed, respected his dreadful secret, and never blew aside the veil. But still good Mr. Hooper sadly smiled at the pale visages of the worldly throng as he passed by.

44 Among all its bad influences, the black veil had the one desirable effect, of making its wearer a very efficient clergyman. By the aid of his mysterious emblem—for there was no other apparent cause—he became a man of awful power, over souls that were in agony for sin. His converts always regarded him with a dread peculiar to themselves, affirming, though but figuratively, that before he brought them to celestial light, they had been with him behind the black veil. Its gloom, indeed, enabled him to sympathize with all dark affections. Dying sinners cried aloud for Mr. Hooper, and would not yield their breath till he appeared; though ever, as he stooped to whisper consolation, they shuddered at the veiled face so near their own. Such were the terrors of the black veil, even when Death had bared his visage! Strangers came long distances to attend service at his church, with the mere idle purpose of gazing at his figure, because it was forbidden them to behold his face. But many were made to quake ere they departed! Once, during Governor Belcher's[27] administration, Mr. Hooper was appointed to preach the election sermon. Covered

[27] **Governor Belcher:** Jonathan Belcher (1682–1757), governor of Massachusetts Bay Colony from 1730 until 1741.

ANALYZE LITERARY ELEMENTS

Annotate: Mark the phrases in paragraph 44 that explain the role Mr. Hooper played in political life.

Infer: What can you infer about the role of the clergy in Puritan Massachusetts?

with his black veil, he stood before the chief magistrate, the council, and the representatives, and wrought so deep an impression that the legislative measures of that year were characterized by all the gloom and piety of our earliest ancestral sway.

45 In this manner Mr. Hooper spent a long life, irreproachable[28] in outward act, yet shrouded in dismal suspicions; kind and loving, though unloved, and dimly feared; a man apart from men, shunned in their health and joy, but ever summoned to their aid in mortal anguish. As years wore on, shedding their snows above his sable veil, he acquired a name throughout the New England churches, and they called him Father Hooper. Nearly all his parishioners, who were of a mature age when he was settled, had been borne away by many a funeral: he had one congregation in the church, and a more crowded one in the churchyard; and having wrought so late into the evening, and done his work so well, it was now good Father Hooper's turn to rest.

46 Several persons were visible by the shaded candlelight in the death chamber of the old clergyman. Natural connections[29] he had none. But there was the decorously grave, though unmoved physician, seeking only to **mitigate** the last pangs of the patient whom he could not save. There were the deacons, and other eminently pious members of his church. There, also, was the Reverend Mr. Clark, of Westbury, a young and zealous divine, who had ridden in haste to pray by the bedside of the expiring minister. There was the nurse, no hired handmaiden of death, but one whose calm affection had endured thus long, in secrecy, in solitude, amid the chill of age, and would not perish, even at the dying hour. Who, but Elizabeth! And there lay the hoary head of good Father Hooper upon the death pillow, with the black veil still swathed about his brow and reaching down over his face, so that each more difficult gasp of his faint breath caused it to stir. All through life that piece of crape had hung between him and the world: it had separated him from cheerful brotherhood and woman's love, and kept him in that saddest of all prisons, his own heart; and still it lay upon his face, as if to deepen the gloom of his darksome chamber, and shade him from the sunshine of eternity.

47 For some time previous, his mind had been confused, wavering doubtfully between the past and the present, and hovering forward, as it were, at intervals, into the indistinctness of the world to come. There had been feverish turns, which tossed him from side to side and wore away what little strength he had. But in the most convulsive struggles, and in the wildest vagaries of his intellect, when no other thought retained its sober influence, he still showed an awful solicitude lest the black veil should slip aside. Even if his bewildered soul could have forgotten, there was a faithful woman at his pillow, who, with averted eyes, would have covered that aged face, which

[28] **irreproachable:** without fault; blameless.

[29] **Natural connections:** relatives, kin.

mitigate
(mĭt´ĭ-gāt) *v.* to lessen.

LANGUAGE CONVENTIONS

Annotate: In paragraph 46, circle the nouns and underline the appositives that follow them.

Analyze: What information do the appositives reveal about the nouns they modify?

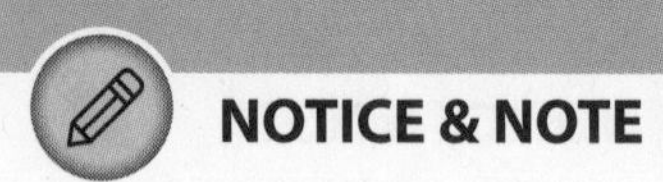

NOTICE & NOTE

ANALYZE LITERARY ELEMENTS

Annotate: Mark the sentence in paragraph 53 that describes Reverend Mr. Clark's action.

Infer: What is the motivation for Mr. Clark's action?

ANALYZE LITERARY ELEMENTS

Annotate: Mark the sentence that describes Mr. Hooper's response to Mr. Clark.

Connect: Why does Mr. Hooper insist on keeping the veil in place?

she had last beheld in the comeliness of manhood. At length the death-stricken old man lay quietly in the torpor[30] of mental and bodily exhaustion, with an imperceptible pulse, and breath that grew fainter and fainter, except when a long, deep, and irregular inspiration[31] seemed to prelude the flight of his spirit.

48 The minister of Westbury approached the bedside.

49 "Venerable Father Hooper," said he, "the moment of your release is at hand. Are you ready for the lifting of the veil, that shuts in time from eternity?"

50 Father Hooper at first replied merely by a feeble motion of his head; then, apprehensive, perhaps, that his meaning might be doubtful, he exerted himself to speak.

51 "Yea," said he, in faint accents, "my soul hath a patient weariness until that veil be lifted."

52 "And is it fitting," resumed the Reverend Mr. Clark, "that a man so given to prayer, of such a blameless example, holy in deed and thought, so far as mortal judgment may pronounce; is it fitting that a father in the church should leave a shadow on his memory that may seem to blacken a life so pure? I pray you, my venerable brother, let not this thing be! Suffer us to be gladdened by your triumphant aspect, as you go to your reward. Before the veil of eternity be lifted, let me cast aside this black veil from your face!"

53 And thus speaking, the Reverend Mr. Clark bent forward to reveal the mystery of so many years. But, exerting a sudden energy that made all the beholders stand aghast, Father Hooper snatched both his hands from beneath the bedclothes and pressed them strongly on the black veil, resolute to struggle, if the minister of Westbury would contend with a dying man.

54 "Never!" cried the veiled clergyman. "On earth, never!"

55 "Dark old man!" exclaimed the affrighted minister, "with what horrible crime upon your soul are you now passing to the judgment?"

56 Father Hooper's breath heaved; it rattled in his throat; but with a mighty effort, grasping forward with his hands, he caught hold of life, and held it back till he should speak. He even raised himself in bed; and there he sat shivering, with the arms of death around him, while the black veil hung down, awful, at that last moment, in the gathered terrors of a lifetime. And yet the faint, sad smile, so often there, now seemed to glimmer from its obscurity, and linger on Father Hooper's lips.

57 "Why do you tremble at me alone?" cried he, turning his veiled face round the circle of pale spectators. "Tremble also at each other! Have men avoided me, and women shown no pity, and children screamed and fled, only for my black veil? What, but the mystery which it obscurely typifies, has made this piece of crape so awful? When the friend shows his inmost heart to his friend; the lover to his best beloved; when man does not vainly shrink from the eye of his

[30]**torpor:** lifelessness, inactivity.

[31]**inspiration:** inhalation of air into the lungs.

Creator, loathsomely treasuring up the secret of his sin; then deem me a monster, for the symbol beneath which I have lived, and die! I look around me, and, lo! On every visage a Black Veil!"

58 While his auditors shrank from one another, in mutual affright, Father Hooper fell back upon his pillow, a veiled corpse, with a faint smile lingering on his lips. Still veiled, they laid him in his coffin, and a veiled corpse they bore him to the grave. The grass of many years has sprung up and withered on that grave, the burial stone is moss-grown, and good Mr. Hooper's face is dust; but awful is still the thought, that it mouldered beneath the Black Veil!

NOTICE & NOTE

ANALYZE LITERARY ELEMENTS

Annotate: Circle the phrases that show the town's actions over time. Underline the actions Father Hooper suggests they should have done.

Draw Conclusions: What themes do Father Hooper's last words suggest?

CHECK YOUR UNDERSTANDING

Answer these questions before moving on to the **Analyze the Text** section on the following page.

1 What is the topic of the first sermon Mr. Hooper gives when wearing the veil?

A Death

B Sorrow

C Secret sin

D Salvation

2 Why does the congregation send a deputation to talk to Mr. Hooper?

F To tell him he is fired

G To ask why he is wearing the veil

H To protest his behavior at the wedding

J To plead with him to marry Elizabeth

3 Which of the following does the story reveal about Puritan beliefs?

A Strict separation of church and state

B Strong belief in witches and witchcraft

C Exclusion of children from Sunday services

D Deep concern with sinfulness

RESPOND

ANALYZE THE TEXT

Support your responses with evidence from the text. NOTEBOOK

1. **Analyze** Mr. Hooper's conversation with Elizabeth is the first time that readers learn about the minister from his own words. What insight does this conversation provide about Mr. Hooper's character?
2. **Evaluate** What evidence in the text hints at or suggests Mr. Hooper's reasons for wearing the black veil? What effect does the ambiguity surrounding the veil add to the overall meaning of the story?
3. **Interpret** What does the veil symbolize? How does the meaning of the symbol change over the course of the story? Cite specific details from the story to support your interpretation.
4. **Synthesize** What themes does the story suggest to you? Cite text evidence in your response.
5. **Notice & Note** Why is it surprising that no one in the congregation talks to Mr. Hooper about the veil when he first starts wearing it? What might this reaction reveal about Puritan society and beliefs?

RESEARCH

Nathaniel Hawthorne's life shaped his thought and work. Research some of the key points of his biography to learn the answers to these questions.

QUESTION	ANSWER
What famous event was his ancestor John Hathorne involved in?	
What political jobs did Hawthorne hold?	
Which of those jobs was used in part in *The Scarlet Letter*?	

Extend Research Hawthorne's relationship with other famous authors of the period, such as Ralph Waldo Emerson and Herman Melville. How did he get along with them? What did he think of them? Share your ideas with the class.

RESEARCH TIP

Combine search terms, such as "Nathaniel Hawthorne" and "John Hathorne" by putting them in quotation marks to get more relevant search results.

CREATE AND DISCUSS

Write an Essay Write an argumentative essay in which you interpret the real causes of the villagers' discomfort in the minister's presence.

- ❑ Choose one of the following pairs of scenes to analyze: (1) first sighting of Mr. Hooper and the parishioners' comments after services; (2) Mr. Hooper's participation in the funeral and the wedding; (3) the delegation's visit and the early days afterward.
- ❑ Determine your thesis statement on the cause of the villagers' discomfort.
- ❑ Craft the essay with clear organization and adequate evidence to support your position.
- ❑ Use the characteristics of the genre, such as making a clear statement of your position and addressing counterarguments.

Go to **Writing Arguments** in the **Writing Studio** for help.

Discuss with a Small Group Explore your views in a moderated discussion. Join with other students who chose the same two scenes as you did.

- ❑ Take turns presenting your interpretations of the congregation's behavior.
- ❑ When you ask questions about the clarity or coherence of others' positions, do so respectfully to engage in a meaningful discussion.

Go to **Participating in Collaborative Discussions** in the **Speaking and Listening Studio** for help.

RESPOND TO THE ESSENTIAL QUESTION

What do we secretly fear?

Gather Information Review your annotations and notes on "The Minister's Black Veil." Then, add relevant details to your Response Log. As you determine which information to include, think about:

- how difficult it can be to face fear alone
- how uncertainty complicates facing fear
- how peer pressure affects our ability to face fear

ACADEMIC VOCABULARY

As you write and discuss what you learned from the story, be sure to use the Academic Vocabulary words. Check off each of the words that you use.

- ❑ **analogy**
- ❑ **denote**
- ❑ **quote**
- ❑ **topic**
- ❑ **unique**

RESPOND

CRITICAL VOCABULARY

WORD BANK
emblem **obstinacy**
pathos **plausibility**
ostentatious **mitigate**

Practice and Apply Complete each of the following sentence stems in a way that reflects the meaning of the Critical Vocabulary word.

1. The painting evoked **pathos** in the viewer because ________.
2. The **obstinacy** of her response was made clear by ________.
3. The runner treasured his race number as an **emblem** of ________.
4. The **ostentatious** display of wealth made visitors uncomfortable because ________.
5. Proponents of the new law sought to **mitigate** opposition by ________.
6. The **plausibility** of her statement was supported by ________.

VOCABULARY STRATEGY: Nuances in Word Meanings

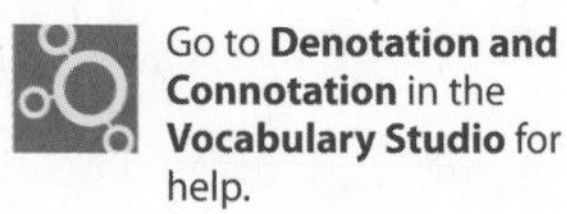

Go to **Denotation and Connotation** in the **Vocabulary Studio** for help.

When you analyze nuances in the meaning of words with similar **denotations,** or dictionary meanings, you look for subtle differences in shades of meaning. The **connotation** of a word refers to the feelings or ideas associated with it. For example, consider the connotation of the Critical Vocabulary word *ostentatious* in this sentence from "The Minister's Black Veil":

> **Some gathered in little circles, huddled closely together, with their mouths all whispering in the centre; some went homeward alone, wrapped in silent meditation; some talked loudly, and profaned the Sabbath day with ostentatious laughter.**

The word *ostentatious* carries a negative connotation of disapproval, in contrast to the synonym *loud*, which has a more neutral connotation. This emphasizes the narrator's reproach of the congregants' behavior on what should have been a solemn day of worship.

Practice and Apply Work with a partner to explore nuances in word meanings. Follow these steps:

- List five words from the story that have a strong positive or negative connotation.
- Use a dictionary and a thesaurus to find definitions and synonyms of the words.
- Discuss how synonyms with different connotations would affect meaning.

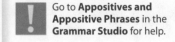

LANGUAGE CONVENTIONS: Appositives and Appositive Phrases

An **appositive** is a noun or pronoun that identifies or renames another noun or pronoun, providing more information about the word it refers to. An **appositive phrase** is simply an appositive and its modifiers.

An appositive or an appositive phrase can be either **essential** or **nonessential.** An **essential appositive** provides information that is necessary to identify what is referred to by the preceding noun or pronoun.

In the following example, the appositive specifies which brother the writer is referring to:

> **Essential appositive:** "My brother **Mychal** was always active."

A **nonessential appositive** provides additional but supplementary information about the preceding noun or pronoun. Nonessential appositives are always set off from the word they refer to by commas or dashes.

> **Nonessential appositive:** "Elaine, **a diligent student,** reviewed her extensive notes the night before the test."

Appositive phrases can be used in place of dependent clauses to make sentences more concise:

> **Dependent clause:** "The Reverend Mr. Hooper, **who was a persuasive but not forceful preacher,** delivered sermons that guided rather than scolded."

> **Appositive phrase:** "The Reverend Mr. Hooper, **a persuasive but not forceful preacher,** delivered sermons that guided rather than scolded."

Practice and Apply Find two examples of appositive phrases in "The Minister's Black Veil" and identify whether they are essential or nonessential. Then, write two sentences that include either an appositive or an appositive phrase.

Go to **Appositives and Appositive Phrases** in the **Grammar Studio** for help.

COLLABORATE & COMPARE

SHORT STORY

THE PIT AND THE PENDULUM

by **Edgar Allan Poe**

pages 293–307

ESSENTIAL QUESTION:

What do we secretly fear?

COMPARE THEMES

Now that you have read Hawthorne's "The Minister's Black Veil," you are ready to compare Edgar Allan Poe's exploration of some of the themes of Dark Romanticism. Look for details that show the setting of this story and how those details shape Poe's approach to his theme.

SHORT STORY

THE MINISTER'S BLACK VEIL

by **Nathaniel Hawthorne**

pages 271–285

The Pit and the Pendulum

QUICK START

Why do you think people like watching horror or suspense movies? What makes the experience of being frightened enjoyable?

ANALYZE MOOD

As a complement to the American Dark Romantics, the European Romantic period gave rise to the Gothic novel. These tales used the stone vaults and dark dungeons of medieval settings to evoke mystery and fear. The term **Gothic** was later applied to any fiction that depicted strange events in a haunting environment.

Poe, a master of Gothic style, sets "The Pit and the Pendulum" during the Spanish Inquisition, which was established in 1480 to punish people accused of heresy—having beliefs that differed from Catholic Church doctrine. The setting allows Poe to evoke an eerie mood. **Mood** refers to the atmosphere the writer creates in a work of literature. Poe uses unique diction and syntax to describe the narrator's situation and state of mind, creating a haunting mood. In the chart below, you can find examples from "The Pit and the Pendulum" that show how diction and syntax can impact the story's mood.

LITERARY ELEMENT	EXAMPLE FROM STORY	IMPACT ON MOOD
Diction word choice	"I was sick—sick unto death with that long agony"	"sick," "death," and "agony" are words that immediately create a frightening mood
Syntax sentence structure	"This only for a brief period; for presently I heard no more. Yet, for a while, I saw; but with how terrible an exaggeration!"	The narrator speaks in brief bursts, creating a tense mood.

As you read, note the way Poe uses diction and syntax to create a mood.

ANALYZE PLOT STRUCTURE

A writer's decisions on how to structure a plot contribute to a story's overall meaning. Typically, a short story begins by introducing the characters, setting the scene, and providing background information. Then, a conflict arises and builds to a resolution. In this story, however, Poe makes some choices to create an immediate atmosphere of terror.

As you read, think about how Poe structures the plot and uses literary elements like character, setting, and imagery to shape your understanding of events. Consider the beginning and ending the story and how his choices build suspense and reveal the narrator's situation.

GENRE ELEMENTS: SHORT STORY

- is a short work of fiction that centers on a single idea
- can experiment with plot structure to build suspense
- conveys a particular mood or atmosphere

GET READY

CRITICAL VOCABULARY

indeterminate	**tumultuous**	**insuperable**	**pertinacity**
lucid	**supposition**	**prostrate**	**avert**

Complete each sentence with the correct Critical Vocabulary word.

1. The __________ that she was honest proved to be a naïve one.
2. It's normal to __________ one's gaze from such a horrific sight.
3. She could describe the incident in a __________ way, even though it occurred years ago.
4. The ship left on a perilous voyage toward a distant and __________ shore.
5. The peasant lay __________ at the baron's feet, fearful of his decision.
6. His __________ feelings overwhelmed him and left him incapable of action.
7. The goal seemed __________, but the team labored to achieve it.
8. The woman devoted herself to her work with a __________ remarkable for her years.

LANGUAGE CONVENTIONS

Semicolons A writer's **style** is the particular way he or she uses language to communicate ideas. One characteristic of Edgar Allan Poe's distinctive style is his use of **semicolons** to create long, uninterrupted sentences.

As you read, note Poe's use of semicolons and how it impacts your understanding of the narrator's state of mind.

ANNOTATION MODEL

NOTICE & NOTE

As you read, look for how Poe creates a particular mood through his use of diction and syntax. Note how he uses literary elements to develop the plot. Here are one student's notes about "The Pit and the Pendulum."

I had swooned; but still will not say that all of consciousness was lost. What of it there remained I will not attempt to define, or even to describe; yet all was not lost. In the deepest slumber—no! In delirium—no! In a swoon—no! In death—no! even in the grave all *is not* lost. Else there is no immortality for man. Arousing from the most profound of slumbers, we break the gossamer web of *some* dream.

Punctuation shows agitation, excitement.

Preoccupation with death is spooky.

BACKGROUND

Edgar Allan Poe *(1809–1849) is considered one of literature's "most brilliant, but erratic stars." Poe explored such distinctive themes as madness, untimely death, and obsession. He was orphaned at an early age, and for most of his life he struggled to earn a living. The 1845 publication of his poem "The Raven" made Poe famous. This success, however, was soon marred by the death of his wife and his own illness. Although Poe's life was brief, his literary influence was great, especially on the development of the horror story and detective fiction.*

THE PIT AND THE PENDULUM

Short Story by Edgar Allan Poe

PREPARE TO COMPARE

You have analyzed how Hawthorne developed theme through the use of characterization and symbols. Look for clues in Poe's text for his theme and the literary elements he uses to develop it.

Impia tortorum longos hic turba furores
Sanguinis innocui, non satiata, aluit.
Sospite nunc patria, fracto nunc funeris antro,
Mors ubi dira fuit vita salusque patent.[1]

[Quatrain composed for the gates of a market to be erected upon the site of the Jacobin[2] Club House at Paris.]

1 I was sick—sick unto death with that long agony; and when they at length unbound me, and I was permitted to sit, I felt that my senses were leaving me. The sentence—the dread sentence of death—was the last of distinct accentuation which reached my ears. After that, the sound of the inquisitorial voices seemed

Notice & Note

Use the side margins to notice and note signposts in the text.

ANALYZE PLOT STRUCTURE

Annotate: Mark the first two sentences of paragraph 1.

Analyze: What is happening to the narrator in these two sentences? How does the beginning of the story create dramatic tension?

[1] **Impia . . . patent:** *Latin:* Here the wicked crowd of tormentors, unsated, fed their long-time lusts for innocent blood. Now that our homeland is safe, now that the tomb is broken, life and health appear where once was dread death.

[2] **Jacobin** (jăk´ə-bĭn): a radical political group active in the French Revolution and later known for implementing the Reign of Terror.

indeterminate
(ĭn-dĭ-tûr´mə-nĭt) *adj.*
not precisely known.

ANALYZE MOOD

Annotate: Beginning with when he first sees them, mark the words the narrator uses to describe the lips of the judges.

Infer: What mood, or atmosphere, does this description help create?

merged in one dreamy **indeterminate** hum. It conveyed to my soul the idea of *revolution*—perhaps from its association in fancy with the burr of a millwheel. This only for a brief period; for presently I heard no more. Yet, for a while, I saw; but with how terrible an exaggeration! I saw the lips of the black-robed judges. They appeared to me white—whiter than the sheet upon which I trace these words—and thin even to grotesqueness; thin with the intensity of their expression of firmness—of immoveable resolution—of stern contempt of human torture. I saw that the decrees of what to me was Fate, were still issuing from those lips. I saw them writhe with a deadly locution.[3] I saw them fashion the syllables of my name; and I shuddered because no sound succeeded. I saw, too, for a few moments of delirious horror, the soft and nearly imperceptible waving of the sable draperies which enwrapped the walls of the apartment. And then my vision fell upon the seven tall candles upon the table. At first they wore the aspect of charity, and seemed white slender angels who would save me; but then, all at once, there came a most deadly nausea over my spirit, and I felt every fiber in my frame thrill as if I had touched the wire of a galvanic battery,[4] while the angel forms became meaningless specters, with heads of flame, and I saw that from them there would be no help. And then there stole into my fancy, like a rich musical note, the thought of what sweet rest there must be in the grave. The thought came gently and stealthily, and it seemed long before it attained full appreciation;[5] but just as my spirit came at length properly to feel and entertain it, the figures of the judges vanished, as if magically, from before me; the tall candles sank into nothingness; their flames went out utterly; the blackness of darkness supervened; all sensations appeared swallowed up in a mad rushing descent as of the soul into Hades.[6] Then silence, and stillness, and night were the universe.

2 I had swooned;[7] but still will not say that all of consciousness was lost. What of it there remained I will not attempt to define, or even to describe; yet all was not lost. In the deepest slumber—no! In delirium—no! In a swoon—no! In death—no! even in the grave all *is not* lost. Else there is no immortality for man. Arousing from the most profound of slumbers, we break the gossamer web of *some* dream. Yet in a second afterward, (so frail may that web have been) we remember not that we have dreamed. In the return to life from the swoon there are two stages; first, that of the sense of mental or spiritual; secondly, that of the sense of physical, existence. It seems probable that if, upon reaching the second stage, we could recall the impressions of the first, we should find these impressions eloquent in memories of the gulf beyond. And that gulf is—what? How at

[3] **locution:** style of speech.
[4] **galvanic battery:** a device for producing electricity with series of voltaic cells.
[5] **appreciation:** understanding.
[6] **Hades:** in Greek mythology, the underworld where the dead reside.
[7] **swooned:** fainted.

least shall we distinguish its shadows from those of the tomb? But if the impressions of what I have termed the first stage, are not, at will, recalled, yet, after long interval, do they not come unbidden, while we marvel whence they come? He who has never swooned, is not he who finds strange palaces and wildly familiar faces in coals that glow; is not he who beholds floating in midair the sad visions that the many may not view; is not he who ponders over the perfume of some novel flower—is not he whose brain grows bewildered with the meaning of some musical cadence which has never before arrested his attention.

3 Amid frequent and thoughtful endeavors to remember; amid earnest struggles to regather some token of the state of seeming nothingness into which my soul had lapsed, there have been moments when I have dreamed of success; there have been brief, very brief periods when I have conjured up remembrances which the **lucid** reason of a later epoch assures me could have had reference only to that condition of seeming unconsciousness. These shadows of memory tell, indistinctly, of tall figures that lifted and bore me in silence down—down—still down—till a hideous dizziness oppressed me at the mere idea of the interminableness of the descent. They tell also of a vague horror at my heart, on account of that heart's unnatural stillness. Then comes a sense of sudden motionlessness throughout all things; as if those who bore me (a ghastly train!) had outrun, in their descent, the limits of the limitless, and paused from the wearisomeness of their toil. After this I call to mind flatness and dampness; and that all is *madness*—the madness of a memory which busies itself among forbidden things.

lucid
(lo͞o´sĭd) *adj.* easily understood.

4 Very suddenly there came back to my soul motion and sound—the **tumultuous** motion of the heart, and, in my ears, the sound of its beating. Then a pause in which all is blank. Then again sound, and motion, and touch—a tingling sensation pervading my frame. Then the mere consciousness of existence, without *thought*—a condition which lasted long. Then, very suddenly, thought, and shuddering terror, and earnest endeavor to comprehend my true state. Then a strong desire to lapse into insensibility. Then a rushing revival of soul and a successful effort to move. And now a full memory of the trial, of the judges, of the sable draperies, of the sentence, of the sickness, of the swoon. Then entire forgetfulness of all that followed; of all that a later day and much earnestness of endeavor have enabled me vaguely to recall.

tumultuous
(to͝o-mŭl´cho͞o-əs)
adj. stormy, intense.

ANALYZE MOOD

Annotate: Mark the different changes in the narrator's thoughts and feelings in paragraph 4.

Interpret: How does Poe convey the rapid succession of ideas in the narrator's mind? How does this contribute to the mood?

5 So far, I had not opened my eyes. I felt that I lay upon my back, unbound. I reached out my hand, and it fell heavily upon something damp and hard. There I suffered it to remain for many minutes, while I strove to imagine where and *what* I could be. I longed, yet dared not to employ my vision. I dreaded the first glance at objects around me. It was not that I feared to look upon things horrible, but that I grew aghast lest there should be *nothing* to see. At length, with a wild desperation at heart, I quickly unclosed my eyes. My worst thoughts, then, were confirmed. The blackness of eternal night

NOTICE & NOTE

supposition
(sŭp-ə-zĭsh´ən) *n.* a belief or assumption.

ANALYZE PLOT STRUCTURE
Annotate: Mark details in paragraph 6 that help you picture the narrator's situation.
Analyze: How do these details help build suspense?

encompassed me. I struggled for breath. The intensity of the darkness seemed to oppress and stifle me. The atmosphere was intolerably close. I still lay quietly, and made effort to exercise my reason. I brought to mind the inquisitorial proceedings, and attempted from that point to deduce my real condition. The sentence had passed; and it appeared to me that a very long interval of time had since elapsed. Yet not for a moment did I suppose myself actually dead. Such a **supposition**, notwithstanding what we read in fiction, is altogether inconsistent with real existence;—but where and in what state was I? The condemned to death, I knew, perished usually at the *autos-da-fé*,[8] and one of these had been held on the very night of the day of my trial. Had I been remanded to my dungeon, to await the next sacrifice, which would not take place for many months? This I at once saw could not be. Victims had been in immediate demand. Moreover, my dungeon, as well as all the condemned cells at Toledo, had stone floors, and light was not altogether excluded.

6 A fearful idea now suddenly drove the blood in torrents upon my heart, and for a brief period, I once more relapsed into insensibility. Upon recovering, I at once started to my feet, trembling convulsively in every fiber. I thrust my arms wildly above and around me in all directions. I felt nothing; yet dreaded to move a step, lest I should be impeded by the walls of the *tomb*. Perspiration burst from every pore and stood in cold big beads on my forehead. The agony of suspense grew at length intolerable, and I cautiously moved forward, with my arms extended, and my eyes straining from their sockets, in the hope of catching some faint ray of light. I proceeded for many paces; but still all was blackness and vacancy. I breathed more freely. It seemed evident that mine was not, at least, the most hideous of fates.

7 And now, as I still continued to step cautiously onward, there came thronging upon my recollection a thousand vague rumors of the horrors of Toledo. Of the dungeons there had been strange things narrated—fables I had always deemed them—but yet strange, and too ghastly to repeat, save in a whisper. Was I left to perish of starvation in the subterranean world of darkness; or what fate, perhaps even more fearful, awaited me? That the result would be death, and a death of more than customary bitterness, I knew too well the character of my judges to doubt. The mode and the hour were all that occupied or distracted me.

8 My outstretched hands at length encountered some solid obstruction. It was a wall, seemingly of stone masonry—very smooth, slimy, and cold. I followed it up! stepping with all the careful distrust with which certain antique narratives had inspired me. This process, however, afforded me no means of ascertaining the dimensions of my dungeon; as I might make its circuit, and return to the point whence I set out, without being aware of the fact; so perfectly uniform seemed the wall. I therefore sought the knife which had been in my pocket,

[8] **autos-da-fé** (ou-tōz-də-fā´): Portuguese for *acts of faith*; public executions of people condemned by the Inquisition and carried out by the civil authorities.

when led into the inquisitorial chamber; but it was gone; my clothes had been exchanged for a wrapper of coarse serge.[9] I had thought of forcing the blade in some minute crevice of the masonry, so as to identify my point of departure. The difficulty, nevertheless, was but trivial; although, in the disorder of my fancy, it seemed at first **insuperable**. I tore a part of the hem from the robe and placed the fragment at full length, and at right angles to the wall. In groping my way around the prison I could not fail to encounter this rag upon completing the circuit. So, at least I thought: but I had not counted upon the extent of the dungeon, or upon my own weakness. The ground was moist and slippery. I staggered onward for some time, when I stumbled and fell. My excessive fatigue induced me to remain **prostrate**; and sleep soon overtook me as I lay.

insuperable
(ĭn-so͞o´pər-ə-bəl) *adj.* impossible to overcome.

prostrate
(prŏs´trāt) *adj.* lying down with the head facing downward.

9 Upon awakening, and stretching forth an arm, I found beside me a loaf and a pitcher with water. I was too much exhausted to reflect upon this circumstance, but ate and drank with avidity. Shortly afterward, I resumed my tour around the prison, and with much toil, came at last upon the fragment of the serge. Up to the period when I fell I had counted fifty-two paces, and upon resuming my walk, I counted forty-eight more;—when I arrived at the rag. There were in all, then, a hundred paces; and, admitting two paces to the yard, I presumed the dungeon to be fifty yards in circuit. I had met, however, with many angles in the wall, and thus I could form no guess at the shape of the vault; for vault I could not help supposing it to be.

10 I had little object—certainly no hope—in these researches; but a vague curiosity prompted me to continue them. Quitting the wall, I resolved to cross the area of the enclosure. At first I proceeded with extreme caution, for the floor, although seemingly of solid material, was treacherous with slime. At length, however, I took courage, and did not hesitate to step firmly; endeavoring to cross in as direct a line as possible. I had advanced some ten or twelve paces in this manner, when the remnant of the torn hem of my robe became entangled between my legs. I stepped on it, and fell violently on my face.

11 In the confusion attending my fall, I did not immediately apprehend a somewhat startling circumstance, which yet, in a few seconds afterward, and while I still lay prostrate, arrested my attention. It was this—my chin rested upon the floor of the prison, but my lips and the upper portion of my head, although seemingly at a less elevation than the chin, touched nothing. At the same time my forehead seemed bathed in a clammy vapor, and the peculiar smell of decayed fungus arose to my nostrils. I put forward my arm, and shuddered to find that I had fallen at the very brink of a circular pit, whose extent, of course, I had no means of ascertaining at the moment. Groping about the masonry just below the margin, I succeeded in dislodging a small fragment, and let it fall into the abyss. For many seconds I hearkened to its reverberations as it dashed against the sides of the chasm in its descent; at length there was a

ANALYZE MOOD

Annotate: Mark the details in paragraph 11 that appeal to the senses.

Interpret: How does the diction in this paragraph contribute to the story's mood?

[9] **serge** (sûrj): a type of woolen fabric.

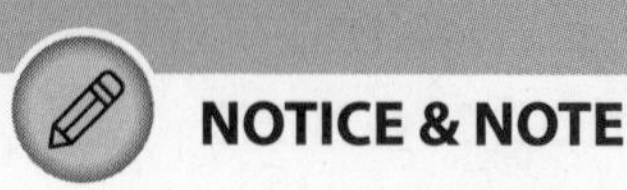

sullen plunge into water, succeeded by loud echoes. At the same moment there came a sound resembling the quick opening, and as rapid closing of a door overhead, while a faint gleam of light flashed suddenly through the gloom, and as suddenly faded away.

ANALYZE PLOT STRUCTURE

Annotate: Mark the sentence in paragraph 12 that states the narrator's understanding of the fate that may await him.

Analyze: How does knowing the narrator's thoughts build suspense in the story?

12 I saw clearly the doom which had been prepared for me, and congratulated myself upon the timely accident by which I had escaped. Another step before my fall, and the world had seen me no more. And the death just avoided, was of that very character which I had regarded as fabulous and frivolous in the tales respecting the Inquisition. To the victims of its tyranny, there was the choice of death with its direst physical agonies, or death with its most hideous moral horrors. I had been reserved for the latter. By long suffering my nerves had been unstrung, until I trembled at the sound of my own voice, and had become in every respect a fitting subject for the species of torture which awaited me.

13 Shaking in every limb, I groped my way back to the wall; resolving there to perish rather than risk the terrors of the wells, of which my imagination now pictured many in various positions about the dungeon. In other conditions of mind I might have had courage to end my misery at once by a plunge into one of these abysses; but now I was the veriest of cowards. Neither could I forget what I had read of these pits—that the *sudden* extinction of life formed no part of their most horrible plan.

14 Agitation of spirit kept me awake for many long hours; but at length I again slumbered. Upon arousing, I found by my side as before, a loaf and a pitcher of water. A burning thirst consumed me, and I emptied the vessel at a draft. It must have been drugged; for scarcely had I drunk, before I became irresistibly drowsy. A deep sleep fell upon me—a sleep like that of death. How long it lasted of course, I know not; but when, once again, I unclosed my eyes, the objects around me were visible. By a wild sulphurous luster,[10] the origin of which I could not at first determine, I was enabled to see the extent and aspect of the prison.

ANALYZE MOOD

Annotate: Mark the phrases in paragraphs 15–16 that describe the dungeon.

Infer: What does the narrator's description suggest about his state of mind? Why does he feel that way?

15 In its size I had been greatly mistaken. The whole circuit of its walls did not exceed twenty-five yards. For some minutes this fact occasioned me a world of vain trouble; vain indeed! for what could be of less importance, under the terrible circumstances which environed me, than the mere dimensions of my dungeon? But my soul took a wild interest in trifles, and I busied myself in endeavors to account for the error I had committed in my measurement. The truth at length flashed upon me. In my first attempt at exploration I had counted fifty-two paces, up to the period when I fell; I must then have been within a pace or two of the fragments of serge; in fact, I had nearly performed the circuit of the vault. I then slept, and upon awaking, I must have returned upon my steps—thus supposing the circuit nearly double what it actually was. My confusion of mind prevented

[10] **sulphurous luster:** a pale, yellow glow.

me from observing that I began my tour with the wall to the left, and ended it with the wall to the right.

16 I had been deceived, too, in respect to the shape of the enclosure. In feeling my way around I had found many angles, and thus deduced an idea of great irregularity; so potent is the effect of total darkness upon one arousing from lethargy or sleep! The angles were simply those of a few slight depressions, or niches, at odd intervals. The general shape of the prison was square. What I had taken for masonry seemed now to be iron, or some other metal, in huge plates, whose sutures or joints occasioned the depression. The entire surface of this metallic enclosure was rudely daubed in all the hideous and repulsive devices to which the charnel superstitions[11] of the monks has given rise. The figures of fiends in aspects of menace, with skeleton forms, and other more really fearful images, overspread and disfigured the walls. I observed that the outlines of these monstrosities were

[11] **charnel superstitions:** irrational beliefs about death and dying.

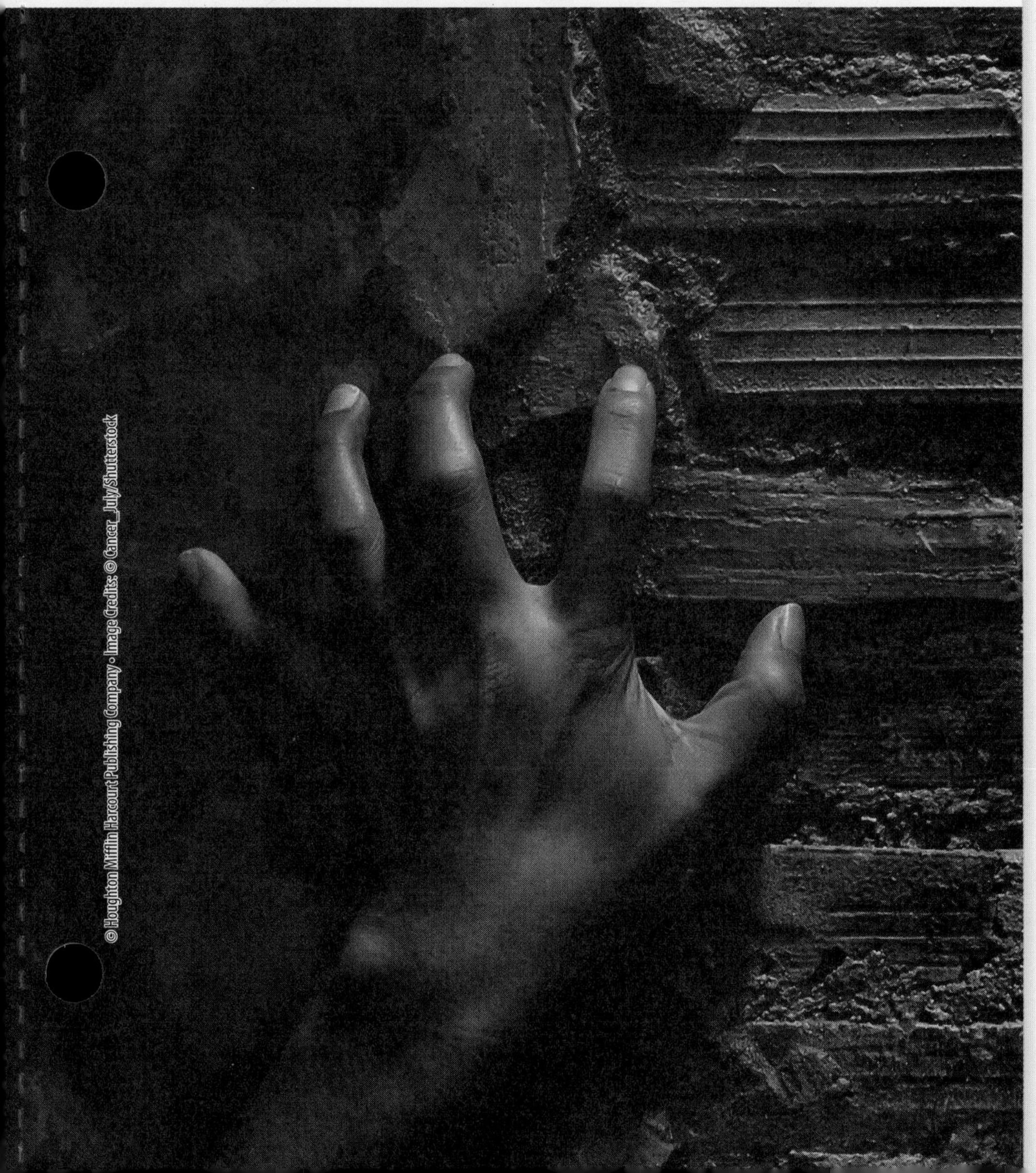

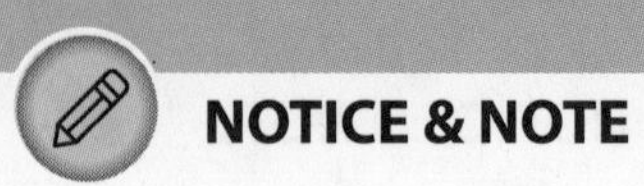

NOTICE & NOTE

ANALYZE PLOT STRUCTURE

Annotate: Mark the words in paragraph 17 that tell you the narrator's situation has changed.

Synthesize: How do these descriptions shape your understanding of the plot?

ANALYZE MOOD

Annotate: Underline details in paragraph 20 that describe the pendulum.

Interpret: How does the description of the pendulum contribute to the mood?

sufficiently distinct, but that the colors seemed faded and blurred, as if from the effects of a damp atmosphere. I now noticed the floor, too, which was of stone. In the center yawned the circular pit from whose jaws I had escaped; but it was the only one in the dungeon.

17 All this I saw distinctly and by much effort: for my personal condition had been greatly changed during slumber. I now lay upon my back, and at full length, on a species of low framework of wood. To this I was securely bound by a long strap resembling a surcingle.[12] It passed in many convolutions about my limbs and body, leaving at liberty only my head, and my left arm to such extent that I could, by dint[13] of much exertion, supply myself with food from an earthen dish which lay by my side on the floor. I saw, to my horror, that the pitcher had been removed. I say to my horror; for I was consumed with intolerable thirst. This thirst it appeared to be the design of my persecutors to stimulate: for the food in the dish was meat pungently seasoned.

18 Looking upward I surveyed the ceiling of my prison. It was some thirty or forty feet overhead, and constructed much as the side walls. In one of its panels a very singular figure riveted my whole attention. It was the painted figure of Time as he is commonly represented, save that, in lieu of a scythe, he held what, at a casual glance, I supposed to be the pictured image of a huge pendulum such as we see on antique clocks. There was something, however, in the appearance of this machine which caused me to regard it more attentively. While I gazed directly upward at it (for its position was immediately over my own) I fancied that I saw it in motion. In an instant afterward the fancy was confirmed. Its sweep was brief, and of course slow. I watched it for some minutes, somewhat in fear, but more in wonder. Wearied at length with observing its dull movement, I turned my eyes upon the other objects in the cell.

19 A slight noise attracted my notice, and, looking to the floor, I saw several enormous rats traversing it. They had issued from the well, which lay just within view to my right. Even then, while I gazed, they came up in troops, hurriedly, with ravenous eyes, allured by the scent of the meat. From this it required much effort and attention to scare them away.

20 It might have been half an hour, perhaps even an hour, (for I could take but imperfect note of time) before I again cast my eyes upward. What I then saw confounded and amazed me. The sweep of the pendulum had increased in extent by nearly a yard. As a natural consequence, its velocity was also much greater. But what mainly disturbed me was the idea that it had perceptibly *descended*. I now observed—with what horror it is needless to say—that its nether extremity was formed of a crescent of glittering steel, about a foot in length from horn to horn; the horns upward, and the under edge evidently as keen as that of a razor. Like a razor also, it seemed massy

[12]**surcingle:** a belt used to hold a saddle or pack onto a horse's back.
[13]**dint:** force.

 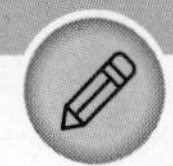

and heavy, tapering from the edge into a solid and broad structure above. It was appended to a weighty rod of brass, and the whole *hissed* as it swung through the air.

21 I could no longer doubt the doom prepared for me by monkish ingenuity in torture. My cognizance of the pit had become known to the inquisitorial agents—*the pit* whose horrors had been destined for so bold a recusant[14] as myself—*the pit*, typical of hell, and regarded by rumor as the Ultima Thule[15] of all their punishments. The plunge into this pit I had avoided by the merest of accidents, and I knew that surprise, or entrapment into torment, formed an important portion of all the grotesquerie of these dungeon deaths. Having failed to fall, it was no part of the demon plan to hurl me into the abyss; and thus (there being no alternative) a different and a milder destruction awaited me. Milder! I half smiled in my agony as I thought of such application of such a term.

22 What boots it[16] to tell of the long, long hours of horror more than mortal, during which I counted the rushing vibrations of the steel! Inch by inch—line by line—with a descent only appreciable at intervals that seemed ages—down and still down it came! Days passed—it might have been that many days passed—ere it swept so closely over me as to fan me with its acrid breath. The odor of the sharp steel forced itself into my nostrils. I prayed—I wearied heaven with my prayer for its more speedy descent. I grew frantically mad, and struggled to force myself upward against the sweep of the fearful scimitar.[17] And then I fell suddenly calm, and lay smiling at the glittering death, as a child at some rare bauble.

23 There was another interval of utter insensibility; it was brief; for, upon again lapsing into life there had been no perceptible descent in the pendulum. But it might have been long; for I knew there were demons who took note of my swoon, and who could have arrested the vibration at pleasure. Upon my recovery, too, I felt very—oh, inexpressibly sick and weak, as if through long inanition.[18] Even amid the agonies of that period, the human nature craved food. With painful effort I outstretched my left arm as far as my bonds permitted, and took possession of the small remnant which had been spared me by the rats. As I put a portion of it within my lips, there rushed to my mind a half formed thought of joy—of hope. Yet what business had I with hope? It was, as I say, a half formed thought—man has many such which are never completed. I felt that it was of joy—of hope; but I felt also that it had perished in its formation. In vain I struggled to perfect—to regain it. Long suffering had nearly

ANALYZE PLOT STRUCTURE

Annotate: Mark the phrases in paragraph 21 that describe the narrator and his antagonists.

Synthesize: What do you learn about the narrator's crime? What details are left out? Explain.

[14] **recusant:** a heretic or dissident.

[15] **Ultima Thule** (ŭl´tə-mə thōō´lē): according to ancient geographers, the most remote region of the world—here used figuratively to mean "most extreme achievement; summit."

[16] **What boots it?:** What good is it?

[17] **scimitar:** a curved sword of Middle Eastern origin.

[18] **inanition:** weakness from starvation.

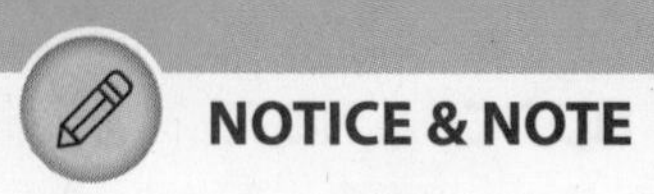

NOTICE & NOTE

annihilated all my ordinary powers of mind. I was an imbecile—an idiot.

24 The vibration of the pendulum was at right angles to my length. I saw that the crescent was designed to cross the region of the heart. It would fray the serge of my robe—it would return and repeat its operations—again—and again. Notwithstanding its terrifically wide sweep (some thirty feet or more) and the hissing vigor of its descent, sufficient to sunder these very walls of iron, still the fraying of my robe would be all that, for several minutes, it would accomplish. And at this thought I paused. I dared not go farther than this reflection. I dwelt upon it with a **pertinacity** of attention—as if, in so dwelling, I could arrest *here* the descent of the steel. I forced myself to ponder upon the sound of the crescent as it should pass across the garment—upon the peculiar thrilling sensation which the friction of cloth produces on the nerves. I pondered upon all this frivolity until my teeth were on edge.

pertinacity (pûr-tn-ăs´ĭ-tē) *n.* firm, unyielding intent.

25 Down—steadily down it crept. I took a frenzied pleasure in contrasting its downward with its lateral velocity. To the right—to the left—far and wide—with the shriek of a . . . spirit; to my heart with the stealthy pace of the tiger! I alternately laughed and howled as the one or the other idea grew predominant.

26 Down—certainly, relentlessly down! It vibrated within three inches of my bosom! I struggled violently, furiously, to free my left arm. This was free only from the elbow to the hand. I could reach the latter, from the platter beside me, to my mouth, with great effort, but no farther. Could I have broken the fastenings above the elbow, I would have seized and attempted to arrest the pendulum. I might as well have attempted to arrest an avalanche!

LANGUAGE CONVENTIONS

Annotate: Mark the semicolon in paragraph 27.

Analyze: How does the semicolon help you comprehend the narrator's shift in thought?

27 Down—still unceasingly—still inevitably down! I gasped and struggled at each vibration. I shrunk convulsively at its every sweep. My eyes followed its outward or upward whirls with the eagerness of the most unmeaning despair; they closed themselves spasmodically at the descent, although death would have been a relief, oh! how unspeakable! Still I quivered in every nerve to think how slight a sinking of the machinery would precipitate that keen, glistening axe upon my bosom. It was *hope* that prompted the nerve to quiver—the frame to shrink. It was *hope*—the hope that triumphs on the rack[19]—that whispers to the death-condemned even in the dungeons of the Inquisition.

28 I saw that some ten or twelve vibrations would bring the steel in actual contact with my robe, and with this observation there suddenly came over my spirit all the keen, collected calmness of despair. For the first time during many hours—or perhaps days—I *thought*. It now occurred to me that the bandage, or surcingle, which enveloped me, was *unique*. I was tied by no separate cord. The first stroke of

[19] **rack:** a device for torture that stretches the victim's limbs.

the razor-like crescent athwart[20] any portion of the band, would so detach it that it might be unwound from my person by means of my left hand. But how fearful, in that case, the proximity of the steel! The result of the slightest struggle how deadly! Was it likely, moreover, that the minions[21] of the torturer had not foreseen and provided for this possibility! Was it probable that the bandage crossed my bosom in the track of the pendulum? Dreading to find my faint, and, as it seemed, my last hope frustrated, I so far elevated my head as to obtain a distinct view of my breast. The surcingle enveloped my limbs and body close in all directions—*save in the path of the destroying crescent.*

29 Scarcely had I dropped my head back into its original position, when there flashed upon my mind what I cannot better describe than as the unformed half of that idea of deliverance to which I have previously alluded, and of which a moiety[22] only floated indeterminately through my brain when I raised food to my burning lips. The whole thought was now present—feeble, scarcely sane, scarcely definite,—but still entire. I proceeded at once, with the nervous energy of despair, to attempt its execution.

30 For many hours the immediate vicinity of the low framework upon which I lay, had been literally swarming with rats. They were wild, bold, ravenous; their red eyes glaring upon me as if they waited but for motionlessness on my part to make me their prey. "To what food," I thought, "have they been accustomed in the well?"

31 They had devoured, in spite of all my efforts to prevent them, all but a small remnant of the contents of the dish. I had fallen into an habitual seesaw, or wave of the hand about the platter, and, at length, the unconscious uniformity of the movement deprived it of effect. In their voracity the vermin frequently fastened their sharp fangs into my fingers. With the particles of the oily and spicy viand[23] which now remained, I thoroughly rubbed the bandage wherever I could reach it; then, raising my hand from the floor, I lay breathlessly still.

32 At first the ravenous animals were startled and terrified at the change—at the cessation of movement. They shrank alarmedly back; many sought the well. But this was only for a moment. I had not counted in vain upon their voracity. Observing that I remained without motion, one or two of the boldest leaped upon the framework, and smelt at the surcingle. This seemed the signal for a general rush. Forth from the well they hurried in fresh troops. They clung to the wood—they overran it, and leaped in hundreds upon my person. The measured movement of the pendulum disturbed them not at all. Avoiding its strokes they busied themselves with the anointed bandage. They pressed—they swarmed upon me in ever accumulating heaps. They writhed upon my throat; their cold

[20] **athwart:** across, from one side to the other.
[21] **minions:** followers, servants.
[22] **moiety:** one of two equal parts.
[23] **viand:** food.

NOTICE & NOTE

ANALYZE PLOT STRUCTURE

Annotate: Mark the sentence in paragraph 29 that shows the narrator's shift from having an idea for freeing himself to beginning to implement it.

Analyze: What does Poe achieve by not having the narrator tell us his plan?

lips sought my own; I was half stifled by their thronging pressure; disgust, for which the world has no name, swelled my bosom, and chilled, with a heavy clamminess, my heart. Yet one minute, and I felt that the struggle would be over. Plainly I perceived the loosening of the bandage. I knew that in more than one place it must be already severed. With a more than human resolution I lay *still.*

33 Nor had I erred in my calculations—nor had I endured in vain. I at length felt that I was *free*. The surcingle hung in ribands from my body. But the stroke of the pendulum already pressed upon my bosom. It had divided the serge of the robe. It had cut through the linen beneath. Twice again it swung, and a sharp sense of pain shot through every nerve. But the moment of escape had arrived. At a wave of my hand my deliverers hurried tumultuously away. With a steady movement—cautious, sidelong, shrinking, and slow—I slid from the embrace of the bandage and beyond the reach of the scimitar. For the moment, at least, *I was free*.

34 Free!—and in the grasp of the Inquisition! I had scarcely stepped from my wooden bed of horror upon the stone floor of the prison, when the motion of the hellish machine ceased and I beheld it drawn up, by some invisible force, through the ceiling. This was a lesson which I took desperately to heart. My every motion was undoubtedly watched. Free!—I had but escaped death in one form of agony, to be delivered unto worse than death in some other. With that thought I rolled my eyes nervously around the barriers of iron that hemmed me in. Something unusual—some change which at first I could not appreciate distinctly—it was obvious, had taken place in the apartment. For many minutes in a dreamy and trembling abstraction, I busied myself in vain, unconnected conjecture. During this period, I became aware, for the first time, of the origin of the sulphurous light which illuminated the cell. It proceeded from a fissure, about half an inch in width, extending entirely around the prison at the base of the walls, which thus appeared, and were, completely separated from the floor. I endeavored, but of course in vain, to look through the aperture.

35 As I arose from the attempt, the mystery of the alteration in the chamber broke at once upon my understanding. I have observed that, although the outlines of the figures upon the walls were sufficiently distinct, yet the colors seemed blurred and indefinite. These colors had now assumed, and were momentarily assuming, a startling and most intense brilliancy, that gave to the spectral and fiendish portraitures an aspect that might have thrilled even firmer nerves than my own. Demon eyes, of a wild and ghastly vivacity, glared upon me in a thousand directions, where none had been visible before, and gleamed with the lurid luster of a fire that I could not force my imagination to regard as unreal.

NOTICE & NOTE 

ANALYZE PLOT STRUCTURE

Annotate: In the plot of a story, a resolution reveals the outcome of events. Mark the sentences in paragraph 33 that indicate a resolution.

Predict: The resolution usually comes at the end and ties up the loose story threads. Do you think the character's problems are over? What do you predict will happen?

NOTICE & NOTE

ANALYZE MOOD

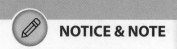

Annotate: Mark the words and phrases in paragraph 36 that provide clues to what is happening.

Analyze: What is happening? What effect on the mood does Poe achieve by not stating what is happening explicitly?

avert
(ə-vûrt´) *v.* to turn away.

36 *Unreal!*—Even while I breathed there came to my nostrils the breath of the vapor of heated iron! A suffocating odor pervaded the prison! A deeper glow settled each moment in the eyes that glared at my agonies! A richer tint of crimson diffused itself over the pictured horrors of blood. I panted! I gasped for breath! There could be no doubt of the design of my tormentors—oh! most unrelenting! oh! most demoniac of men! I shrank from the glowing metal to the center of the cell. Amid the thought of the fiery destruction that impended, the idea of the coolness of the well came over my soul like balm. I rushed to its deadly brink. I threw my straining vision below. The glare from the enkindled roof illumined its inmost recesses. Yet, for a wild moment, did my spirit refuse to comprehend the meaning of what I saw. At length it forced—it wrestled its way into my soul—it burned itself in upon my shuddering reason.—Oh! for a voice to speak!—oh! horror!—oh! any horror but this! With a shriek, I rushed from the margin, and buried my face in my hands—weeping bitterly.

37 The heat rapidly increased, and once again I looked up, shuddering as with a fit of the ague.[24] There had been a second change in the cell—and now the change was obviously in the form. As before, it was in vain that I, at first, endeavored to appreciate or understand what was taking place. But not long was I left in doubt. The Inquisitorial vengeance had been hurried by my twofold escape, and there was to be no more dallying with the King of Terrors. The room had been square. I saw that two of its iron angles were now acute—two, consequently, obtuse. The fearful difference quickly increased with a low rumbling or moaning sound. In an instant the apartment had shifted its form into that of a lozenge. But the alteration stopped not here—I neither hoped nor desired it to stop. I could have clasped the red walls to my bosom as a garment of eternal peace. "Death," I said, "any death but that of the pit!" Fool! might I have not known that *into the pit* it was the object of the burning iron to urge me? Could I resist its glow? or, if even that, could I withstand its pressure? And now, flatter and flatter grew the lozenge, with a rapidity that left me no time for contemplation. Its center, and of course, its greatest width, came just over the yawning gulf. I shrank back—but the closing walls pressed me resistlessly onward. At length for my seared and writhing body there was no longer an inch of foothold on the firm floor of the prison. I struggled no more, but the agony of my soul found vent in one loud, long, and final scream of despair. I felt that I tottered upon the brink—I **averted** my eyes—

38 There was a discordant hum of human voices! There was a loud blast of many trumpets! There was a harsh grating as of a thousand thunders! The fiery walls rushed back! An outstretched arm caught my own as I fell, fainting, into the abyss. It was that of General Lasalle. The French army had entered Toledo. The Inquisition was in the hands of its enemies.

[24] **ague:** an illness, like malaria, that causes fever and shivering.

CHECK YOUR UNDERSTANDING

Answer these questions before moving on to the **Analyze the Text** section on the following page.

1 What are the rats doing when the narrator first encounters them?

A Fleeing the fire

B Trying to take his food

C Chewing on his bonds

D Crawling on his body

2 Which method of execution does the narrator fear the most?

F The pit

G The pendulum

H The fire

J The contracting walls

3 What detail contributes to the horrific mood?

A *I breathed more freely*

B *I found beside me a loaf and a pitcher with water*

C *at length I again slumbered*

D *I struggled violently, furiously, to free my left arm*

ANALYZE THE TEXT

Support your responses with evidence from the text. NOTEBOOK

1. **Synthesize** Review the elements of Gothic fiction on the Get Ready page. Which of these elements does Poe include in "The Pit and the Pendulum"?
2. **Infer** The narrator is often uncertain about how much time has elapsed and about the physical details of the prison. What does this uncertainty suggest about the narrator's state of mind?
3. **Analyze** Poe's narrator's personal qualities are revealed through his responses to the horrors of imprisonment. How does discovering his character in this way affect your understanding of the plot? Cite text evidence in your response.
4. **Infer** How would you describe the mood of the story? How does Poe create this mood? Cite examples of diction and syntax in your response.
5. **Synthesize** How does Poe begin and end the story? What does this structure suggest about the story's overall meaning?

RESEARCH

RESEARCH TIP
When searching for information on the literary influence of an author, be sure to use reliable sources, such as books by expert authors or websites that are reliable and accurate.

Edgar Allan Poe's life, though brief, had a lasting literary impact, as he is credited with having influenced later writers. Find out more about Poe's literary heritage by answering these questions.

QUESTION	ANSWER
Which Stephen King story is modeled on Poe's "Tell-Tale Heart"?	
Which famous author of detective fiction wrote, "Where was the detective story until Poe breathed the breath of life into it?"	
Which French poet acclaimed Poe's poetry and helped establish his reputation as a poet?	

Extend Read more about Poe's influence on the horror story, the detective story, or science fiction. Write a brief paragraph summarizing your findings on the views of his influence.

CREATE AND PRESENT

Write an Adaptation Poe's "The Pit and the Pendulum" is an intense study of a man suffering petrifying terror, fighting despair, and trying desperately to find a method of escape. Such a dramatic work could be adapted to another form, such as a radio or television script or a graphic novel.

- ❑ Choose the medium you prefer for your adaptation.
- ❑ Break the overall narrative into individual scenes that accurately convey a sense of character, setting, plot, and the theme of the original work.
- ❑ Write a narrative that includes text, stage directions (if appropriate), and visuals.
- ❑ Review your adaptation to ensure that it builds dramatic tension and conveys the main character's state of mind and the work's mood.

Go to **Writing Narratives** in the **Writing Studio** for help.

Present an Adaptation Turn your adaptation into a presentation either by recording the script or making a visual presentation out of your graphic novel.

- ❑ Practice using volume, tone of voice, and expression to convey effectively the thoughts, feelings, and state of mind of the narrator.
- ❑ Scan or copy visuals into a digital format to facilitate displaying them to classmates.
- ❑ Give a dramatic reading of your script or graphic novel to classmates, using voice and nonverbal communication to add impact to the presentation.

Go to **Using Media in a Presentation** in the **Speaking and Listening Studio** for help.

RESPOND TO THE ESSENTIAL QUESTION

What do we secretly fear?

Gather Information Review your annotations and notes on "The Pit and the Pendulum." Then, add relevant details to your Response Log. As you determine which information to include, think about the:

- fear of being in the power of another
- impact of the unknown on people's fears
- appeal of stories with elements of horror

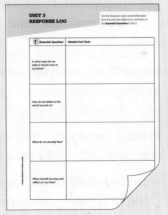

ACADEMIC VOCABULARY

As you write and discuss what you learned from the story, be sure to use the Academic Vocabulary words. Check off each of the words that you use.

- ❑ **analogy**
- ❑ **denote**
- ❑ **quote**
- ❑ **topic**
- ❑ **unique**

RESPOND

CRITICAL VOCABULARY

WORD BANK
indeterminate **insuperable**
lucid **prostrate**
tumultuous **pertinacity**
supposition **averted**

Practice and Apply Choose the correct term to complete each sentence.

1. The __________ figure of the dog sprawled on the hearth.
2. Her response was remarkably __________ for one so young.
3. "Determination is an admirable trait," he cautioned, "but __________ will not make up for lack of preparation."
4. By following well-thought-out plans, the team __________ the disaster.
5. The rebellion launched a period of __________ and wrenching change.
6. The staff was told to prepare for a(n) __________ number of visitors, making it difficult to secure sufficient supplies.
7. The odds were __________ for anyone with less determination than he.
8. The confident __________ that we would meet the deadline faded.

VOCABULARY STRATEGY: Context Clues

Go to **Using Context Clues** in the **Vocabulary Studio** for help.

When you come across an unfamiliar word in a text, you can use context clues, or information in surrounding phrases and sentences, to determine the word's meaning. For example, you can use context clues to determine the meaning of the word *indeterminate* in this passage from "The Pit and the Pendulum":

> **I was sick—sick unto death with that long agony; and when they at length unbound me, and I was permitted to sit, I felt that my senses were leaving me. The sentence—the dread sentence of death—was the last of distinct accentuation which reached my ears. After that, the sound of the inquisitorial voices seemed merged in one dreamy indeterminate hum.**

The word *dreamy* provides a clue that *indeterminate* means "not precisely known." The clause "I felt that my senses were leaving me" also hints at this meaning. In addition, the word *distinct* contrasts what the narrator hears when the sentence is announced from the sound of the voices that follow.

Practice and Apply Work with a partner to use context clues to help determine or clarify the meaning of unknown words. Follow these steps:

- Identify unfamiliar words in the story.
- Look for synonyms, antonyms, and other clues in surrounding words and sentences that help you infer the word's meaning. Consult a thesaurus if needed to identify synonyms and antonyms.
- Verify your preliminary determination of each word's meaning by checking the definition in a print or digital college-level dictionary.

LANGUAGE CONVENTIONS: Semicolons

Go to **Semicolons and Colons** in the **Grammar Studio** for help.

Semicolons are used syntactically in various ways to help writers construct compound and compound-complex sentences.

One use is to separate two independent clauses that are linked by a conjunction (*and, or, but*), especially when one of the clauses contains a number of commas:

> **How long it lasted of course, I know not; but when, once again, I unclosed my eyes, the objects around me were visible.**

Semicolons are also used to separate parts of a compound sentence that are not joined by a coordinating conjunction or adverb:

> **They shrank alarmedly back; many sought the well.**

Semicolons are used to link an independent clause with another independent clause preceded by a **conjunctive adverb** (*then, however, thus,* or *therefore*) to closely connect the two ideas:

> **With the particles of the oily and spicy viand which now remained, I thoroughly rubbed the bandage wherever I could reach it; then, raising my hand from the floor, I lay breathlessly still.**

Semicolons are also used to separate items in a list when one or more of the items within the list has a comma:

Poe was a master of many genres, as evidenced by such impressive works as "The Raven" and "The Bells," lyric poems; "The Tell-Tale Heart" and "The Fall of the House of Usher," short stories; and many pieces of literary criticism.

Practice and Apply Write four original sentences, each following one of the four examples of uses of semicolons.

Collaborate & Compare

THE PIT AND THE PENDULUM
by Edgar Allan Poe

COMPARE THEMES

Collaborate to Synthesize Comparing works of literature from the same historical period can deepen your understanding of each work's themes and provide an insight into issues and ideas important in that period. "The Minister's Black Veil" and "The Pit and the Pendulum" represent two different strains of American Romanticism. Poe is considered a master of Gothic literature. Hawthorne's work is subtler and more psychologically probing, but reflects a shared interest in the darker side of the human mind.

In a small group, complete the chart with similarities and differences in the two texts you read. One example is completed for you. Add rows as your group generates more ideas.

SIMILARITIES	DIFFERENCES
	"Minister": main character interacts with others "Pit": other characters unseen

ANALYZE THE TEXTS

Discuss these questions in your group, paraphrasing and summarizing the text when needed and using academic vocabulary.

1. **Cite Evidence** What is the setting of each story? How does each setting relate to ideas and themes the writer presents?
2. **Synthesize** Compare and contrast the social context of the characters in both stories. How do their interactions with others contribute to the themes of the two works?
3. **Analyze** Select two short passages from each story and identify details that contribute to a dark and ominous mood. How do these details support the themes of each work? Consider word choice, imagery, and plot details in your response.
4. **Analyze** How does each author use ambiguity or uncertainty to add interest and to advance his themes? Cite an example of ambiguity in each story and describe its effect.

COLLABORATE AND PRESENT

Now your group can continue exploring the ideas in these texts by identifying and comparing their themes. Follow these steps:

1. **Decide on the most important details** With your group, review your chart to identify the key similarities and differences in the two stories. Identify points you agree on and collaboratively offer ideas, resolving disagreements through discussions based on evidence from the texts.

2. **Create theme statements** Determine a theme statement for each story. Remember, it is up to you and your group to use details to infer the themes and determine the implicit meaning of the texts. You can use a chart to determine the themes each writer suggests.

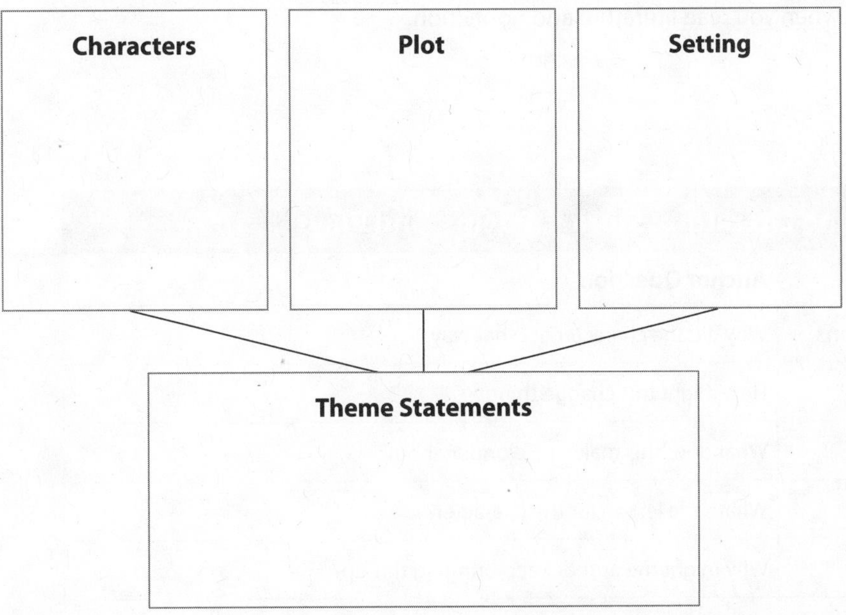

3. **Compare themes** With your group, discuss whether the themes of the stories are similar or different. Listen actively to the members of your group and ask them to clarify any points you do not understand. Be sure to use text evidence supplemented by original ideas.

4. **Present to the class** Finalize your ideas as a group. Create a formal presentation that has a logical structure, smooth transitions, accurate evidence, and well-chosen details. Present your ideas to the class. Be sure to include clear statements on the themes of each story. Compare and contrast the stories' themes to highlight the different purposes of the two authors. Think about using visuals to help convey information to the class. Make sure every member of the group takes part in the presentation.

Go to **Giving a Presentation** in the **Speaking and Listening Studio** for help.

INDEPENDENT READING

Reader's Choice

ESSENTIAL QUESTION:

Review the four Essential Questions for this unit on page 205.

Setting a Purpose Select one or more of these options from your eBook to continue your exploration of the Essential Questions.

- Read the descriptions to see which text grabs your interest.
- Think about which genres you enjoy reading.

NOTICE & NOTE

In this unit, you practiced noticing and noting the signposts and asking big questions about nonfiction. As you read independently, these signposts and others will aid your understanding. Below are the anchor questions to ask when you read literature and nonfiction.

Reading Literature: Stories, Poems, and Plays	
Signpost	**Anchor Question**
Contrasts and Contradictions	Why did the character act that way?
Aha Moment	How might this change things?
Tough Questions	What does this make me wonder about?
Words of the Wiser	What's the lesson for the character?
Again and Again	Why might the author keep bringing this up?
Memory Moment	Why is this memory important?

Reading Nonfiction: Essays, Articles, and Arguments	
Signpost	**Anchor Question(s)**
Big Questions	What surprised me? What did the author think I already knew? What challenged, changed, or confirmed what I already knew?
Contrasts and Contradictions	What is the difference, and why does it matter?
Extreme or Absolute Language	Why did the author use this language?
Numbers and Stats	Why did the author use these numbers or amounts?
Quoted Words	Why was this person quoted or cited, and what did this add?
Word Gaps	Do I know this word from someplace else? Does it seem like technical talk for this topic? Do clues in the sentence help me understand the word?

You can preview these texts in Unit 3 of your eBook.

Then, check off the text or texts that you select to read on your own.

ESSAY

***from* Nature**

***from* Self-Reliance**

Ralph Waldo Emerson

How can you live as an individual, relate to nature, and be your own master?

ARTICLE

The Pointlessness of Unplugging

Casey N. Cep

What happens when people unplug from their digital devices?

POEM

The Raven

Edgar Allan Poe

Does the raven relieve a grieving man of his painful burden of memories?

POEM

Pastoral

Jennifer Chang

Find out how a poet's vivid images and wordplay can place you in a field of flowers.

Collaborate and Share With a partner, discuss what you learned from at least one of your independent readings.

- Give a brief synopsis or summary of the text.
- Describe any signposts that you noticed in the text and explain what they revealed to you.
- Describe what you most enjoyed or found most challenging about the text. Give specific examples.
- Decide if you would recommend the text to others. Why or why not?

Go to the **Reading Studio** for more resources on **Notice & Note.**

Write an Explanatory Essay

Go to the **Writing Studio** for help writing an explanatory essay.

This collection focuses on understanding ourselves and the relationship among self, society, and nature. For this writing task, you will write an explanatory essay—a type of informational writing that examines and analyzes a topic or explains a topic. For an example of a well-written explanatory essay you can use as a mentor text, review the excerpt from *Last Child in the Woods*.

As you write your explanatory essay, you can use the notes from your Response Log which you filled out after reading the texts in this unit.

Writing Prompt

Read the information in the box below.

This is the context for your explanatory essay.

> **Society is made up of individuals who share space, share natural resources, and rely on each other.**

Think carefully about the following question.

How might stopping and reflecting help people who rely on each other?

> **When should we stop and reflect on our lives?**

What information will you use to develop a topic and support a thesis in your explanatory essay?

Write an explanatory essay exploring this question, using your own ideas as well as ideas from two or more of the selections in this unit.

Be sure to include—

- ❑ an introduction with a clear thesis statement about the relationships of the individual and society
- ❑ ideas from at least two selections from the unit
- ❑ a logically structured body that thoroughly develops the topic with relevant examples, details, and quotations from the texts
- ❑ transitions to clarify the relationships between sections of your essay and to link ideas with the textual evidence that supports them
- ❑ a conclusion that follows from the ideas in the body of the essay
- ❑ precise use of language with appropriate tone and style

Review these points as you write and again when you finish. Make any needed changes.

1 Plan

Before you start writing, you need to research and plan your essay. First, review your notes from the unit's selections on the individual and society. Work with a group to share ideas and discuss the following questions. Be prepared to discuss specific textual evidence.

- Which authors described ways to maintain a balance between the self and society? Did they engage with the outer world? Did they retreat from the issues of the day?
- Overall, did the authors present society and individuals in opposition or in harmony?

Now that you have discussed the topic with others, consider your own approach to the question "How can we maintain balance between the individual and society?" Decide which texts contain ideas about the connection between the self and society, and choose two or three that you feel best demonstrate these connections. Reread these selections, taking notes about what each one says about the relationship between the individual and society. Add quotations or ideas from the work. Be sure to note which selection you are using for quotations or ideas.

Explanatory Essay Planning Table	
Genre	
Topic	
Audience	
Ideas from Selection 1	
Ideas from Selection 2	
Ideas from Selection 3	

Background Reading Review the notes you have taken in your Response Log that relate to the question, "When should we stop and reflect on our lives?" Texts in this unit provide background reading that will help you formulate the key ideas you will include in your essay.

Go to **Using Textual Evidence: Summarizing, Paraphrasing, and Quoting** for help planning your explanatory essay.

Notice & Note

From Reading to Writing

As you plan your explanatory essay, apply what you've learned about signposts to your own writing. Remember that writers use common features, called signposts, to help convey their message to readers.

Think how you can incorporate **Contrasts and Contradictions** into your essay.

Go to the **Reading Studio** for more resources on **Notice & Note**.

Use the notes from your Response Log as you plan your explanatory essay.

UNIT 3 RESPONSE LOG

Use this Response Log to record information from the texts that relates to or comments on the **Essential Questions** in Unit 3.

? Essential Question	Details from Texts
In what ways do we seek to remain true to ourselves?	
How do we relate to the world around us?	
What do we secretly fear?	
When should we stop and reflect on our lives?	

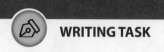

Go to **Writing Informative Texts: Organizing Ideas** for help organizing your ideas.

Organize Your Ideas After you have gathered ideas from your planning activities, you need to organize them in a way that will help you draft your explanatory essay. Develop a strong thesis statement. Choose which textual evidence is the most relevant to your thesis statement and your main ideas. Select an interesting quotation or detail to accompany your thesis statement in the introduction. List some ideas for your concluding section. You can use the chart below to map out the organizational structure of your essay.

Ideas for Introduction
Interesting quotation or detail for Introduction:
Thesis Statement:

Main Idea	Main Idea	Main Idea
Text Evidence	**Text Evidence**	**Text Evidence**

Ideas for Conclusion

2 Develop a Draft

You might prefer to draft your essay online.

Once you have completed your planning activities, you will be ready to begin drafting your explanatory essay. Refer to your Graphic Organizers as well as any notes you took as you studied the texts in this unit. These will provide a kind of map for you to follow as you write. Using a word processor or online writing application makes it easier to make changes or move sentences around later when you are ready to revise your first draft.

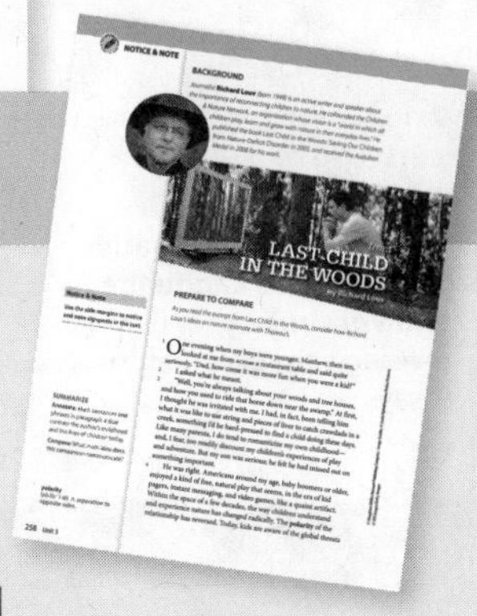

Use the Mentor Text

Structure and Purpose

Contrasts and comparisons are important in all types of writing. Fiction writers create characters with stark contrasts to highlight their differences or similarities. Informational writers include comparisons to help readers understand a new fact or process. Richard Louv compares his own childhood and modern childhood to show how the world has changed.

Not that long ago, summer camp was a place where you camped, hiked in the woods, learned about plants and animals, or told firelight stories about ghosts or mountain lions. As likely as not today, "summer camp" is a weight-loss camp, or a computer camp.

Louv shows the way our attitudes toward nature have changed by using a "then and now" example regarding summer camp.

Apply What You've Learned Consider how you could use contrasts and comparisons to strengthen your main ideas. Can you compare being alone with being part of society, or being in nature with being in a city? What contrasts can help address the important distinctions between the individual and society?

Supporting Main Ideas

Writers of explanatory essays use a variety of evidence and details to support their thesis and main ideas. Personal experiences, quotations from famous authors, references to pop culture, and facts and statistics are all fair game—the art of the essay is tying it all together. Notice how Richard Louv uses examples from history and pop culture to introduce ideas and elaborate on them.

A recent television ad depicts a four-wheel-drive SUV racing along a breathtakingly beautiful mountain stream—while in the backseat two children watch a movie on a flip-down video screen, oblivious to the landscape and water beyond the windows.

Louv gives an example of how children today do not appreciate nature. They would rather watch screens than look at nature.

Apply What You've Learned Choose one or two places in your plan where you can include evidence or details from history—for example, a charismatic individual or important event—or an element of pop culture, such as an advertisement or movie. Note these ideas in your Graphic Organizer.

3 Revise

Go to **Writing Informative Texts: Precise Language and Vocabulary** for help revising your explanatory essay.

On Your Own Once you have written your draft, you'll want to go back and look for ways to improve your explanatory essay. As you reread and revise, think about whether you have achieved your purpose. The Revision Guide will help you focus on specific elements to make your writing stronger.

Revision Guide

Ask Yourself	Tips	Revision Techniques
1. Does my introduction engage the reader and contain a thesis statement that clearly identifies the topic?	**Highlight** sentences that get the audience interested. **Underline** your thesis statement.	**Add** vivid language and details to interest the reader. **Reword** your thesis statement to **clarify** the topic.
2. Do I present relevant text evidence to support my thesis statement and central ideas?	**Highlight** each central idea. **Underline** evidence that supports each idea and **note** evidence that seems weak.	**Add** evidence for any idea that is not supported. **Change** evidence that does not offer strong support.
3. Is my essay logically organized with smooth transitions linking ideas and evidence?	**Note** major sections that reflect your organization. **Underline** each transitional word or phrase.	**Reorder** paragraphs if needed. **Add** transitions to **clarify** relationships between ideas.
4. Do I use formal, precise language?	**Highlight** slang and informal language.	**Reword** text to avoid informal language.
5. Does my conclusion follow logically from the ideas I present?	**Note** where the conclusion summarizes your ideas.	**Add** a closing statement if needed to sum up the information your essay presents.

ACADEMIC VOCABULARY

As you conduct your **peer review,** be sure to use these words.

- ❑ **analogy**
- ❑ **denote**
- ❑ **quote**
- ❑ **topic**
- ❑ **unique**

With a Partner Once you and your partner have worked through the Revision Guide on your own, exchange explanatory essays and evaluate each other's draft in a **peer review.** Focus on providing revision suggestions for at least three of the items mentioned in the chart. Explain why you think your partner's draft should be revised and what your specific suggestions are.

When receiving feedback from your partner, listen attentively and ask questions to make sure you fully understand the revision suggestions.

4 Edit

Once you have addressed the organization, development, and flow of ideas in your explanatory essay, you can look to improve the finer points of your draft. Edit for the proper use of standard English conventions and make sure to correct any spelling or grammatical errors.

Go to **Semicolons and Colons** in the **Grammar Studio** to learn more.

Language Conventions

Use Semicolons Authors have unique styles to communicate information. One characteristic of Richard Louv's style is his use of semicolons to form compound and compound-complex sentences. He often uses semicolons rather than a comma and conjunction to mimic the way people think or speak and to create a rhythm in his writing. Semicolons also add clarity to writing and can draw attention to specific ideas or closely connect two ideas.

Notice how Louv uses semicolons to connect ideas in *Last Child in the Woods*.

Purpose	Example
To separate two independent clauses that are linked by a conjunction when the sentence already contains a number of commas	The postmodern notion that reality is only a construct—that we are what we program—suggests limitless human possibilities; but as the young spend less and less of their lives in natural surroundings, their senses narrow, physiologically and psychologically, and this reduces the richness of human experience.
To separate parts of a compound sentence that are not joined by a coordinating conjunction or adverb	But my son was serious; he felt he had missed out on something important. But I knew my woods and my fields; I knew every bend in the creek and dip in the beaten dirt paths.

5 Publish

Finalize your explanatory essay and choose a way to share it with your audience. Consider these options:

- Present your essay as a speech or video recording.
- Post your essay as a blog on a classroom or school website.

WRITING TASK

Use the scoring guide to evaluate your essay.

Writing Task Scoring Guide: Explanatory Essay

	Organization/Progression	Development of Ideas	Use of Language and Conventions
4	• The organization is effective and logical and appropriate to the task and purpose. • Transition words and phrases effectively link related ideas and evidence.	• The introduction engages the reader's attention and includes a thesis statement that clearly addresses the prompt. • The topic is strongly developed with relevant facts, concrete details, interesting quotations, and examples from the texts. • The concluding section follows from and supports the ideas presented.	• The writing reflects a formal style. • Language is vivid and precise. • Sentence structures vary and have a rhythmic flow. • Spelling, capitalization, and punctuation are correct. • Grammar and usage are correct.
3	• The organization is for the most part appropriate to the task and purpose. • Progression of ideas mostly flows smoothly. Transitions are needed in a few places to link related ideas and evidence.	• The introduction could do more to attract the reader's curiosity; the thesis statement identifies the topic. • One or two key points could use additional support in the form of relevant facts, concrete details, quotations, and examples from the texts. • The concluding section mostly follows from and supports the ideas presented.	• The style is inconsistent in a few places. • Vague language is used in a few places. • Sentence structures vary somewhat. • Some spelling, capitalization, and punctuation mistakes occur. • Some grammatical and usage errors are repeated in the report.
2	• The organization is confusing in some places and often doesn't follow a logical order. • More transition words and phrases are needed throughout to link ideas and evidence.	• The introduction provides some information about a topic, but the thesis statement is weak or unclear. • Most key points need additional support in the form of relevant facts, concrete details, quotations, and examples from the texts. • The concluding section is confusing and does not follow from the ideas presented.	• The style and tone are too informal. • Vague, general language is used in many places. • Sentence structures barely vary, and some fragments or run-on sentences are present. • Spelling, capitalization, and punctuation are often incorrect but do not make reading the report difficult. • Grammar and usage are incorrect in many places, but the writer's ideas are still clear.
1	• A logical organization is not used; information is presented randomly. • Transitions are not used, making the essay difficult to understand.	• The response to the prompt is vague or confused. • The thesis statement is missing or unclear. • Facts, details, quotations, and examples from the texts are missing or unrelated to the topic or thesis. • The essay lacks an identifiable concluding section.	• The style and tone are inappropriate for the essay. • Language is too vague or general to convey the information. • Repetitive sentence structure, fragments, and run-on sentences make the writing monotonous and difficult to follow. • Spelling, capitalization, and punctuation are incorrect throughout. • Many grammatical and usage errors change the meaning of the writer's ideas.

Reflect on the Unit

By completing your explanatory essay, you have created a writing product that pulls together and expresses your thoughts about the reading you have done in this unit. Now is a good time to reflect on what you have learned.

Reflect on the Essential Questions

- Review the four Essential Questions on page 205. How have your answers to these questions changed in response to the texts you've read in this unit?
- What are some examples from the texts you've read that show how people interact with others and society while remaining true to themselves?

Reflect on Your Reading

- Which selections were the most interesting or surprising to you?
- From which selection did you learn the most about the relationship between the individual and society?

Reflect on the Writing Task

- What difficulties did you encounter while working on your explanatory essay? How might you avoid them next time?
- What part of the explanatory essay was the easiest to write? the hardest to write? Why?
- What improvements did you make to your explanatory essay as you were revising?

UNIT 3 SELECTIONS

- **from "Song of Myself"**
- **"My Friend Walt Whitman"**
- **Poems of Emily Dickinson: "The Soul selects her own Society," "Because I could not stop for Death," "Much Madness is divinest Sense," "Tell all the Truth, but tell it slant"**
- **"In the Season of Change"**
- **from *Walden***
- **from *Last Child In the Woods***
- **"The Minister's Black Veil"**
- **"The Pit and The Pendulum"**

RESOURCES

HMH *INTO LITERATURE* STUDIOS

For more instruction and practice, visit the HMH *Into Literature* Studios.

Reading Studio

Writing Studio

Speaking & Listening Studio

Grammar Studio

Vocabulary Studio

UNIT 1 RESPONSE LOG

Use this Response Log to record information from the texts that relates to or comments on the **Essential Questions** in Unit 1.

? Essential Question	Details from Texts
Why are we bound to certain places?	
What motivates people to explore the unknown?	
What does it mean to be a stranger in a strange land?	
What happens when cultures collide?	

UNIT 2 RESPONSE LOG

Use this Response Log to record information from the texts that relates to or comments on the **Essential Questions** in Unit 2.

? Essential Question	Details from Texts
What does oppression look like?	
How do we gain our freedom?	
How can we share power and build alliances?	
How do we transform our lives?	

UNIT 3 RESPONSE LOG

Use this Response Log to record information from the texts that relates to or comments on the **Essential Questions** in Unit 3.

? Essential Question	Details from Texts
In what ways do we seek to remain true to ourselves?	
How do we relate to the world around us?	
What do we secretly fear?	
When should we stop and reflect on our lives?	

UNIT 4 RESPONSE LOG

Use this Response Log to record information from the texts that relates to or comments on the **Essential Questions** in Unit 4.

? Essential Question	Details from Texts
When is self-determination possible?	
What divides us as human beings?	
How do we face defeat?	
What is the price of progress?	

UNIT 5
RESPONSE LOG

Use this Response Log to record information from the texts that relates to or comments on the **Essential Questions** in Unit 5.

? Essential Question	Details from Texts
To what degree do we control our lives?	
Why do humans cause harm?	
What are the consequences of change?	
What makes a place unique?	

UNIT 6 RESPONSE LOG

Use this Response Log to record information from the texts that relates to or comments on the **Essential Questions** in Unit 6.

? Essential Question	Details from Texts
How do we deal with rejection or isolation?	
For whom is the American Dream relevant?	
When should personal integrity come before civic duty?	
What would we do if there were no limits?	

Using a Glossary

A glossary is an alphabetical list of vocabulary words. Use a glossary just as you would a dictionary—to determine the meanings, parts of speech, pronunciation, and syllabification of words. (Some technical, foreign, and more obscure words in this book are defined for you in the footnotes that accompany many of the selections.)

Many words in the English language have more than one meaning. This glossary gives the meanings that apply to the words as they are used in the selections in this book.

The following abbreviations are used to identify parts of speech of words:

adj. adjective *adv.* adverb *n.* noun *v.* verb

Each word's pronunciation is given in parentheses. A guide to the pronunciation symbols appears in the Pronunciation Key below. The stress marks in the Pronunciation Key are used to indicate the force given to each syllable in a word. They can also help you determine where words are divided into syllables.

For more information about the words in this glossary or for information about words not listed here, consult a dictionary.

Pronunciation Key

Symbol	Examples	Symbol	Examples	Symbol	Examples
ă	**pat**	m	**mum**	ûr	**urge, term, firm, word, heard**
ā	**pay**	n	**no, sudden*** (sŭd′n)	v	**valve**
ä	**father**	ng	**thing**	w	**with**
âr	**care**	ŏ	**pot**	y	**yes**
b	**bib**	ō	**toe**	z	**zebra, xylem**
ch	**church**	ô	**caught, paw**	zh	**vision, pleasure, garage**
d	**deed, milled**	oi	**noise**	ə	**about, item, edible, gallop, circus**
ĕ	**pet**	o͝o	**took**	ər	**butter**
ē	**bee**	o͞o	**boot**	**Sounds in Foreign Words**	
f	**fife, phase, rough**	o͝or	**lure**	KH	*German* **ich, ach;** *Scottish* **loch**
g	**gag**	ôr	**core**	N	*French*, **bon** (bôN)
h	**hat**	ou	**out**	œ	*French* **feu, œuf;** *German* **schön**
hw	**which**	p	**pop**	ü	*French* **tu;** *German* **über**
ĭ	**pit**	r	**roar**		
ī	**pie, by**	s	**sauce**		
îr	**pier**	sh	**ship, dish**		
j	**judge**	t	**tight, stopped**		
k	**kick, cat, pique**	th	**thin**		
l	**lid, needle*** (nēd′l)	*th*	**this**		
		ŭ	**cut**		

*In English the consonants *l* and *n* often constitute complete syllables by themselves.

Stress Marks

The relative emphasis with which the syllables of a word or phrase are spoken, called stress, is indicated in three different ways. The strongest, or primary, stress is marked with a bold mark (**′**). An intermediate, or secondary, level of stress is marked with a similar but lighter mark (′). The weakest stress is unmarked. Words of one syllable show no stress mark.

GLOSSARY OF ACADEMIC VOCABULARY

adapt (ə-dăpt´) *v.* to make something suitable for a particular situation; to adjust to an environment.

ambiguous (ăm-bĭg´yo͞o-əs) *adj.* open to more than one interpretation.

analogy (ə-năl´ə-jē) *n.* a similarity in some respects between things that are otherwise dissimilar or a comparison based on such similarity.

clarify (klăr´ə-fī) *v. tr.* to make clear or easier to understand.

coherent (kō-hîr´ənt) *adj.* holding together in an orderly, logical, or consistent way.

confirm (kən-fôrm´) *v.* to support or establish the certainty or validity of; verify.

contemporary (kən-tĕm´pə-rĕr-ē) *adj.* belonging to the same period of time; of about the same age; current or modern.

contrary (kŏn´trĕr-ē) *adj.* opposite or opposed in character or purpose.

definitely (dĕf´ə-nĭt-lē) *adv.* in a clearly defined manner; explicitly precisely; decidedly.

denote (dĭ-nōt´) *tr. v.* to mark; indicate; to serve as a symbol or name for the meaning of; signify.

deny (dĭ-nī´) *tr. v.* to declare untrue; assert to be false; to refuse to believe.

device (dĭ-vīs´) *n.* something made for a specific purpose; a literary technique used to achieve a certain effect.

displace (dĭs-plās´) *v.* to move or force from one place or position to another.

dynamic (dī-năm´ĭk) *adj.* characterized by change, movement, or activity.

format (fôr´măt) *n.* a plan for the organization and arrangement of a specified production.

founder (foun´dər) *n.* someone who sets up, establishes, or provides the basis for something.

global (glō´bəl) *adj.* spherical in shape; worldwide; total.

ideological (ī-dē-ə-lŏj´ĭ-kəl) *adj.* based on ideas, beliefs, or doctrines.

implicit (ĭm-plĭs´ĭt) *adj.* implied or understood though not directly expressed.

infinite (ĭn´fə-nĭt) *adj.* having no boundaries or limits; immeasurably great or large.

publication (pŭb-lĭ-kā´shən) *n.* the act of making public in printed or electronic form; the product of this act.

quote (kwōt) *v.* to repeat or copy words from a source such as a book usually with an acknowledgment of the source; to give a quotation; *n.* a quotation.

revise (rĭ-vīz´) *v. intr.* to alter or edit; to reconsider and change or modify.

revolution (rĕv-ə-lo͞o´shən) *n.* the overthrow and replacement of a government, often through violent means.

simulated (sĭm´yə-lā-tĭd) *adj.* made in resemblance of or as a substitute for another; performed or staged in imitation of a real event or activity.

somewhat (sŭm´wŏt, -hwŏt, -wŭt, -hwŭt) *adv.* to some extent or degree.

topic (tŏp´ĭk) *n.* the subject of a speech, essay, discussion, or conversation.

unify (yo͞o´nə-fī) *v.* to make into or become a unit; consolidate.

unique (yo͞o-nēk´) *adj.* being the only one of its kind; remarkable or extraordinary.

virtual (vûr´cho͞o-əl) *adj.* existing or resulting in essence or effect though not in actual form; existing in the mind.

GLOSSARY OF CRITICAL VOCABULARY

abandonment (ə-băn´dən-mĕnt) *n.* a lack of restraint or inhibition.

abdicate (ăb´dĭ-kāt) *v.* to relinquish or cede responsibility for.

abhor (ăb-hôr´) *v.* to regard with horror or loathing; detest.

abject (ăb´jĕkt) *adj.* miserable and submissive.

abstraction (ăb-străk´shən) *n.* something that is not part of the concrete, material world.

acrid (ăk´rĭd) *adj.* unpleasantly sharp, pungent, or bitter to the taste or smell.

adamant (ăd´ə-mənt) *adj.* inflexible and insistent, unchanging.

affect (ə-fĕkt´) *v.* to cause or influence.

affluence (ăf´lo͞o-əns) *n.* wealth.

anomalous (ə-nŏm´ə-ləs) *adj.* unusual.

apprehension (ăp-rĭ-hĕn´shən) *n.* fear or anxiety; dread.

archaic (är-kā´ĭk) *adj.* relating to, being, or characteristic of a much earlier period.

artifice (är´tə-fĭs) *n.* a clever means to an end.

atrocious (ə-trō´shəs) *adj.* evil or brutal.

augment (ôg-mĕnt´) *v.* to make (something already developed or well underway) greater, as in size, extent, or quantity.

automation (ô-tə-mā´shən) *n.* the automatic operation or control of equipment, a process, or a system.

avert (ə-vûrt´) *v.* to turn away.

belatedly (bĭ-lā´tĭd-lē) *adv.* done too late or overdue.

bravado (brə-vä´dō) *n.* a show of bravery or defiance, often in order to make a false impression or mislead someone.

cabal (kə-băl´) *n.* a group united in a secret plot.

calamity (kə-lăm´ĭ-tē) *n.* an event that brings terrible loss or lasting distress.

caliber (kăl´ə-bər) *n.* level of ability.

capacity (kə-păs´ĭ-tē) *n.* ability to hold or have something; function or role.

cardinal (kär´dn-əl) *adj.* most important; prime.

catalyst (kăt´l-ĭst) *n.* a substance, usually used in small amounts relative to the reactants, that modifies and increases the rate of a reaction without being consumed in the process.

cede (sēd) *v.* to yield or give away.

circumlocution (sûr-kəm-lō-kyo͞o´shən) *n.* the use of unnecessarily wordy language.

circumvent (sûr´kəm-vənt) *v.* to avoid or get around by artful maneuvering.

clave (klāv) *v.* past tense of ***cleave:*** to cling; to adhere.

codified (kŏd´ĭ-fīd´) *v.* systematically categorized and arranged.

compelled (kəm-pĕld´) *v.* forced (a person) to do something; drove or constrained.

composed (kəm-pōzd´) *adj.* self-possessed; calm.

conceivable (kən-sēv´ə-bəl) *adj.* formed or developed in the mind.

configuration (kən-fĭg-yə-rā´shən) *n.* arrangement of parts into a whole structure or pattern.

conjure (kŏn´jər) *v.* to influence or effect by or as if by magic.

conquistador (kŏng-kē´stə-dôr, kŏn-kwĭs´tə-dôr) *n.* a 16th-century Spanish soldier-explorer who took part in the defeat of the Indian civilizations of Mexico, Central America, or Peru.

consolation (kŏn´sə-lā´shən) *n.* act of giving comfort.

constitute (kŏn´stĭ-to͞ot) *v.* to amount to; equal.

contrive (kən-trīv´) *v.* to plan skillfully; to design.

contrived (kən-trīvd´) *adj.* obviously planned or calculated; not spontaneous or natural.

conventional (kən-vĕn´shə-nəl) *adj.* based on or in accordance with general agreement, use, or practice; customary.

copious (kō´pē-əs) *adj.* extensive.

defection (dē-fĕkt´shŭn) *n.* the abandonment of one social or political group in favor of another.

delicacy (dĕl´ĭ-kə-sē) *n.* something pleasing and appealing, especially a choice food.

delinquency (dĭ-lĭng´kwən-sē) *n.* shortcoming or misbehavior.

delinquent (dĭ-lĭng´kwənt) *adj.* failing to do what law or duty requires.

demurred (dĭ-mûrd´) *v.* disagreed politely or politely refused to accept a request or suggestion.

deprecate (dĕp´rĭ-kāt) *v.* to express disapproval.

deprive (dĭ-prīv´) *v.* to keep from possessing or enjoying; deny.

diligence (dĭl´ə-jəns) *n.* consistent, thorough effort and dedication.

discord (dĭs´kôrd) *n.* disagreement or conflict.

disposed (dĭ-spōzd´) *adj.* having a preference, disposition, or tendency.

disposition (dĭs-pə-zĭsh´ən) *n.* character or temperament.

distinction (dĭ-stĭngk´shən) *n.* difference in quality.

divers (di´vərz) *adj.* various; several.

efface (ĭ-fās´) *tr. v.* to rub or wipe out; erase.

elusive (ĭ-lo͞o´sĭv) *adj.* difficult to define.

emblem (ĕm´bləm) *n.* an identifying mark or symbol.

engross (ĕn-grōs´) *v.* to completely engage the attention or interest.

eradicate (ĭ-răd´ĭ-kāt) *v.* tear up by the roots; eliminate.

establish (ĭ-stăb´lĭsh) *v.* to formally set up; institute.

estrangement (ĭ-strānj´mənt) *n.* to make hostile, unsympathetic, or indifferent; alienate.

evince (ĭ-vĭns´) *v.* to reveal or give evidence of.

eviscerate (ĭ-vĭs´ə-rāt) *v.* to remove the necessary or important parts of.

exclusive (ĭk-sklo͞o´sĭv) *adj.* not allowing something else.

expedience (ĭk-spē´dē-əns) *n.* a self-interested means to an end.

expedition (ĕk-spĭ-dĭsh´ən) *n.* a journey, especially a difficult or hazardous one, undertaken after extensive planning and with a definite objective in mind.

extenuating (ĭk-stĕn´yo͞o-ā-tĭng) *adj.* serving to make a fault or an offense seem less serious.

extortionist (ĭk-stôr´shən-ĭst) *n.* one who obtains something by force or threat.

extremity (ĭk-strĕm´ĭ-tē) *n.* the outermost or farthest point or portion; the hand or foot.

façade (fə-säd´) *n.* false or misleading appearance.

facile (făs´əl) *adj.* easy to make or understand.

felicity (fĭ-lĭs´ĭ-tē) *n.* great happiness.

ferry (fĕr´ē) *v.* to transport (people or goods) by vehicle.

fixed (fĭkst) *adj.* firmly in position; stationary.

flotilla (flō-tĭl´ə) *n.* a fleet of small water craft.

formidable (fôr´mĭ-də-bəl) *adj.* difficult and intimidating.

frantically (frăn´tĭ-kəl-lē) *adv.* excitedly, with strong emotion or frustration.

gape (gāp, găp) *intr. v.* to stare wonderingly or stupidly, often with the mouth open.

grope (grōp) *v.* to reach about uncertainly; feel one's way.

illumination (ĭ-lo͞o-mə-nā´shən) *n.* awareness or enlightenment.

imperative (ĭm-pĕr´ə-tĭv) *adj.* of great importance; essential.

impertinent (ĭm-pûr´tn-ənt) *adj.* rude; ill-mannered.

impunity (ĭm-pyōō´nĭ-tē) *n.* exemption from punishment, penalty, or harm.

inclination (ĭn-klə-nā´shən) *n.* a characteristic disposition or tendency to act in a certain way; a propensity.

incorrigible (ĭn-kôr´ĭ-jə-bəl) *adj.* incapable of being reformed or corrected.

indeterminate (ĭn-dĭ-tûr´mə-nĭt) *adj.* not precisely known.

indigenous (ĭn-dĭj´ə-nəs) *adj.* native to a land.

induced (ĭn-dyōōst´) *v.* led or moved, as to a course of action, by influence or persuasion.

ineffable (ĭn-ĕf´ə-bəl) *adj.* beyond description; inexpressible.

infinitesimal (ĭn-fĭn-ĭ-tĕs´ə-məl) *adj.* immeasurably or incalculably minute.

infraction (ĭn-frăk´shən) *n.* the act or instance of infringing, as of a law or rule; a violation.

ingenious (ĭn-jēn´yəs) *adj.* having great inventive skill and imagination.

inhumanity (ĭn-hyōō-măn´ĭ-tē) *n.* lack of pity or compassion.

insuperable (ĭn-sōō´pər-ə-bəl) *adj.* impossible to overcome.

insurgency (ĭn-sûr´jən-sē) *n.* rebellion or revolt.

intangible (ĭn-tăn´jə-bəl) *adj.* unable to be defined or understood.

interminable (ĭn-tûr´mə-nə-bəl) *adj.* seemingly endless.

internalize (ĭn-tûr´nə-līz) *v.* to take in and make an integral part of one's attitudes or beliefs.

invest (ĭn-vĕst´) *v.* to grant or endow.

lucid (lōō´sĭd) *adj.* easily understood.

malign (mə-līn´) *tr. v.* to make evil, harmful, and often untrue statements about (someone).

metaphysical (mĕt-ə-fĭz´ĭ-kəl) *adj.* based on speculative or abstract reasoning.

miscellany (mĭs´ə-lā-nē) *n.* a collection of various items, parts, or ingredients, especially one composed of diverse literary works.

mitigate (mĭt´ĭ-gāt) *v.* to lessen.

narcotic (när-kŏt´ĭk) *adj.* inducing sleep or stupor; causing narcosis.

noblesse oblige (nō-blĕs´ ō-blēzh´) *n.* the responsibility of people in a high social position to behave in a noble fashion.

oblige (ə-blīj´) *v.* to compel or require (someone) to do something.

obstinacy (ŏb´stə-nə-sē) *n.* stubbornness.

ostensibly (ŏ-stĕn´sə-blē) *adv.* apparently.

ostentatious (ŏs-tĕn-tā´shəs) *adj.* conspicuous and vulgar.

panic (păn´ĭk) *n.* sudden, overpowering feeling of fear.

parity (păr´ĭ-tē) *n.* equality, being equivalent.

patent (păt´nt) *n.* an official document granting ownership.

pathos (pā´thŏs) *n.* something that evokes pity or sympathy.

peril (pĕr´əl) *n.* imminent danger.

pertinacity (pûr-tn-ăs´ĭ-tē) *n.* firm, unyielding intent.

perturbation (pûr-tər-bā´shən) *n.* disturbance or agitation.

pigmentation (pĭg-mən-tā´shən) *n.* coloration of tissues by pigment.

platoon (plə-tōōn´) *n.* a subdivision of a company of troops consisting of two or more squads or sections and usually commanded by a lieutenant.

plausibility (plô-zə-bəl´ĭ-tē) *n.* likelihood; believability.

pliable (plī´ə-bəl) *adj.* easily bent or shaped; easily influenced, persuaded, or controlled.

poignant (poin´yənt) *adj.* physically or mentally painful.

GLOSSARY OF CRITICAL VOCABULARY

polarity (pō-lăr´ĭ-tē) *n.* separation to opposite sides.

ponder (pŏn´dər) *v. tr.* to think about (something) with thoroughness and care.

posse (pŏs´ē) *n.* a group of civilians temporarily authorized by officials to assist in pursuing fugitives.

postulate (pŏs´chə-lāt) *v.* to assume or assert the truth, reality, or necessity of, especially as a basis of an argument.

presaging (prĕs´ĭj-ĭng) *adj.* predicting.

pristine (prĭs´tēn) *adj.* pure or unspoiled.

project (prə -jĕkt´) *v.* to communicate or put forth.

proposition (prŏp-ə-zĭ´shən) *n.* a plan suggested for acceptance; a proposal.

prostrate (prŏs´trāt) *adj.* lying down with the head facing downward.

protrude (prō-trōōd´) *v.* to stick out or bulge.

provision (prə-vĭzh´ən) *n.* food supply.

provocation (prŏv-ə-kā´shən) *n.* the act of provoking or inciting.

recalcitrant (rĭ-kăl´sĭ-trənt) *adj.* uncooperative and resistant of authority.

reckless (rĕk´lĭs) *adj.* acting or done with a lack of care or caution.

reckoning (rĕk´ə-nĭng) *n.* a settlement of accounts.

recompense (rĕk´əm-pĕns) *n.* payment in return for something, such as a service.

regenerate (rĭ-jĕn´ə-rāt) *v.* to form, construct, or create anew.

regimen (rĕj´ə-mən) *n.* a system or organized routine of behavior.

remunerative (rĭ-myōō´nər-ə-tĭv) *adj.* bringing in money or profit.

reparations (rĕp-ə-rā´shəns) *n.* compensation or payment from a nation for damage or injury during a war.

rudiment (rōō´də-mənt) *n.* basic form.

sceptical (skĕp´tĭ-kəl) *adj.* marked by or given to doubt; questioning.

segregated (sĕg´rĭ-gāt-əd) *adj.* separated; isolated.

sentiment (sən´tə-mənt) *n.* a thought, view, or attitude, especially one based mainly on emotion instead of reason.

settlement (sĕt´l-mənt) *n.* a small community in a sparsely populated area.

sliver (slĭv´ər) *n.* a small narrow piece, portion, or plot.

specter (spĕk´tər) *n.* a ghostly apparition; a phantom.

stem (stĕm) *v.* to have or take origin or descent.

stoically (stō´ĭk-lē) *adv.* without showing emotion or feeling.

straits (strāts) *adj.* a position of difficulty, distress, or extreme need.

strive (strīv) *v.* to struggle or fight forcefully; contend.

subservience (səb-sûr´vē-əns) *n.* the condition of being subordinate in capacity or function.

summarily (sə-mĕr´ə-lē) *adv.* quickly and without ceremony.

sundry (sŭn´drē) *adj.* various or assorted.

superfluous (sōō-pûr´flōō-əs) *adj.* unnecessary.

supplant (sə-plănt´) *v.* to take the place of.

supposition (sŭp-ə-zĭsh´ən) *n.* the act of supposing; a belief or assumption.

systematize (sĭs´tə-mə-tīz) *v.* to form something into an organized plan or scheme.

tableau (tăb´lō) *n.* a dramatic scene or picture.

tepid (tĕp´ĭd) *adj.* lukewarm; indifferent.

tidings (tī´dĭngs) *pl. n.* information or news.

timid (tĭm´ĭd) *adj.* lacking self-confidence; shy.

transient (trăn´zē-ənt) *adj.* temporary; short-term.

transition (trăn-zĭsh´ən) *n.* process of change.

trifling (trī´flĭng) *adj.* frivolous; inconsequential.

truculent (trŭk´yə-lənt) *adj.* eager for a fight; fierce.

tumultuous (to͞o-mŭl´cho͞o-əs) *adj.* stormy, intense.

tyrannical (tĭ-răn´ĭ-kəl) *adj.* characteristic of a tyrant or tyranny; despotic and oppressive.

unalienable (ŭn-āl´yə-nə-bəl) *adj.* impossible to be taken away.

unassailable (ŭn-ə-sā´lə-bəl) *adj.* undeniable.

undulation (ŭn-jə-lə´shən, ŭn-dyə-, -də-) *n.* a regular rising and falling or movement to alternating sides; movement in waves.

unfathomed (ŭn-făth´əmd) *adj.* located at the deepest place.

unimpeded (ŭn-ĭm-pēd´əd) *adj.* not delayed or obstructed in its progress.

unremitting (ŭn-rĭ-mĭt´ĭng) *adj.* constant; never stopping.

vacant (vā´kənt) *adj.* blank, expressionless.

vanquish (văng´kwĭsh) *v.* to defeat in a contest or conflict.

venture (vĕn´chər) *v.* to risk or dare.

vindicate (vĭn´dĭ-kāt) *v.* to demonstrate or prove the validity of; justify.

virtuous (vûr´cho͞o-əs) *adj.* having or showing virtue, especially moral excellence.

virulent (vîr´yə-lənt) *adj.* extremely hostile or malicious.

volatile (vŏl´ə-tl) *adj.* evaporating readily at normal temperatures and pressures.

watershed (wô´tər-shĕd) *n.* a turning point, a crucial dividing line.

wring (rĭng) *v.* to obtain through force or pressure.

INDEX OF SKILLS

M

N

INDEX OF TITLES AND AUTHORS

ACKNOWLEDGMENTS

"Ambush" from *The Things They Carried* by Tim O'Brien. Text copyright © 1990 by Tim O'Brien. Audio copyright © 1990 by Tim O'Brien. Reprinted by permission of Houghton Mifflin Harcourt Publishing Company, Tim O'Brien, HarperCollins Publishers Ltd., and Janklow and Nesbit Associates.

"Balboa" from *Tales of the New World* by Sabina Murray. Text copyright © 2011 by Sabina Murray. Reprinted by permission of Grove/Atlantic, Inc. Any third-party use of this material, outside of this publication, is prohibited.

"Because I could not stop for Death," "Much madness is divinest sense," "The soul selects her own society," and "Tell all the truth but tell it slant" from *The Poems of Emily Dickinson* edited by Thomas H. Johnson. Text copyright © 1951, 1955, renewed 1979, 1983 by the President and Fellows of Harvard College. Text copyright © 1914, 1918, 1919, 1924, 1929, 1930, 1932, 1935, 1937, 1942 by Martha Dickinson Bianchi. Text copyright © 1952, 1957, 1958, 1963, 1965 by Mary L. Hampson. Reprinted by permission of The Belknap Press of Harvard University Press, Cambridge, Mass.

"Building the Transcontinental Railroad" from *The Chinese in America: A Narrative History* by Iris Chang. Text copyright © 2003 by Iris Chang. Reprinted by permission of Viking Books, an imprint of Penguin Publishing Group, a division of Penguin Random House LLC. All rights reserved. Any third-party use of this material, outside of this publication, is prohibited. Interested parties must apply directly to Penguin Random House LLC for permission.

The Crucible by Arthur Miller. Text copyright 1952, 1953, 1954, renewed © 1980, 1981, 1982 by Arthur Miller. Reprinted by permission of Viking Books, an imprint of Penguin Publishing Group, a division of Penguin Random House LLC, and The Wylie Agency LLC. All rights reserved. Any third-party use of this material, outside of this publication, is prohibited. Interested parties must apply directly to Penguin Random House LLC for permission.

"A Desperate Trek Across America" by Andrés Reséndez from *American Heritage*, Fall 2008, Vol. 58, Issue 5. Text copyright © 2008 by American Heritage Publishing. Reprinted by permission of American Heritage Publishing via Copyright Clearance Center.

Excerpt from *Fast Food Nation: The Dark Side of the All-American Meal* by Eric Schlosser. Text copyright © 2001 by Eric Schlosser. Reprinted by permission of Houghton Mifflin Harcourt Publishing Company, Penguin Books Ltd., the author, and Random House Audio Publishing Group, a division of Random House LLC. Any third-party use of this material, outside of this publication, is prohibited. Interested parties must apply directly to Random House, Inc. for permission. All rights reserved.

Excerpt from *1491: New Revelations of the Americas Before Columbus* by Charles C. Mann. Text and illustration copyright © 2005 by Charles C. Mann. Map by Nick Springer and Tracy Pollack of Springer Cartographics LLC. Reprinted by permission of Alfred A. Knopf, an imprint of the Knopf Doubleday Publishing Group, a division of Penguin Random House LLC, Roam Agency on behalf of Charles C. Mann, and Granta Publications. All rights reserved. Any third-party use of this material, outside of this publication, is prohibited. Interested parties must apply directly to Penguin Random House LLC for permission.

Excerpt from *The Great Tree and the Longhouse: The Culture of the Iroquois* by Hazel W. Hertzberg. Text copyright © 1966 by American Anthropological Association. Reprinted by permission of American Anthropological Association.

"In the season of change" by Teresa Palomo Acosta. Text copyright © 1994 by Teresa Palomo Acosta. Reprinted by permission of the author.

From *Last Child in the Woods* (Introduction) by Richard Louv. Text copyright © 2005 by Richard Louv. Reprinted by permission of Algonquin Books of Chapel Hill. All rights reserved.

"The Latin Deli: An Ars Poetica" by Judith Ortiz Cofer from *The Americas Review*, Vol. 19, No. 1. Text copyright © 1991 by Arte Público Press - University of Houston. Reprinted by permission of Arte Público Press - University of Houston.

Excerpt from *Lean In: Women, Work, and the Will to Lead* by Sheryl Sandberg. Text copyright © 2013 by Lean In Foundation. Reprinted by permission of Alfred A. Knopf, an imprint of the Knopf Doubleday Publishing Group, a division of Penguin Random House LLC and William Morris Endeavor Entertainment, LLC. All rights reserved. Any third-party use of this material, outside of this publication, is prohibited. Interested parties must apply directly to Penguin Random House LLC for permission.

"The Lowest Animal" from *Letters from the Earth* by Mark Twain, edited by Bernard DeVoto. Text copyright © 1938, 1944, 1946, 1959, 1962 by The Mark Twain Company. Text copyright 1942 by The President and Fellows of Harvard College. Reprinted by permission of HarperCollins Publishers.

"My Dungeon Shook: Letter to My Nephew on this One Hundredth Anniversary of the Emancipation" by James Baldwin. Text copyright © 1962 by James Baldwin. Copyright renewed. Originally published in *The Progressive*. Collected in *The Fire Next Time*, published by Vintage Books. Reprinted by arrangement with the James Baldwin Estate.

"My Friend Walt Whitman" from *Blue Pastures* by Mary Oliver. Text copyright © 1995 by Mary Oliver. Reprinted by permission of Houghton Mifflin Harcourt Publishing Company.

"Poetry" from *The Collected Poems of Marianne Moore* by Marianne Moore. Text copyright © 1935, renewed 1963 by Marianne Moore. Reprinted with the permission of Scribner, a Division of Simon & Schuster, Inc. and Literary Estate of Marianne Moore, David M. Moore, Executor.

"A Rose for Emily" from *Collected Stories of William Faulkner* by William Faulkner. Text copyright 1930, renewed © 1958 by William Faulkner. Reprinted by permission of Random House, an imprint and division of Penguin Random House LLC, Curtis Brown Group Ltd., and W. W. Norton & Company, Inc. All rights reserved. Any third-party use of this material, outside of this publication, is prohibited. Interested parties must apply directly to Random House LLC for permission. All rights reserved.

ACKNOWLEDGMENTS

"Runagate Runagate" from *Collected Poems of Robert Hayden* by Robert Hayden, edited by Frederick Glaysher. Text copyright © 1966 by Robert Hayden. Reprinted by permission of Liveright Publishing Corporation.

"A Soldier for the Crown" from *Soulcatcher and Other Stories* by Charles Johnson. Text copyright © 1998 by Charles Johnson. Reprinted by permission of the WGBH Educational Foundation.

Excerpt from "Speech on the Vietnam War, New York City, April 4, 1967" by Martin Luther King, Jr. Text copyright © 1967 by Dr. Martin Luther King, Jr., renewed 1991 by Coretta Scott King. Reprinted by permission of Writers House on behalf of the Heirs of the Estate of Martin Luther King, Jr.

"Thomas Jefferson: The Best of Enemies" by Ron Chernow from *Time Magazine*, July 5, 2004. Text copyright © 2004 by Time, Inc. Reprinted by permission of Time, Inc. All rights reserved.

"The Universe as Primal Scream" from *Life on Mars* by Tracy K. Smith. Text copyright © 2011 by Tracy K. Smith. Reprinted by permission of The Permissions Company, Inc. on behalf of Graywolf Press, Minneapolis, Minnesota. www.graywolfpress.org

Excerpt from *The Warmth of Other Suns* by Isabel Wilkerson. Text copyright © 2010 by Isabel Wilkerson. Reprinted by permission of Random House, an imprint and division of Penguin Random House LLC. All rights reserved. Any third-party use of this material, outside of this publication, is prohibited. Interested parties must apply to Penguin Random House LLC for permission.

"Why Everyone Must Get Ready For the 4th Industrial Revolution" by Bernard Marr from Forbes.com, April 5, 2016. Text copyright © 2016 by Bernard Marr. Reprinted by permission of Bernard Marr.